1999

DUNS SCOTUS
on the Will and Morality

DUNS SCOTUS
on the Will and Morality

Selected & Translated
with an Introduction by Alan B. Wolter, O.F.M.

Translation Edition
Edited by William A. Frank

The Catholic University of America Press
Washington, D.C.

Copyright © 1986, 1997
The Catholic University of America Press
All rights reserved
Printed in the United States of America

The paper used in this publication meets the minimum requirements
of American National Standards for Information Science—Permanence
of Paper for Printed Library materials, ANSI Z39.48-1984.
∞

Library of Congress Cataloging-in-Publication Data
Duns Scotus, John, ca. 1266–1308.
   [Selections. English. 1997]
   Duns Scotus on the will and morality / selected and translated
with an introduction by Allan B. Wolter : edited by William A.
Frank.—Translation ed.
      p. cm.
   Includes bibliographical references and index.
   1. Ethics, Medieval. 2. Will—Early works to 1800. I. Wolter.
Allan Bernard, 1913–   . II. Frank, William A. III. Title.
B765.D73D8613 1997
171'.2—dc21
97–2325
ISBN 0–8132-0895–5 (alk. paper)

Contents

Preface to This Edition   ix

Preface to the Original Edition   xvii

Introduction   1

I. General Remarks   3

   1. Scotus' metaphysical notion of God   5
   2. How divine free will differs from ours   9
   3. God's voluntary self-love as both free and necessary   11
   4. Right reason governs God's relationship to creatures   16
   5. The moral law as accessible to reason   25

II. Notes on the Specific Selections   31

Part I. The will and intellect   31

   1. Practical science   32
   2. The will as a rational faculty   35
   3. How the will controls thought   37
   4. Coercion and free will   39

Part II. The will and its inclinations   39

   5. The will and its inclinations   39
   6. Natural will and natural volition   41
   7. Happiness   42
   8. Synderesis and conscience   45

Part III. Moral goodness   47

   9. The nature of moral goodness   47
   10. The source of moral goodness   48
   11. Degrees of moral goodness and badness   48
   12. Does the end alone justify actions?   51
   13. Morally indifferent acts   52
   14. Is moral goodness conformity to God's will?   53

Part IV. God and the moral law   54

   15. God's justice   54
   16. God's absolute and ordained power   56

Part v. The moral law in general   57

    17. Natural law and divine positive law   57
    18. The decalogue and the law of nature   60
    19. On marriage and bigamy   64
    20. Divorce and the Mosaic law   72
    21. Positive law and civil authority   73

Part vi. The intellectual and moral virtues   75

    22. The will as the seat of the moral virtues   75
    23. Moral virtue and the gifts and fruits of the Spirit   78
    24. Are the moral virtues connected?   84

Part vii. The love of God, self, and neighbor   89

    25. The infused virtue of charity   89
    26. Love of God and neighbor   94
    27. Love of God and self   97

Part viii. Sin   98

    28. Is the power to sin from God?   98
    29. The sin of Lucifer   100
    30. The sin of malice   105
    31. Lying   106
    32. Perjury   110
    33. The obligation to keep secrets   113
    34. The sin of enslavement   114

Texts in Translation

Part i. The Will and Intellect   127

    1. Practical science   127
    2. The will as a rational faculty   136
    3. How the will controls thought   150
    4. Coercion and free will   151

Part ii. The Will and Its Inclinations   153

    5. The will and its inclinations   153
    6. Natural will and natural volition   154
    7. Happiness   155
    8. Synderesis and conscience   162

Part iii. Moral Goodness   167

    9. The nature of moral goodness   167

10. The source of moral goodness　169
11. Degrees of moral goodness and badness　173
12. Does the end alone justify actions?　176
13. Morally indifferent acts　178
14. Is moral goodness conformity to God's will?　181

Part IV. God and the Moral Law　183

15. God's justice　183
16. God's absolute and ordained power　191

Part V. The Moral Law in General　195

17. Natural law and divine positive law　195
18. The decalogue and the law of nature　198
19. On marriage and bigamy　208
20. Divorce and the Mosaic law　212
21. Positive law and civil authority　219

Part VI. The Intellectual and Moral Virtues　223

22. The will as the seat of the moral virtues　223
23. Moral virtue and the gifts and fruits of the Spirit　237
24. Are the moral virtues connected?　252

Part VII. The Love of God, Self, and Neighbor　275

25. The infused virtue of charity　275
26. Love of God and neighbor　287
27. Love of God and self　291

Part VIII. Sin　293

28. Is the power to sin from God?　293
29. The sin of Lucifer　295
30. The sin of malice　302
31. Lying　304
32. Perjury　314
33. The obligation to keep secrets　323
34. The sin of enslavement　325

Bibliography　331
Topical Index　341

Preface to This Edition

Since the appearance of the original edition of *Duns Scotus on the Will and Morality*, there has been a remarkable growth of interest in the thought of this early fourteenth-century Franciscan master. In part, this renaissance reflects the spate of scholarly activity associated with the official recognition of the cult of John Duns Scotus when John Paul II confirmed his status as blessed during a Solemn Vespers in the Basilica of St. Peter in 1993. It is also the case that Allan Wolter's book on Scotus' volitional and ethical doctrine has itself provoked and guided a good deal of the recent inquiry.

Whatever the source of the activity, it has become evident since the recent international Scotus conferences held in Rome and Bonn that there is active interest among philosophical scholars along several lines of investigation directly connected with *Duns Scotus on the Will and Morality*. The following three areas deserve special mention: (1) Scotus' metaphysics of freedom and contingency (e.g., Vos, 1994; Dumont, 1995; Frank, 1992; Honnefelder, 1991; and Wolter, 1990a), (2) his anthropological doctrine of the will (e.g., Boler, 1990, 1993; Incandela, 1992; and Adams, 1987, 1995), and (3) Scotistic ethical theory (e.g., Adams, 1986; Santogrossi, 1994; Shannon, 1995, and especially Ingham, 1996). In fact, these investigations have enabled us to begin to see more critically a unity of concern in Scotistic thought. In the balance of my remarks I shall try to sharpen the focus on this unifying thread.

The problem of freedom. The lodestone of Scotus' theological vision is the idea of Divine Love, as understood both within the mutuality of the Trinitarian Persons and in God's relation to creation. His philosophical thought expresses this fundamental reality under the aspects of the metaphysics of contingency and the experience of freedom. Scotistic freedom, however, is a subtle notion that does not easily adjust itself to classical Greek or medieval concepts of nature and science, nor does it happily jibe with prevailing modern libertarian strains of thought. It is precisely this seminal understanding of freedom that has been increasingly brought to the fore in the last ten or fifteen years of scholarship.

The correct understanding of the God/world relationship is one of the more important metaphysical questions in which freedom is a central issue. This is especially true in the case of Christian thinkers, and

Duns Scotus' account of the relationship is a particularly challenging instance. One of the critical problems Christian thinkers face is the tension between the idea of a world possessed of an intelligible structure and the notion of creatures appearing out of nothingness by the fiat of a transcendent God. The basis of the tension is that philosophers expect to find the rational foundations of the world in necessary reasons, but a "fiat," even if it is divine, seems arbitrary, if not uncertain. Thus, when Scotus claims that the Divine Will in his relations with creatures is an exemplar of orderly, reasonable volition, he asserts that the world's intelligibility is founded on the reason of Divine Freedom. One might ask, however: "What is to count as reasonable?" The Scotistic answer falls between two polarized positions, and it is important to see that it cannot be assimilated to either of them.

One position, which we can call Aristotelian essentialism, bases intelligibility on the fact that things have natures, and God is bound to respect the requirements of these essences. This strategy, however, fails to honor the unqualified primacy Scotus gives to Divine Freedom in his dealings with the world. The second pole asserts voluntarism in its radical, unmitigated form and emphasizes the arbitrariness of God's choices in regard to his creatures. This second theory, which we might call anarchical, fails to express Scotus' thought, because he rejects the idea of an arbitrary willy-nilly in the Divine Will. It is interesting to note that both the essentialist and anarchical theories share a common idea of what counts for "rationality." At the origin of this notion of rationality is a metaphysical order that requires each actual being to exclude the simultaneous real possibility of its opposite. For instance, in the Aristotelian framework, to take the classical formulation, cosmic and ethical order finally comes to rest in ultimate ontological essences or natures. By contrast, where such forms are eliminated in the name of divine liberty and omnipotence, cosmology and morality lose their substantive, rational foundation. In the often told story of the history of ideas, the philosopher-theologians of the late medieval and early renaissance period opted for the nominalist, anarchical alternative and in the process put an end to what Louis Dupré, in *Passage to Modernity*, has called the classical "ontotheological vision of the real." Most versions of this narrative portray Duns Scotus as a patriarch of later nominalistic theologians.

The truth of Scotus' theodicy, however, is otherwise. He is no standard essentialist, nor is he a familiar nominalist, for the reason that he has not put freedom and reason in a fundamental ontological opposition to one another. The order or the reason of nature and action, of cosmology and morality, unfold within *the architectonic form of freedom*. And this explains why, when Duns Scotus says that God is a debtor to his own generosity (*debitor ex liberalitate sua* [*Ord.* IV, dist. 46]) and that in his creative action his volition is most orderly (*ordinatissime volens* [*Ord.* III, suppl., dist. 32]), Scotus is under the sway of a single idea: *Liberality—the freedom that is generosity—has its own order*. Interpretations of Scotus' doctrine of freedom will continue in a disorienting oscillation between the poles of essentialism and nominalism until we have a sufficiently cogent account of "freedom's reason."

Metaphysics of contingency. Part of what makes current Scotus studies so interesting and philosophically fruitful is that we find ourselves in search of what is, for our time, a fresh paradigm of reason, one that is common to both metaphysics and ethics, and which belongs essentially and centrally to a fundamental narrative of freedom. We find this enthusiasm of discovery in the work of the John Duns Scotus Research Group, headed by Antoine Vos Jaczen, at the Franciscan Study Centre and Theological Faculty at Utrecht University. Confirming and extending ideas independently developed by Simo Knuutilla, they have identified the centrality of the notion of "synchronic contingency" in Duns Scotus' systematic thought (Vos, 1994, pp. 23–37, 127–29). According to this modal theory, "the opposite of what is actually the case is both logically and really possible at the very time when it is actually the case" (Dumont, 1995, p. 160). This radical contingency derives from the distinctive potency that distinguishes the free will as its own species of active power. The resultant ontology is a remarkable achievement, for it means that any finite created entity subsists over against the simultaneous and real possibility that it could be otherwise. Accordingly, to say that something is contingent is to state something about the modality of its present existence, and not only to describe the present fact as a succession from past reality that was otherwise—nor simply to affirm that in the succeeding future it will be otherwise.

Freedom is thus the glue of the universe, for the Divine Will actively causes finite things to exist and persist in the way they do. Within a Parmenidean or even an Aristotelian framework, ultimately what-is is and could not not-be, and thinking comes to rest either in the necessity of the great cycles and rhythms of nature, or even more finally in the Unmoved Mover's contemplation. If, however, our notion of being is inextricably bound up with the concept of possibility and synchronic contingency, as it is with Scotus, then actuality discovers its reason in the logic of the will's freedom. Such voluntarist considerations find their complement in an account of the foundation of possibility in the divine intellect (Wolter, 1993). As yet, however, there is no standard study that adequately integrates the various strains of the metaphysical and cosmological issues of freedom in an account of the rational order of the universe. It is likely that this cannot be done until we have a better grasp of Scotus' theory of personhood. Recent anthropological and ethical studies of Scotus have made some progress along these lines.

Anthropology. Two of Scotus' doctrines, the key sources for which are found in Part II and Parts IV–V, lie particularly close to our concern with the architectonic form of freedom. One centers on Scotus' intriguing doctrine of natural law, and the other concerns his teaching on the *affectio justitiae*. Regarding the latter, John Boler's three studies of the doctrine of *affectio justitiae*, which Scotus calls the innate freedom of the will, has demonstrated in great detail how Scotistic morality requires a radical transcendence of the natural. "For Scotus . . . morality arises precisely with the possibility of somehow 'transcending' the pursuit of the agent's 'natural' potential in favor of a concern for the 'good in itself' of things. The presence of *affectio justitiae* . . . transforms the whole appetitive structure of the agent" (Boler, 1994, p. 27). This transformation lies at the heart of rational personhood. In Scotus' philosophy, "nature" underdetermines the content of morality and the good we achieve through our free will. "'Action in accord with right reason,' therefore, picks out what is reasonable or rational. . . . But it is not something suited to the *nature of the agent*. Being moral cannot be analyzed in terms of an agent's nature, because being free is precisely not being 'in' a nature" (Boler, 1990, p. 38). In effect, morality arises from the discontinuity between the natural and the voluntary. "Nature" does not suffice to specify the content of morality: it can only give us the good in the eudaemonistic form of the *bonum sibi*. Transcending freedom, of course, has its measure; it is not arbitrarily open-ended, for its object is the *bonum in se* of things and, most especially, the love of God. But how is it that we recognize the moral good for what it is? Scotus seems to believe that the moral agent's right reason suffices to discern the ethical truth in a moral situation.

Ethical theory. In discussions of moral obligation, it is important to distinguish the *subjective* problem of explaining how what is morally obligatory makes a claim upon us from the question of the *objective* basis of moral obligation. The second, more fundamental question asks for the origin of the moral rightness or wrongness of a given action. Why, for instance, ought one not murder? Or why should one love God? For Scotus, the first principle of morality, promulgated in the first tablet of Moses' decalogue, is "God is to be loved," and it obligates because it is axiomatic; it is a self-evident consequence of the very meaning of God and love. The principle holds universally—under all possible circumstances, for all rational agents, always. All other precepts that are not logically necessary inferences from the primary prin-ciple and which in fact govern the large majority of our practical, workaday situations oblige for a different reason. In order to explain why these precepts (such as those against murder, adultery, and theft) oblige, Scotus introduces contingency into his account of moral obligation.

In the act of creation God ordered all things to participation in Divine Love (Wolter, 1980; Adams, 1986; Santogrossi, 1994). It is easy enough to understand the claim that all angelic and human beings are intended to be co-lovers of God, but Scotus insists that *all* created reality exists in some subordination, whether immediate or remote, to the dynamic principle, "God is to be loved." Thus even "a tree exists insofar as it enables me to love God more in himself" (*Ord.* suppl., dist. 32). Now the interesting point here is that among the interrelationships connecting creatures to one another, especially the ones binding man to man, but also man to nature, those that are morally obligatory do not express anything that could not logically or really be otherwise. As such, the content of morality participates in the radical contingency of finite reality. But that is not to say that the moral order is in this respect arbitrary. The checkrein on moral relativism is Divine Authority. The order of creation reflects a judgment on God's part that certain relationships ought to obtain among finite entities because it is a most suitable and exceedingly fitting way for all things to participate in Divine Love. In the act of creation, therefore, God's decision concerning the harmony of goodness in the universe becomes natural law. Now this means that the demands of what is good, both with respect to things in themselves (*bonum in se*) and for us (*bonum sibi*), embody an intelligible structure, but one much better understood as analogous to the aesthetic judgment of a creative artist than the proof of a mathematician. One of the challenges to properly interpreting Scotus' ethical theory lies in the difficulty of appreciating this kind of rationality. Mary Elizabeth Ingham has made a brilliant contribution to the effort in her book, *The Harmony of Goodness: Mutuality and Moral Living According to John Duns Scotus.*

With regard to the subjective concern of how moral obligation makes its claim in the actual deliberations and actions of moral agents, Scotus is a right reason theorist. Man's dignity partially consists in the fact that God has given us the capacity for moral reason, which in principle can correctly estimate the entire ensemble that goes into the make up of a moral act, namely, its object, agent, end, and circumstances. If the acting person goes on to will in accordance with the judgment of right reason, then the resultant action—a real alteration in the complex web constituting the creative order—advances God's own purpose of bringing all things into harmony, as it were, with Divine Love.

Among the questions raised by this dual teaching on right reason and the contingency of natural law precepts of the second tablet of Moses' decalogue, the one provoked by the way Scotus deals with dispensations from the natural law that God is supposed to have made in the Old Testament has emerged as a particularly important ethical issue. In the view of standard medieval exegesis, God seems to have lifted his injunctions against acts of murder, theft, and adultery, as when he ordered Abraham to sacrifice his son and when he bade Hosea marry a harlot. Scotus readily absorbs these kinds of events in his ethical theory. To begin with, the rationale of the original, standard precepts rests in the fact that God has seen some special harmony in a life lived in accordance with such laws. But, let us say, the conditions of the world have changed due to some natural disaster or to an evolved and incorrigible hardheartedness on the part of mankind, and in his judgment the primary good of raising co-lovers might be more fittingly attained by sacrificing what in the earlier scheme of things was an inviolable, but secondary, good. Given these terms, God *could* dispense with the requirements of the natural law governing our behavior with the secondary goods. It must be added, though, that he would in no way be obligated to do so, for he might address the crisis more fittingly in other imaginable ways. We are even less able to predict what God will deem fitting than we can anticipate the particulars of a creative artist's next masterpiece. What we do know, however, is that, whatever the content of the moral law, it will be evident to us and will make its claim to govern our actions through the deliberations of right reason. With the exception of Andre McGrath's Ph.D. dissertation (1979) on the ethical doctrine of Scotus' *Ordinatio* treatment of marriage, the historical-critical exegesis of Scotus' teaching on the dispensations from the natural law has not significantly advanced beyond Robert Prentice's excellent study (1967). Nevertheless, critical discussion of the meta-ethical issue and its practical significance has been brought into prominence by Thomas Shannon (1993, 1995) and the pointed opposition of Ansgar Santogrossi (1994).

The notion that morally obligatory laws are revisable in response to changing circumstances and the prospect that the moral agent's right reason can discern what is morally obligatory captivates Shannon. He finds in Scotus' development of these ideas an enriching inspiration for a contemporary ethical theory that prizes the autonomy of the moral agent and emphasizes the dependence of moral value on the individuating circumstances of action. Santogrossi (1994) thinks that Shannon has overstated the case for human autonomy in the act of determining moral values. If Shannon were right, then Scotistic morality would be a kind of ethical deism. In other words, according to his interpretation, it would appear that God has given us a sufficient capacity for moral reasoning, placed us in a contingent, dynamic world of moral values, and released us to our freedom. The problem as Santogrossi sees it, however, is that authentic dispensations need to be ratified by an historical event of special revelation. It may be that right reason suffices to authenticate the original positive ordination of contingent, innerworldly, secondary goods to the primary good of Divine Love, but he argues that alterations to the original intent of creation require the confirmation of some form of special revelation. The difficulty with Santogrossi's doctrine, from Shannon's point of view, is that this introduces authority and the need for obedience to divine positive law, a move that would compromise his ideals of freedom and mature rational autonomy. Besides the exegetical question of getting Scotus' doctrine right, there is the critical philosophical issue which can be posed in the following way. To what extent does the autonomy of a moral agent find its perfection not only in transcending eudaemonistic interests in favor of a personally indifferent service to the intrinsic good of another, but also in the actual conformity to divine positive judgment? At issue in this meta-ethical dispute are judgments regarding the degree of mutuality required between God and man, and the form it must take, in the process of moral action.

This edition. Among those who have tried to understand perennial philosophical issues from within an architectonic of freedom, John Duns Scotus stands as one of history's seminal thinkers. Many of his teachings regarding liberty, contingency, and an ethics attuned to the concerns of mutuality and historical circumstance resonate with modern sensibilities. These prefatory remarks highlight the interesting and fruitful work now being done along these lines in the last decade. Much of this inquiry has been instigated by the publication of Allan Wolter's *Duns Scotus on the Will and Morality*. It is still the standard source book in the field. We hope that by publishing it in an affordable English-only edition we can make Duns Scotus' thought on the will and morality more widely available to scholars and students. In this edition the original thirty-four selections of texts from Scotus' works have been maintained as they were in the first edition. We have eliminated the Latin texts and retained only the English translations. Allan Wolter's General Remarks in the Introduction and his Notes on the Specific Selections have been retained and only slightly amended,

either to correct errors or to remove irrelevant references to the delet-
ed Latin texts. The bibliography has been expanded substantially,
mainly in order to reflect much of the philosophical scholarship on
Scotus' ethical and volitional doctrine since the 1986 publication of
the first edition.

William A. Frank
University of Dallas
July 15, 1996

Preface to the Original Edition

These selections were originally chosen for use in a graduate course on a specific topic in the history of philosophy, Duns Scotus' theory of ethics. The main aim was twofold: first, to correct the common misconceptions that arose because of his voluntaristic notions of God's relationship to creation, but more important, to show the unity of his ethical system based on right reason, for it is his rational approach to what he believed as an *ex professo* theologian that makes his conceptions of morality and especially the will of more than historical interest.

As an original philosopher, Scotus was perhaps more of a metaphysician or a philosophical psychologist than an ethician. He did, however, solve enough ethical questions in the course of his two major theological works, the *Ordinatio*, or revised commentary on the *Sentences* of Peter Lombard, and his magisterial *Quodlibet*, to develop a distinctive approach to moral philosophy. In subsequent decades this became so popular that the Cistercian moral theologian John Caramuel y Lobkowicz, writing in the mid-seventeenth century, was able to say that "the school of Scotus is more numerous than all the others combined" and to use this fact as a theological argument against the counterview that God himself could not dispense from any aspect of the natural law (Bak, 1956).

I have often suggested that most of what seems distinctive about Scotus' ethics has its roots in his theory of the will's native liberty, and when this is properly understood the unity of his ethics becomes apparent and the antinomies some claimed to find in it are dissolved. It seemed inappropriate, then, to publish a collection of texts on his moral philosophy without including some relevant items about the will that would substantiate this opinion.

Since Scotus' ethical system systematically presupposes his whole metaphysical conception of God's nature and the world's dependence on his will, it might seem fitting to include some texts on this topic as well. However, since so much of this is readily available in texts and translations I have published earlier, it seemed sufficient simply to sum up what I thought might be relevant in the Introduction, as well as point out there to what extent specific ethical insights might be logically independent of his system and hence of interest to those who do not share his metaphysical conceptions or religious faith.

The selection of items, for better or worse, was governed by what seemed to me most important for putting Scotus' ethical views in proper perspective, particularly in view of the distressing repetition of old errors by professional philosophers. It is my hope that this reworking of the rough translations done for my students over the past decade may be of some use to a wider group of scholars, particularly those with no working knowledge of Scotus' cryptic Latin style or those limited to using the presently available editions. Most of the material relevant to his ethical theory has not yet appeared in the new critical Vatican edition. Also much of the material used in the past was taken from what are now recognized as unexamined student reports (*Reportata*), rather than from more reliable texts such as Scotus' own earlier *Lectura* (now partially edited for the first time), or his late revised *Ordinatio*, and magisterial *Quodlibet*. Where the text of the Vatican press was not available, I tried to correct the Wadding edition on the basis of some of the better manuscripts recommended by the late C. Balić, former president of the Scotistic Commission in charge of the Vatican edition. I have also allowed myself the liberty of a quasi-commentary style, rather than a literal translation, in view of the face-to-face edition of the original text.

Without the initial interest of my graduate students, friends, and colleagues who occasionally sat in on my seminars on Scotus or encouraged my work on his thought, I might never have undertaken the tedious task of translating so difficult a thinker. I am grateful to them all, especially to Dean Jude Dougherty and to Professors John Wippel and Marilyn McCord Adams, who suggested or encouraged the publication of these selections, to Dr. William A. Frank for permission to include parts of his corrected Latin text of the *Quodlibet*, to the staff of The Catholic University of America Press for their gracious editorial assistance, and particularly to Frank Hunt, who had the thankless task of carefully reading and correcting the entire typescript. As usual I owe much to all my Franciscan confreres at the Old Mission for their kindly support and congeniality that makes it possible to work here under such pleasant circumstances.

Old Mission, Santa Barbara
March 27, 1985

Introduction

I

General Remarks

he dual primary purpose of editing these texts was to present a sufficient number of John Duns Scotus' ethical writings to enable historians of medieval philosophy, first of all, to correct some common misconceptions as to his theory of morality, and secondly to perceive its inner coherence. If this were accomplished, then I would hope—as my secondary aim—that they and others interested in ethical theory might better appreciate the value of his more interesting insights and see their relevance for contemporary ethical issues. Before turning to a brief analysis of the particular items, then, it seems well to address a few general remarks to the concerns that prompted the publication of the present collection.

Let us begin with what is perhaps the most persistently recurring objection to his moral philosophy. An article on British philosophy in *The Encyclopedia of Philosophy* sums it up well in a single line: "Things are good because God wills them and not vice versa, so moral truth is not accessible to natural reason" (Quinton, 1965, p. 373). This same claim has been made from the very beginning of the neoscholastic revival initiated by Pope Leo XIII (Erdmann, 1896, p. 214; Willmann, 1896, p. 508f; Siebeck, 1898; Landry, 1922, pp. 33f, 343f, etc.), and though effectively refuted periodically (Minges, 1905; Klein, 1916; Longpré, 1922; Schwendinger, 1934; De Wulf, 1936; Copleston, 1950; Stratenwerth, 1951; Hoeres, 1958; Wolter, 1972), tends to be repeated, especially by those dependent on material available in present editions, where unexamined student reports are credited with the same value as Scotus' own more carefully worded remarks.

More discriminating scholars, like Vernon Bourke, recognize that

Scotus "died before he could say his best word on the problems of ethics" and that "until recently his writings have been badly edited and they are not yet wholly available in critical texts." Nevertheless, he could see—even on the limited basis of what has been critically edited—that Scotus "was one of the most brilliant intellects produced in the British Isles" and "in spite of his general opposition to the philosophy of Thomas Aquinas, Duns Scotus supports the view that right reason is the basis on which to judge good human action. He offers, in fact, one of the clearest explanations of the meaning of *recta ratio*" (Bourke, 1970, p. 150f). Copleston, too, was well aware of Scotus' genius and importance, yet he admits at the beginning of his relatively short, but excellent, introductory account of Scotus' ethics that "my aim is not to propound all the ethical doctrines of Scotus, but rather to show that the accusation which has been brought against him of teaching the purely arbitrary character of the moral law, as though it depended simply and solely on the divine will, is, in the main, an unjust accusation" (Copleston, 1950, p. 545).

While his work is largely successful in accomplishing this limited but important goal, it does not show in any detail the inner coherence of Scotus' ethical theory and how he uses right reason to develop specific ethical conclusions. The same is true of Gilson's more extended account, which is not surprising in view of what he says about the scope and limitations of this work. "On n'y trouvera pas non plus un 'système' de Duns Scot, mais, cette fois, la seule raison en est que nous ne l'avons pas trouvé nous-même" (Gilson, 1952, p. 7).

C. R. S. Harris, it seems to me, put his finger on the keystone that gives Scotus' ethical philosophy its distinctive unity when he wrote: "His insistence on the distinction between will and desire enables him to grapple more adequately with the psychological analysis of ethical problems and lends his thinking a deeper insight into the facts of moral experience than was displayed by any Christian thinker since the days of Augustine" (Harris, 1927, p. 303). Yet Harris himself fails to see the full import of this distinction when he treats of Scotus' moral philosophy *ex professo*. For while he admits that "it is a mistake to interpret Duns' ethical theory solely in the light of [his] voluntaristic passages, as Landry, Jourdain, Schwane, Werner and many other of his critics have seen fit to do," Harris himself is unable to comprehend how these statements can be reconciled with Scotus' equally strong assertion that "the goodness of an action is dependent on conformity with right reason. That there is a latent contradiction in Scotus' thought," he goes on to say, "cannot be doubted, nor can we find any satisfactory solution to the antinomy . . . It is only by a frank recognition of this antinomy that we can hope to avoid the one-sided interpretation in which his teaching has so often been distorted" (pp. 331–35).

It seems incredible, however, that Duns, whom his most understanding yet outspoken critic admired "because of the great knowledge he had of logic" (Ockham, 1970, p. 344), was not aware of such a glaring antinomy at the very core of his ethics. For that reason, it seems well to begin the first and general part of this introduction with a brief account of the following presuppositions that underlie Scotus' ethical system. The first is his metaphysical notion of God; the second, his conviction that God must have free will and how it is to be understood; the third, how God's love for his infinitely perfect nature is both voluntary and steadfast, and hence is, in a special sense, necessary; the fourth, how this dual aspect of his will affects his relationship to creatures, with whom he always deals according to right reason and in some ordained and methodical way; and the last, in what sense God could be said to have revealed his will naturally to creatures, particularly in regard to the moral law. Once all this is properly understood, I think two points become very clear. First, Scotus had every reason to think moral truth was accessible to man's natural mental powers; second, his ethical philosophy as a whole is remarkably coherent.

1. *Scotus' metaphysical notion of God*

Though an *ex professo* theologian, Scotus—like the generality of his university colleagues in the tradition of Anselm's *Faith Seeking Understanding*—made wide use of philosophy, which in his day included all knowledge acquired by natural reason. And living in an age that intellectually at least was pluralistic, embracing not only Jewish philosophers like Maimonides and Avicebron, but Moslem Aristotelians like Avicenna and Averroes, Scotus was concerned to separate out the rational component of his beliefs from those "that are the subject of belief, wherein reason is held captive—yet to Catholics, are the more certain since they rest firmly upon [revealed] truth and not upon our intellect which is blind and weak in many things" (*De Primo Principio* 4.86; Wolter, 1983, p. 146). Hence his attitude towards what reason could prove:

If there are some necessary reasons for what we believe, it is not dangerous to set them forth, neither for the sake of believers nor for the sake of unbelievers. Not for believers, for Catholic doctors, inquiring into the truth of their beliefs and trying to understand them, did not intend thereby to destroy the merit of faith. Indeed Augustine and Anselm believed they labored meritoriously in trying to understand what they believed, according to that text

from Isaiah 7:[9] (in the other [i.e., Septuagint] translation): "Unless you believe, you will not understand"; for as believers they inquired, that they
might understand the reasons for what they believed . . . Neither is it dangerous so far as unbelievers are concerned. If one could find necessary reasons to
prove the possibility of some fact, it would also be useful to confront unbelievers with such, because by so doing one might to some extent persuade
them not to resist such beliefs as impossibilities. On the other hand, it could
be dangerous to present such unbelievers with sophisms as demonstrations,
because by so doing one could expose the faith to derision (and this is also
true of all other matters, also those which are [theologically] indifferent, such
as geometry). Rather than proposing fallacious arguments in place of demonstrations, it is better for one who lacks knowledge to recognize that he is ignorant than to think he knows on the basis of such sophisms. (Ord. II, dist. 1,
nn. 138–39; Vatican ed. VII, pp. 69–70)

Hence the theologian's need for critical analysis, rather than a funda-
mentalistic naivete or pietistic attitude.

If you say, otherwise, that God gives such knowledge to whom he wills, then
it would follow that we labor in vain in our study and inquiry into the truth.
A far better and easier way of coming to theology would be to sit in church
and ask God to give us this light. [Si dicas, quod non dat sic, sed cui vult (sc.
Deus) etc., sequeretur quod laboraremus frustra in studio et inquirendo veri-
tatem, et esset multo melior via et levior veniendi ad scientiam theologiae
sedere in ecclesia et rogare Deum, ut daret nobis illud lumen.] (Ord. III,
suppl. dist. 24; Codex A, f. 167ra)

Because theology has God as its subject, Scotus was most interested
in what philosophy could offer in the way of rational knowledge of
God's existence and nature. John Duns felt that metaphysics, as the
first and highest of the theoretical sciences outlined by Aristotle, had
the most to contribute to his enterprise. Aristotelians like Avicenna
and Averroes, however, had been at odds as to its subject and its goal.
William of Alnwick, Scotus' secretary, gave the following edited account of John's own words as to why he sided with the former:

We must first see whether metaphysics, the first and highest of the naturally
acquired habits [of knowledge or science] perfecting man's intellect in the
present life, has God as its first object. On this point there is a controversy
between Avicenna and Averroes. Avicenna claims that God is not the subject of metaphysics, because no science proves [the existence of] its own subject. The metaphysician, however, proves that God exists. Averroes reproves
Avicenna in his final comment on the Physics, Bk. I, because he wished, by
using the same major premise against Avicenna, to prove that God and the
pure spirits are the subject of metaphysics, and that God's existence is not
proved in metaphysics, since it is only by means of motion, which pertains to
the science of natural philosophy [or physics], that any kind of pure spirit can

be proved to exist.—It seems to me, however, that of the two, Avicenna has spoken better. Wherefore, I argue against Averroes as follows . . . If the philosopher of nature can prove that God exists, then God's existence is a conclusion of natural philosophy. Now if metaphysics cannot prove the existence of God in this way, then God's existence is presupposed as a principle of metaphysics. Consequently, a conclusion of natural philosophy is a principle of metaphysics, and therefore the philosophy of nature is prior to metaphysics . . . Now it is not just such properties of the effect as are treated in the philosophy of nature that are possible only on condition that God exists, for the same is true of the properties treated in metaphysics. Not only does motion presuppose a mover, but a being that is posterior presupposes one that is prior. Consequently, from the priority that exists among beings, the existence of the First Being can be inferred, and this can be done in a more perfect way than the existence of a Prime Mover can be established in natural philosophy. We can infer, then, in metaphysics from act and potency, finiteness and infinity, multitude and unity, and many other such metaphysical properties, that God or the First Being exists . . . Hence I concede with Avicenna that God is not the subject of metaphysics. The Philosopher's statement (*Metaphysics*, Bk. I) that metaphysics is concerned with the highest causes, presents no difficulty. For he speaks here as he did in the *Prior Analytics*, Bk. I, where he says: "First it is necessary to determine with what [Prior Analytics] is concerned and what it has to do. It is concerned with demonstration and has to do with the demonstrative branch of learning, that is with the general science of demonstrating or syllogizing". Hence "concerned with" denotes properly the circumstance of the final cause just as much as it does that of the material cause. Wherefore, metaphysics is concerned with the highest causes as its end. In knowing them, metaphysical science attains its goal. (Wolter, 1962, pp. 9–12)

Though he developed his metaphysical proof with slight variations in all his commentaries on the *Sentences*, its final form appears in what was to become a philosophical classic, his *Tractatus de Primo Principio*. Fittingly—since metaphysics has "being" as its subject—Scotus opens with a prayer to the God who revealed himself to Moses as "the I am who am." "Help me then, O Lord," he prays, "as I investigate how much our natural reason can learn about that true being which you are if we begin with the 'being' which you predicated of yourself." And in the closing pages he sums up what he thinks metaphysics can offer a believing Catholic:

O Lord, our God, Catholics can infer most of the perfections which philosophers knew of you from what has been said. You are the first efficient cause, the ultimate end, supreme in perfection, transcending all things. You are uncaused in any way and therefore incapable of becoming or perishing; indeed it is simply impossible that you should not exist, for of yourself you are necessary being. You are therefore eternal, because the span of your existence is

without limit and you experience it all at once, for it cannot be strung out in
a succession of events. For there can be no succession save in what is continually caused, or at least in what is dependent for its existence upon another, and this dependence is a far cry from what has necessary being of itself.
You live a most noble life, because you are understanding and volition. You
are happy, indeed you are by nature happiness itself, because you are in possession of yourself. You are the clear vision of yourself and the most joyful
love, and although you are self-sufficient and happy in yourself alone, you still
understand in a single act everything that can be known. At one and the
same time you possess the power to freely and contingently will each thing
that can be caused and by willing it through your volition cause it to be. Most
truly then you are of infinite power. You are incomprehensible, infinite, for
nothing omniscient or of infinite power is finite . . . Neither is the ultimate
end, nor what exists of itself in all simplicity, something finite. You are the
ultimate in simplicity, having no really distinct parts, or no realities in your
essence which are not really the same. In you no quantity, no accident can be
found, and therefore you are incapable of accidental change, even as I have
already expressed, you are so in essence. You alone are simply perfect, not just
a perfect angel, or a perfect body, but a perfect being, lacking no entity it is
possible for anything to have. Nothing can formally possess every perfection,
but every entity can exist in something either formally or eminently, as it
does in you, O God, who are supreme among beings, the only one of them
who is infinite. Communicating the rays of your goodness most liberally, you
are boundless good, to whom as the most lovable thing of all every single
being in its own way comes back to you as to its ultimate end. (Wolter, 1983,
pp. 142–44)

In describing how we form concepts of God (*Ord.* I, dist. 3, n. 58;
Vatican ed. III, p. 48), Scotus points out that there are two ways in
which we can speak and think of his infinite perfection. One is to enu-
merate all his perfections in the manner Scotus does above; the other
is by using a simpler, but less perfect, concept (i.e., one that does not
spell out formally all it implies), namely, "infinite being," which virtually includes all of the above. And in his *Quodlibet*, q. 5, he explains
in some detail how we go about forming such a concept or how we give
conceptual meaning to the term "infinite" as applied to God (see
Alluntis-Wolter, 1975, pp. 108–12).

The point of all this is that God, for Scotus, is equated with a being
of infinite perfection, whether unqualified perfection be conceived of
intensively or extensively. This will explain much of what he says
about what is necessarily binding on God, both with respect to what
he is and with respect to what he owes his own goodness, if and when
he creates (selections 15 and 16). It also accounts for what will be
binding in an absolute sense on whatever moral beings God might
create (selections 18, 25, 26, 27, and 32). And in all these matters,

Duns will point out, God never acts contrary to what right reason or prudence would dictate, for God is always *ordinatissime volens*.

2. How divine free will differs from ours

Equally certain to Scotus was the experiential fact that we possess free will (see selection 2) and that contingency exists in the world around us. He considered the latter to be a "primary truth not demonstrable *a priori*." Those who deny such manifest things, he says, quoting Aristotle, "need punishment or senses," not argument.

For as Avicenna puts it . . . "Those who deny a first principle should be beaten or exposed to fire until they concede that to burn and not to burn, or to be beaten and not to be beaten, are not identical". And so too, those who deny that some being is contingent should be exposed to torments until they concede it is possible for them not to be tormented. (Wolter, 1962, p. 9)

From the existence of our free will and the fact of contingency in the world, he believed we could prove that God also has free will and that this fact is a necessary condition, though not a sufficient reason, why something is contingent. His proof for this was in the aforesaid metaphysical argument for God, but is repeated in summary fashion in dist. 39 of his lectures on the first book of the *Sentences*, where he goes on to analyze in some detail how God's will must differ from ours. This discussion appears in several forms, including that of the original *Lectura* (XVII, pp. 481–513) and a substantially revised and expanded form that follows the plan of the *Lectura*, but depends upon the *Reportatio examinata* I, dists. 38–40. The editors of the Vatican edition think this later version, though expressing the most mature thought of Scotus, may have been completed by a disciple using materials from Scotus' notebooks and other sources no longer extant. Since it is found in all the principal manuscripts in substantially the same form, the editors believe they all depend upon a single apograph, and they have prepared a critical edition of this text in Appendix A of volume VI, pp. 401–44. Scotus' argument there runs as follows.

Granted contingency exists, what must we presuppose about God, the first cause, as a necessary condition for the possibility of such contingency? We must assume that he does not create, conserve, or cooperate with the causes he creates in any necessary way. There must be some positive cause or reason, which cannot be his intellect as such, but must have its roots in his free will. To understand how we can ascribe will to God we must first analyze what our own freedom involves. It has a triple aspect. First, we are free in regard to opposite acts. This refers to what Scotus described in some detail in selection 2, namely, that our will is an active potency, and as such can do something, i.e., it can determine itself in opposite or contrary ways. Second, as the root cause of such opposite acts of volition, it can also tend to opposite objects and, third, produce opposite effects. The first sort of freedom, as it exists in us, involves a certain imperfection, for we are not only the cause of our volition, but the recipient of this immanent action as well, and in causing it, we are changed from a state of not willing to willing. Passivity and mutability, then, are imperfections associated with this first sense of freedom. It will require further analysis, Scotus explains, to extract from this amalgam of positive perfection, passivity, and mutability what is a matter of pure perfection and hence could exist in God. Scotus finds this kernel of unqualified perfection to be what is implied in the will's peculiar character as an active potency or causal principle, namely, the positive or superabundant indeterminacy that enables the will to act in opposite or contrary ways. The second and third aspects of freedom, the will's ability to tend to opposite objects and produce opposite effects, is the sort of freedom required for artistic creativity and is also a matter of pure or unqualified perfection. The two aspects are separable, however, for one can love or hate something without necessarily producing or destroying it. Scotus describes the second aspect, as characteristic of our freedom, in the following way:

I maintain that one obvious power for opposites is associated with this freedom, for although it does not include the power to will and not will simultaneously (since this is nothing), it still includes the power to will after not willing, or a power for opposites in succession. This power for opposite acts in succession, however, is not peculiar to the will, but is characteristic of all mutable things. Nevertheless, the will has another, less evident power for opposites apart from any succession. For suppose that a created will existed for but one instant and had this particular volition at that instant, it would not have it at that moment in a necessary manner. Proof: If it did, then since it is a cause only at the instant it causes that volition, the will would cause it then in a simply necessary fashion. (For the present situation would not obtain, where the will is said to be a contingent cause, because prior to the instant it causes, it could either cause or not cause. Just as this being, then, when it exists, is necessary or contingent, so too a cause, when it causes, does so then either necessarily or contingently.) At this instant, then, [this cause which exists but for an instant] causes contingently, and hence has at that moment, in the absence of any succession, the power for the opposite of what it actually causes. And this real power (as first act [i.e., as actually existing]) is a power that is naturally prior to those opposites, which (as second acts [i.e., as its actual volitions]) are naturally posterior. For the first act [i.e., something as existing], considered in its natural priority to second act, gives to its effect, as contingent, its existence in such a way that, as naturally prior, it could just as well have done the opposite.

Concomitant with this real active power that is naturally prior to what it produces is a logical power, which is a compatibility of terms. For even when the will produces this particular volition, the opposite volition is not inconsistent with the will as first act [i.e., as an actually existing causal power]. The reason is twofold, first because the will is a contingent cause with respect to its effect, and second, insofar as the will is also the recipient subject of its immanent act, it is related to what informs it only contingently, because no subject is opposed to what inheres in it only as an "incidental accident."

Therefore, both a power for opposites in succession and a power for opposites at the same instant, are associated with the liberty of our will; or to put it another way, either of these real powers could exist without the other. But it is this second real power—as naturally prior to the concomitant third, or logical, power—that is the real cause of the volitional act. But the "fourth power"—viz., to have opposite acts simultaneously—is not associated with the will, because this represents no power whatsoever.

Using the logical tool of the distinction between the composite and divided senses, Scotus goes on to show both in what sense the ambiguous statement "When the will wills A, it can also not will A" can be both true and false and why Aristotle's controversial statement in *De interpretatione* II, ch. 9 (19a23–24), that "whatever exists, when it is, must necessarily exist" needs qualification. Since Duns' detailed explanation is covered by what he says in selection 2, we need not go into the matter further. Suffice it to say that just as we—at the instant we freely decide and will one alternative—have both a real and a logical potentiality for the opposite, so too does God. For this is what the essential perfection of free will implies. And while such coexists in us only with the imperfection associated with passivity and mutability, this factual mutability is lacking in God, who from all eternity freely decides to create, conserve, and cooperate with the free actions of his creatures in a contingent way. For despite the steadfastness of his free will, it always has at root its potentiality to have caused the opposite of what it *de facto* causes. This point will be treated in selection 16, which deals with the absolute and ordained power of God.

3. God's voluntary self-love as both free and necessary

In selection 4 we have Scotus' interpretation of the twofold "affection" St. Anselm of Canterbury ascribes to the created will. The first is its affection for the advantageous (*affectio commodi*). This makes it a rational or intellectual appetite that seeks what the intellect shows is advantageous to the creature, particularly what makes it happy (selection 6). Under the aspect of its inclination for the advantageous we can speak of a "natural will" (selection 5). This refers primarily not to an elicited action of the will, but rather to an inclination or bias the will has as a "nature." For like all natures, according to Aristotle, it seeks or "loves"—whatever perfects its nature. This affection for the advantageous is also characteristic of all human sense appetites. Hence it is not something proper or peculiar to a rational creature possessing intellect.

It is the second inclination that is proper to a rational being whose mind is governed by right reason, namely, its "affection for justice." This is essentially an inclination towards something intrinsically good (*bonum honestum*). By reason of this affection, the will is invited to love or tend towards that good "for its own sake." We experience such an objective attraction where beauty is to be found. There we are drawn out of ourselves, as it were, and are involved with and absorbed by the beautiful object itself. We "love it for its own sake" with a "love" that is neither private nor jealous, but rather one that inclines us to invite others to admire and share it with us. Richard of St. Victor was to develop this notion to explain the inner life of the Trinity (Richard de Saint-Victor, 1958, pp. 136ff), wherein he was followed by St. Bonaventure (Hayes, 1979, p. 23f). Scotus uses it primarily to show the rationale behind God's creativity (Wolter, 1980, p. 157).

As Richard conceives of this "love," it has an aspect of necessity. Indeed, because this inner divine life is as necessary as is God's nature itself, Richard is convinced that he can give not just "probable but necessary reasons" why God is the sort of being he is (p. 89). Anselm's original approach is to stress the other aspect, the inner freedom or essential "liberty" of God's will-act or "love" of what is intrinsically good about himself. He had earlier corrected a common misconception about human liberty, viz., that our will is free because it has the capacity to sin, a *potestas peccandi* that permits it to depart from justice or what right reason dictates. As such, *will* cannot exist in God; neither is will in any unqualified sense a perfection (*perfectio simpliciter*). Hence, Anselm's revolutionary definition of *freedom* as a pure perfection, viz., as the capacity to preserve justice for its own sake (*potestas servandi rectitudinem propter seipsum*) and his definition of *justice* itself as "rectitude-of-will served for its own sake" (*iustitia est rectitudo voluntatis propter se servata*), cited by Scotus in selection 15. Under this aspect, freedom is not opposed to necessity, for "necessary" and "necessity" are terms with many meanings, as we shall shortly see.

But before going into that, however, let us note that the rectitude and justice Anselm apparently had in mind was that supernatural or "gratuitous grace," something infused by God which so sanctifies the soul as to make it capable of sharing in the inner life of the Trinity in the hereafter. As such it liberates us from the need to seek God only as our ultimate perfection and happiness, and permits us to love him honestly for his own sake and above all else (see selection 25). Scotus seemingly carried this notion of liberation even further than Anselm, for he described this "affection for justice" as "libertas innata," i.e., something inborn, native, or congenital to the human will. In fact he goes still further; not only is it an essential component of the will, but it represents what an Aristotelian would call the "ultimate specific difference" that elevates a "rational appetite" and transforms it into an appetite that is "free." He refers to this "affectio iustitiae" either as "innata libertas" (which I have translated as "native liberty") or as "ingenita libertas," which could be translated literally more properly as "unbegotten liberty" (but which I have translated, as characteristic of creatures, and man in particular, as "congenital"). Though it is a bias and an inclination, like the affection for the advantageous, and hence is not an elicited act as such, the affection for justice already introduces a measure of freedom from nature. For nature, according to Aristotle, always seeks its own perfection, either as concretized in the individual or as characteristic of the species. But liberty comes to its full perfection when the human will (which is physically free to elicit an act in regard to either inclination) freely determines itself in accord with this higher inclination and elicits an act that tends towards a good in an objective and honest manner, namely, in accord with the intrinsic value or goodness of the object as such. Where the human will is well ordered, its first act of love of any good, then, will be in accord with this affection for justice. But since man is finite in perfection and tends to perfect himself by actively acquiring what he needs to be perfect, he must also—to be true to himself and his God-given nature—will what is to his advantage as well as what is good in itself. Hence, secondarily, persons with well-ordered wills will love what most accords with their own perfection, namely, what fulfills their personal needs and thus brings happiness and contentment. Happiness itself can thus become a sort of reflex object of well-ordered love (see Klein, 1916, p. 157, and selection 25).

In the supernatural order, man is destined to be perfected by union with the Trinity, because God, as a perfect lover, wills that what he loves be loved by others, "willing others to love with him the very object of his love" (Wolter, 1980, p. 157). Hence the will's affection for the advantageous (affectio commodi) is perfected supernaturally by the infused theological virtue of hope, whereas its affection for justice is perfected by the theologically infused virtue of charity or sanctifying grace (selection 25). In selection 25, art. 2, Scotus will explain how a well-ordered love can regard God under all three aspects, (1) as a good in himself, (2) as our good, and (3) as a source of happiness, and in that order of priority of values.

According to what was said in the previous section, God possesses whatever is a matter of pure perfection in our human will. Hence, the full conception of God's free will must include not only his ability to will opposites or to produce contrary effects (something Scotus thought was well described by Aristotle; see selection 2), but also what St. Anselm considered to be a pure perfection, i.e., the will's affection for justice (see selection 5; also Hoeres, 1958, 1962). Mutability, as we noted in the previous section, is an imperfection of the will, like the *potestas peccandi* that permits a finite agent to "depart from justice" and to will some finite good immoderately in one of the several ways Scotus explains that Lucifer might have sinned (selection 29). Mutability in this sense must also be lacking in God, where it would imply that he could cease to love his infinitely lovable divine nature with the objectivity that the affection for justice demands. If we can, and right reason dictates we should, love our own nature and whatever perfects it and makes us happy (selection 27), something we are already inclined by nature to do in virtue of our *affectio commodi*, then God too—in some analogous way—must also love this aspect of his infinitely lovable nature, namely, that it is a good for him, and also a source of infinite happiness. For, according to our way of thinking, this dynamic unselfish love for what is intrinsically good also perfects his will and makes God happy in much the same way as our well-ordered love of God for his own sake has two other accompanying sorts of love for him, one because he loves and perfects us, the other because he is our ultimate happiness. Now, in the aforesaid selection on Lucifer's sin, Scotus explains how the blessed in heaven can love their own happiness that results from the beatific vision and the love it engenders, and do so out of an affection for justice. In the same way Anselm explains that God could have necessarily loved what pertained to the perfection of his nature and satisfied his will, as it were, making it happy and content, with no compelling need to seek further perfection. For this is something that becomes his nature, and to fail to love himself, or to have the capacity we have of turning away from what we are most inclined to love by reason of our affection for justice, would imply an "infirmity" or weakness in God's essence, something metaphysically incompatible with the infinite perfection Scotus ascribes to it.

If such mutability is also lacking in God, then by the same token his will must have the pure perfection we call "firmness of purpose" or a "steadfast will." It is under this aspect that Scotus admits that, where God is concerned and with respect to his inner love-life, the freedom associated with his "unbegotten liberty" (*ingenita libertas*) must also be associated with a certain immutability or necessity. It is this notion that he proposes in his *Quodlibet*, q. 16. We are indebted to William A. Frank for a critical reading of a portion of that text which has been erroneously transcribed in all of our presently available editions. For "firmitas est perfectio" they have substituted "libertas est perfectio" where Scotus is explaining how "libertas voluntatis et necessitas naturalis possint se competi in eodem respectu eiusdem actus" (Frank, 1982, p. 215). The important passage from Frank's edition, based on three of the earliest manuscripts (described in Alluntis-Wolter, 1975, pp. xxxii–iii), reads as follows:

Dico quod cum necessitate ad volendum stat libertas in voluntate . . . Probatur idem "propter quid." Et hoc primo sic: Actio circa finem ultimum est actio perfectissima; in tali actione firmitas in agendo est perfectionis; igitur necessitas in ea non tollit sed magis ponit illud quod est perfectionis; si est libertas.

This necessitates the following change in the Alluntis-Wolter translation, *God and Creatures* (16.32, p. 378), which should read:

Action that has to do with the ultimate end is most perfect. But firmness pertains to the perfection of such an action. Therefore, the necessity that is to be found there does not do away with, but rather demands, what is needed for perfection, namely, freedom.

The context in which the relevant passage occurs is as follows. Scotus has first shown that the act by which God loves himself is necessary in an unqualified sense, for "God is necessarily happy, and hence beholds and loves the beatific object." John Duns then undertakes to prove that this is not inconsistent with the essential freedom associated with every elicited act of God's will. No pure perfection excludes another pure perfection, says Scotus (Wolter, 1949, p. 167). This need to love what is infinitely lovable, if we may call it a "need," is also a matter of pure perfection. Hence it is *per se* compatible, according to Anselm, with perfect liberty. Anselm explicitly tells us such, says Scotus, in ch. 1 of *Free Choice*: "Whoever has what is appropriate and advantageous in such a way that it cannot be lost is freer than he who has this in such a way that it can be lost." From this Anselm concludes: "The will then which cannot cease to be upright is freer" (Alluntis-Wolter, 1975, p. 378). Augustine too could be quoted in confirmation, but—says Scotus—we can give rational proofs as to why this is so, the first of which is the one based on the notion of "firmitas." We might note that Scotus considers it a self-evident fact that "firmness pertains to the perfection of such an action," because he speaks of the proof based on this notion as "propter quid." This is the sort of proof Aristotle says is not just a demonstration of the simple fact, but rather a proof that gives the essential reason why this fact is true.

The point of all this is to show why Scotus believed that in God, at least, the perfection of his love for his own nature is not only free but necessary. It is free, in the sense that it is a will-act and *will*, as opposed to *nature*, never tends to anything except in the spontaneous, self-determining, and liberated way that is peculiar to it as *will*. But it is also in some sense necessary. For "necessary"—he points out—is a multifaceted word with a multiplicity of meanings. And in addition to the ones that are cited explicitly in *God and Creatures* (Alluntis-Wolter, 1975), p. 379, we need to add the necessity entailed by "firmness of purpose" or a "steadfast will."

Finally, we should stress that this too is a consequence of God's "affection for justice," which, as Scotus will point out in selection 15, obliges him to do justice to his own goodness. And this brings us to our next point, how this dual aspect not only affects the relationship of God's will to his own goodness, but also modifies his creative act.

4. Right reason governs God's relationship to creatures

The two selections in Part IV deal with the dual aspect of God's relationship to creatures in general and to the moral law binding on man in particular. If God's will is infinitely perfect and all creatures have only a finite degree of being and goodness, then it is clear that from an Aristotelian point of view, the finite goodness of a creature cannot be the final cause that moves God to give it existence, even if "moves" be taken in the metaphorical sense of a motive (*Finis movet metaphorice*). As we shall see in explaining the background of item 16, the scholastics to a man rejected the theory of Abelard that anticipated in some sense Leibniz's belief that one could find a sufficient reason for God's creating the world he actually did in the degree of goodness characteristic of this "best of all possible worlds." It is this conviction—rooted let us note in the fact that God's creative will is governed by right reason—that caused the Parisian theologians to reject the Averroistic necessitarianism that had invaded the arts faculty and prompted Bishop Stephen Tempier to issue the condemnations of "errors" in 1270 and 1277. Here is where we find the rationale of the controversial statement that "things are good because God wills them, and not vice versa."

As I noted in an earlier publication (Wolter, 1972, pp. 366–68), the context in which this oft-quoted expression occurs is in reference to the merits of Christ and reads in full:

I say that just as everything other than God is good because it is willed by God and not vice versa, so this merit was good to the extent that it was accepted. It was not the other way around, namely, because it was merit and good, therefore it was accepted. (*Ord.* III, suppl. dist. 37, n. 6)

Scotus is concerned here specifically with meritorious goodness, rather than natural or moral goodness as such. Since merit is dependent on grace or charity (selection 11), it has to do, not with the natural order, but with the supernatural state to which man has been gratuitously elevated by God. If any human act is to be rewarded with an increase of grace in this life and a face-to-face vision and love of God in the next, this is obviously a pure gift on God's part and transcends anything our human nature needs or requires. Hence, the particular application of this principle should not create any problem or appear as a violation of anything demanded by right reason. However, the principle itself is unquestionably broader in scope, and may even have a transcendental or metaphysical interpretation, as well as application to "moral goodness" in the broad sense in which this term is taken in selection 11. In either case, however, right reason and the affection of the will for justice seem to play a significant role. This will become clear if we consider how Scotus regarded natural goodness, and secondly, what moral goodness adds to the natural goodness of a voluntary act.

a. Natural goodness. Scotus is not denying that possibles by reason of their nature can have an essential or natural goodness; the same is true not only of substantive natures but also of actions, including voluntary acts that are elicited freely. In selection 11, for instance, he refers to "volition's natural goodness, which pertains to it as something positive and which is characteristic of any positive thing according to the grade of entity it has (the more the entity, the more the goodness; the less the entity, the less the goodness)." Obviously, such natural goodness, or the "primary or essential goodness" Scotus speaks of in selection 10—if these be the same—is not arbitrarily will-dependent. Otherwise, there would be no point in what he says about God as "ordinatissime volens," something we shall take up shortly. What he is trying to rule out is the suggestion that this natural goodness somehow moves God's creative will in the way his own infinite goodness does, for no creature has a claim to actual existence simply in virtue of the sort of thing it happens to be.

In the case of God's intellect, Scotus had argued that it would be derogatory to the perfection of God's mind if it depended for its knowledge on the intelligibility of a created object. For any such object is finite, limited in perfection, and to that extent, it represents a mixture of perfection and imperfection, and as such it does not move God's intellect to know it. God is rather like the poet or sculptor, who first models his masterpiece in his mind before putting it on paper or embodying it in marble or bronze, for his infinitely fertile intellect mentally creates each possible creature as an object of thought, thus giving that created nature or essence its first intelligibility or *esse intelligibile*. Hence, for Scotus it is true to say: "God does not know creatures because they are intelligible; but vice versa, creatures are intelligible because God knows them" (*Ord.* I, dist. 35, nn. 31–32; Vatican ed. VI, p. 258). If creatures have an ideal being or essence, they also have an ideal or essential goodness. But being finite in degree, it cannot force or compel the divine will first to give it being as a willed object (*esse volitum*) from all eternity, and then actual existence at some moment in time. Hence, when Scotus says that "everything other than God is good because it is willed by God and not vice versa," if natural goodness is meant, the statement can only refer to real or actual existing goodness. And it would mean nothing more than that the divine creative will is contingently related to whatever created good exists.

So understood, the controversial maxim would be a logical consequence of the fact that God's will is governed by an affection for justice. For this would mean it tends to something good in terms of its intrinsic or true value. Only where the good is infinite can it bind or necessitate God's infinitely perfect will. In all other cases, God is free to love or not to love creatively.

Does this mean God is free to deal with his creatures in a purely arbitrary and whimsical fashion? Or to put the question another way, in what sense is God constrained to create a cosmos rather than something bizarre or chaotic? Does the affection for justice characteristic of his will impose any obligation on him as to what or how he will create? Scotus addresses himself to this problem in selection 15, where he asks: Is there justice in God? and in selection 16: Could God have created things otherwise than he did?

In answer to the first question he points out in what sense God is just and upright both in respect to what he owes himself and in his dealings with others. To begin with, the law or practical truth "God must be loved" is prior to any decision on the part of the divine will. Furthermore, he is bound by his affection for justice to be true to his own goodness. This obligation, if we can call it that, is also something anterior to any act on the part of his will. While he is obliged, so to speak, to love his infinitely lovable divine nature as an infinite good, he is not so necessitated towards any finite entity. Creative love is always a free gift on his part, something contingently given. But granted he does create, does God owe creatures anything in justice? Not in a strict sense, says Scotus, since these are finite and cannot compel or force an infinite will to do anything it does not freely choose to do. Nevertheless, the justice which obliges God to be true to his own goodness does modify his creative act in regard to whatever he chooses

to create. Scotus expresses this most succinctly when he writes in selection 15:

I say that God is no debtor in any unqualified sense save with respect to his
own goodness, namely, that he love it. But where creatures are concerned he
is debtor rather to his generosity, in the sense that he gives creatures what
their nature demands, which exigency in them is set down as something just,
a kind of secondary object of this justice, as it were. But in truth nothing
outside of God can be said to be definitely just without this added qualification. In an unqualified sense where a creature is concerned, God is just only
in relation to his first justice, namely, because such a creature has been actually willed by the divine will.

In a word, if he actually creates something, God must be true to
himself and to his infinitely good and perfect nature. As I noted elsewhere (Wolter, 1972, p. 367), it has often been said of fine artists or
master craftsmen that they cannot turn out a product badly done. I
think this might serve as a model for what Scotus is saying equiva-
lently. For God is obviously the most perfect of artists, a craftsman like
no other. He owes it to himself that whatever he chooses to create will
have a beauty and natural goodness about it. Yet no particular creation
is so perfect, beautiful, or good that it exhausts his infinite powers of
creativity. While the goodness of creation is thus, in some sense, a
consequence of the affection for justice inherent in his will, no creation or creature is such that its goodness can be regarded in an Abelardian or Leibnizian sense as a sufficient reason for its existence.

This latter point is stressed in selection 16, which points out that
God could always create otherwise than he actually has, since to do so is
not self contradictory. For though he has ordered things wisely, his absolute power extends beyond what he has actually ordained. And while
absolute power is defined in terms of what is not self-contradictory,
this does not mean—as an initial objection suggests—that "he could
have made things inordinately." If what Scotus has just said of God's
justice be true, then it would be simply self-contradictory if he did not
do justice to his own goodness and in his generosity make creatures in
a fitting way. And in the examined report of his late Paris lectures he
says expressly, paraphrasing St. Augustine: "Whatever God made, you
know that God has made it with right reason" ("Quidquid Deus fecit,
hoc scias, Deum cum recta ratione fecisse"; *Reportatio* I A, dist. 44,
q. 2; Vienna, cod. palatinus 1453, f. 122va).

Put in another way, God is always "ordinatissime volens." In the
section entitled "How God's Love Extends to All Things" (Wolter,
1980, pp. 155ff), Scotus describes the actual order of creation as the
theologian conceives of it.

Everyone who wills in a reasonable way, first wills the end and secondly that which immediately attains the end, and thirdly other things that are more remotely ordered to the attainment of his end. And so it is [with] God, who is most reasonable, not of course by different acts, but in one single act which is said to tend in different ways to the different objects ordered in some way to one another—first wills the end, and in this his act is perfect, and his intellect is perfect, and his will is happy. Secondly, he wills those things which are immediately ordered to him . . . Hence, he first loves himself ordinately and consequently not inordinately in an envious or jealous manner. Secondly, he wills to have co-lovers, and this is nothing else than willing that others have his love in themselves . . . Thirdly, however, he wills those things which are necessary to attain his end, namely, the gift of grace. Fourthly, he wills for their sakes other things that are more remote, for instance this sensible world in order that it may serve them, so that what is stated in the second book of Aristotle's *Physics* is true: 'Man is in some way the end of all sensible things', for these are willed in the fourth place because of man's being willed in the second place. Also that which is closer to the ultimate end is customarily said to be the end of the sensible world, whether it be because God wills the sensible world to be ordered to predestined man or whether it be because his more immediate concern is not that the sensible world exist, but rather that man love him.

Even though he is speaking of a supernatural order, something beyond anything Aristotle dreamed of, there is no suggestion the principle does not apply to the natural order as well. God is always "ordinatissime volens"—a most methodical lover. Grace builds on nature, after all, and the supernatural on the natural.

So much for natural goodness and meritorious goodness. But what of moral goodness? Can the controversial maxim be applied to this, as Quinton suggests, and if so, how is it to be understood?

b. Moral goodness. Moral goodness is formally something inherent in a human act, namely, its suitability or conformity to what right reason dictates (selections 9, 10, and 12). Hence its existence as well as its possibility in some degree depends on the fact that God has freely created man not merely with an intellectual but with a free appetite. One could interpret this reductively of course as meaning merely that a morally good act has a special form of natural goodness. But Scotus apparently had something more in mind. As he points out in selections 10 and 11, moral goodness is something over and above the natural or essential goodness characteristic of a voluntary act, though it presupposes such antecedent goodness as a relational entity presupposes its relata and foundation for the relationship. The will's affection for justice or its native freedom liberates it in some degree from the servitude of human nature that always seeks its own individual perfection or that of the species. Consequently, one would suspect that the will too is not bound morally merely by some principle of self-actualization, or obligation that arises automatically and exclusively from the fact that creatures are perfectible in certain ways. It can be bound only by an infinite or absolute good, or by a higher will that has authority because it authored man as free, i.e., with an inclination or affection for justice as dictated by right reason.

To explain. As ethicians have often argued, one cannot logically go from what is the case to what ought to be. Because justice determines what ought to be, Scotus sees the will as somehow morally bound by reason of what is essential to it as will, its affection for justice (selection 5) and the fact it is a "rational potency" or guided by right reason (selection 2). As such, it tends to things in terms of their intrinsic values, or what it owes to such. Where the value is absolute, such as in the case of the infinitely good God, "God should be loved" is an obligation according to right reason simply in virtue of the object to be loved. Scotus, in selection 11, distinguishes two grades of moral goodness antecedent to meritorious goodness. One is generic, the other specific; the former regards the object willed; the latter regards the attendant circumstances and particularly the end for which the object in question is loved or hated. Generic goodness is concerned with the question: "According to right reason is it suitable, appropriate, or just to love or hate such an object?" Specific goodness asks: "Is the purpose or other attendant circumstances such that according to right reason such and such an object should be loved or hated, sought or avoided?" There is only one case where a voluntary act is completely good simply in virtue of its object or generic goodness, that is, where God is the object of friendship love (*amor amicitiae*). For by such a voluntary act, God is loved for his own sake, and thus, we could say, the appropriate end is built into the initial act itself. Furthermore, as an infinite good, God cannot be loved too much, or too often, or under any other inappropriate conceivable circumstance.

As for generic goodness, this fitting relationship between the will-act and its object, like natural goodness, is not something that depends solely upon God's will. God wills such because it is good, and it is not good just because God wills it. Take the case where an act is generically good or bad by reason of the object alone, e.g., love of God as an intrinsically good act, or hatred or disrespect of God as an intrinsically bad act. In selection 15, referred to above, Scotus makes it clear that the "law" or "practical truth" "God should be loved" or "God must not be shown irreverence" holds good antecedent to any will or decision on God's part. It is on this score that Scotus concedes that "legal justice, could be postulated of God if there were some other law antecedent to any decision of his will, with which 'law and its legislator' as other his own will could rightly agree." There is such a law, he goes on to say, namely, "'God should be loved'—if one ought to call it a 'law' rather than a practical principle of law." In any case, he insists, "it is a practical truth that is prior to any decision on the part of the divine will." If God's will itself is "bound by such a law," so too, *a fortiori*, is the free will of any creature he has authored.

But what is to be said of the other specific obligations that ethical philosophers agree are morally binding on man? All of these, unless they can be shown to follow logically from a law such as "God should be loved" or "God should not be hated," are indifferent *per se* generically, and become morally good or bad dependent on the circumstances, as the selections in Part III make clear. In regard to such actions, natural goodness becomes a necessary condition for generic moral goodness; generic moral goodness, for specific moral goodness; specific moral goodness, for meritorious goodness. Conversely, the absence of anything demanded by right reason suffices to induce some measure of moral badness or lack of moral goodness, according to the principle taken over from pseudo-Dionysius, namely, "Good requires that everything about the act be right" (selection 11).

Like the generality of his contemporaries and medieval colleagues, Scotus equates the complete requirements of the moral law with what is enjoined on man by either natural law, divine positive law, or legitimate positive legislation imposed by proper ecclesiastical, civil, or parental authority (see Part V, "The Moral Law in General"). Obligations of divine positive law obviously depend upon the will of God; ecclesiastical or civil authority is legitimate if it is directly or indirectly sanctioned by God. The question of the will-dependence of the remaining obligations then comes down to how far the precepts of natural law can be said to be dependent on God's will.

In selection 18, Scotus explains at great length the twofold meaning of "law of nature," reflected in its division into two tables. The initial three commandments that make up the first table concern our relationship and obligations towards God. The second table, comprising the last seven commandments, concerns our social and political relationship and obligations towards our neighbor. Now, the intrinsic and objective values safeguarded by the precepts of these two tables are vastly different. Inasmuch as the first table can be equated with this law, "God should be loved," God himself could not dispense man from its obligations. And hence in this sense, the actions commanded or prohibited by the first table are morally good or bad independently of the fact that God commands or prohibits such (see *Ord.* II, dist. 21,

q. 2, n. 3; Wadding reprint ed. XIII, p. 141; *Reportatio* II A, dist. 22, n. 3; ibid., XXIII, p. 104). Specifically the third commandment (regarding the obligation "to keep holy the Sabbath") represents positive divine law, explicating affirmatively how "God should be loved" is to be fulfilled, and to that extent this action is good because God wills it. But the first two precepts, insofar as they prohibit the worship of "strange gods" or any irreverence towards the true God, are precepts that "belong strictly to the natural law, taking law of nature as that which follows necessarily if God exists and he alone must be loved as God." Since God himself could never dispense from these two, the meaning of the controversial maxim cannot be that these commandments bind only because God wills such.

But what of the obligations imposed by the second table? Here, there were diverse opinions among the scholastics as to how such commandments were expressions of the law of nature, and on what, if any, grounds God could dispense with them. One thing all seemed to agree upon, however, was that only in its broad outlines was the natural law "written into the heart of man" and to that extent evident to all who had not sinfully blinded their intellect to the truth in the way Paul speaks of in the opening chapter of his Epistle to the Romans. We shall have occasion to refer to this again in the following section.

We might note here parenthetically, however, that many of Scotus' colleagues, following Augustine, made use of an idea borrowed from the Stoics. They considered the entire decalogue as a reflection of some impersonal "eternal law" that was written into nature, and saw it as binding on God by reason of what he is and the sort of created nature he decided to make. As we said above, Scotus—instead of making use of this Stoic conception—develops an insight of St. Anselm; he sees the moral law as grounded rather in the will's affection for justice; this native liberty frees it, to some extent, from what "nature" demands, and allows it to "moderate its affection for the advantageous" (selection 29).

One could put this another way, by stressing that the values protected by the second table of the natural law cannot have the same absolute value as those preserved by the first table. Neither are they as independent of, or antecedent to, what God wills, in the way the values safeguarded by the precepts of the first table are. For the natural good each precept is intended to save or secure concerns some aspect of what is of individual, social, and political value to mankind. As such it represents only what pertains to man's natural perfection. Like human nature itself, this is only a finite good; furthermore, it represents an ideal for which one should strive, rather than the actual condition in which man exists. As a Christian theologian like his contemporaries, Scotus views man's actual condition as tainted by original sin. As selections 25 and 26 indicate, man was destined for a supernatural end, from which he fell, and to which he was restored through the merits of Christ. Now, none of the intrinsic or ideal natural perfections protected by the second table of the law are absolutely or necessarily connected with the attainment of man's actual supernatural end, which is union with God in the afterlife. Hence, Scotus maintains (selection 18) that while the second table represents what is "valde consonans" with natural law, certain aspects of the second table of the decalogue can be dispensed with according to right reason, when their observation would entail more harm than good. But God could obviously not dispense from all its precepts at once, for this would be equivalent to creating man in one way and obligating him in an entirely different fashion, something contrary to what he "owes to human nature in virtue of his generosity."

All of these aspects would have to be considered, Scotus would say, in answering whether some specific voluntary act was morally good or bad only because God willed such. The important qualification here is "only," for what is naturally good or evil, as we said, is a precondition for moral goodness or moral badness. And the natural goodness or badness of an act, as the subsequent section will make clear, is something we can reason to philosophically or logically. Natural goodness, as we said, does not automatically guarantee moral goodness, though the rational analysis of what constitutes such natural goodness can tell us much about the actual content of the law of nature. Copleston (1950, p. 547) explains this point rather well when he writes:

Inasmuch as the divine intellect, considered as preceding an act of the divine will, perceives the acts which are in conformity with human nature, the eternal and immutable moral law is constituted in regard to its content; but it acquires obligatory force only through the free choice of the divine will. One can say then, that it is not the content of the moral law which is due to the divine will, but the obligation of the moral law, its morally binding force. 'To command pertains only to the appetite or will' [*Ord.* IV, dist. 14, q. 2, n. 5]. The intellect says that this is true or untrue, in the practical as in the speculative sphere, and though it inclines to action of a certain type, it does not dictate that one ought to act in that way. Scotus is not simply saying that obligation actually bears on human beings only because God has willed to create them, which would be obvious enough, since they could not be obliged if they did not exist; he is saying that the divine will is the font of obligation. It seems to follow that if God had not chosen to impose obligation, morality would be a matter of self-perfection, in the sense that the intellect would perceive that a certain course of action is what befits human nature and would judge that it is reasonable and prudent to act in that way. One would have an ethic of the type represented by Aristotle's ethics. Actually, however, God has willed that course of action, and that will is reflected in moral obligation: to transgress the law is thus not simply irrational, it is sin in the theological sense of the word.

If the will of God underpins it, then the law of nature, especially as regards the second table, loses something of its impersonal and inflexible character. Its personal dimension cannot be ignored. Where other scholastics, following Augustine, who in turn was influenced by the Stoics, link it with the *lex aeterna*, Scotus eliminates this last vestige of impersonalism. To legislate or command is a function of will, not of a nature as such, even if it be the most perfect of natures (Wolter, 1972, p. 370; Stratenworth, 1951, pp. 5–7). However, this does raise a crucial question: How do we know the will of God? Does this not require a special revelation on his part?

5. *The moral law as accessible to reason*

What is often overlooked in the studies of the ethics of Scotus is that the notion that God reveals himself in nature as well as through the Scriptures was something the great scholastics took for granted. After all, had not Peter Lombard formulated this basic principle in their theological textbook (I, dist. 3, c. 1, p. 69):

That the truth [about the *invisibilia Dei*] might be made clear to him, man was given two things to help him, a nature that is rational and works fashioned by God. Hence the Apostle says [in Romans 1:19] "God has revealed to them," namely, when he made works in which the mind of the artisan somehow is disclosed.

And Hugh of St. Victor (PL 176, 268), whose influence on the Franciscan school can hardly be overestimated, had even earlier made specific application of this principle to ethics and the will of God:

Was it not like giving a precept to infuse into the heart of man discrimination and an understanding of what he should do? What is such knowledge but a kind of command given to the heart of man? And what is the knowledge of what should be avoided but a type of prohibition? And what is the knowledge of what lies between the two but a kind of concession, so that it is left up to man's own will where either choice would not harm him? For God to command, then, was to teach man what things were necessary for him, to prohibit was to show what was harmful, to concede was to indicate what was indifferent.

That Scotus accepted this principle is clear from what he says about the law of nature being, in the words of St. Paul, "written interiorly in the heart" (*Ord.* I, prol., n. 108; I, p. 70; also II, dist. 28) and in selection 18 (in answer to initial arguments): "In every state all the commandments have been observed and should be observed . . . In the state of innocence also all were bound by these precepts, which were either prescribed interiorly in the heart of everyone, or perhaps by some teaching given exteriorly by God." The same idea recurs in selection 17 where the criterion of whether something belongs to the law of nature or not is whether it would hold for any state in which man existed. "The reason is that if [something] were a matter of natural law, the obligation would have held for any state of law—which is false. For no such obligation existed in the state of innocence or during the tenure of the Mosaic law."

But how far can human reason go in determining specific obligations of natural law, particularly something that pertains to the natural law only in the secondary sense that it is "valde consonans" or in harmony with those primary or self-evident principles that involve natural law in the primary sense? By way of answer, Scotus makes two points clear.

The first is that the human intellect, as such, has the capacity to reach reasonable conclusions about ethical matters, just as it has the capacity to reason to other theoretical or practical conclusions, beginning with principles that are more or less self-evident. In selection 10 from his *Quodlibet*, he explains how agents that act "by virtue of intellectual knowledge . . . are suited by nature to have an intrinsic rule of rectitude for their actions. Only they can have an act whose goodness is moral." He goes on to explain that to infer whether an action is suitable to man as a moral agent and is therefore morally good we need premises that are certain. For this, knowledge of three things suffices, viz., the nature of the agent, the nature of the faculty by which he acts, and the essential notion of the act ("natura agentis et potentia secundum quam agit et ratio quidditativa actus"). "If these three notions are given, no other knowledge is needed to judge whether or not this particular act is suited to this agent and this faculty," and hence is in accord with right reason. It is clear from all he says that he thought this sort of knowledge posed no particular problem, at least to a philosopher skilled in reasoning.—Even the sort of dispensations Scotus sees God making, we might also note, are always in accord with right reason, and are something the human mind did figure out, or might have if emotions did not blind one's reason. For they concern such things as are good for man in relation to his fellowman, where there is a hierarchy of values involved, and where to obtain the principal value, certain aspects of lesser value may have to be sacrificed, in view of a less than ideal environmental situation. In short, Scotus in his analysis of the two specific areas where he believes God dispensed the Jewish patriarchs (selections 19 and 20) is using right reason to clarify what he believes to be the objective priority of values.

The second point Scotus makes is that matters pertaining to the law of nature in the primary sense are far more clear, and universally agreed upon, than those pertaining to the second table of the decalogue. Scotus, like the scholastics generally, did not think the finer details of what might be natural law were as readily discernible as were its broad outlines. Particularly is this true—he says—of those things that pertain to the second table. In *Ordinatio* IV, dist. 26, n. 9, explaining why the indissolubility of marriage is not evident to everyone, he admits:

But even if the law of nature were to obligate a couple to the indissolubility of their bond, which they entered into in virtue of their marriage contract, this would not be the law of nature of the most evident kind, but rather that of the second sort. Whatever is not manifest to everyone is not a law of nature, except in the second sense; and it therefore requires that the necessity of the precept be determined by positive law. . . . Those precepts that are far removed from the practical principles of the law of nature are not apparent to everyone in the way the universally known practical principles are because they are not explicated, and they are not explicated because no legislator other [than God] is able to do so. (Ord. 4, d. 26, n. 9)

This same notion comes through when Scotus explains why specific actions are sinful or not in accord with right reason. For theologians may often agree that something, such as lying, is sinful, yet the reasons they give why such is so differ widely.

Given the fact that Scotus, in determining what pertains to natural law, continually falls back on what is naturally good for human nature, it is not surprising that for him, as well as for Ockham, who followed him, that the substantive content of the natural law seems to be roughly the same as it was for the generality of the scholastics. It is only in their interpretation of why and how it binds that we discover a significant difference, as Copleston pointed out in the text cited earlier. It is a "law" and to that extent "obliges" inasmuch as it represents an expression of God's will in man's regard. For as Scotus puts it, "'To command,' I say, could only pertain to an appetite or the will" ("Hoc 'imperare' non convenit nisi appetitui vel voluntati"; Ord. IV, dist. 14, q. 2, n. 5; Codex A, f. 230rb). A specific application of this way of thinking is found in selection 29 where Scotus explains why we have an obligation to moderate our desire for happiness, even though it stems from a natural inclination. Scotus argues that Lucifer sinned when—despite his intellectual knowledge that it was morally wrong— he deliberately willed his own happiness in some immoderate fashion.

For from the fact that Lucifer's free will, in virtue of its affection for justice, could moderate its affection for the advantageous, says Scotus, "it is bound to do so according to the rule of justice it has received from a higher will" (selection 29). In other words, if we know from metaphysics that God exists and has made us, and we know from a psychological analysis of our affections that we have this capacity to moderate the affection for what is advantageous, we have thereby a moral obligation according to right reason to do so.

This refers to cases where the failure to do so would involve serious consequences, for Scotus points out that though we are bound to God by creation in regard to whatever we are able to do, we are left free to do what we will so long as we keep the precepts of the decalogue. ("Licet homo ex creatione Deo teneatur in omnibus quae potest, tamen Deus non tantum exigit ab homine, imo dimittit liberum eum sibi, solummodo exigens quod servet praecepta decalogi"; *Ord.* IV, dist. 26; Codex A, f. 249ra.)

If we consider the above points carefully, we see that the logical antinomy Harris thought he found at the heart of Scotus' ethics is largely a myth. Scotus' system rather manifests a remarkable coherence, given the premises from which he begins. Before concluding these general remarks, however, it might be worthwhile to note the following points that make his moral philosophy interesting even to those who do not accept all his premises. Thus, although Scotus' ethical system does presuppose knowledge of the existence of God, it is in a sense independent of any particular special revelation on the part of God. In the prologue to the *Ordinatio*, Scotus acknowledges that "the Philosopher, following natural reason, maintained that perfect happiness consists in the acquired knowledge of the pure Spirits, as he apparently wishes to say in Bks. I and X of the *Ethics*, or if he does not categorically assert that this is our highest possible perfection, at least natural reason can argue to no other."

Also, the fact that the second table of the decalogue is only *valde consonans* with man's ultimate (supernatural) end indicates that Scotus considered it more or less loosely connected with this, and consequently with what he believed a Christian theologian might accept as revealed knowledge of his ultimate destiny and how it might be obtained. As he explains in selection 26, I can have a basic love of my neighbor in the sense that I will that he attain God in heaven, without necessarily willing that he observe every item of what the last seven commandments require of him. Also, the Judaic or Moslem believer, or any other ethician who grounds moral obligation on the will of God as revealed to him by a rational analysis of human nature, might still agree with Scotus' fundamental conclusions about what is morally right in our dealings with our fellowmen without necessarily accepting the whole of what he believed God had revealed to him through the Scriptures and positive divine law (selection 17). This is clearly illustrated in the obligation Scotus ascribes to the third precept of the decalogue and to the positive aspects of the first two command-ments (selection 18). For it is only in their negative aspect that these precepts express what pertains strictly to the law of nature, namely, that God be not hated or dishonored or shown irreverence.

It also seems clear that one could use the same evaluative tech-niques that Scotus employs to solve particular ethical problems that fall under the second table of the law without necessarily agreeing with his reasons why they oblige morally. For what right reason tells us—according to the analysis he gives in the *Quodlibet* selection (10)—is what perfects man's human nature naturally, and this should suffice for the development of a rational ethics by those who claim man's moral behavior is not essentially dependent upon a divine com-mand. That is why some who have developed a phenomenological axiology, like Dietrich Von Hildebrand, find their concrete conclu-sions regarding what is morally good or morally bad in factual harmony with Scotus' ethical positions (Von Hildebrand, 1966, p. 8).

A final note before turning to an analysis of the particular items in this selection. As I have indicated in the article "Native Freedom of the Will as a Key to the Ethics of Scotus" (Wolter, 1972, p. 370):

There is another important consequence that seems implicit at least in a Scotistic approach to ethics. If nature's perfection is not an absolute value that must be placed above all else, then God, for whom a 'thousand years are as one day', is under no constraint to see that it be attained at once. The conception of a nature that achieves its end or perfection only gradually and by an internal mechanism that allows for a trial and error method of progres-sion does not seem foreign to or incompatible with the conception of God that Scotus held. Though he states the principle of evolutionary develop-ment *Deus ordinate agens procedit de imperfecto ad perfectum* in reference to God's supernaturally revealed law, there seems no reason why it cannot be extended to his promulgation of the law of nature as well, viz., to a gradual growth in moral awareness, protracted over a period of centuries or even mil-lennia if you will. *In processu generationis humanae, semper crevit notitia veritatis* [*Ord.* IV, dist. 1, q. 3, n 8; XIV, p. 136].

II

Notes on the Specific Selections

A s the title of this collection indicates, the selections fall roughly into two main sections, the first dealing with the will, the second with morality as such. The first of these includes the headings of the first two parts; the second the remaining six parts.

PART I: THE WILL AND INTELLECT

The four selections in this part are meant to express Scotus' conception of how the will and intellect interact. The will, insofar as it is a rational faculty according to Aristotle (selection 2), always works "with reason" and hence needs "practical knowledge" as the proper basis for practice or praxis (selection 1). Of the two faculties, it is the will alone that has the power to command, as Scotus points out in *Ordinatio* IV, dist. 14, q. 2, n. 5 (Wadding reprint ed. XVIII, p. 52; Codex A, f. 230rv), cited above under general remarks, n. 4. Selection 3 shows how Scotus believed the will could exercise such thought control. The last selection shows the converse influence of intellect upon the will. For by presenting the will with the distasteful consequences of any particular choice, the intellect can bring pressure on the will to choose what amounts to the lesser of two evils, even though, physically speaking, the will is causally free and must determine itself to will the distasteful action. For even by his absolute power, God could not force the human will to elicit an act of volition or nolition, since to do so would entail a contradiction.

1. Practical science

Scotus admits that ethics or moral philosophy is a practical, rather than a theoretical, science, but being primarily a theologian rather than a moral philosopher, he deals most explicitly with the subject of what makes science or knowledge practical in the prologue to his two commentaries on the *Sentences* of "the Master," Peter Lombard. To begin with we must keep in mind that "science," whether practical or theoretical, has the technical epistemic meaning given to it by Aristotle in his *Posterior Analytics* I, ch. 2. For the Latin term *scientia* has a dual meaning. It refers initially to the single or individual conclusions of a demonstrative syllogism or reasoning process, which could best be translated as "scientific knowledge." But it also has the more contemporary sense of a unified body or corpus of such reasoned conclusions, where *scientia* is more reasonably translated as "science," though as we use the term today, this would also include principles as well as conclusions. Just what sort of "unity" such conclusions must have to be considered one science, he discusses explicitly in Bk. VI of his *Questions on the Metaphysics of Aristotle*. He alludes to this briefly in suggesting how the various specific prudential judgments or "prudences" can form one virtue of prudence, and how the corresponding habit has the same unity as the universal science of geometry (selection 24, art. 2, part 2). The same sort of unity, he thought, characterized the reasoned conclusions of the theologian. And it is in this sense that the medieval scholastics of his day considered it a science. But they disagreed whether it was primarily practical or theoretical. It is this topic he discusses in the prologue to his commentaries on the *Sentences*.

There are two edited versions in the critical Vatican edition, the early *Lectura* and his expanded revision intended for publication and general circulation, known as the *Ordinatio*. In both versions, two interrelated questions are raised, namely, whether theology is a theoretical or a practical science and secondly whether a science is called theoretical or practical because of its end. Since the way the initial question is answered will depend upon how one replies to the second, Scotus in both versions begins his discussion with the latter question, namely, "Is a science called speculative or practical because of its end?" We choose this, then, as our first question and take our text from the relatively simpler *Lectura* (prol., nn. 127, 133–77; XVI, pp. 46–59) rather than the greatly expanded and involved development characteristic of the *Ordinatio*.

Both versions, however, begin the discussion with a principle generally accepted by Scotus' contemporaries, namely, that practical knowledge "extends to practice," where "practice" or "praxis" (its transliterated Greek form, is the common designation for either action or making. The qualification "extends to praxis" indicates that practical knowledge, in contrast to theory, is never knowledge for knowledge's sake. To deserve the name "practical" it must play a directive role as regards the action of some faculty other than intellect, and for this reason, Scotus does not consider logic to be a practical science, since it directs only discursive reasoning, which is an action of the intellect. Practical knowledge is said to be "directive" in the sense that it allows one to make a sound choice, where several behavioral alternatives or procedures are presented. As Scotus points out, praxis therefore involves of necessity some act of the will, either the elicited choice itself or the action of some other faculty under the control of the will. Since the will cannot issue a command without an initial elicited act of self-determination, praxis refers primarily to the will's own elicited act and only secondarily to the action to be done by some other potency under its command.

Parenthetically we might note that Scotus maintains that each and every elicited act of the will is free (selections 2 and 4), and in later selections we shall deal more specifically with the powers of the will and in what sense, if any, it is constrained to seek something good, should it freely choose to act, rather than not act (selections 7 and 30). But here in referring to the view of Henry of Ghent that theology is speculative rather than practical (since it has to do with God as our end), Scotus does distinguish between good in general as the end of a will-act and a particular or specific good such as God as the ultimate end of man. What is more, he accepts, for the sake of argument, the fact that practical knowledge has as its purpose to enable the will to make a choice in accord with right reason or sound knowledge, namely, in a way that the intended good (whether it be real or apparent, or whether it be a better or a lesser good) be expeditiously obtained. Hence, like Aristotle before him, Scotus considers "knowledge," in the proper sense of the term, to refer to true or correct knowledge. And where the knowledge in question is practical, rather than theoretical, it is what he calls "right knowledge," namely, knowledge that by its nature not only *enables* the will to act rightly, but as we shall see later in his discussion of the sin of Lucifer (selection 29), *positively inclines* the will to act in accord with right reason. For the present it is enough to note that the role of right reason is never far from Scotus' mind in discussing the freedom of the will. In this first selection, for example, he cites Aristotle's remark in the *Nicomachean Ethics*,

Bk. VI, ch. 2 (1139a22–25), that both intellect and appetite must be right if the choice is to be right (Lect., prol., n. 135; Vatican ed. XVI, p. 47). This natural inclination of the free will to act in accord with right reason must be kept in mind if we are to assess correctly the extent to which Scotus believes a rational ethics is possible.

In the present selection, Scotus prefaces his answer to the question as to why a science is called practical with certain preliminary notions, the first of which is a clarification of what is meant by praxis. In addition to the aforesaid requirement that it be the act of some power or faculty other than the intellect, two other properties are mentioned, namely, that it naturally follows an act of intellection or knowledge, and secondly that it is suited by nature to be elicited in accord with right reason. These last two properties also explain in what way practical knowledge is said to *extend to praxis*. As he explains in greater detail in the *Ordinatio*: "This extension consists in a twofold aptitudinal relationship, namely, [1] of conformity, and [2] of natural priority." Priority, because knowledge is a natural precondition for any act of the will; conformity, because, as Aristotle puts it in VI *Ethics*, ch. 3: "The truth of a practical consideration consists in its agreement with right desire." Scotus goes on to explain: "I have said 'aptitudinal,' because neither relation needs to be actual. For so far as the practical consideration itself is concerned, whether the action which follows is actually in accord with such correct knowledge is wholly contingent and accidental to that consideration as such. For if actual extension were required to call a thing 'practical,' nothing would be necessarily practical, but the same knowledge would be at times practical and at other times purely theoretical, which amounts to nothing. Therefore, it suffices that the twofold extension is only aptitudinal—in other words, that the knowledge in question has an aptitude to be extended to praxis" (*Ord.*, prol., nn. 236–37; Vatican ed. I, pp. 161–62).

In showing just why he thinks theology is a practical science, Scotus also makes reference to other forms of practical knowledge, such as moral philosophy and the virtue of prudence. Ethics or moral philosophy in its most general sense embraces both principles and conclusions, both of which are more or less directly connected with praxis or proper behavior. Prudence, on the other hand, is regarded by Scotus as an intellectual rather than a moral virtue, since it resides in the cognitive, rather than the appetitive, portion of the soul. Where the prudential choice refers to an action that is naturally or morally good, however, prudence plays an important role not only in guiding the will but in inclining it to act in accord with right reason. Hence, it is even more directly connected with praxis or practice than is ethics as a moral science. This comes to the fore in connection with an objection based on the apparent claim of the *Nicomachean Ethics* VI, chs. 4 and 5, that "prudence" is neither an art nor a science, since by definition it is "a habit involving true reasoning that enables one to act well." As it stands, Scotus says, this "definition" needs to be glossed, since it would also apply to any form of moral philosophy or ethical knowledge, whether this be a knowledge of primary moral principles or knowledge of the conclusions that follow therefrom.

In later selections (22 to 24) we shall have more to say about the cardinal virtues of prudence, justice, temperance, and fortitude, and in what portion of the soul Scotus believes them to be located. For the present it suffices to note that virtues (or vices) are referred to as "habits" and, like the respective acts which produce them, fall under the first subdivision of the Aristotelian category of "quality." Habits differ from acts, however, in that, like a "second nature," they are relatively permanent and, once acquired, difficult to overcome or remove. We should also keep in mind that since acquired habits, at least, are the result of some naturally prior act, it is not surprising that terms like "prudent," "just," "temperate," etc., may refer indiscriminately to either the act or the habit.

The fact that prudence is related to praxis more directly than are dictates of ethics as a moral science recalls another point that will be discussed later, in selection 8, namely, the distinction made by the scholastics between the intellect as "conscience" and the intellect as "synderesis," the former being an intellectual judgment about the goodness or badness of a concrete, individual action to be performed or omitted here and now, whereas the judgment of the intellect qua synderesis will always be of a general or universal nature. Needless to say, a logical gap exists between the dictates of synderesis and those of conscience. Prudence, as we shall see, enables one to bridge that gap, and that is why Scotus can argue here that prudence is more directly related to praxis than is any scientific ethical conclusion, and hence a person may possess moral science without having the virtue of prudence, and one who has always acted prudently may very well have acquired through experience the virtue of prudence, without being able to justify his behavior in concrete situations in terms of some broader or more universal moral principle.

2. *The will as a rational faculty*

The second selection is taken from Scotus' questions on Aristotle's *Metaphysics* (a work entitled in the Wadding reprint edition of Scotus'

Opera omnia, tom. VII, *Quaestiones subtilissimae super libros Meta-physicae Aristotelis*). These "questions" may have been discussed as a scholastic exercise in a local Franciscan convent with various students playing the role of opponents and respondents and Scotus the role of a regent master. According to the best manuscripts this work ends with the fifteen questions on Bk. IX, devoted to unraveling the linguistic ambiguities in the Aristotelian notions of "act" and "potency." Hence, the present question would in all probability seem to represent the very last item of this collection. In *Ordinatio* I, dist. 8, n. 25 (Vatican ed. IV, p. 294), Scotus expresses the benign attitude he has in inter-preting the Philosopher, a courtesy he extends to another favorite thinker, Avicenna. "Regarding the mind of these philosophers, Aris-totle and Avicenna, I do not wish to attribute to them anything more absurd than they may actually have said or which necessarily follows from what they did say, and from their remarks I wish to take the most reasonable interpretation I am able to give them." Perhaps nowhere is the application of this principle better illustrated than in this fifteenth and last question on the *Metaphysics*. There he defends Aristotle's dis-tinction between rational and nonrational faculties, but shows that it leads to the curious conclusion, noticed also by Henry of Ghent, that the will, rather than the intellect *per se*, is the only rational faculty man possesses. Despite its intricacy this interesting question deserves to be quoted in its entirety. For the Latin original I have used the Wadding reprint text (VII, pp. 606–17) modified somewhat on the basis of an early fourteenth-century manuscript (Balliol College, Oxford, 234, ff. 132rb–34vb).

In reading this question, we should keep in mind that in the preced-ing q. 14 (Can something be moved by itself?) Scotus has effectively challenged the so-called metaphysical principle "Whatever is moved is moved by another," commonly attributed to Aristotle and defended so emphatically by Scotus' contemporary Godfrey of Fontaines. Among other instances of "self-movement" Scotus singles out the human will's ability to determine itself. As an active potency, the will is formally distinct from, but really identical with, the soul substance, and is ei-ther the exclusive or at least the principal efficient cause of its own volition. This volition in turn, like the act of intellection, is an imma-nent action that falls under the Aristotelian category of quality, and resides in the soul as subject. When the will makes a positive decision, and thus elicits a voluntary act of either nolition or volition, there-fore, it is determining itself, and hence one can correctly say the soul "moves itself" from a state of indeterminacy to a positive state or deci-sion. Not only does Scotus believe the will has this power of self-determination, but he insists this is precisely why it is called an active "potency," "because there is something it can do, for it can determine itself." I have referred to this "superabundant sufficiency" of the will to act in this way as being a state more suitably called "positive indeterminacy" rather than "negative indeterminacy." Other Franciscan thinkers before Scotus, such as Olivi, had defended this same theory of the will but considered it to be anti-Aristotelian. Scotus' merit was to show one could reconcile the Franciscan thesis with what is essential to Aristotle's metaphysics if this be properly understood. And so, with Godfrey of Fontaines apparently in mind, he writes: "What is added about metaphysical principles being most universal is true enough, but none of them suffers exception in a particular instance. For the mark of true statements is the fact that they are illustrated in what is manifest. But how can that be called a principle from which so many absurdities follow? I don't believe Aristotle could have assumed any proposition to be—not a first, no! not even a *tenth* principle, which has, in so many particular instances, such obviously absurd consequences." And with the will in mind, he goes on to add: "If the following be a metaphysical principle: 'Nothing identical can be both in virtual act and still in potency to the formal perfection of which this virtual act is the effective principle'—if, I say, this be a first metaphysical principle, I know it is not inscribed in Aristotle's *Metaphysics*. If those who hold it have another metaphysics, how is it that they alone have the sort of intellect that can grasp the terms of this 'principle', which everyone else is unable to comprehend?" (q. 14, n. 23; Wolter, 1981, p. 60); see also Roy Effler's excellent study, *John Duns Scotus and the Principle 'Omne quod movetur ab alio movetur'* (Effler, 1962).

With this in mind consider the text as such. It is presented in the customary tripartite format of a scholastic question, beginning with the case for the opposition, and after a long and detailed discussion of the problem, closing with an answer to these initial objections. Those who find Scotus' involved argumentation difficult to follow may be helped by reading a detailed analysis I have given of this question elsewhere in an article entitled "Duns Scotus on the Will as a Rational Potency" (Wolter, 1990).

3. *How the will controls thought*

If sin or moral malice is primarily an act of the will, how can one sin in thought, word, and deed, as Augustine, Jerome, and other Fathers of the Church have traditionally maintained? In dist. 42 of the second book of his commentary on the *Sentences*, Scotus discusses this prob-

lem, setting up the following as a general principle: "Malice is primarily and formally only in some act of the will . . . Although sin can
not be formally in anything other than the will or its act, materially it
can be in the aforesaid acts, namely, thought, word, and deed, because
according to Anselm [On Original Sin], the will is the motor or moving
cause throughout the whole realm of the soul, and all else obeys it.
Just as the will is bound to have rectitude in its own act, therefore, so
it is required to have it in all the exterior acts in which it cooperates as
moving cause. Thus by moving the inferior potencies rightly, their
acts become right by a participated rectitude, and so also in the opposite way, by not moving them rightly, the rectitude the will ought to
give them is lacking and they are not right. And thus by moving them
in an unrighteous way, the will deprives them of that rectitude" (Opus
oxoniense II, qq. 1–4, nn. 1–2; Wadding reprint ed. XIII, pp. 448–
49). With this in mind Scotus takes up the present interesting question that throws considerable light on his theory of how will is related
to intellect. How is it that the will, despite the fact that it must work
with reason and requires enlightenment before it can freely choose at
all, is able nevertheless to command the intellect and turn it from one
consideration to another?

The question is found in the Wadding edition of the Opus oxoniense, but according to Balić it does not belong to the Ordinatio and is
missing from Codex A and other manuscripts of Bk. II. However, a
variation of the edited text is found in William of Alnwick's Additiones
to Bk. II, which the explicit of Codex V (Vat. 876) says he "extracted
from the Paris and Oxford lectures of the aforesaid Master John [of
Duns]" (f. 310va). I have suggested elsewhere that perhaps the reason
why it is not found in the Ordinatio is that Scotus had completed in
great part his revision of the first two books of his Oxford lectures before leaving for Paris, and that Alnwick thought there was sufficient
reason in the later material Scotus presented at Paris to warrant an
update of what Scotus had done earlier on Bks. I and II. Be that as it
may, from what we have seen of the Reportatio examinata on Bk. I and
the text of the Additiones magnae published in the Wadding edition as
the first book of the Reportata parisiensia, it would seem that Alnwick
was trying to reproduce the substance of Scotus' Paris lectures with
some clarifications from what he had said earlier at Oxford. Perhaps
the same can be said of Alnwick's additions to the second book. At
any rate, the material of the present selection seems to represent the
mind of Scotus, if not his actual words. We have translated the Latin
text as found in the Wadding reprint edition, dist. 42, qq. 1–4, nn.
10–11 (XIII, pp. 460–61); for the text of the Additiones, see Codex V,
f. 309ra–b.

4. Coercion and free will

Some philosophers interpret free will as freedom from external coercion and nevertheless maintain a certain causal determinism rules even the human will, in terms of its natural dispositions, habits of mind, etc. They assert that freedom and necessity are not incompatible notions. While this may be true in the case of God's inner love life, and for very special and sophisticated reasons Scotus discusses in Bk. I, dist. 39, he is equally firm in asserting that even God could not violate the will or force its consent, for the simple reason that this is a contradiction in terms (*Ord.* II, dist. 37, q. 2: "Voluntatem violentari includit contradictionem"; Codex A, 136vb). In the present selection, he mentions this fact in passing, and then goes on to explain how and why psychological pressure can be brought to bear on persons so that they are forced to make certain choices they would not otherwise make, and do so even according to right reason.

The original text is taken from *Ord.* IV, dist. 29, where Scotus is concerned to explain in what sense one can speak of forced consent and why it does not suffice to contract a valid marriage.

PART II: THE WILL AND ITS INCLINATIONS

5. The will and its inclinations

Following St. Anselm of Canterbury Scotus accepts the fact that the will has a twofold inclination or bias, one described by Aristotle and Plato before him as "natural" in the sense that it inclines one to seek whatever perfects the nature of the agent, either as concretized in this individual or as conserving the species to which it belongs. This inclination towards self-perfection or self-actualization Anselm refers to as an "affection for the advantageous," or *affectio commodi*. In virtue of this natural inclination, will can be called an "intellective" or "rational appetite," i.e., an appetite guided in its quest for self-perfection by intellect and reason. As Scotus notes in the subsequent selection about natural will and natural volition, this inclination is not an elicited act, but a tendency or bias to act in a particular way when the will freely elicits some act.

Every elicited act of the will is free in the sense of its being an act of self-determination elicited contingently and not deterministically, as the preceding selection indicated. However, there is a prior sort of "liberty" or "innate freedom" possessed by the will, a liberty that frees it from the need to seek self-perfection as its primary goal, or as a supreme value. It consists in free will's congenital inclination towards the good in accord with its intrinsic worth or value rather than in terms of how it may perfect self or nature. Anselm calls this higher inclination the will's "affection for justice," or *affectio iustitiae*. In virtue of this "innate justice," as Scotus calls it, the will is able to love God for his own sake as a supreme value. But it also inclines the will to love other lesser goods "honestly" or in accord with right reason, namely, in terms of their intrinsic worth rather than in terms of how they perfect one's individual person or nature.

According to an interesting text found among the *Reportata examinata*, or "examined reports," of Scotus' lectures, the first or natural inclination only gives the will its generic perfection as a rational appetite or "nature," but the second represents its specific difference as "will" or an active potency that is free to determine itself in an objective way towards good (*Reportata parisiensia* II, dist. 6, q. 2, n. 9; Wadding reprint ed. XXII, p. 621).

In another sense, however, the will with its affection for justice can be called "natural," namely, where this term is contrasted with the supernatural order of grace or charity (see, for example, the next selection on natural will and natural volition). For Scotus, in contrast to many of his contemporaries, believed that man by reason of his natural powers could love God above self or any other created good, and that this capacity was not something he possessed only in virtue of some special grace or the infused theological virtue of charity. In this he seems to have gone further, perhaps, than Anselm himself. Pierre Rousselot, in his historical study of this "problem of love" (Rousselot, 1908), calls the Aristotelian or Platonic theory of love "physical" (in the sense that it tends to perfect one's nature or *physis*) and contrasts it with its polar opposite, the "ecstatic theory" characteristic of the mystics, who in their love for God at least tend to forget self completely.

Scotus adopts a mediating position between the two theories in that he recognizes that both tendencies or inclinations of the will are God-given and lead to him in different ways. Where the affection for justice inclines us to love God for the beautiful and good being he is in himself, the affection for the advantageous inclines us to seek him as *our* greatest good, because by union with him through knowledge and love, our nature as "capax Dei" is perfected in the highest way. Hence the inclination for the advantageous does not need to be eradicated as something bad, but rather controlled or moderated lest it lead to excess. He will point this out in some detail in the selection on the sin of Lucifer (selection 29). Here he is more concerned with how the supernatural or theological virtues of faith, hope, and charity build on or perfect nature, for the question from which this item is taken asks: Is hope a theological virtue distinct from faith and charity ("Utrum spes sit virtus theologica distincta a fide et caritate")? Hope may be a virtue distinct from faith, but since it, like charity, resides in the will as subject, one can legitimately ask: Is hope also distinct from charity? Scotus argues that since the formal subject of hope is the will as inclined to self-perfection, whereas the formal subject of charity is the will as inclined towards justice, the virtue of hope will be distinct from that of charity, since these affections represent specifically distinct innate inclinations. In the supernatural order, the infused virtue of hope perfects the will's inclination for the advantageous, whereas the infused virtue of charity perfects its higher inclination or affection for justice.

6. Natural will and natural volition

The sixth selection is taken from Scotus' question: Were there only two wills in Christ ("Utrum in Christo fuerint tantum duae voluntates")? The Second and Third Councils of Constantinople had settled the monophysite and monotheletite heresies by insisting that hypostatically united in the person of Christ, as the God-man, was not only the uncreated divine nature and will the Word shared with the Father and the Holy Spirit, but also a complete and perfect human nature endowed with intellect and will. In Scotus' day this doctrine was no longer in question. Peter Lombard's comments on Christ's agony in the garden, where he prayed to his Father, "Take this cup away from me; but let it be as you would have it" (Mark 14:36), however, had raised another question in the minds of the scholastics. Did Christ's prayer, expressing as it did both his natural revulsion to bodily suffering and death as well as his willingness to accept such as the will of his Father, imply a dual will in his human nature?

Scotus begins by calling attention to the fact that in an extended and improper sense of the word, "will" could also refer to the non-rational sensitive appetite, found in human nature and falling under the classification of "nature" as opposed to "will" in the sense of the distinction he had made in our second selection. In this extended sense, then, one could speak of more than one human will in Christ. Scotus notes, however, that psychologically speaking man has not just a single sense appetite but many, one corresponding to each of the senses whereby he apprehends things.

But there are also three other meanings one could give to the expression "natural will" or "natural volition" that are more directly connected with the human will as such. As a self-determining rational potency the will has a twofold aspect, one active, whereby it elicits its free act of choice, and the other passive, where it is the recipient of its own act. Now according to Aristotelian terminology, everything is said to desire or will its own perfection, where "desire" and "will" refer not to elicited acts, but rather to an ontological relationship or innate inclination towards what perfects the nature or agent as such. In this sense, even primary matter can be said to be inclined towards and to desire form, or a heavy body to be naturally inclined to move towards the center of the earth and to remain there when reaching it. See the following selection on the natural will and happiness as well as what I have written elsewhere (Wolter, 1949).

Prior to eliciting any act, the will is naturally inclined towards receiving such an act as something that perfects it as a potency. Hence, this is one sense that can be given to "natural will" and "natural volition." "I say that 'natural will' according to its formal meaning is neither a power nor a will, but rather an inclination of the will, being a tendency by which it tends passively to receive what perfects it." And again, "I say . . . natural will is really not will at all, nor is natural volition true volition. For the term 'natural' effectively cancels or negates the sense of both 'will' and 'volition.' Nothing remains but the relationship a power has to its proper perfection."

In a second sense "natural" is contrasted with "supernatural," and refers to the will in terms of what it can do naturally, as distinguished from what it could do when informed by the supernatural gifts of grace.

Finally, there is a third sense in which "natural volition" could refer to a freely elicited act whereby one deliberately seeks one's self-perfection or self-actualization, since this is in accord with one's natural inclination in the first sense. But this would also be using "nature" and "natural" as opposed to freedom in the sense of the "innate justice" Scotus had spoken of earlier. For the free will, which can elicit an act in conformity with either of the Anselmian "affections," is following its affection for the advantageous rather than its affection for justice.

The Latin text I have translated is from the supplement to *Ordinatio* III, dist. 17, as found in Codex A (f. 160ra-b), with correction where the manuscript has an obvious homoeoteleutonic omission. See the Wadding reprint ed. XIV, pp. 653b–55b.

7. Happiness

Having pointed out, in the previous selection, the various meanings of natural will and natural volition and their connection with the will's affection or inclination for the advantageous, Scotus raises two further related questions in regard to happiness or beatitude: Do all men will happiness necessarily and above all else? And do they will whatever they will because of happiness? Both Aristotle and Augustine seem to argue that man cannot fail to desire happiness, and make this in some sense the ultimate good of man. But how is the ultimate good to be understood? Is "good" simply a general term or universal that is predicable of any good whatsoever, or does it refer to a particular good that *de facto* is man's ultimate end, namely, the beatific possession of God, as a Trinity of Persons, in the afterlife? Like the medieval theologians generally, Scotus believed that we have been gratuitously elevated to a supernatural order, and—unlike some theologians in a latter age—he was more interested in man's actual end than in what it might have been had man been created and remained in a purely natural state. Hence, Scotus' very first question in the prologues to both the *Lectura* and *Ordinatio* was: Does man in his present state necessarily need some revealed doctrine? He points to the controversy between theologians, who insist on the need for such, and philosophers like Aristotle and Averroes, or their followers, who seem to think that the intellect can acquire all the knowledge necessary for man in a purely natural way. As a Christian theologian he refutes this latter claim, but with his usual subtlety points out that if one takes seriously the theologians' claim that grace builds on nature and even the beatific vision does not do violence to, but perfects, man's intellect, then there must be a sense in which man can be said to "naturally desire the supernatural" and yet be unable to attain the happiness this entails without supernatural assistance. (See Wolter, 1950.)

But if man's knowledge of God in the afterlife perfects his intellect, his love of God and the happiness it entails perfects his will as well. Hence, there is also a sense in which he may be said to naturally desire and be inclined naturally toward supernatural beatitude, even though one has no conscious knowledge of the afterlife or assurance by reason alone that the soul is immortal. This paradoxical situation makes sense if "desire" is nothing more than an ontological relationship towards whatever perfects a thing. Indeed, the example Scotus cites of primary matter desiring form would seem to reduce "inclination" to a mere metaphor.

However, it is clear that if the expression "to desire" or "to will" is obviously an equivocal term, it certainly implies a certain bias or pull when applied to a causal agent or active potency such as the will. Scotus makes this clear in the present selection when he indicates that a natural inclination is more powerful than any acquired habit of acting, though habits of this sort are often enough referred to as "second nature," and Scotus definitely accords them the status of an active potency. Referring to Aristotle's claim that "all the arts or productive forms of knowledge are potencies, for they are the originative sources of change in another thing qua other or in the artist himself qua other" (*Metaphysics* IX, ch. 2, 1046b2−3), Scotus argues these are not just passive potencies capable of receiving what perfects them, as some claim. "A habit that resides in an active power is an active principle, which is what Aristotle wants to say expressly in the above text," he insists. (See his *Questions on the Metaphysics, Bk. IX,* q. 8; Wolter, 1981, p. 40.)

In discussing the previous selection (6), however, we referred to Scotus' distinction between the will regarded as the passive recipient of its own volition and its role as an active agent in producing that volition. We can regard the desire of something passive to receive such perfection as mostly metaphorical speech, but the same is not to be said for the will as an active potency. To understand the difference here we should keep in mind Scotus' theory of how intellect (with its knowledge) interacts with the will. Originally he believed the will was the sole efficient cause of its action, but could not on this assumption explain why one wills certain things more intensely or in disproportion to their objective value. Eventually he revised his position, according to William Alnwick, and admitted that the intellect, as showing the object to the will, functions as a partial cause enabling it to elicit a positive act in regard to the object in question (Bonansea, 1965).

The relationship between intellect and will in this case is that of two essentially ordered causes, similar to the case of the object and intellect as regards intellection. In the case of volition, however, the will is the principal cause and the intellect with its knowledge the less important cause; for that reason, the elicited act will always be free and not determined by the knowledge in question.

This should be kept in mind when evaluating Scotus' admission, in answer to an objection based on Augustine's claim that we cannot wish to be miserable, that there is some limitation on what the will can will or nill. For, if it is presented with something good, it is free to will it or refrain from willing it, but it cannot elicit an act of hatred towards it. Similarly, when confronted with something evil, it can refrain from hating or nilling it or, as he points out elsewhere, will it under the aspect of an apparent good, but one cannot—it seems— love evil as such (selection 30). To explain why this limitation does not imply that the will is necessitated or determined in eliciting an act or refusing to do so, he appeals to a somewhat obscure example based on a theory of color Aristotle borrowed from Plato (*Timaeus* 67E), namely, that white, as a piercing color, produces fine particles that di-late the medium, whereas black produces large particles that compress the medium (*Metaphysics* X, ch. 7, 1057b8–12). Hence, black is not suited by nature to be seen by the sort of act of vision that white is, namely, an act of vision produced by dilating the medium (*actus videndi disgregando*).

The questions in this selection are taken from the supplement to Bk. IV of the *Ordinatio*, dist. 49 (Codex A, ff. 281va–82va), where they are listed as questions 9 and 10; a similar text is found in the Wadding reprint edition, as part of the *Reportata parisiensia*, dist. 49, qq. 8–9 (XXIV, pp. 658a–68b).

8. Synderesis and conscience

St. Jerome, in the opening chapter of his *Commentary on Ezechiel* (PL 25, 22B), is credited with introducing the Greek term "synteresis" into Latin, referring to it as the spark of conscience (*scintilla conscientiae*) which even Cain's sin could not eradicate from his nature. Derived from the Greek verb "syntereo" (to watch closely, to preserve or keep safe) it seems to have been nothing more than a poetic way of describing conscience. According to De Blic (1949), it was a medieval scribe who made the error of writing "synteresis" (conservation) for "syneidesis" (conscience) in copying Jerome's work on Ezechiel. The error was incorporated into the popular *Glossa ordinaria* and, through Peter Lombard's *Sentences*, passed on to the scholastic theologians, who speculated as to its exact nature, usually giving it a special function distinct from conscience.

Just where to locate synderesis and conscience, however, was a matter of dispute. In attempting to explain why man is naturally attracted towards goodness, Peter Lombard cites various views as to what "weighs human nature towards good." Referring to Jerome's commentary, he says: "Man is rightly said to will good naturally, because he was established with a good and right will. For the higher 'spark of reason,' which also, as Jerome says 'could not be extinguished in Cain,' always wills good and hates evil" (*Sent.* II, dist. 39). This suggests that synderesis might be either in the intellect or in the will or simply in the soul as possessing both. In one of the first known commentaries on Peter's book, attributed to Udo (Lottin, 1948, pp. 107–8), synderesis is identified with Augustine's *ratio superior*. One of the first Franciscan masters at Paris, John of La Rochelle, went along with this interpretation of Udo. St. Bonaventure, on the other hand, interprets conscience as a habit of the practical intellect, which inclines a person to know both general principles of moral rectitude and the goodness or badness of particular actions, whereas he sees synderesis as the "weight

of the will whose function it is to incline it towards the good in itself"
(II *Sent.*, dist. 39, art. 2, q. 1; *Opera* II, p. 910). Thus it seems to
perform much the same function as Scotus ascribes to the affection for
justice (selection 4). But this "affection," for Scotus, is not an action,
or elicited act, of any faculty. Peter Lombard, however, speaks of synderesis more as an action or "movement" (*motus*) associated with the
higher portion of the rational soul, contrasting it with another "motus
mentis" whereby the "mind, leaving behind the law of higher things,
subjects itself to sins and entertains them." This suggestion that it is
an action of some sort apparently caused Scotus to preface his remarks
with this qualification. If one is considering not just inclinations
(which are not acts) but rather elicited acts, or habits that result from
such acts and incline one towards their repetition, then one will have
to assign such acts or habits of practical moral knowledge to the intellect rather than the will. Here, then, Scotus parts from Bonaventure,
and more specifically and immediately from Henry of Ghent, to side
with the majority of his contemporaries, who concede that synderesis
is simply another name for the practical intellect insofar as it makes
judgments based on general moral principles, whereas conscience refers to particular concrete actions. But insofar as the will, by reason of
its affection for justice, is inclined to follow the judgments of right reason, synderesis and particularly conscience can be said to be a "stimulus to good."

We referred earlier to Scotus' theory that the intellect or its knowledge functions as a partial cause of volition. This same notion recurs
in the present selection, when Scotus speaks of the intellect's practical
moral knowledge playing the role of a partial cause enticing the will to
elicit a morally good act. But because the intellect or its knowledge is
not the principal but the less important of the two essentially ordered
causes of volition, the elicited act of volition is free. What is more, the
will need not follow this inclination of conscience, for in virtue of its
intrinsic freedom it can determine itself in accord with either its affection for justice or its affection for the advantageous. Hence, Scotus
says, there is no necessary or guaranteed assurance that the will actually will follow the better judgment of conscience or synderesis,
though it is clearly inclined to do so.

The text translated here is from the *Ordinatio* II, dist. 39, qq. 1–2
(Codex A, f. 138ra–b).

PART III: MORAL GOODNESS

9. *The nature of moral goodness*

In the selection "What sort of thing is moral goodness?" Scotus comes closest to giving us a definition, describing moral goodness as a kind of moral beauty or comeliness. In terms of the Aristotelian categories, he refers to it here and in the second selection as an "accident," and among the "accidents," it is not something absolute, like quantity or quality, but rather falls into the category of "relation." Like beauty, it "is not some absolute quality," but rather a harmonious interrelationship of many items (the faculty of the will, the object it seeks, the conditions under which it does so, etc.). All these give the act a certain beauty or decor, as it were, when viewed in the light of right reason. Thus moral goodness represents an agreement of the act in question with the dictates of right reason, and it indicates the act is in harmony with all that it should have. So much for the nature of moral goodness.

Scotus, however, is concerned with the problem of its causality. For the dist. 17 of the *Ordinatio* I, where this item occurs, has to do with the theological habit or virtue of charity, why it is needed, the role it plays, and how it is increased. Habits and actions or acts, according to Aristotle, are absolute accidents in the category of "quality." The specific angle Scotus is interested in here is the question of whether virtue functions as an active cause (*principium proprium*) of moral goodness. If moral goodness is formally not something absolute but something relative, then it does not have a proper cause or principle in the way substance or an absolute accident has, but given the existence of the related terms, the relation follows of necessity. And so he writes: "This goodness, like any other relation, does not have an active principle all its own—especially since this respect follows from the nature of the related terms once they are given."

If a habit or virtue plays any causal role, then, it will be with regard to the substance of the act, and once that is given, it will bear a certain relationship to other given items. Nevertheless, since conformity of the act to right reason, expressed in the form of a prudential judgment, is an essential aspect of moral goodness, the presence of prudence as dictating the action in question does function as a "secondary sort of cause" or quasi-reason why an act is said to be morally good or why we call the habit generated by the repetition of such an act a moral virtue.

The original Latin source is from the Vatican ed. V, pp. 163–69.

10. The source of moral goodness

The second selection, "What is the source of moral goodness and badness?" is taken from Scotus' Quodlibet, q. 18, which is concerned with whether the external act adds some moral goodness to the inte-rior act. Scotus argues that it does, but he first prefaces his discussion of why this is so with one of the most extensive explanations we find in any of his works as to what precisely constitutes moral goodness and badness.

The translation is from Alluntis-Wolter, God and Creatures, 18.8–18.23.

11. Degrees of moral goodness and badness

Scotus asks one question in dist. 7 of Bk. II of his Ordinatio: "Does the bad angel will evil necessarily?" This gives him occasion to raise the issue of the various ways in which an act may be morally good. He cites four ways in which an act may be good, where each presupposes the previous way; thus the list he gives represents degrees of goodness, the last three of which are aspects of moral goodness.

He begins by differentiating moral goodness from natural goodness, though there is some ambiguity as to what natural goodness he has in mind. For initially he seems to be talking about that metaphysical or transcendental goodness which accrues to anything insofar as it has entity or being, according to the principle: Omne ens est bonum. We have explained elsewhere how this Neoplatonic idea claims that every being to the extent that it is being or has entity is something good (see Wolter, 1946, pp. 119ff). Scotus' first description seems to refer to this, for he says that "natural goodness . . . is characteristic of any positive thing . . . according to the grade of entity it has (the more the entity, the more the goodness; the less the entity, the less the goodness)." However, when he describes the first grade of moral good-ness, he seems to contrast it to the natural goodness of an act in a different sense, namely, as something accidental, in the way that he said earlier that beauty is something accidental, falling into the Aris-totelian category of relation, rather than quality, for he speaks of it as "something appropriate to this act . . . on natural grounds, as sunlight is suited to an act of vision." One could also distinguish another sense of natural goodness, namely, insofar as volition is an accidental quality that perfects the passive or receptive potency of the will, as Scotus explained earlier in selection 6. But whatever be the ways in which an act of volition could be said to be naturally good, this is obviously not something that concerns Scotus here, since he is only interested, it seems, in showing that moral goodness in any of its three degrees goes beyond any sort of natural goodness, in that it implies a conformity of the act to the dictates of right reason. And this is something in addition to natural goodness, howsoever this be understood.

This first degree, however, serves merely as a sort of ground or base for a morally good act, without formally constituting the act as morally good. There is one exception to this, as I mentioned earlier (I, 4, b), namely, an act of the love of God for his own sake. For this act, stemming as it does from an affection for justice, is morally good *ex genere*, requiring no further specification, since it is obviously performed for a good and proper end, and no other conceivable circumstance could vitiate it. All other loves, by contrast, since they tend towards finite goods or objects, are indifferent in the sense that they can be either good or bad, depending on the circumstances, where the end or purpose is reckoned among the circumstances. This generic goodness of Scotus corresponds to what traditional moralists have referred to as morality derived from the object (as contrasted with that stemming from the circumstances or one's intention). That is to say, that act *per se* is the sort of behavior that apart from intention or circumstances tends either to honor God or to serve one's own objective good or that of a neighbor. The example Scotus gives is to give alms, i.e., to supply for a neighbor's needs. Hence the act described generically as something good needs to be specified further as to its concrete circumstances before it can be pronounced either morally good or morally bad. If the alms given is something belonging to the giver and is needed by the pauper to whom it is given out of love for God, then the act is morally good. We might note that in this example, the purpose indicates conformity to Scotus' primary ethical norm, namely, "God is to be loved" (*Ord.* IV, dist. 46, q. 1, n. 10; *Ord.* III, dist. 27, n. 2).

The third degree refers to the supernatural order and specifically to such acts as merit a supernatural reward, since they are performed "because of that charity that makes one a friend of God, insofar as God views one's works with favor." The qualification refers to his acceptance theory of reward, namely, that no act by its nature automatically, as it were, deserves to be supernaturally rewarded, but it is up to God to determine what he will accept and under what conditions he will accept a morally good act as deserving "de congruo" of a special reward.

He concludes with the remark: "Now, this triple goodness is so ordered that the first is presupposed by the second, but not vice versa, and the second by the third, but not the other way round."

Scotus then shows there is a corresponding moral badness or defect corresponding to the absence of one or the other degree of moral goodness. Moral badness is generic when the object is inappropriate or bad, such as hatred directed to God. The second sort of badness stems from the inappropriate circumstances, even though the act is directed towards a generically good object, whereas the third type of badness is that deserving of demerit and pertains to the supernatural order of grace and glory.

Scotus points out that each form of moral badness can occur either as a contrary or as a privation, the former being based on something positively inconsistent with goodness, whereas the privation is the simple absence of goodness that should be there.

Where generic badness is concerned, contrary and privative badness are coextensive attributes, that is to say, if a person is confronted with any object that right reason says can be morally good or morally bad, then it ought to be wanted or rejected, as the case may be; if there is no object, then there is no question of either act. In other words, Scotus is claiming that an object is either appropriate or inappropriate by its nature to be conformed with right reason, and hence generic goodness and badness represent immediate contraries.

Where circumstances are concerned, however, the contrary and privative differ. Some act can lack some circumstance needed for it to be virtuous, and yet not be a vicious act, for instance, giving alms to a pauper without any specific motive in mind. Such would be a morally indifferent act as opposed to giving alms out of vainglory like the Pharisees Christ spoke of. Here the bad intention makes the act contrarily bad.

Where merit or demerit are concerned, the contrary and privative also differ. As an act that is privatively bad, Scotus cites an otherwise good act that does not proceed from grace or charity; such would be an act in the state of simple innocence, that is, without supernaturally sanctifying grace and prior to any fall from grace. However, *de facto* we are in a supernatural order and as such are either in a state of grace or in a state of sin (at least that of original sin, which Scotus regards as the absence of grace that ought to be there had Adam not sinned). If this be so, then there is no indifferent state except in one case, where an act that is good circumstantially is performed, but one of the circumstances is not the sort of good that supernatural charity would incline one to. And hence the act would be deserving neither of merit nor of demerit. As a possible example of what Scotus has in mind, we might think of saving an animal's life, which is something naturally good and could even be morally good in the sense that it might be performed out of a natural respect for the dictates of right reason, and yet it need not be an act motivated expressly by the love of God or neighbor, as Scotus conceives of such supernatural love. Normally, since one is either in a state of grace or in a state of sin, however, Scotus seems to think that sanctifying grace, if it is present, would tend to incline one to act in accord with it, and in such a case the act would be meritorious as well as morally good from a natural stand-point. But if one performs an act that from a natural viewpoint is against right reason and hence is morally bad, it would also be clearly demeritorious as well, for the prior malice (generic badness) implies moral badness, and moral badness implies demerit, though the converse implication does not obtain. If an act is bad in the second way, then, it is a sinful act, as well; but if an act is performed by one not in the state of grace and hence is not meritorious, and yet is the sort of act that is morally good in the second way, such an act would be neither good nor bad in the third way. Therefore, it would be neutral so far as goodness or badness are contraries of the third type, but it would not be neutral, speaking of the second type.

The Latin source is taken from a corrected text of the *Ordinatio* II, dist. 7, supplied to the author by the courtesy of the Scotistic Commission some years ago. It may not be identical in every respect with what is eventually published in the Vatican edition, volume VIII.

12. *Does the end alone justify actions?*

In dist. 40 of Bk. II of the *Ordinatio*, Scotus raises the question of whether the end or purpose which motivates an act alone suffices to make it morally good, and again he repeats what he said in selections 9 and 10, that all the circumstances must be in accord with right reason. Those authorities quoted to show that the end alone suffices to make an act morally good can be explained if we take them to refer not simply to morally good in the first or second degrees referred to above, but to the third type of moral goodness, namely, that deserving of merit and supernatural reward.

In this selection, however, we notice Scotus distinguishing a two-fold sense of natural goodness. One is what we may call "ontological" in the sense that it is "coextensive with being." This seems to be identical with the natural goodness referred to at the beginning of selection 11. The other meaning of "natural goodness" is "that which is opposed to evil" and seems to refer to the "secondary goodness," rather than the "primary" or "essential goodness," mentioned in selection 10. Such secondary or accidental goodness can also characterize an action as well as a body. If we consider all of the selections where Scotus uses the term "natural goodness," we seem to have at least three distinct ways in which an action that could be morally good or bad possesses some natural goodness. One is ontological or transcendental, which accrues to a human action by reason of its positive entity as an "accident" inherent in the agent as its subject. The second would be its "essential goodness," which would be characteristic of the act inasmuch as it falls into the generic category of quality and comes under the first of the four "species," or divisions, Aristotle gives of "qualities." For genus and species determine the "essence" of any entity. The third would be the accidental goodness opposed to what is naturally bad or evil. Thus one could characterize an action performed with a certain natural grace as good, as opposed to one that is awkward or badly done.

The Latin source for the translation is a revision of the Wadding edition based on Codices A, V, and S.

13. Morally indifferent acts

In dist. 41 of the *Ordinatio* II Scotus has an *ex professo* discussion of indifferent acts. He begins by contrasting the moral aspect of the act with that act as falling into "a determinate species in the category of nature." The assumption here is that the act possesses a natural goodness in virtue of the specific sort of act it is and the way in which it is performed. Hence it would seem to comprise or include all three notions of "natural goodness" referred to above. Here he does not allude to the fact he deals with elsewhere, namely, that a naturally good act could also be morally good if it is done deliberately because it is prudent to do so, or because it is in accord with right reason. It makes no difference, in other words, whether or not it is the initial act of this sort or whether it proceeds from a habit one has acquired of so acting. One such act, according to Scotus, seems sufficient to induce a "habit" or virtue, because a single act of some specific nature could suffice to dispose one to repeat this act rather than its opposite, given the same set of circumstances. Here, he seems to presuppose that one has performed such a naturally good act for a morally good reason before and hence has acquired—in an incipient stage at least—the virtue of justice. The point he wants to make with moral goodness is that one could still perform a naturally good action as a kind of automatic response to a familiar concrete situation without either actually or virtually doing this because it is just and in accord with right reason, or because it is intended as a manifestation of one's love of God. Such an act, he claims, would be naturally good but morally indifferent. Even more so in the case of meritorious acts, where their merit depends on whether one is in the state of grace and, if one is, whether the act actually or virtually proceeds from the virtue of charity. Thus a sinner, lacking grace and the supernatural virtue of charity, could still perform an act that is naturally good, or even morally good, because it is in accord with right reason, without necessarily acquiring sanctifying grace. Or a person in the state of grace might perform a similar action without meriting an increase in the supernatural virtue of charity if an actual or virtual intention of doing such out of love of God is a necessary condition for merit. Hence Scotus' conclusion:

There are many indifferent acts, therefore, which are such not merely because of the being they have as a specific nature, but also according to the being they have as something moral. And there are also acts that are indifferent as regards the goodness that is meritorious or the evil that is demeritorious, for one individual good can be of this sort and another of that sort. Many individual elicited acts can also be indifferent, because they are neither the meritorious sort nor the other, and we are not speaking here of nonhuman acts, such as stroking the beard or brushing off a bit of straw and suchlike, acts which originate with the sense imagination and not from any free impulse, for freely elicited acts can also be indifferent.

The selection is a translation of a revision of the Wadding edition based on Codices A, V, and S.

14. *Is moral goodness conformity to God's will?*

This question occurs only in the *Ordinatio* and not in the earlier *Lectura*. To understand what prompted it, we must look at dist. 48 of the first book of the *Sentences*, where Peter Lombard explains in what way our will ought to conform to the divine will. He writes·

You should realize that sometimes the will of man is bad when it wills what God wills and the will of man is good when it wills something other than what God does. For to recognize what makes the human will good, you must look to what it ought to will and for what purpose. For there is a difference between God's will and man's will, such that in certain matters what it behooves God to will is different from what it behooves man to will. Hence Augustine in his *Enchiridion* says, "Sometimes a man in the goodness of his will desires something that God does not desire, even though God's will is also good, nay much more fully and more surely good (for his will never can be evil): for example, if a good son is anxious that his father should live, when it is God's good will that he should die. Again, it is possible for a man with an evil will to desire what God wills in his goodness: for example, if a bad son wishes his father to die, when this is also the will of God. It is plain that the former wishes what God does not wish, and that the latter wishes what God does wish; and yet the filial love of the former is more in harmony with the good will of God, though the son's desire is different from God's, than the want of filial affection of the latter, though the son's desire is the same as God's. Thus, in determining whether a man's desire is one to be approved of or disapproved of, it is so necessary to consider what it is proper for man and what it is proper for God to desire." For one can will some good that it is not appropriate for that person to will and one can will some good that it is appropriate to will, and yet will it for some purpose that is not right; and therefore, the will in such a case is not good.

Peter Lombard, paraphrasing Augustine, cites the case Scotus quotes in the initial argument to the contrary:

The Jews willed that Christ suffer and die, something which Christ also willed; and still they sinned ("Forgive them, Father," he said, "for they know not what they do").

Obviously Lombard and Augustine have in mind the fact that man has been elevated to a supernatural state and destined to share the inner life of the Trinity. Consequently, actions are called "good" or "bad" not merely from the standpoint of moral goodness, but also from that of meritorious goodness. To be meritorious, however, the act must also be morally good, and Scotus restricts his discussion to this level, reiterating the point he made in the earlier selections that in order for an act to be morally good, it is not enough that the object of the act be good. For this only confers what he previously called "generic goodness." Before the concrete action can be morally good, all the circumstances must be good. "A defect in any one suffices to make the act morally bad." As he says in answer to the counterargument at the beginning, "Goodness depends not solely on the object, but on all the other circumstances as well, particularly upon the end." If one performs an otherwise good action out of love of God, for example, it is clear that the moral and meritorious goodness of the action stems from the fact that it represents a fulfillment of that primary moral law, "God should be loved."

The Latin original is from the Vatican edition VI, pp. 387–89.

PART IV: GOD AND THE MORAL LAW

15. God's justice

This question occurs not in the explicit treatise on God in the first book of the *Sentences*, but in the last portion of Bk. IV, where the "Master" (Peter Lombard) deals with the "four last things"—death, judgment, hell, and heaven. As Scotus says at the beginning:

Because the forty-sixth distinction treats of how both justice and the mercy of God concur in the punishment of evildoers, therefore four questions are raised here: first, whether there is justice in God; second, whether there is mercy in God; third, whether in God justice is distinct from mercy; and fourth, whether in his punishment of evildoers justice and mercy concur on God's part.

We have translated only the first and most important of the four questions, because it has the most bearing on this section. Justice refers primarily to God's dealings with creatures in rewarding and punishing them—in short, in giving them what is their due. In the present question, Scotus first discusses the nature of justice, initially in terms used by St. Anselm of Canterbury. The saint was concerned with showing, first, that freedom is not primarily or even essentially the power to sin, but rather the power to preserve justice, and second, that the will is able to do so because of its affection for justice, which frees it from the need to seek everything other than self only insofar as it serves the interests of self or nature. Anselm went on to define the justice that the will seeks in the words Scotus quotes here: "Justice is rectitude of will observed, preserved, served, for its own sake." The Latin "servatus" has all three connotations. It means simply that our will loves things objectively for what they are in themselves, and not just for what they are in relation to ourselves. When the will does act in this way, that act is just, upright, and honest, and the will acquires the virtue of justice.

Scotus goes on to specify "this most general notion" (ratio generalissima) by adding to it Aristotle's notion of justice, viz., that "it has to do with others," namely, with rendering them what is their due. He spells out briefly some of the main divisions of justice that Aristotle gives and then turns to the question at issue. How much of all this is applicable to God in his dealings with creatures?

As we shall see again in the subsequent question, Scotus will not accept the Averroistic necessitarianism that was current in the arts faculty at Paris, and had sparked the condemnations of 1270 and 1277 by Stephen Tempier, bishop of Paris. God, the theologians contended, was not necessitated by his nature to create at all, and was free to create otherwise than he did. This freedom introduced a radical contingency at the basis of the whole natural order, something that seemed to be the very antithesis of what one could logically reason to about God's relationship to creation. Scotus, however, was concerned to save both the freedom of God and the contingency of his relationship to creatures, and at the same time show he was ordinatissime volens, i.e., one who willed first things first and each honestly in accord with its intrinsic value.

In spelling out how this Anselmian-Aristotelian conception of justice he had worked out in his own mind can be applied to God, he also gives us the best insight into why he did not consider God free to act whimsically or irrationally.

It is clear, says Scotus, that God has justice in Anselm's sense, for "he has rectitude of will; indeed a will that cannot be gainsaid, because it is the rule or norm," as it were, both for himself and for us.

The Latin source is a revision of the Wadding edition based on Codex A, f. 270ra–va.

16. God's absolute and ordained power

Peter Abelard (d. 1142) first raised the question: Could God have created otherwise than he did? He came to a solution, much like that of Leibniz, that God being the good and rational creator that he was, he could only have made things the way he did and at the time he did (*Theologia Christiana* V, nn. 29–58; PL 178, 1324–30). This seemed logically equivalent to saying creation had to be what it was and hence was necessary, and not contingent. Hugh of St. Victor (d. 1141), St. Bernard (d. 1153), and others promptly challenged this novel view in the name of tradition, and the Council of Sens condemned it along with other errors that Abelard saw fit to retract in his *Apologia seu Fidei confessio* (PL 178, 107).

Peter Lombard devoted dists. 42–44 of Bk. I of his *Sentences* to the refutation of Abelard's views, thus insuring a discussion of this question by the bachelor theologians, who used his work as their basic textbook from the time Alexander of Hales introduced its study at Paris. With the advent of Averroism in the latter part of the thirteenth century, Abelard's necessitarianism reappeared as a philosophical challenge to the views of the theology faculty at the University of Paris. At the instigation of the theologians, this with other necessitarian views was condemned as "erroneous" by Stephen Tempier, bishop of Paris, first implicitly in the Parisian condemnations of 1270 and explicitly in those of 1277.

Since Scotus' "voluntarism" with its stress on the contingency of creation and God's freedom to do otherwise than he did was part and parcel of the common reaction of theologians of his day to these earlier condemnations, it is not surprising to find him raising this question in both the *Lectura* (Vatican ed. XVII, pp. 535–36) and the *Ordinatio* (VI, pp. 363–69). As with other theologians of his day, Scotus' answer to the question centers on clarifying the meaning of God's absolute and ordained power (*potentia Dei absoluta et ordinata*). The brief discussion in the *Lectura* is expanded considerably in the *Ordinatio*, where it is tied in with the juridical distinction of what one can do *de jure* and *de facto*.

Scotus' solution is not greatly different from that of Aquinas, Ockham, and others (Gál, 1976; Pernoud, 1972) for whom "potentia absoluta" had the meaning of "power" considered simply and absolutely without any restriction or qualification. In the case of God, whose omnipotence was considered to be limited only in terms of what implied a contradiction, it was usually defined in terms of what God could or might have done without contradicting himself, in short, what was possible for him in virtue of his omnipotence. Hence, Scotus' counterargument in the present question, which sets the stage for his own position, reads: "That things could have been made otherwise is not self-contradictory, neither is the world necessary." "Potentia ordinata" was not always uniformly defined, since "ordinata" could be translated in several ways. The commonly accepted meaning referred to what God has *de facto* ordained, which is the basic juridical sense Scotus refers to. But acting "ordinate" and "ordinatissime" can also have the meaning of acting "orderly" and "most methodically," terms Scotus applies to God as "ordinatissime volens." And hence the suggestion that God's absolute power *de jure* extends beyond what he has *de facto* ordained suggests to an unnamed opponent in the opening argument of the "Pro and Con" that if God could have created otherwise than he did, he could only have done so by acting inordinately, a point Scotus rejects vehemently. For whatever God does by his absolute power, he does *de jure* and in a manner that does justice to his own goodness. For though God is free to create otherwise, he is not free to do violence to his own goodness or act contrary to the inclination or affection for justice that is part of the pure perfection of the "innate liberty" of his will, as described by Anselm and Scotus (Wolter, 1972).

As this point must be kept in mind in reading Scotus' answer to this question, it is well to review what I said in answer to Anthony Quinton's statement that "things are good because God wills them and not vice versa, so moral truth is not accessible to natural reason" (Wolter, 1972).

The Latin source is in the Vatican edition VI, pp. 363–69.

PART V: THE MORAL LAW IN GENERAL

17. *Natural law and divine positive law*

Scotus has a short but excellent treatment of natural law and divine positive law in *Ordinatio* IV, dist. 17, where he discusses the sacrament of penance and the reason why there is an obligation to confess a person's serious sins orally to a priest.

Here, as in the following selection, he distinguishes between what belongs properly to the law of nature and what can be called "natural law" only in a secondary or extended sense. To be a law of nature in the proper sense, the proposition expressing such must be either (1) self-evident or analytic, i.e., known from an analysis of the meaning of its terms, or (2) a conclusion that follows logically from one or more such propositions. That God is to be loved and shown no irreverence would be an example of the first; that deliberate perjury is always gravely wrong would be an instance of the second sense, since it follows logically from the precept that God's name should not be taken in vain, i.e., God should be shown no irreverence.

In an extended sense, natural law would be "a practical truth that is immediately recognized by all to be in accord with such a law." In the following selection he points out that the second table of the decalogue, i.e., the last seven of the ten commandments, is of the natural law in this secondary or extended sense. The same would be true of the example he gives here when he says: "I grant that we know by the natural light of the mind that a guilty person must be judged" and that "no sin should be left unpunished anywhere if there is one ruler of the universe and he is just."

Note what he says of practical or moral truths that express "natural law" in this extended sense. They are "immediately recognized by all" to be very much in accord with natural law in the primary sense, and hence they represent conclusions that any reasoning person can readily know or infer. No special revelation, in other words, seems to be required. However, in the subsequent selection, he clarifies this somewhat in answer to an objection based on St. Paul's remark in his letter to the Romans ("It was only through the law [i.e., the revelation of the Old Testament Scriptures] that I came to know sin. I should never have known what evil desire was unless the law had said, 'You shall not covet'"). By way of reply, Scotus admits two points. One, that "although God's existence could have been inferred by natural reason from principles known in themselves, nevertheless, for the ignorant people unskilled in intellectual matters, it would be known only from revealed law." The same conclusion, then, would seem to apply also to moral truths that are ascertained only after a certain amount of reasoning. Secondly, Scotus concedes that sinful habits could blind the intellect and hence "to corrupt men it would not be known that their lusts were against the natural law, and therefore, it would have been necessary to explain—either by the law that was given, or in some other way—that sins of lust are prohibited by the second table. One could concede that such things are not known *per se*." Hence, one could interpret this "recognition by all" in one of three ways. (1) It refers only to the more general aspects of the moral law, rather than the finer details. Thus Scotus admits in discussing the indissolubility of marriage that this is something that pertains only to natural law in the second or extended sense and that "those things that pertain to the law of nature only in the second way are not manifest to all, and therefore, it was necessary that this precept of the natural law be determined by divine positive law" (*Ord.* IV, dist. 26, n. 9; Codex A, f. 248vb: "But even if the law of nature were to obligate a couple to the indissolubility of their bond, which they entered into in virtue of their marriage contract, this would not be the law of nature of the most evident kind, but rather that of the second sort. Whatever is not manifest to everyone is not a law of nature, except in the second sense; and it therefore requires that the necessity of the precept be determined by positive law.") Or (2) it could refer to the generality of mankind, rather than to each and every individual. Or finally (3) it could refer to the possibility, rather than the actuality, of what can be recognized by the light of natural reason, particularly by someone who is not "unskilled in intellectual matters" and whose ability to reason objectively has not been blinded by emotional attachments or who has not become so corrupt that he no longer recognizes that his "lusts were against the natural law." Scotus here seems to be referring to St. Paul's earlier remarks in Romans 1:18–32 on those "who have stultified themselves" and "their senseless hearts are darkened," and "in consequence God has delivered them up in their lusts to unclean practices." For any or all of these reasons, then, Scotus would say it was fitting for God to have revealed the entire decalogue or ten commandments, even though the precepts pertaining to natural law in the strict sense, or to the more general aspects of natural law in the secondary sense, could have been known naturally.

Because the precepts of "the law of nature"—whether this be understood in the strict or extended sense—stem implicitly from human nature being what it is and God being what he is, Scotus can say: "If it [i.e., confession to a priest] were a matter of natural law, the obligation would have held for any state of law." That it did not hold for the "state of innocence," i.e., the state mankind was in before the fall of Adam and Eve from grace, and did not oblige the Jews before the coming of Christ, says Scotus, is indicative or proof of the fact that confession to a priest is a matter of natural law in neither the primary nor the extended sense. He will make the same point in the subsequent selection when he writes: "I say that in every state all the commandments have been observed and should be observed."

Though Scotus does not do so here, perhaps one ought to distinguish also between positive divine law in a strict and in a more extended sense. The former would refer to those specific obligations God required of mankind that could only be known by way of some special divine revelation. This would refer to the examples Scotus gives here, such as the sacrifices and other details of worship God required of the Jews that are mentioned in the Old Testament. Circumcision, the observance of the Sabbath, abstaining from certain foods, etc., would be specific instances of divine positive law in the strict sense. However, one of the purposes of positive law, whether divine or human, is to clarify the more obscure aspects of natural law or apply its more general principles to more specific concrete situations. Inasmuch, then, as the finer details of natural law, at least, are not "manifest to all," and hence God has revealed many such explicitly in the Scriptures, perhaps we ought to say only this. Objectively these pertain to the law of nature in an extended sense and could be recognized as such by a skillful moralist; for a great many others, or even the majority of individuals, however, they can be known practically only by way of some positive divine law. If this be so, we could say further that these are, subjectively speaking, at least, matters of divine positive law in an extended sense, rather than of natural law in the extended sense.

Scotus also notes that Gratian, the canon lawyer, used "natural law" in a third and still different sense, namely, "to include all that is in the Old and New Testament Scriptures." Scotus, however, thinks this is too broad an interpretation and hence an unacceptable linguistic usage of the term.

The text translated here is from Codex A, f. 238va–b.

18. The decalogue and the law of nature

The question Scotus raises here is whether all the precepts of the decalogue or ten commandments belong to the law of nature. He begins with citing the arguments for the opposition, the first of which is that God cannot dispense from what pertains to natural law, yet he has dispensed certain patriarchs or prophets from the fifth, sixth, and seventh commandments, according to the Scriptures. The incidents most frequently cited were God's command that Abraham kill his son, Isaac, as a sacrifice; his permitting the Jews to steal from or "despoil the Egyptians" as they fled from Egypt; and his command to the prophet Hosea to take to wife a harlot or one given to fornication and "have of her children of fornication."

From the way in which Scotus develops the body of the question, it seems clear that the problem that occasioned it was a rather common view held by some of his colleagues or predecessors (e.g., St. Thomas in the *Summa theologiae* IaIIae, q. 100, arts. 1 and 8). These tried to account for such apparent "dispensations," while insisting at the same time that all the precepts of the decalogue belong to the natural law in the strict and proper sense Scotus had defined (in selection 17). If this is true, Scotus argues, then "it seems the reply to the first argument should be that God simply cannot dispense from such cases, for what is unlawful of itself cannot, it seems, become licit through any [act of God's] will."

Scotus first explains this "view of others" and how those who hold it attempt to account for the aforesaid "dispensations."

The law of nature is a law proceeding from first principles known to hold for actions; these are seminal practical principles known from their terms. The intellect is naturally inclined to their truth because of their terms, and the will is naturally inclined to assent to what they dictate. From such principles everything in the decalogue follows either mediately or immediately. For all that is commanded there has a formal goodness whereby it is essentially ordered to man's ultimate end, so that through it a man is directed towards his end. Similarly, everything prohibited there has a formal evil which turns one from the ultimate end. Hence, what is commanded there is not good merely because it is commanded, but commanded because it is good in itself. Likewise, what is prohibited there is not evil merely because it is prohibited, but forbidden because it is evil.

While Scotus admits this account may be true of some of the precepts of the decalogue, namely, those which "regard God immediately as object" and pertain to the "first table of the decalogue," they do not generally hold for those of the "second table," namely, the last seven commandments, which have to do with our relations to our fellowmen. For if God or union with God in the afterlife is our "ultimate end," then it is possible that this be attained, or at least it is not self-contradictory that such be attained, without all the details commanded or prohibited by the last seven commandments being necessarily observed. Furthermore, it is difficult to explain how God could have dispensed with certain aspects of the decalogue—as he seems to have done according to the Old Testament.

Hence, Scotus distinguishes—as he did in the previous selection—between (1) a strict or proper sense in which something belongs to the law of nature, namely, practical principles known from their terms or conclusions necessarily entailed by such, from which there can be no dispensation, and (2) a secondary or broader sense of the term, namely, precepts that "are exceedingly in harmony" with the above sense of law, "even though they do not follow necessarily from those first practical principles known from their terms, principles which are necessarily grasped by any intellect understanding those terms."

Scotus also explains the notion of a dispensation and then raises the question of whether God can dispense from such commandments as "No neighbor should be hated or killed" or "Theft should never be committed":

To dispense does not consist in letting the precept stand and permitting one to act against it. To dispense, on the contrary, is to revoke the precept or declare how it is to be understood. For there are two kinds of dispensations — one revokes the law, the other clarifies it.

My question then is this. Granted that all the circumstances are the same in regard to this act of killing a man except the circumstances of its being prohibited in one case and not prohibited in another, could God cause that act which is circumstantially the same, but performed by different individuals, to be prohibited and illicit in one case and not prohibited but licit in the other? If so, then he can dispense unconditionally, just as he changed the old law when he gave a new law. And he did this in regard to the ceremonial functions he required, not by letting the ceremonial precepts stand, but not requiring them to be observed, but rather by letting an act remain the same, but not requiring anyone to do this as he did before. This is also the way any legislator dispenses unconditionally when he revokes a precept of positive law made by himself. He does not allow the prohibited act or precept to remain as before, but removes the prohibition or makes what was formerly illicit now licit. But if God cannot cause this act [of killing], which under such and such circumstances was formally prohibited, to be no longer prohibited, even under the same circumstances, then he cannot make killing licit—but that he did so is clear in the case of Abraham and in many other instances.

Arguing against the position of Thomas that all the precepts of the decalogue belong to the law of nature in the strict or proper sense, he adds a further clarification about laws of this sort and shows that the precepts against killing or theft do not fall into this strict meaning of natural law.

Propositions which are true by reason of their terms, whether they be immediately so or conclusions therefrom, have their truth value prior to any act of the will, or at least they would be true, even if, to assume the impossible, no act of willing existed . . . [For] apart from all volition the divine intellect would see such propositions as true of themselves, and then the divine will would necessarily agree with them.

Where the law of nature in the strict sense is concerned, therefore, it is clear that moral goodness or badness of actions prescribed or prohibited is not simply due to the fact that God willed it so. Rather it was because such actions are morally good or morally bad that God commanded or prohibited them respectively.

Neither are moral truths of this sort "inaccessible to human reason." Quite the contrary, he insists:

It is to these that the canon of the *Decrees of Gratian* refers, where it is said that "the natural law begins from the very beginnings of rational creatures, nor does time change it, but it is immutably permanent"—and this I concede.

The same point is made in the second argument at the beginning: "What is known from the law of nature is recognized as something to be done or not to be done, even though it is not written [in the Scriptures], just as what is known naturally in theoretical matters would still be known naturally, even if it were not revealed." From Scotus' reply to this argument, it is clear that he accepts its validity so far as the precepts of natural law in the strict sense are concerned.

But how much of the decalogue pertains to natural law in the strict sense and how much to natural law in the extended sense or to divine positive law? After a lengthy discussion, he sums up his main conclusions as follows:

First we deny that all the commandments of the second table pertain strictly to the law of nature; second, we admit that the first two commandments belong strictly to the law of nature; third, there is some doubt about the third commandment of the first table; fourth, we concede that all the commandments fall under the law of nature, speaking broadly.

Since the commandments of the second table according to St. Paul can all be summed up in a single precept, "You shall love your neighbor as yourself," Scotus raises the interesting question of whether the perfect or well-ordered love of God does not also imply the above precept, and hence whether his first conclusion that all the commandments of the second table do not belong to the strict law of nature is not false. He suggests three possible answers one could give that would allow him to maintain his thesis. They are indicative of what he considered "love of neighbor" to imply, and it is helpful in this connection to read selection 26, where he shows how the supernatural virtue of charity extends to one's fellowman.

In the previous selection 17, Scotus argued that what belongs to the law of nature in an extended sense is "immediately recognized by all to be in accord with [natural law in the strict sense]." And also "whatever pertains to the law of nature, either properly or extensively, is uniform," i.e., it holds for any state of human existence. In his reply to the initial arguments in the present selection, he reaffirms this fact "that in every state all the commandments have been observed and should be observed," but he qualifies his previous claim—as we noted above in regard to selection 17—that all individuals "immediately recognize" the precepts of the second table. For those not skilled in intellectual matters or those whose immoral habits have so corrupted their intellect that they can no longer reason unemotionally or objectively, revelation of the law may well be necessary, particularly if some measure of inference or reasoning is required to know it naturally. As he puts it: "If some sin [of lust] could [only] be inferred to be against the law of nature, nevertheless to corrupt men it might not be known that their lusts were against the natural law." And of these—as well as of the finer details of the natural law, he might have added—"one could concede that [they] are not known _per se_."

The text translated here is a revision of the Wadding edition based on Codices A and S.

19. On marriage and bigamy

In dist. 33 of the fourth book of the _Ordinatio_, Scotus raises two questions that illustrate interesting cases where God seems to have dispensed the Jewish nation from two of the "natural laws" pertaining to the second table of the decalogue, namely, the prohibition of bigamy and divorce. "Was bigamy ever licit?" he asks, and "Was divorce licit under the Mosaic law?"

The questions are among the twenty-four Scotus devotes to discussing matrimony, both as a divine institution by God as the author of nature and as a grace-conferring sacrament reflecting the union of Christ with his mystical body, the Church. His initial question on the subject of marriage is whether matrimony was immediately instituted by God (_Ord._ IV, dist. 26). Let us consider the contents of this fundamental question for a moment before attempting to analyze these two questions on bigamy and divorce, for they are fully understandable only in light of what he considers an ideal marriage to be.

After a long discussion of the nature of marriage, its various aspects, its purpose in the plan of God, etc., he concludes as a theologian that it was immediately instituted by God primarily for the purpose of propagation of the human race and, from a supernatural viewpoint, for peopling the kingdom of God by the procreation and religious education of children. In the initial arguments pro and con, Scotus first cites the conventional arguments against this view, and one argument (under the opposition) for the position he himself will eventually adopt. The argument he sees as most effective is the reply of Christ to the Pharisees as reported in the Gospel of Matthew (19:3–6). It may help to consider, for a moment, the context of the passage Scotus quotes.

Though bigamy was regarded as permissible from the very beginnings of the Jewish nation and was already practiced by the patriarchs Abraham, Isaac, and Jacob, divorce was tolerated, but only as the lesser of two evils. When Babylon fell to the Persians under Cyrus II in

539 B.C., the Jews who had been taken into exile after the destruction of Jerusalem in 587 by Nebuchadnezzar were allowed to return and rebuild the temple. Though the Jewish marriage laws frowned on mixed marriages with the natives of the area, many of the Jews divorced the "wife of their youth" to marry younger and more attractive foreigners. The prophet Malachi refers to this practice and condemns it when he writes: "The Lord is witness between you and the wife of your youth, with whom you have broken faith, though she is your companion, your betrothed wife. Did he not make one being, with flesh and spirit: and what does that one require but godly offspring? You must then safeguard life that is your own and not break faith with the wife of your youth. For I hate divorce, says the Lord, the God of Israel" (2:14–16).

Though this attempt to restore the indissolubility of the Jewish marriage bond ruled out divorce for frivolous reasons, it did not outlaw divorce as such. Neither did it overrule the earlier prohibitions of remarrying one's divorced wife mentioned in Deuteronomy 24:1–4: "When a man, after marrying a woman and having relations with her, is later displeased with her because he finds in her something indecent, and therefore he writes out a bill of divorce and hands it to her, thus dismissing her from his house: if on leaving his house she goes and becomes the wife of another man, and the second husband, too, comes to dislike her and dismisses her from his house by handing her a written bill of divorce; or if this second man who has married her, dies; then her former husband who dismissed her, may not again take her as his wife after she has become defiled." Though the law here deals only indirectly with divorce, its object being the prevention of reunion of the partners after separation, it acknowledges the custom, and its vague description of the grounds justifying it, viz., "displeasure with something indecent," became the source of heated controversy among the rabbis at the time of Christ. The school of Shammai permitted divorce only for adultery; the school of Rabbi Hillel, on the other hand, allowed divorce if the husband fell in love with another woman or for something as trivial as inferior cooking.

According to Matthew's Gospel (19:3–6) the Pharisees tried to force Christ to takes sides with Shammai or Hillel when they asked: "May a man divorce his wife for any reason whatever?" to which Christ replied—in the text cited by Scotus—"Have you not read that at the beginning the Creator made them male and female and declared, 'For this reason a man shall leave his father and mother and cling to his wife, and the two shall become as one'? Thus they are no longer two but one flesh. Therefore, let no man separate what God has joined."

Scotus sees Christ not only as restoring the pristine indissolubility of marriage, but primarily—in view of his question: Was marriage immediately instituted by God?—as reaffirming that marriage was an institution authored by the divine lawgiver himself, a fact confirmed by the texts of Genesis to which Christ, and earlier, the prophet Malachi, had referred.

What is the purpose of marriage? As a theologian, basing himself on what Scripture says, Scotus finds only two express purposes mentioned, one primary, the procreation and fitting education of children, reflected implicitly in the words "they are no longer two but one flesh," and more explicitly in the words of Genesis 1:27–28 "God created man in his image . . . male and female . . . blessed them, saying 'Be fertile and multiply; fill the earth and subdue it.'" The same notion is expressed in the citation from Malachi mentioned earlier: "Did he not make one being, with flesh and spirit: and what does that one require but godly offspring?"

Scotus' lengthy description of marriage reflecting this primary purpose is presented in the following five conclusions:

The first main conclusion: For the procreation of offspring to be educated fittingly it is honorable and upright for a man and a woman to be mutually joined together or bound by an indissoluble bond.

Second conclusion: It is honorable and upright that a man and woman mutually transfer the power of their bodies to serve one another for the procreation of offspring to be educated fittingly.

Third conclusion: It is appropriate that this mutual gift to one another be instituted and blessed by God, and so it was done.

Fourth conclusion: It is fitting that some grace-giving sacrament be annexed to the contract that seals this gift to one another, and so it was done.

Fifth conclusion: Several distinct elements concur in matrimony; just what are they?

He proves each of these from Scripture and from reason, applying the criteria he gave for actions that are both generically and specifically morally good, often with enlightening insights as to how such a relationship benefits not only the married partners and their children but the community in which they live as well. In explaining and proving the fifth conclusion he points out that marriage is a multifaceted affair. First of all, it involves above all a lifetime commitment or dedication of two persons to one another, which is not a transient but a permanent relationship abiding in the souls of the spouses. Secondly, it is initiated by a solemn bilateral contract in the presence of God. Thirdly, in pronouncing their vows to each other, the partners administer to one another the grace-giving sacrament God has associated with such a solemn mutual contract. Scotus views these three—the lifetime commitment, the initial contract or convenant, and the conferring of the sacrament—as distinct elements that make up the complex personal relationship called "matrimony" as God intended it to be. In the proper sense, sacrament is not only a sacred sign, but an efficacious one, in the sense that the sign not only signifies but confers grace. As such, "sacrament" is something instituted by Christ and given to the Church, his mystical body. That Christian marriage is a sacrament in this sense is something we know with certainty from tradition and the authority of the Church, says Scotus. For though it was instituted by God, marriage as characteristic of the age of innocence, or during the tenure of the Mosaic law, or even as portrayed by the New Testament Scriptures, is not evidently sacramental in the strict sense. Some of Scotus' colleagues, however, apparently appealed to Paul's letter to the Ephesians (5:32) to prove that it was. There the apostle cites the words of Genesis, commonly interpreted as indicative of the indissolubility of marriage as instituted by God, "A man shall leave father and mother and *cling* to his wife, and they shall be made into one," and then goes on to say: "This is a great sacrament: I mean it refers to Christ and the Church." But since "sacrament" in the proper sense is "an efficacious sign of grace," not just a "sacred sign," in Paul's analogy the love of a husband for his wife is sacramental only in this broader sense of a symbol of something sacred (i.e., of Christ's love for his Church). Hence Scotus argues:

Matrimony is not an efficacious sign in regard to union with Christ, but in a certain way we do have an efficacious sign of such a union; thus the vow of virginity can be an efficacious sign as regards such a union with Christ.

Scotus evidently refers to the common theological conception of the virginal life as a "spiritual marriage" with Christ (an interpretation of the "virgins who follow the Lamb" in Revelation 14:40) and the celibate life of a man for the sake of the kingdom as generating that special sort of personal union the apostles shared with Christ, which Jesus spoke so feelingly of at the Last Supper when he said: "I call you no longer servants, but friends" (John 15:15). Paul too had this motive in mind when he lauded the virginal and celibate life in his first letter to the Corinthians (7:33–34):

The unmarried man is busy with the Lord's affairs, concerned with pleasing the Lord; but the married man is busy with this world's demands and occupied with pleasing his wife. This means he is divided. The virgin—indeed, any unmarried woman—is concerned with things of the Lord, in pursuit of holiness in body and spirit. The married woman, on the other hand, has the cares of this world to absorb her and is concerned with pleasing her husband.

At the beginning of that same chapter, Scotus finds what he regards as the second main purpose Scripture gives for marriage, namely, to avoid immorality. This was something the theologians of his day commonly considered a consequence of man's fall from his original preternatural state, but which would also have existed had man been created in a purely natural state. In answer to questions the church of Corinth had raised, Paul began this chapter with advice that may have been influenced in part by his views on the second coming of Christ:

A man is better for having no relations with a woman, but to avoid immorality, every man should have his own wife and every woman her own husband. The husband should fulfill his conjugal obligations to his wife and the wife hers toward her husband. A wife does not belong to herself, but to her husband; equally a husband does not belong to himself but to his wife. Do not deprive one another, unless perhaps by mutual consent for a time, to devote yourselves to prayer; then return to one another that Satan may not tempt you through your lack of self-control. I say this by way of concession, not as a command. Given my preference, I should like you to be as myself [i.e., celibate]. Still, each one has his own gift from God, one this and another that.

To those not married and to widows I have this to say: It would be well if they remain as they are, even as I do myself, but if they cannot exercise self-control, they should marry. It is better to marry than to be on fire. To those not married, however, I give this command (though it is not mine, it is the Lord's): a wife must not separate from her husband. If she does separate, she must either remain single or become reconciled to him again. Similarly, a husband must not divorce his wife.

There are obviously other values in a successful and happy marriage that contemporary theologians and Christians concerned with the high rate of divorce and broken marriages today are quick to point out—those they see implicit, for example, in the second account of creation in Genesis 2:18: "It is not good for the man to be alone; I will make a suitable partner for him." And creating an ideal marital relationship is not an easy nor a part-time thing. Hence, Deuteronomy 2:24 wisely set down the command: "When a man is newly wed, he need not go out on a military expedition, nor shall any public duty be imposed on him. He shall be exempt for one year for the sake of his family, to bring joy to the wife he has married." Neither is a year sufficient to cement a successful marriage; it is something that needs ongoing, if not continual, attention.

Scotus was not oblivious to these values or to the difficulty of achieving a satisfactory marriage, as is obvious from other *obiter dicta* throughout his writings. In explaining the expression in Genesis 2:24 "he will cling to his wife," for instance, he makes this point. "Clinging" refers to true and mutual love, rooted not just in the senses but in the will, and it is clear that God made such love a condition for matrimony as he originally instituted it. (See *Ord.* IV, dist. 29; Codex A, f. 250vb: "He will cling"—he said—"to his wife" [Gen 2:24], that is, to cling to someone through love. And it is thus clear that God established mutual will and mutual love and consent as the conditions for matrimony, and it is also clear that he instituted [the sacrament].") Scotus also recognized the difficult nature of the mutual obligations persons take upon themselves in entering the married state. Thus he argues God made marriage a sacrament with special graces, something he does not do for the complete consecration of one's person and life to God as a religious, because he believes marriage makes even more demands on a person than the religious life such as he himself lived. (See *Ord.* IV, dist. 26; Codex A, f. 249ra: "Because of the difficulty of the marriage contract, in that it gives rise to an extremely difficult obligation, it is fitting that there be joined to it the conferral of grace. This conferral is established because of the multitude of miseries and infirmities in the midst of which the couple are bound to serve one another until death. Indeed, to the extent that this is true, marriage is more difficult than the religious life.") Scotus clearly saw marriage as "a school in unselfishness" in terms of what it requires to successfully raise and care for a family.

However, in attempting to explain the apparent Scriptural justification of bigamy and divorce in the Old Testament, he simplistically limits his consideration—possibly to better illustrate the principle he believes justifies dispensation from certain aspects of natural law in the secondary sense—to the two main purposes he sees for the institution of marriage, viz., (1) the creation of a family through the procreation and fitting education of children and (2) the natural need of men and women living and working together as man and wife to find adequate sexual satisfaction and comfort in one another if extramarital sins are to be avoided.

What he says about God dispensing from the natural law of monogamy for the patriarchs of the Old Testament and why Moses permitted divorce to avoid greater evils is interesting as exemplary of how moral decisions might be reached through rational analysis where a conflict of values is involved. This is not simply "value clarification" as this term is understood today, for he believed the mind of man was capable of arriving at a rational and not just an emotional evaluation of what is morally good and morally bad. However, if such objective clarification can be reached, as he obviously thought it could (see selection 10), then any proper and reasonable response to a polyvalued situation where some values must be sacrificed to save others must be guided by what is implicit in the following principle:

When there are two reasons why something is ordered, one the principal purpose, the other a less important end, it is reasonable to make use of such in a
manner that favors the chief end, even if this militates to some extent against
the less important purpose.

What he illustrates here with respect to the two distinct purposes of
different values he believes marriage to have could be applied, *mutatis
mutandis*, to other polyvalued situations where a choice must be made
at the cost of some sacrifice, or where one is forced to choose the lesser
of two evils in the sense explained earlier (selection 4).

Let us turn then to the question of bigamy. The question Scotus
raises is phrased in two ways: "So far as the Mosaic law or the law of
nature is concerned, was bigamy ever licit, or were the patriarchs of
old allowed to have several wives joined in the bonds of matrimony?"

After citing from the Old Testament the particular cases that would
seem to illustrate either a negative or positive answer, he proceeds in
the body of the question to discuss what justice requires in the exchange of marital vows. Since matrimony, as he understands it, is initiated with a contract between two individuals in which there is an
exchange of bodily procreative powers, it is commutative justice he
speaks of. This involves an equitable exchange of something in fulfillment of a contractual obligation. As he explained earlier, in selection
15, "in commutative justice, some require quantitative equality, not
only proportional equity." If this be applied to one's procreative ability, which, biologically speaking, is a purely animal function, it is
clear in the human species at least, as in many other animal species,
that the male could be said to have a greater procreative power than
the female if quantity be measured only in terms of the time required
to produce a child. If the primary purpose for which God created male
and female was that the human race might "be fertile and multiply; fill
the earth and subdue it," as Genesis 1:28 seems to imply, then it would
follow—Scotus argued—that, if the human race were in danger of
dying out, or if there were some special need that "members of the
human race needed to be multiplied either in an unqualified sense or
in regard to divine cult, since there were few who worshiped God, it
was necessary that those who did so, beget as much as they could,
since only in their progeny would faith and divine worship continue to
exist." Considered solely under this aspect, then, bigamy would not
seem to be contrary to nature. Whether children could be as fittingly
educated under such circumstances, or the mutual love demanded of
the partners for a successful marriage could be preserved, is another
question. However, what he says of inequality or "commutative injustice"—if you will—in regard to the secondary value exchanged,

could also be applied to these other values of a monogamous marriage.

Because there is definitely no equal exchange as regards the secondary purpose of marriage cited by St. Paul, something Scotus argued "held good for the state of fallen nature," when Adam and Eve's progeny no longer enjoyed the supernatural and preternatural gifts their parents originally possessed that gave them perfect control over their animal instincts, such bigamous marriages were certainly not ideal, nor were they what God originally had in mind. Nevertheless, if women freely choose to enter into such unions for the sake of having children of their own, then, Scotus believed, they could reasonably do so, provided another condition was present, namely, that it was clear God had dispensed from what the natural law demanded.

The reason for this is that God as the author of human nature is also the only one authorized to dispense with precepts that pertain to the law of nature only in a secondary sense. We noted earlier that certain aspects of natural law in the extended sense might also be considered as positive divine laws in an extended sense, and if this be so, then though what such laws concern may be the sort of actions that are naturally good, in the sense of being "exceedingly in harmony" with natural law in the primary and proper sense, the reason that such actions become morally good or morally bad, in the last analysis, is that God has commanded or forbidden them respectively.

Hence, though there may have been no need for a divine dispensation so far as the primary purpose of marriage was concerned, such a dispensation is required—Scotus insists—where the married partners cannot do justice to the secondary purpose, since this too is part of the complete nature of the marital state as instituted by God.

Hence, in answering the initial argument for the negative view, Scotus reiterates his previous thesis regarding natural law and God's power to dispense with it.

Something is said to be of the natural law in two ways, viz., first, what is simply a practical truth known by the natural light of reason alone. Here a practical principle known from its terms represents the strongest form of such a law of nature, only second to which are those conclusions demonstrated from such primary principles. What pertains secondarily to the law of nature, however, is anything that as a general rule is in harmony with a law of nature in the previous sense. There is no dispensation as regards the first class, and therefore anything opposed to such would always seem to be a mortal sin. But for the secondary type, dispensation occurs in a situation where the opposite seems to be generally more in harmony with the primary law of nature. And it is just in this secondary sense of natural that monogamy pertains to the law of nature and bigamy is opposed to such, and hence I concede the validity of the proofs [cited in the initial argument]. But from this it does not follow that in a special case the opposite could not be licit, or even in some cases necessary. In such a case, however, there would be justice on the part of the parties entering marriage as well as in regard to what they gave to each other, for right reason would dictate that their contractual exchange take place in a different way, and in addition the divine precept to enter such a contract would also be there.

He even suggests that bigamy could become licit again if war, pestilence, or some other calamity threatened the existence of the human race, leaving a majority of women and a minority of men, "if one considers only precise justice on the part of the contract and contracting parties." In such a case, "all that would be wanting for complete justice would be divine approbation, which perhaps would then occur and be revealed in a special way to the Church."

In view of what was said earlier (I, 5) about God revealing himself through nature and about the ability of right reason to determine what his positive will is, one could raise several questions in this connection. On the one hand, nuclear war could conceivably be the sort of war that might decimate the human race, but whether it would leave the survivors with a significant disproportionate number of one sex or the other is questionable. On the other hand, some parts of the world are threatened with overpopulation. What happens when the primary purpose Scotus saw for marriage in his day no longer exists? In such a case, does God will that all live a celibate life, or is not some form of natural family planning necessary? Here the secondary purposes of marriage, man's need for comfort and companionship, the need to love and be loved, etc., would seem to justify a different rational approach to marriage.

But let us turn to the next question.

20. Divorce and the Mosaic law

The second question Scotus raises in regard to marriage is whether divorce was licit or not under the Mosaic law. Though Scotus will fall back on the same basic principle he used for bigamy to solve this question, he obviously regarded bigamy and divorce as basically different violations of the natural law in regard to marriage. A bigamous partnership was still a marriage that preserved the primary purpose of that institution, and hence could be regarded as something good, even though it might be less than ideal and not as good as a monogamous marriage might be. Furthermore, for a bigamous marriage to be fully just, it was necessary that God should actually dispense from the natural law in the secondary sense, inasmuch as it prescribed monogamy. Scotus considered divorce, however, to be an unmitigated evil and surely a shattering experience for the wife in question. It could only be justified inasmuch as it was the lesser of two evils, and he believed it was only for that reason that God, by way of dispensation, permitted a man to divorce his wife.

Though Deuteronomy 22:13ff took some steps to protect the rights of a woman from sexual abuse, there is little question that according to Jewish law, she was not regarded legally as the equal of man. For while a man could divorce his wife, strictly speaking no provision was made for a woman divorcing a man who was unfaithful. Both he and his paramour were to be stoned if she was married, but if she was a virgin whom he took by force, he had to pay a fine to her father and take her to wife, with no option of divorce. Scotus obviously considered Christ's restoration of the indissolubility of marriage a step in the direction of correcting what was patent sexual discrimination, condoned by so much of the pre-Christian world.

As to the question itself, Scotus comes to no categorical decision. Did God actually dispense the Jews from the indissolubility of marriage and permit them licitly to divorce their wives? He presents two views current among theologians in his day, one denying that divorce was ever licit, the other asserting that God did permit it, but only to avoid the greater evil of uxoricide. And though the way Scotus sets up the initial arguments and the rational defense he makes for the second view obviously indicates he prefers the latter, he seems to have attributed only probability to this view at best. And in answering the arguments for the view that divorce, even with a written bill of dismissal, was illicit, he admits:

I concede that the delay which writing the bill entailed does suggest that God was displeased with this dismissal; and that it was not merely that it would be better not to dissolve the marriage, but that it was bad to do so, but not so bad that one would sin gravely against marriage in the way one would if this were not licensed by law.

And having made a strong case for the second view, which he seems to prefer, he still admits one could reasonably hold the first view, that divorce of any sort is "still mortally sinful" and was "allowed only to prevent an even graver mortal sin happening," and he concludes with showing how—on such a view—"one could easily reply to the arguments against it."

The Latin source of this and the preceding question is Codex A, ff. 253rb–55ra.

21. *Positive law and civil authority*

Unlike Aquinas, Scotus never commented on Aristotle's *Politics*, nor did he write any significant political tracts like Ockham. The present question from dist. 15 of the *Ordinatio* IV (q. 2) and the parallel account in the report of his Paris lectures on this distinction (qq. 2–4) contain the most extensive statement of his "political and economic philosophy," even though these questions are not concerned *ex professo* with such, but with something pertaining to the sacrament of penance or reconciliation. "Is everyone who has unjustly taken or kept some property belonging to another obliged to make restitution to obtain absolution?" To answer this question Scotus felt it necessary to first discuss two preliminary questions. How can an individual person justly acquire private property to begin with? and secondly, once it is acquired, how can it be transferred to another? It is these two articles that are treated in the present selection, the first in its entirety, the second only briefly.

A word as to why Scotus thought he had to explain the origin of distinct ownership. It was commonly held that in the state of original justice, just as among the early Christians described in the Acts of the Apostles 4:32, "none of them ever claimed anything as his own; rather, everything was held in common." The Franciscans, because of their profession of poverty, were much in sympathy with this view, and Scotus cites the *Decrees of Gratian* in support of it (*Decretum Gratiani cum glossis* [Parisiis, 1542], I, dist. 8, ff. 8va–9ra; see also PL 187, 43, and also the authority from Augustine on which Gratian bases this opinion). If this be so, we can understand Scotus' initial question:

I ask: What is the source of distinct ownership such that this may be called "mine" and that "yours"? For all injustice through misappropriation derives from this as well as all justice through restitution.

He presents his solution in the form of six conclusions, the fifth of which sums up his theory of the origin of civil authority. Brief as that conclusion is, C. R. S. Harris (1937) considered what Scotus had to say there socially significant enough to write:

Scotus is important in the history of political science as one of the pioneers of modern social theory. His doctrines bear a strong resemblance to the later teachings of Locke. Scotus' account of the social contract is a philosophic analysis of the origin of society. Society, he held, was naturally organized into family groups; but when paternal authority was unable to enforce order, political authority was constituted by the people. Accordingly all political authority is derived from the consent of the governed.

In the sixth and last conclusion, Scotus shows how, once society was organized and invested with patriarchal or political authority, positive laws could be passed that would permit the common property of the human race to be divided up among individuals.

In the second article Scotus sets forth in great detail how property, once legitimately acquired, may be transferred to others. Harris gives a brief account of its significance as follows:

Concern for the public welfare is the basis of Scotus' economic doctrines. He regarded private property as a product of positive rather than natural law and insisted that property must not be administered in a way detrimental to the community. He formulated principles for the equitable employment of various commercial contracts, and while he accepted the current concept of a just price he recognized the social importance of a merchant class.

Since Scotus' economic doctrines are of only peripheral interest to the main concern of this book, I have cited only the initial paragraph of this second article.

The text of this selection is from the *Ordinatio* IV, dist. 15, q. 2; Codex A, f. 233rb–va.

PART VI: THE INTELLECTUAL AND MORAL VIRTUES

Scotus begins his treatment of the virtues (theological, intellectual, and moral) with dist. 23 of Bk. III and concludes with the question on the connection of the virtues in dist. 36. Because some codices of the *Ordinatio* end with dist. 14, Balić first believed that this was as far as Scotus had come in his final revision of his commentary on the *Sentences*, even though the most important Codex A extends to dist. 40. Lottin was able to prove by a detailed analysis of the various manuscripts of dist. 36 that Codex A was indeed a revision of Scotus' earlier lectures on the question of the connection of the virtues and argued that the *Ordinatio* III, or final revision of the third book, extends to at least dist. 36. Until the Scotistic Commission, which is still busy with the second book, makes a thorough study of the problem and comes to some definitive conclusion, we may adopt the customary way of referring to the questions in dists. 15 to 40 as "supplements" to *Ordinatio* III. The question of whether all the precepts of the decalogue pertain to the law of nature (selection 18) fell in this category. What I have translated here is the text of the Wadding edition revised on the basis of Codices A and S. We have done the same for the Latin text of the next three questions.

22. *The will as the seat of the moral virtues*

Against Aristotle (*Nicomachean Ethics* III, ch. 10, 1117b23), Aquinas (*Summa theologiae* IaIIae, q. 56, art. 4), and others who place fortitude and temperance in the irascible and concupiscible sense appetites, justice in the will, and prudence in the intellect, Scotus argues that not only justice but fortitude and temperance as well are virtues that reside in the will.

Since those who held the opposite view among his contemporaries did so because of what they attributed to Aristotle, Scotus first shows that one can construct arguments for his own position based on what the Philosopher says in the *Politics* and the *Ethics*. But the most unequivocal authority for his position is clearly Augustine. In his *Morals of the Church*, ch. 15, and in Bk. XIV of the *City of God*, chs. 5 and 6, the saint claims that emotions or passions reside in the higher portion of the soul, specifically in the will, and that the moral virtues are nothing more than "well-ordered love" on the part of the will.

As for philosophical arguments based on reason, Scotus takes the arguments for the opposition and cleverly turns them to his own purposes, concluding that

if we consider these arguments which are adduced to support the other opinion, it is clear how they prove the opposite, [first] because the will is not of itself righteous and is able to be rectified as regards that action that is properly its own; [second] because the will is no less undetermined and determinable than is the intellect to which one attributes virtue; [third] because it is also inclined by nature to delight in its own way in that action that is properly its own, and so it ought to have a habit whereby it can act in a way that gives it delight; [fourth] because it is the principal agent in performing actions that are distinctively human, inasmuch as they are free, and because human actions, if they are to be praiseworthy, require in the principal agent a virtue deserving of praise; [fifth] because the will, if it possesses virtues, can more readily moderate the passions in a fitting way than the sense appetite can.

Hence he concludes in answer to the question:

Just as in the intellect, either through its first act or through frequently elicited acts, the habit of prudence is generated, so also with the first correct choice consonant with the dictates of right reason, or through many such correct choices, there is generated in the will a proper virtue which inclines the will to choose rightly . . .

One can concede, however, that if the will by willing can command the sense appetite (by moderating either its passion or the way it goes after or flees from a thing, if this be an act of the sense appetite), it can also leave behind in the sense appetite by such correct commands some habit that inclines that appetite to move more readily towards sensibles in the way the will commands. And this habit that is left there, although it is not properly a virtue, because it is not an elective habit, nor does it incline one to make choices, can in some sense be conceded to be a virtue, since it inclines one to such things as are in accord with right reason.

In answer to an objection that if moral virtues can exist in the higher or more spiritual portion of the soul, then they can also exist in angels which have no sense appetites, Scotus explains in some detail how an angel, if created in a purely natural state, could also have a moral habit, provided it made many correct choices in regard to such passions as are revealed to it by the intellect. And if one is not content with this answer, one could simply deny the parallel between the soul and the angel, and argue in this way. The soul has a sense appetite that is apt by nature to pull it towards what is pleasing to the senses alone, thus making it difficult for the will to tend to any higher or spiritual good in an objective way. Moral virtue, however, is concerned not with just any good, but with such goods as are difficult to obtain.

Another objection, posed by admirers of Aristotle, is that if moral virtue were in the will, then such virtue would be more noble than prudence, and this contradicts the Philosopher. Scotus replies that from a supernatural viewpoint, in the intellect it is faith, not prudence, that is its most perfect virtue, and in the will it is charity, not moral virtue, that is its highest virtue; but even speaking naturally one can admit that

if there be an act of the practical intellect and an act of the will in regard to the same object such as a moral good, if both act perfectly, one dictating, the other choosing, then the right choice will be simply more noble than the right dictate, and consequently the habit generated by choices of this sort will be simply more perfect than those produced by correct judgments, which I grant.

As for the Philosopher preferring prudence, I reply that prudence is somehow related to the other virtues, insofar as it and its act preceded the generation of either an act or a habit of moral virtue, and because of this priority a moral act and habit is conformed to it as prior and not vice versa. And such priority according to the Philosopher implies that prudence functions as a rule and a measure, and it is in this that its dignity consists, but not in an unqualified sense.

Still another objection states that if it is only because the sense appetite is moved by the will that a habit or virtue is induced in it, then a moral habit could be induced in any part of the body that is frequently moved voluntarily. Scotus admits that this is in a sense true, for one could induce a habit or quasi-virtue in the body, as is clear from the hand of a writer or painter. If the handiwork is a product of a virtuous action, then one could admit that practice could make one skilled in performing a work of moral virtue.

In a broad sense "virtue" means simply a certain inherent power or efficacy an agent possesses. Hence, one could apply the term in this way to bodily skills, and *a fortiori* to a habit produced in the sense appetite by the will acting in accord with right reason. But this is using the term "virtue," or "moral virtue," in a less perfect way than when the term designates "that quality in the will that inclines it to choose rightly."

Scotus concludes the question with a somewhat lengthy discussion of how Henry of Ghent solves the initial argument based on what Aristotle says about reason ruling the sense appetite with "despotic rule" (*Politics* I, ch. 5, 1254b3–5). Henry distinguishes between the will acting (1) as nature, (2) as free, and (3) as deliberative. When it acts as nature no virtue is needed because it tends naturally to the object; neither is virtue required when it acts freely, for virtue is a habit and habits act necessarily; only when the will acts as deliberative is virtue required.

Scotus objects that the will never acts as nature, for all its acts are free, and Henry's third member includes the second, because all deliberate acts are free. He goes on to explain that though virtues or habits act of necessity, when two causes act as a common principle, one free and the other of necessity, the resulting act is still free because the will is the principal cause of the act and the habit only a cooperating cause. Also he points out that what Henry regards as the will acting as nature are those voluntary acts where the time of deliberation is so short as to be imperceptible, i.e., the virtuous person has been so conditioned by prudence to make a correct judgment as to what should be chosen that he seems to act automatically rather than to be making a choice. The rapidity of the action, however, stems from the speed with which the practical judgment is made, in contrast to the slow or reluctant way a person acts who has not acquired the virtue of prudence; for such a one can "syllogize only with difficulty and delay" in making the correct choice.

The Latin source is distinction 33 of the supplement to *Ordinatio* III, revised with the help of Codices A (ff. 174ra–75vb) and S (ff. 215ra–16va).

23. *Moral virtue and the gifts and fruits of the Spirit*

The gifts refer to the workings of the Holy Spirit mentioned in Holy Scripture and manifested in Christ and in the life of his Church. Promised already in Isaiah, the Holy Spirit actually revealed himself at the baptism of Jesus and communicated himself to the apostles at Pentecost and thereafter to the Church. Six gifts are mentioned in the Hebrew version of Isaiah 11:1–3, namely, "a spirit of wisdom and of understanding, a spirit of counsel and of fortitude, a spirit of knowledge and of fear of the Lord." The Greek Septuagint, however, adds a seventh, viz., piety or godliness, and it was this version of the gifts that influenced the scholastics of the thirteenth century.

The beatitudes refer to the eight beatitudes mentioned by Christ in the Sermon on the Mount. According to Matthew 5:3–12, they are (1) poverty of spirit (which Scotus, following Augustine, interprets as humility); (2) meekness; (3) sorrow or mourning; (4) hunger and thirst for justice; (5) mercy; (6) purity of heart; (7) peacemaking; (8) suffering persecution.

The nine fruits of the Holy Spirit refer to St. Paul's list in his letter to the Galatians (5:22–23), viz., "The fruit of the Spirit is love, joy, peace, patient endurance, kindness, faith, mildness, and chastity."

Though most theologians denied the distinction between the virtues, gifts, beatitudes, and fruits, basing themselves on St. Gregory the Great, during the third decade of the thirteenth century, due to the *Summa de bono* of Philip the Chancellor, many theologians, especially at Paris, began viewing the gifts as superior to and distinct from the virtues, whether acquired naturally or supernaturally infused. Thomas Aquinas, for example, after discussing various aspects of the virtues, devotes qq. 68, 69, and 70 of the *Summa theologiae* IaIIae respectively to the nature of the gifts, beatitudes, and fruits, and how they differ from the virtues. In art. 1 of the first of these he writes:

Now it is manifest that human virtues perfect man insofar as it is natural for him to be moved by his reason in his interior and exterior actions. Consequently man needs yet higher perfections if he is to be disposed to be moved by God. These perfections are called gifts, not only because they are infused by God, but also because by them man is disposed to become amenable to divine inspiration.

If the gifts are distinct habits from the virtues, what of the beatitudes and the fruits? Aquinas is clear on this matter. He regards them not as habits (or virtues) but rather as acts proceeding from such habits. In art. 1 of q. 69 he points out that the beatitudes differ from the virtues and gifts, "not as habit from habit, but as act from habit"; and in the first article of q. 70 he explains that the fruits are special sorts of acts:

The word "fruit" has been transferred from the material to the spiritual world. Now fruit, among material things, is the product of a plant when it comes to perfection, and has some attraction for the taste. Accordingly, in spiritual matters, we may take the word "fruit" in two ways: first, in the sense that the fruit of man, who is likened to a tree, is that which he produces; second, in the sense that man's fruit is what he gathers. Yet not all that man gathers is fruit, but only that which is last and gives pleasure . . . In this sense man's fruit is his last end, which is intended for his enjoyment. But if by man's fruits we understand a product of man, human actions are called "fruits," because operation is the second act of the operator, and gives pleasure if suitable to him. If, then, a man's operation proceeds from man in virtue of his reason, it is said to be the fruit of his reason, but if it proceeds from him with respect to a higher power, which is the power of the Holy Spirit, then a man's operation is said to be the fruit of the Holy Spirit.

And in the second article of this question, he explains the difference between beatitude and fruit in this way:

More is required for a beatitude than for a fruit, because it is sufficient for a fruit to be something ultimate and delightful, whereas a beatitude must be something perfect and excellent. Hence all the beatitudes may be called fruits, but not vice versa.

This view of Aquinas, particularly on the relationship of the virtues to the soul and to the gifts, fits in with his overall theory of how the soul and its potencies or faculties are interrelated. He considered the soul as really distinct from its intellectual and volitional powers; hence, he believed special infused virtues, in addition to the sanctifying grace residing in the substance of the soul, are required to fully supernaturalize human nature. Furthermore, he thought the will could be moved naturally (and hence, even necessarily under certain conditions) by right reason and that it was moved in a similar way supernaturally by the Holy Spirit. Hence, he deals with the difference between the virtues and the gifts in terms of what habits condition the will to be moved in these several ways. Among the Franciscan masters, Richard of Mediavilla was particularly impressed with Aquinas' interpretation, and he broke with the earlier tradition that denied any distinction between the virtues and the gifts.

In his initial arguments Pro and Con Scotus refers first to this older view and then to the more recent opinions that sought to differentiate them. He writes:

The number of gifts and beatitudes is not the same; also what is enumerated there clearly does not coincide, for there is a beatitude that is not a gift and a gift that is not a virtue, and the same with the fruits.

Since the argument for the opposition in the introductory Pro and Con usually represents the position Scotus will eventually take, we may assume he believes some sort of distinction must be made in regard to the virtues, gifts, etc. In the present case, however, the distinction he wishes to make is a somewhat intricate one, and it could be said to favor the affirmative view (viz., that the gifts, fruits, and beatitudes are not something other than the intellectual, moral, or theological virtues that perfect man in the natural and supernatural order). At the same time, it respects the negative view in showing that they are distinct, not in the sense that they represent distinct species of supernatural gifts on the part of God, but rather in the sense of the inadequate distinction that exists between a genus and some particular species that falls under it, or between a species and a subspecies. Furthermore, his view of the distinction is presented only as a possible or probable theory, "without asserting it categorically."

Before developing it, however, Scotus first presents three opposing opinions as to how these four items differ. The first is that of Henry of Ghent, to which as usual Scotus devotes the most attention. According to Henry, one can face adversity in a threefold way: humanly, superhumanly, and in an "inhuman" or heroic way. Through the virtues a person faces such humanly; through the gifts, superhumanly; through the beatitudes, heroically. Scotus plays upon the meaning of the term "inhumano modo"—which Henry understands in a positive and transcendent sense, rather than in either the quasi-neutral sense of "nonhuman" or the negative or contrary sense of "inhuman." The triple distinction itself is drawn from what Aristotle says in the opening chapter of Bk. VII of the *Nicomachean Ethics*, where—as Henry interprets it—he contrasts the three moral states to be avoided, namely, "vice, incontinence, and brutishness," to three opposing virtuous states, namely, "virtue, superhuman virtue, and a heroic or godlike kind of virtue."

To this Scotus objects that, since it is the supernatural virtues one is talking about, charity—according to St. Paul—is better than superhuman or even heroic fortitude. "If I have fortitude and hand over my body to be burned, but have not charity, I gain nothing" (1 Corinthians 13:3).

Furthermore, since the virtues are acquired and increase in strength with practice, Scotus sees no reason why they cannot be developed to an even heroic degree without altering their specific nature, and hence the principle of parsimony would apply, viz., species should not be multiplied without necessity.

Likewise, if we take the term "inhumano modo" seriously, it is difficult to see how anyone could at the same time act both humanly and inhumanly in any meaningful sense. This goes back to Scotus' basic thesis that the human intellect and will are naturally open at least to being supernaturally perfected, even though such perfection cannot be acquired without the intervention of some voluntary and transcen-

dent action on the part of the divine will (see, for instance, his opening question of the prologue to his commentaries on the *Sentences*;
Wolter, 1949, 1951). If Henry's theory were correct, Scotus argues,
any previously acquired or infused virtue would be "rendered null by
an acquired gift, or if it did remain, it would be unable to go into action," because "its function would be replaced by the more perfect
gift." The same would obviously be true of the beatitudes, which the
blessed enjoy in heaven. Yet this seems both incongruous and contrary
to Scripture, for—according to Paul—"in heaven charity will not pass
away, nor will faith and hope in this life."

In a more summary fashion Scotus deals with the views of Bonaventure and Richard of Mediavilla. The first stresses the activity and autonomy of the will; the second, the fact that the will always tends to
be moved by another.

Bonaventure (*Sent.* III, dist. 34, art. 1, q. 1) believed that virtue
gives the will the capacity to act rightly; the gifts, to act perfectly; and
the beatitudes, to act quickly. Since it is the will Bonaventure is talking of, the virtues in question appear to be those we call "moral,"
rather than those called "theological." Because Scotus regards these
moral virtues as acquired, rather than infused, he argues that the virtues that enable one to act "rightly" are also those that enable one to
act easily and quickly, something the infused virtues (of faith, hope, or
charity) do not. (We might note that Scotus held that the acquired
virtues become supernaturalized by the fact that they exist in a soul
that has been elevated by sanctifying grace, which is only formally distinct from the infused virtue of charity residing in the will. Since the
will and the soul-substance are only formally, not really, distinct, what
elevates or supernaturalizes one, supernaturalizes the other.) According to Aristotle, acquired virtues are a species of habit, and habits—as
a second nature—enable one to act quickly and easily. If the habit is a
virtue rather than a vice, then it perfects the potency or faculty in
question. Consequently, given Scotus' account of the nature of the
will and the fact that it is the immediate subject of the moral virtues of
justice, temperance, and fortitude, he obviously cannot accept Bonaventure's account of the distinction.

As Lottin points out (1954, p. 695), Richard of Mediavilla (*Sent.*
III, dist. 34, art. 1, q. 1), whose views resemble those of Aquinas, is
the second target of Scotus' criticism.

Another says that something is necessary to dispose the will so that it is able
to be moved by right reason, and that is virtue. But something else is needed
so that the Holy Spirit can move it, and that is the gift; and these two are
postulated as moving the will.

Understandably Scotus objects to this because "it falsely assumes that reason causes the will's movement"—the assumption being that it is the total or principal cause of its movement. Furthermore, Richard's theory assumes it is the virtue—acquired or infused—rather than the innate "affection for justice," that naturally or exclusively disposes the will to act in accord with right reason. He also argues that this view of Richard "fails to distinguish the beatitudes from the gifts and virtues."

In the body of the question Scotus simplifies the interrelationship of these various agents of virtuous behavior by reducing the gifts, beatitudes, and fruits to some form of "virtue." There he presents this basic thesis: even though man is in a supernatural order, "the only virtues necessary in this life are the moral virtues, the intellectual virtues, and the theological virtues." The first two are acquired, the last infused supernaturally by God.

Scotus, however, understands the moral virtues as "generic virtues," each with a host of species or subspecies under it, for each specifically different moral act can generate a corresponding habit or virtue. Since this question of the distinction of virtues and gifts has to do with the moral life, he points out that his sevenfold classification of the virtues is not meant to cover those habits of knowledge that are theoretical, as these "intellectual virtues" are as numerous as are the various arts and sciences. In his classification, then, "intellectual virtues" refer to those which produce prudential judgments. Since such judgments can refer to specifically different subjects, "prudence" too is taken in a generic sense as covering all practical habits of knowledge needed to guide moral behavior.

Despite the fact that the question is obviously theological, dealing as it does with notions of how the Holy Spirit cooperates supernaturally with morally good human actions so as to make them meritorious as well as naturally and morally good, the question is of interest philosophically, for Scotus—in developing his "probable thesis"—is always careful to point out how far one can go using natural reason before indicating its natural limitations and where faith and revealed knowledge is necessary to complement what we can know naturally. Thus he writes, for instance:

Natural reason infers the necessity of . . . intellectual habits . . . covering theoretical and practical knowledge . . . [and] of a habit perfecting the appetite in regard to what is desirable for oneself and what one can seek in relationship to others . . .

Although one may conclude perhaps by natural reason that man is not sufficiently perfected by these habits . . . other information is required to indicate just what additional cognitive and appetitive habits are needed, for natural reason alone does not show clearly enough what intellectual and what appetitive virtues there are other than these. But one may reasonably hold . . . that besides these there is a necessity for that cognitive habit and that appetitive habit which the Catholic Church says is necessary, and by faith we hold that three theological virtues are necessary, and that they perfect the soul immediately with respect to the uncreated object [God].

Scotus divides his discussion into two articles, the first dealing with the virtues, the second with gifts, beatitudes, and fruits. The treatment of the first is almost purely philosophical, and is noteworthy for Scotus' conception of "generic virtue" and how the distinction of "irascible and concupiscible" appetites is to be understood. The second portion, since it treats of the relationship of the various supernatural gifts to the virtues, is obviously more theological. Nevertheless, what he says there throws considerable light on how Scotus, as a philosopher, in the tradition of Aristotle, understood the moral virtues. The discussion in both articles is relatively clear and straightforward.

The Latin text translated here is from the supplement to *Ordinatio* III, dist. 34, and represents a revision of the Wadding reprint edition (XV, pp. 464–575) based on Codex A (ff. 175vb–77rb) and Codex S (ff. 206vb–18vb).

24. Are the moral virtues connected?

Lottin (1954, pp. 551–666) has traced the origin of this question and the various answers given to it by the scholastics. He sees the systematic treatise on the virtues by William of Auxerre, written around 1220, as first raising this question of the acquired virtues as distinct from the infused moral virtues given at baptism. William argues that if acts of temperance could exist without acts of fortitude, obviously the corresponding habits or virtues are not necessarily connected. However, many Fathers of the Church, including St. Bernard, following the classical philosophers like Seneca and Cicero, praised the harmonious interconnection of all the virtues. Thus Master Peter Lombard, in dist. 36 of his third book of the *Sentences*, credits Saints Jerome and Augustine with the idea that they are somehow one. For Jerome had written in the beginning of ch. 56 of his *Commentary on Isaiah*: "All the virtues hang together, so that if one is lacking, all are. Hence, one who has one virtue has them all." And Peter quotes Augustine in praise of charity in these words:

Where charity is, what could be wanting? But where it is not, what else could be of any value? Why then should we not say that he who has this virtue, has all the virtues, since charity represents the complete fulfillment of the law?

The more it is in a man, the more is that individual endowed with virtue, and the less charity he has, the less virtue he possesses, and the less virtue is in him, the more he has of vice.

The scholastic theologians were loath to repudiate this traditional position completely. Around 1230 Philip the Chancellor found a solution. He distinguished between a broad sense of the cardinal virtues and a narrow sense; in the broad sense, for example, temperance is a necessary prerequisite for any virtue, since virtue has traditionally been recognized as a middle position between two extremes. The same is true of fortitude, prudence, and justice, for any virtue enables one to face a difficult situation with courage, and to act in a way that is both prudent and just. In the narrow sense, however, a cardinal virtue is defined by its object, namely, some formal specific good; in this sense temperance designates a moderation of the passions of the concupiscible appetite; fortitude is concerned with the irascible appetites; justice with rendering to each his due. Odo Rigaud, Bonaventure, Albert the Great, and others adopted this opinion. But when the complete translation of Aristotle's *Nicomachean Ethics* became available shortly after 1245, the problem was presented in a new way. The four cardinal virtues are no longer treated as a block, but "moral virtue" refers to the three that reside in the appetitive faculties (justice, temperance, and fortitude) and these are distinguished from the virtue of prudence, which resides in the practical intellect. The Aristotelian solution is no moral virtue without prudence, and no prudence without moral virtue. It is in this way that the four cardinal virtues are interconnected.

But this view did not totally replace the older view which envisaged the connection of the virtues among themselves; the two coexisted throughout the second half of the thirteenth century. Many combined the two views, like Aquinas, who distinguished between the imperfect and the perfect state of a moral virtue (*Summa theologiae* IaIIae, q. 65, art. 1). In the imperfect state "moral virtue is nothing but an inclination in us to do some kind of good deed, whether such an inclination be in us by nature or by habituation." Here there is no connection. But "the perfect moral virtue is a habit that inclines us to do things well, and if we take moral virtues in this way we must say they are connected." Aquinas gives two reasons, one the argument of Philip the Chancellor that if we look to the general properties, we discover a connection; the other reason is based on the Aristotelian thesis "No moral virtue without prudence, no prudence without moral virtue." Towards the end of the century those who sought to defend the Aristotelian thesis introduced a distinction between two forms of prudence similar to that in regard to moral virtue. One form of prudence was particular; it was proper not only to each moral virtue, but also to the concrete differences between acts falling under each of these virtues. The other form of prudence was general, viz., that which unifies all human activity in view of man's unique final end, that common end towards which all moral virtue is directed.

Around 1280 Henry of Ghent, however, adopted a particularly vulnerable thesis. As for the patristic claim of the connection of the virtues among themselves, he distinguishes various stages and substages in the acquisition or formation of a virtuous habit. In the first two, i.e., the inchoative stage, or where the virtue exists only to a mediocre degree, there is no connection between the moral virtues. Only where the virtue has been developed to perfection, in the third stage, or where it is truly heroic, in the fourth stage, is there any connection.

Scotus divides his treatment of the question into four articles, in the first three of which he seems to have Henry of Ghent mainly in mind:

In this question there are many articles, the first of which concerns the interconnection of the specific moral virtues among themselves on the basis of whether they are species of the same or different genera; the second article treats of the connection of each of the moral virtues with prudence; the third, of the link between the moral and the theological virtues; and the fourth article, of the nexus between the theological virtues themselves.

The second article is subdivided on the basis of the two meanings of "prudence": one dealing with prudence as a particular virtue directed to a specific sort of moral action; the other, with prudence as a general or generic virtue.

The third and fourth articles seem to have been occasioned by the fact that the quotation from St. Augustine Peter Lombard cites in his *Sentences* apparently refers to the infused or theological virtue of charity. Once Scotus has clarified his views on the first two articles, he is in a position to show that the "moral virtues do not require the theological virtues in order to be perfect as regards their own specific nature, though without such, they do not have that further extrinsic perfection they could have." The theological virtues, infused as they are, e.g., in baptism of an infant, obviously do not necessarily impart acquired moral virtue. Neither are the three theological virtues of faith, hope, and charity necessarily connected, since—according to the Scriptures—in heaven "the habits and acts of charity exist without the habits and acts of faith and hope." Even in this life, one who sins mortally can lose sanctifying grace or charity and yet retain the virtue of faith or hope.

As for the first article—namely, the connection of the moral virtues among themselves—Scotus takes on Henry of Ghent as his principal protagonist, but also touches briefly on what seems to be Aquinas' solution, though he generalizes and applies what Aquinas says of prudence to all the virtues. Neither view seems to be sufficient to justify a necessary connection of the acquired moral virtues. Hence—as Lottin points out—Scotus breaks completely with Philip the Chancellor's defense of the Fathers of the Church, and denies categorically that there is any necessary connection among the acquired moral virtues, whether one treats of them particularly or generically.

I concede there is no connection either of the generically different moral virtues, commonly referred to as justice, fortitude, and temperance, or of the even more general types I distinguished earlier [i.e., in selection 23], namely, those disposing one's affects towards self and others respectively.

For this opinion one can argue persuasively as follows. While virtue is a perfection of man, it does not represent complete perfection, for then one moral virtue would suffice. But when something has several partial perfections, it can be simply perfect according to one perfection and simply imperfect according to another, as is apparent in the case of a man, who has many organic perfections, and can have one in the highest degree, and not have another; for example, someone may be disposed in the highest way as to sight and touch but lack any hearing. Someone can possess the highest degree of perfection in matters of temperance and not have the perfection required as regards another perfection, and consequently can be simply temperate also in regard to any act of temperance, although he is not brave. But one is not simply a moral person without all the virtues, just as one is not simply sentient without all one's senses. But this does not make one less perfectly temperate because one is less perfectly moral, just as one's vision or hearing is no less acute because one is less perfectly sentient in other ways.

He goes on to discuss how the points Henry brought up that seem to be true could be explained in terms of the above.

As for the second article, viz., the connection of each moral virtue with prudence, Scotus asks whether it is a specific or a generic virtue of prudence one is speaking of. If one is speaking of particular prudence, one can admit only the first half of the Aristotelian solution proper (viz., no moral virtue without prudence). Moral virtue does require a measure of prudence. Hence Scotus will admit that "what is necessary is not conformity of one moral virtue to another, because no one is the rule for the other, but conformity of each moral virtue to prudence." And he goes on to acknowledge the probability of the view that one morally good act can produce both a moral habit of virtue in the will and, at the same time, a particular prudential habit in the intellect. But he is particularly concerned to show that the prudential choice is not limited to the means to an end, but may also refer to a particular end that represents the aim of a particular moral virtue.

As for the second part of the Aristotelian solution (viz., no prudence without moral virtue), Scotus wants to defend the freedom of the will to choose the opposite of what right reason dictates and, by its control over the intellect (see selection 3), the will's ability to turn the intellect's consideration to sophistical reasons or to irrelevant matters—"lest that actual displeasure remain that consists in that remorse for choosing the opposite of what one knows to be right." Hence, his general conclusion as regards particular prudence:

This habit, generated by correct judgments, whether about the means to an end or about the ends themselves (at least certain particular ones which are properly speaking the ends of distinct moral virtues and where perhaps there is no other judgmental habit about such ends), is prudence, even though a correct choice does not follow . . . But the converse relationship is different, for no choice can be morally right unless it is conformed to some rule or measure, which is a correct dictate. Such a right dictate, however, is suited by nature to generate prudence, even though this prudence refers only to this particular matter. Therefore, one can concede the existence of the converse connection, since a moral virtue cannot exist without there being a prudential habit concerned with its respective matter.

As for the connection of all moral virtues with one general or generic prudential habit that comprises all the particular "prudences," Scotus concludes:

How all these "prudences" form one habit and how all habits of geometry pertain to one universal science has been explained in my first question on Bk. VI of the *Metaphysics*, for one should understand this not as a formal but as a virtual unity. Just as a habit which is about a first subject is formally one by reason of that subject, and is virtually concerned with all those things contained in that first subject, though it is not formally about them, so this habit, which is formally about some end of certain actions, is virtually, but not formally, concerned with all of these possible actions, the practical knowledge of which is virtually included in that end. And so, by extending the name "prudence" to that habit which is an understanding of first practical principles, that prudence, which is formally one in itself, is virtually concerned with all the virtues.

This reference to his *Metaphysics* is one of two Scotus makes in this question. Lottin, on the basis of his study of manuscripts other than Codex A where Scotus treats of this problem of the connection of virtues, was of the opinion that Scotus' revision of his earlier lectures extended to at least this distinction in the third book, if not further.

Balić, who at first thought otherwise, came to admit that if the version contained in the Assisi manuscript (Codex A) was not intended as his "ordinatio," it must at least be included as part of the supplement to that book. What is more, Scotus' two references to his questions on the *Metaphysics* of Aristotle, where he gives a detailed critique of Henry's view of prudence as one virtue, led Lottin to date the composition of these questions between Scotus' earlier lectures on the *Sentences* and the "ordinatio" revision of Bk. III (See Lottin, 1953).

The Latin text for this supplement to *Ordinatio* III, dist. 36, is a revision of the Wadding reprint edition (XV, pp. 597–729), based on Codices A (ff. 177rb–79va) and S (ff. 218vb–21rb).

PART VII: THE LOVE OF GOD, SELF, AND NEIGHBOR

25. *The infused virtue of charity*

In Bk. III, dists. 27 to 29, Scotus raises three questions in regard to the supernatural or infused virtue of charity. The first concerns the love of God; the second, love of neighbor; and the third, love of self. Much of what he has to say, especially in the first and longest of the three, is of philosophical interest, because it concerns the love of God insofar as it is a moral virtue and is enjoined on man by natural law in the strictest sense. The question reads: "Is there some theological virtue inclining one to love God above all?"

Before answering the main question, Scotus points out that there are three preliminary questions to be answered: First, is the love of God above all an act that is morally right? Second, what is the precise object or aspect under which God is loved by an act or by the virtue of charity? Third, is human nature capable of loving God above all without a supernaturally infused virtue?

First, is the love of God above all an act that is morally right? Scotus replies:

As for the first, I say that to love God above all is an act conformed to natural right reason, which dictates that what is best must be loved most; and hence such an act is right of itself; indeed, as a first practical principle of action, this is something known *per se*, and hence its rectitude is self-evident. For something must be loved most of all, and it is none other than the highest good, even as this good is recognized by the intellect as that to which we must adhere the most.

Scotus' answer, like the question itself, requires a word of explanation, since he seems to be talking simply of a morally good act, rather than a meritorious one, and of an act that could, by repetition, produce an acquired virtue of charity, rather than the supernaturally infused virtue. Yet it is the nature and function of the latter that he is primarily concerned with in this distinction and the two that follow. There are two things to keep in mind to understand what he has to say, especially in this twenty-ninth distinction.

(a) One is the generally accepted theological principle that grace (and the supernatural virtue of charity which is really identical with grace) builds on nature, and the supernatural presupposes the natural as a necessary, though not a sufficient, condition. Now, every virtue, be it supernaturally infused or naturally acquired, implies that the act that stems from it is also something naturally good and morally right. It is this fact that prompts Scotus' first preliminary question, "Is it morally right to love God above all?" He answers this question by showing that the love of God above all is a morally good act dictated by right reason and hence something towards which we are naturally inclined by reason of the will's affection for justice. This obviously raises further questions, among them the third preliminary question of whether we need a supernaturally infused virtue to love God above all, something that many of his colleagues claimed we did. This brings us to the other point we must keep in mind.

(b) "Charity" for Scotus is just another name for "justice," as he explained in selection 23. Now, justice can be either naturally acquired or supernaturally infused. As we said earlier, though Scotus began by distinguishing Anselm's "affection for justice" from the will's "affection for the advantageous," he definitely extended and amplified the saint's notion of "justice." For Anselm never clearly distinguished the will's natural inclination for justice from the supernaturally infused "justice" that Scotus regarded as identical in reality with grace or charity. Just as Scotus made the inclination or affection for justice something essential to the nature of the will, so now he argues that the will's ability to love God above all is something man is already inclined to do by nature. Furthermore, it is something he is obliged to do by virtue of natural law as well as by express divine command. Incidentally, this poses a special problem for him, one that he will answer before concluding his discussion of the question, namely, why is the infused habit of charity necessary if we can love God above all by our natural resources?

Whatever be the precise role of this infused virtue, however, the first point Scotus wishes us to keep in mind is that the love of God above all is an act that "is known to be right," and "from this it follows that there can be a virtue inclining one naturally towards such an act." But as something supernaturally given rather than naturally acquired, this special virtue of charity, though "based immediately upon the first rule of human action," has to be "infused by God," for it has to do with the highest portion of the soul, and this "cannot be perfected in the best possible way except immediately by God." This supernatural virtue of charity is distinct from the infused virtue of faith, "because its act is one neither of belief nor of understanding." It is likewise distinct from the infused virtue of hope which perfects the will insofar as it has an affection for the advantageous. "This virtue," he says, "which thus perfects the will insofar as it has an affection for justice, I call 'charity.'"

This already indicates how Scotus will answer the second preliminary question about the specific aspect under which God is the formal object of charity. There are three ways in which God can be an object of love. He can be loved for his intrinsic worth, i.e., for his own sake. He can be loved because he loves us and shares himself with those who love him. And finally, because there is a satisfaction or happiness that accompanies a well-ordered love, he can be loved because he makes us happy. Properly speaking, charity tends to God as its formal object only in the first sense, even though in a secondary and tertiary sense we can speak of him being an object in the other two ways.

As for the third question, "Does nature suffice to love God above all?" there are various views. Aquinas (*Summa theologiae* IaIIae, q. 109, art. 3) and Henry of Ghent (*Quodl.* IV, q. 11) ask similar questions, and the editors of the Wadding edition cite these authors as the probable protagonists Scotus had in mind in what he says in this third article. However, the way they answer the question and the arguments they give as to why man in his present fallen state, at least, needs either grace or infused charity or both to love God above all by an elicited act, do not correspond precisely to those cited here by Scotus. As he presents the question, there are two main positions held by his contemporaries. The first, according to Duns, "assumes that nature is not sufficient for this act of love without an infused habit." The second "argues against this." The Assisi manuscript, Codex A, has a marginal note here (f. 171va) designating the first view "Opinio Thomae" and the second "Opinio Henrici." Francis Lychetus in his commentary on this passage (see the Wadding reprint ed. XV, p. 365) cites Godfrey of Fontaines's *Quodlibet* IV, q. 6, as proposing this second view. At any rate, Scotus believes the arguments it employs against the first view to be inconclusive, and John Duns does not rest content with such but presents two of his own. These he sums up as follows in his solution to the question.

As for this article, because of these two reasons—conformity of the will to right reason and the case of the brave citizen—I concede the conclusion that by purely natural means any will could love God above all, at least as human nature existed in the state in which it was instituted. To clarify this, then, I explain first how "above all" is to be understood; then, second, to what extent a rational creature is bound to such love; and third, why, despite this natural capacity, the habit of charity is still necessary.

(A) As for the first (i.e., what "above all" means in this context), Scotus says there are two senses. The expression is understood either extensively or intensively. Extensively a person loves God above all if he or she "out of affection for him would will more readily that all else should cease to be rather than that God not exist." Intensively one loves God above all if one "wills God well with a greater measure of affection than one has for any other person's welfare." Intensity, therefore, seems to refer to the emotional ardor of one's voluntary act, for as Scotus conceives of the will, it too, as an affective appetite, is capable of emotions of varying intensities.

He cites here first the "opinion of others" that one love, like that of a mother for her child, may exceed another because it is more fervent or tender, whereas another, like a father's love for his offspring, may be stronger and firmer, if less effusive, than the former. And that "love of God above all ought to be of this latter sort . . . but it is not necessary that he be loved above all as to tenderness and fervor and sweetness." Scotus argues against this on the grounds that "only one who loves more firmly loves more . . . And I am speaking of that love which is an act of the will, and not about that which is a feeling in the sense appetite." The more effusive manifestation Scotus ascribes to "sensible sweetness." This is really no measure of the solidity or firmness of a love that would not stop short of martyrdom for God's sake. Sensible sweetness that may accompany the will-act, says Scotus, is only a "certain rewarding feeling . . . whereby God nourishes his little ones and draws them to himself lest they fall by the way." Hence his conclusion:

I say, then, that this "above all" must be understood in both ways, extensively and intensively, for just as I am held to love God above all extensively, so I am held to love him also intensively with a greater affection than simply anything else. I say "greater affection" because it is more opposed to anything incompatible with it, in the sense that one could more easily be turned against loving anything else than turned against loving God.

(B) As for how this precept obliges or how it can be expected to be fulfilled, Scotus points out that "the affirmative precept . . . not only always obliges us to refrain from the opposite, viz., an act of hatred, but also obliges us to elicit an act that is directed to God as our end." This we do through divine worship, specifically by hearing mass according to the precept of the Church. But he admits we are not so totally absorbed in the contemplative love of God as we might be under special conditions where all sensible distractions were absent, "so that the will could exert the sort of effort it could if our powers were all united and recollected and all impediments were removed." Putting this in another way we could say that Scotus admits that we can love God "above all" in this substantial sense; if confronted with a concrete instance of choice between displeasing God or giving up some created treasure or object we value highly, we refrain from the former and elect to surrender the latter. Nevertheless, in this life, we cannot love God above all according to "all the conditions which are implied by the words 'with your whole heart, your whole soul,' etc., because in this life there cannot be that recollection of our faculties with all impediments removed." It is on this ground that Scotus explains the claim of Augustine and Peter Lombard that "this precept is not fulfilled in this life, for the propensity of the inferior powers in the present state impedes the superior powers from acting perfectly."

(C) As to why the infused habit of charity is necessary, despite our natural ability to love God above all in the aforesaid sense, Scotus replies that "this habit adds to the substantial intensity of the act a further intensity, which the will alone could also have given to the act by exerting an equal effort." He spells out what "greater" implies in mathematical terms, referring back to what he said in Bk. I, dist. 17, where he discusses to what extent a virtuous habit plays an active role in regard to the goodness of a will-act. There he uses this same distinction of arithmetic versus geometric increase in perfection to answer the objection that charity is not necessary in heaven, since even without it each will would love God as much as was possible. Scotus argues that this is not so, for "no potency that is capable of being perfected by a habit can perform an act as perfectly without such a habit as it can with a habit; indeed the more perfect the power, the less could it have an act in proportion to its perfection if it lacked every habit. For if the increase produced by the habit in each case is similar geometrically speaking, there will still be some arithmetic proportion according to which the more perfect power will be simply more deficient without the habit than the less perfect potency would be" (*Ord.* I, dist. 17, n. 181; Vatican ed. V, p. 225).

The point Scotus is making is that the infused habit of charity increases any will's natural ability to love according to some geometric proportion—say it doubles, triples, or quadruples the intensity of its love. Viewed from the converse aspect of what it is missing by reason of not having charity, though geometrically there is no difference, arithmetically speaking the more perfect the natural capacity of the will, the greater its loss of perfection. Suppose, for example, the natural capacity is doubled; then a will capable of loving naturally with an intensity of only two will be able to love with an intensity of four, whereas a more perfect will capable of loving naturally with an intensity of eight will be able, with charity, to love with an intensity of sixteen. Hence, by not having charity the more perfect will will lose eight possible degrees in the intensity of its capacity to love, whereas the less perfect will will lose only two degrees, arithmetically speaking. Scotus' point in brief is that even though without charity the less perfect will might—with greater natural effort—equal the capacity of will with less effort to will (for instance, one that ordinarily wills with an intensity of four or eight), nevertheless that same natural effort, arithmetically speaking, would be immensely increased proportionally were infused charity present. Hence, speaking simply or in an unqualified sense, the more perfect the will's natural capacity to love God is, the more it has to gain by having charity.

Apart from increasing the natural capacity of the will to love, charity also is responsible for a morally good act becoming meritorious, i.e., meriting an increase in grace or charity in this life and beatitude in the life to come. Since this refers to the supernatural order, namely, the capacity to share more intensely in the inner life of God through acts of love, it is a gratuitous gift dependent on what God freely deigns to give as a reward for loving him. In *Ordinatio* I, dist. 17, n. 129 (Vatican ed. V, pp. 202–3), Scotus explains that over and above the added intensity a habit like charity imparts to one's act of love of God, the habit also serves as a lasting mark in the soul, even when it is not eliciting an act of love. Charity indicates that the nature possessing it "is formally accepted by God as habitually able to be beatified and that the acts elicited with its help are accepted as meritorious." Using Augustine's simile comparing the will to a horse and habitual grace or charity to its rider, Scotus explains that the horse is free to throw its rider (destroy charity through mortal sin) or it may not follow the guidance of the rider (and then its actions are not meritorious, but are either indifferent or venially sinful) or, thirdly, it may choose to follow where charity leads (and then its action is meritorious) (ibid., n. 155, p. 213). It is with this simile in mind that Scotus can say here that "as for this added circumstance, that the act has the special character of being accepted by God, this is something due principally to charity and less so to the will."

26. *Love of God and neighbor*

In this second of the three distinctions devoted to infused charity, Scotus raises the question: "Is it by the same habit by which we love God that we are bound to love our neighbor?" What prompts the question is that, according to the first epistle of St. John (4:21), "the commandment we have from [Christ] is this: Whoever loves God must also love his brother," yet charity as a theological virtue has God as its formal object. Hence, in the first article, Scotus aims to explain how this habit whereby God is loved refers to our neighbor as well. His second article is devoted to answering the question: "Who is my neighbor?"

In answer to the first question, "How does charity towards God refer to neighbor?" Scotus recalls his earlier discussion of the nature and function of the supernatural habit of charity (*Ord.* I, dist. 17), and uses Richard of St. Victor's definition of perfect love to solve the paradox of how love of God entails love of neighbor.

To the first I say, as in dist. 17 of the first book, that charity is defined as the habit by which we hold God to be dear. Now, it could be that someone is considered dear because of some private love where the lover wants no co-lovers, as is exemplified in the case of jealous men having an excessive love of their wives. But this sort of habit would not be orderly or perfect. Not orderly, I say, because God, the good of all, does not want to be the private or proper good of any person exclusively, nor would right reason have someone appropriate this common good to himself. Hence, such a love or habit, inclining him to this good as exclusive to himself and not to be loved or had by another, would be an inordinate love. Neither would it be perfect, because one who loves perfectly wants the beloved to be loved by others, as is clear from Richard [of St. Victor] . . . Therefore, God, in infusing the love by which all tend towards him in a perfect and orderly way, gives this habit by which he is held dear as a good that is to be loved by others as well. Thus this habit which regards God in himself, inclines also to this, that he be loved by another, at least by anyone whose friendship he is pleased to have, or whose friendship is pleasing to him . . .

From this it is clear how the habit of charity is one, because it does not refer to a plurality of objects, but regards as its primary object God alone insofar as he is good and is the first good. Secondarily, it wills that God be loved by anyone whose love is perfect and directed to loving him as he is in himself, for this is what perfect and orderly love of God means. And in so loving, I love both myself and my neighbor out of charity, viz., by willing that both of us love God in himself. And this is something that is simply good and an act of justice. Thus the first object of charity is only God in himself; all the others, however, are certain intermediate objects. They are objects of quasi-reflex acts by means of which one tends to the infinite good, who is God. It is the same habit, however, that has to do with both direct and reflex acts.

The second article discusses the problem "Who is my neighbor?" with reference to this supernatural infused habit. Scotus explains:

My neighbor is anyone whose friendship is pleasing to the beloved, namely, anyone by whom God would want to be loved. But I am not obligated rationally to want that the one loved above all be loved also by one by whom he does not care to be loved, or whose love is not pleasing to him.

This qualification is understandable if we realize that Scotus is speaking of a love of neighbor that stems exclusively from the infused virtue of charity. For it is only under this aspect that, at the close of this question, he can answer the initial arguments against his position. If one loves God, not for God's own sake or out of an affection for justice, but only because he represents a good for the lover, then that sort of love stems rather from the affection for the advantageous. While such love is something good, since it is based on our God-given needs, at the supernatural level it is reinforced by the virtue of hope, rather than charity. In qualifying the scope of charity, then, Scotus does not have this less perfect sort of love in mind. He goes on to say:

Since it is certain that the love of the blessed in heaven is pleasing to him, however, it follows that I must want God to be loved by them in an unqualified sense. Since in this life, however, there is some doubt as to any specific individual, I ought to want such to love God conditionally, namely, if it pleases God to be loved by him or to be loved now or whenever it pleases God to be so loved. As for pilgrims in this life in general, since one must always presuppose there are some whose love is pleasing to God, or not displeasing to him, one can will absolutely that God be loved by them also. I ought not will that God be loved by the damned, the devils, or also those displeasing men who are blind to him.

This last observation about the damned, the devils, and those displeasing men who are blind to him is found only in Codex A. While it may sound strange or even paradoxical, it is a logical consequence of what Scotus has been saying about the extent and the limitations of the infused virtue of charity. Since this has God and his interests as its primary aim, it can extend to ourselves or others only if what we will for these is pleasing to God. If our love of God prompts us to pray even for sinners, then, it is only under the aspect that this is not displeasing to him. For, like God, we ought not "derive any pleasure from the death of the sinner," but "rather rejoice when he turns from his evil way that he may live" (Ezechiel 18:23). But, according to Scotus at least, love of neighbor under this aspect would seem to fall under the scope of more the infused virtue of hope than the infused virtue of charity.

The Latin source is from the supplement to *Ordinatio* III, dist. 28, and is a revision of the Wadding reprint ed. (XV, pp. 377–85) based on Codices A (f. 172rb–vb) and S (f. 212rb–vb).

27. Love of God and self

In the third distinction devoted to the infused virtue of charity Scotus asks: "Is everyone bound to love self most after God?"

From what he has said in the previous question, it is clear that what is said of love of neighbor applies also to oneself.

For insofar as charity is the principle of tending directly towards God by a direct act, it is also the principle for reflecting on those acts whereby one tends to God; and on this account, as was pointed out there, it is the principle for wanting everyone able to love God to do so.

Hence, the real question being asked here is, why does the above apply to oneself more than it does to one's neighbor? An obvious psychological answer would be that in the last analysis, it is only the individual person as a free and responsible agent who has the power to make the ultimate decision to love God. We may hope that our neighbor makes that choice, we may encourage, exhort, help him or her to do so, but we cannot force the issue. As Scotus remarked earlier, even God, by his absolute power, cannot force the will, for this implies a contradiction. Though, in virtue of principles he expresses elsewhere, Scotus could have argued in this way, he chooses here to take another tack, based on the fact that both neighbor and self represent "reflex objects" of the infused virtue of charity.

Among all the acts of the same nature, however, the principle of tending to God is also the principle of reflecting most directly upon the act one elicits; this is the act by which one having charity loves God. Therefore, most directly after loving God, charity inclines a person to love that by which he tends to God, or by which he wants himself to love God. In wanting himself to love God, he loves himself out of charity, because he wills for himself a just and honorable good. Therefore, immediately after love of God, he loves himself out of charity.

Scotus adds a confirmatory argument based on one's natural inclination, which seeks self-perfection as its highest aim. What he says there should be read in light of his earlier remarks in selection 6 about the third meaning of "natural will" (i.e., "the will insofar as it elicits an act in conformity with its natural inclination, which would always be aimed at its own advantage") and in selection 7 about our natural inclination to seek happiness, and also what he said in selection 29 about how this desire for happiness may be willed out of "an affection for justice," as well as out of an affection for the advantageous, since it is only under the former aspect that charity, rather than the virtue of hope, is involved.

The text translated here is from the supplement to *Ordinatio* III, dist. 29, and is a revision of the Wadding reprint ed. (XV, pp. 389–90) based on Codices A (f. 172vb) and S (ff. 212vb–13ra).

PART VIII: SIN

28. Is the power to sin from God?

At the end of Bk. II of the *Sentences*, Peter Lombard raises the question: Is the power to sin in man and the devil from God? This occasioned a discussion of the present question among the scholastics, beginning with the *Summa fratris Alexandri* IIaIIae, n. 8, and continued in the *Sentence* commentaries of Bonaventure (art. 1, q. 1), St. Thomas (q. 1, art. 1), and a great many others. It was a favorite question because it allowed the young bachelor of theology to introduce a number of distinctions based on the positive and negative aspects of what was meant by the "power to sin." Scotus opens his discussion with an argument for the opposition based on a principle he himself accepts as a valid insight of St. Anselm of Canterbury (as we noted earlier in the introduction to selection 15), namely, that freedom consists essentially in the power to preserve justice for its own sake, rather than in the power to sin. From this it would seem to follow that "to be able to sin is not liberty or any part of liberty." In replying to the argument Scotus has the opportunity to explain in general how Anselm understood the notion of pure perfection (*perfectio simpliciter*) and what is implied by the admission that pure perfections are characteristic of creatures, but as found there, they are associated with imperfection as well, for though their formal notion does not imply imperfection, this is only because the notion prescinds from any question as to the degree or intensity of the perfection in question.

As for the body of the question, Scotus' discussion, like that of most of his colleagues, is based on the Augustinian idea that evil is not something positive, as the Manichaeans, and Augustine himself as a member of that sect, had once held. After his conversion, the saint fought for some fifteen years to save the Bible from a Manichaean interpretation, and his analysis of evil as a privation and sin as a deformity, rather than the effect of some evil god of darkness, had a strong influence on all the great scholastics.

Scotus' specific approach and solution are not greatly different from that of his colleagues, but they do bring into play a number of his particular conceptions of the created will as a pure perfection, as well as some of its actual limitations. He begins by distinguishing between "the act that is the basis for sin" and the lack of goodness or "deformity that is present in the sinful act."

The "power to sin either [1] expresses the immediate order of poten- tiality to the act of sinning or else [2] refers to the foundation of such a potentiality, by virtue of which the one having such is said to be able to sin." The first of these, says Scotus, can be interpreted in two ways: (a) the act that is the basis for sin or (b) the deformity present in that act.

If the first is meant, then this order is from God, . . . [for] God has power also over that act which underlies or is the basis for sin, and not just the created will, according to one opinion. If the second is meant, then there is no such ordering to sin, even as the term [i.e., the deformity or lack of goodness] is nothing, and hence is not from God.

What Scotus is arguing for here is the position that God not only creates and conserves the human will as an active potency, but also cooperates with it in eliciting its act, whatever that act may be. The rationale for this is his conviction that inasmuch as the act, as a voli- tion or nolition, is a positive quality in the will, it has a measure of entity or being at the moment it comes into existence. God as the primary cause of all being, therefore, has a creative finger, so to speak, in its coming into existence. The contrary opinion he is opposing is the doctrine that God's cooperation with the actions of his creatures consists essentially in his creating and conserving the creatural essence or nature with its active potencies as such, and that this suffices for them to act on their own, given the proper external conditions. In this sense, God would not function formally as a primary "moving" cause and the creature, with respect to him, as secondary cause.

On the other hand, if (b) is meant, then since there is no positive entity involved, no causality on God's part is required either. But what of case [2]?

If one is speaking of the basis or foundation of this order, however, I say that something positive lies at the root of this order in both senses [i.e., something positive underlies both the act that is the basis of sin and the deformity itself]. For as is the case of passive or receptive potencies, where the same subject can either have something or be deprived of it, so too where the subject is a power that is free to act deficiently. Such a power is the immediate basis or source of its opposite states by either acting or being deficient. By acting it is a power for righteousness, by being deficient it is a power to sin. And this abso- lute entity [i.e., the will] is the proper power for both in the respective way that there can be a power for both [righteousness and sin], namely, by the power being either effective or defective. And in this sense the power to sin is from God, i.e., God is the source of that nature which enables its possessor to commit sin by using its powers not effectively but defectively, of which deficient usage, however, this positive entity is the proximate ground.

Scotus mentions a counterthesis, also mentioned and refuted by Bonaventure, that the power to sin stems from the inevitable fact that the will is created from nothing and not from any positive power it contains. This gives Scotus occasion to reiterate that as free, the will has the option of either following the dictates of right reason and the inclination of the affection for justice or following its counterinclination, the affection for the advantageous. How this leads to sin is spelled out in great detail in the subsequent selection on the sin of Lucifer.

The Latin source is a revision of the Wadding reprint (XIII, pp. 496–98) based on Codex A (ff. 138vb–39ra).

29. The sin of Lucifer

One of the clearest presentations of how the various acts of the will are hierarchically interrelated when ordered according to right reason is found in *Ordinatio* II, dist. 6, q. 2: "Was the sin of the first angel formally a sin of pride?" Since Lucifer, as a pure spirit, could not be tempted by the desire for any sensible good, many sought to explain the fallen angel's sin as one of pride. Scotus, however, sees his initial fall from innocence rather as a sin of inordinate self-love, an abuse of friendship or benevolent love. This led immediately to a sin of desire wherein the devil sought his own happiness in an inordinate fashion, a sin which Scotus sees as related more closely to the capital sin of lust (*luxuria*) than to that of pride. Because of the undue length of the question, we have dealt only with the first portion that explains how the various orderly and disorderly acts would be related rationally according to Scotus. He begins with the proper order that would obtain between the various acts of the will.

First we must examine the order that exists among the acts of the will. And here I say there is a twofold act of the will, namely, to like [*velle*] and to dislike [*nolle*], for dislike is a positive act of the will whereby it turns away from the distasteful and shuns the inconvenient, whereas to like or love is the act whereby it accepts some appropriate or suitable object. Furthermore, there is a twofold like or love, one which can be called the love of friendship [*velle amicitiae*], another called the love of desiring or wanting or coveting [*velle concupiscentiae*]. Friendship or benevolent love concerns an object of well-wishing, whereas the love of desire concerns some object I want for some other beloved.

The order among these acts is clear, for every dislike presupposes some liking, for I turn away from something only because it is inconsistent with something I regard as suitable . . . And the order that exists among the two forms of love is also evident, because the coveting presupposes the other love of friendship. For, with respect to what is desired, the one befriended becomes a quasi-end for the sake of whom I want this good (since it is for the sake of the beloved that I desire the good I wish that person to have). And since the end has the distinction of being the first object willed, it is clear that friendship or benevolent love precedes the love of desire or coveting.

In light of this, Scotus proceeds to lay out the sequence that would obtain among disorderly acts of the will, as follows:

There is a similar process in disorderly acts, for the first inordinate act can never be one of dislike, since it is only in virtue of something liked or loved that an act of dislike is possible. And if the love is orderly as to its object and all the circumstances, then the dislike that is a consequence of such a love would also be in order. By the same token, if the friendship-love would not be inordinate, the consequent love of desire would also be ordinate. For if that for which I desire some good is loved ordinately, then the will whereby I desire something for the one I wish well will also be in order.

Scotus then proceeds to apply this analysis to the sin of Lucifer. His initial sin, then, would have to be one of benevolent love rather than one of desire. The object of such love could not have been God, because it is impossible to love God by a benevolent or friendship-love that would be inordinate. Neither would such an act of love be disorderly by reason of any circumstance, for an act of love of God for his own sake, proceeding as it does from the *affectio iustitiae* for what is infinitely good, is itself morally good generically (i.e., by reason of its object alone, apart from any specification by circumstances, including that of the end). Hence, Scotus writes:

It follows, then, that [Lucifer's] very first inordinate act of will was the first benevolent love he had towards one to whom he wished well. But this object was not God, for God could not have been loved inordinately, speaking intensively of friendship-love. God is so lovable solely by reason of the object he is, that he renders the most intensive act of love completely good. Neither is it likely that something other than oneself could have been loved too much by an act of friendship-love, first because a natural inclination tends more towards self than towards any other creature, and also because friendship, according to Bk. VIII of the *Ethics*, is based on oneness, and (from Bk. IX) what is amicable for others has its roots in what is amicable for oneself. The first inordinate act, therefore, was one of benevolence towards himself.

Scotus then proceeds to theorize as to what the first initial act of desire might have been, and he concludes that it was an inordinate quest for happiness, for the following reasons:

The initial inordinate desire did not proceed from an affection for justice, as no sin proceeds from such. Hence, it must have come from an affection for the advantageous, because every act elicited by the will stems from an affection either for justice or for the advantageous, according to Anselm. And a will that fails to follow the rule of justice will seek most of all what is most advantageous, and thus it will seek such first, for nothing else rules that unrighteous will but an inordinate, immoderate appetite for that greatest beneficial good, namely, perfect happiness . . . The second proof is this. The first sin of covetousness will be one of love or desire (for nothing is shunned to avoid disaster except it be that one desires the opposite of such a calamity). And this first love called "desire" is either just, utilitarian, or hedonistic (for nothing is loved save in one of these three ways). But it was not a just or honorable love, for then the angel would not have sinned; neither is it utilitarian, for this is never first (inasmuch as this regards someone for whom it is useful, and no one covets the useful first, but rather that for which it is useful). Hence he first sinned by loving something excessively as his supreme delight. What is supremely delightful, however, is the honorable good and as such is beatitude itself [viz., God].—And this argument is based on what the Philosopher says in Bk. VIII of the *Ethics* and the commonly accepted distinction of good into what is useful, delightful, and honorable.

Scotus cites two further "persuasive arguments." The first is based on the fact that associated with any cognitive power is a corresponding appetite that hungers to know and delights when that hunger is satisfied. The will, as the appetite associated with knowledge, will first hunger for such happiness as comes from knowing the most perfect of all knowable objects. The second is this:

If justice did not regulate it, what the will would want first is something it would want if such alone existed and in the absence of which nothing else would be wanted. Now, delight is such a thing. For if one were sad, what one would want would be not some excellence or any other such thing, but happiness or something like it . . . A will unassociated with any sense appetite, then, and consequently not attracted to anything by the inclination of such an appetite, if deserted by justice, follows that inclination the will has in itself as will. For what perfects the intellect most, perfects the appetite corresponding to this cognitive power. Hence, [the angel's first sin of covetousness] was an immoderate desire for happiness, for happiness is the object of the will.

Scotus goes on to raise and answer some objections, and in the course of his discussion other aspects of his theory of will come to light. One of the most notable of these is his development of Anselm's thought in a very important way. In speaking of justice, Anselm seems to have had in mind "infused justice," which is identical with sanctifying grace and the theological virtue of charity. This is something supernatural that man cannot earn or deserve by reason of anything native or congenital to human nature as such. But Scotus, as we said earlier, extends the idea of Anselm's twofold affection to the natural order, and conceives of the "affection for justice" as rooted in the very nature of the will; indeed—according to a report of his Paris lecture—he regards it as the ultimate specific difference of the will as an active potency.

He refers to Anselm's famous *Gedankenexperiment* as to what an angel or pure spirit would be like if God gave it only an affection for the advantageous, where its intellectual or reasoning power served exclusively the self-interest of the agent. (The same would apply *mutatis mutandis* to the spiritual soul of man.) An active potency of this sort might well be associated with intellectual knowledge, without such a rational agent possessing free will. Rationality does not explain human freedom, contrary to what many Aristotelians believed. For an angel of this sort would still be chained or imprisoned within the confines of self-fulfillment, unable to view any good in terms of its intrinsic or objective value. Such an appetite would be "rational" in the sense that intelligence and reason would be put into the service of self-perfection and self-actualization. It would not be "free," however, in the way a person is who, possessing an inclination or affection for justice, is able to love what is good as it deserves to be loved.

If one were to think, according to that fictitious situation Anselm postulates in *The Fall of the Devil*, that there was an angel with an affection for the beneficial, but without an affection for justice (i.e., one that had a purely intellectual appetite as such and not one that was free), such an angel would be unable not to will what is beneficial, and unable not to covet such above all. But this would not be imputed to it as sin, because this appetite would be related to intellect as the visual appetite is now related to sight, necessarily following what is shown to it by that cognitive power, and being inclined to seek the very best revealed by such a power, for it would have nothing to restrain it. Therefore, this affection for justice, which is the first checkrein on the affection for the beneficial, inasmuch as we need not actually seek that towards which the latter affection inclines us, nor must we seek it above all else (namely, to the extent to which we are inclined by this affection for the advantageous)—this affection for what is just, I say, is the *liberty innate* to the will, since it represents the first checkrein on this affection for the advantageous. (Italics added.)

Scotus goes on to justify his statement that this affection for justice is something natural or congenital to the will on the grounds that Anselm's description of how the affections for justice and the advantageous interact is not only applicable to supernatural or "infused justice," but applies equally well to an appetite guided by right reason. For such an "affection" would incline one to love things objectively in terms of their true worth or value, and not just in terms of how they benefit us. Hence, he writes:

Anselm may often be speaking not just of the actual justice which is acquired, but of infused justice, because he says it is lost through mortal sin, something true only of infused justice. Nevertheless by distinguishing *from the nature of the thing* the two primary characteristics of this twofold affection (one inclining the will above all to the advantageous, the other moderating it, as it were, lest the will in eliciting an act should have to follow its inclination), he makes these aspects out to be *nothing other than the will itself insofar as it is an intellective appetite and insofar as it is free*. For . . . qua pure intellective appetite, the will would be actually inclined to the optimum intelligible, . . . whereas qua free, it could restrain itself in eliciting its act from following this natural inclination, as to either the substance of the act or its intensity. (Italics added.)

Scotus sees an obligation stemming from this fact that God gives man this inclination and ability to moderate self-love. As he puts it:

From the fact that [the will] could moderate this, it is bound to do so according to the rule of justice it has received from a higher will. It is clear, then, from this that a free will is not bound in every way to seek happiness (in the way a will that was only an intellective appetite without liberty would seek it). Rather it is bound, in eliciting its act, to moderate the appetite qua intellective, which means to moderate the affection for the advantageous, namely, lest it will immoderately.

Precisely how does one argue from fact to moral obligation? Obviously, one must do so under the aspect explained earlier (I, 5) as to how Hugh of St. Victor understood God to reveal his will to us. By understanding fully what we are and what we are capable of accomplishing, we become aware also of the reason why God created us and cognizant of our obligations.

Another point that Scotus has to explain is how the angelic will, in following the dictates of a natural inclination, can will happiness inordinately, and why the blessed in heaven can legitimately will and take complacency in their own happiness.

The first problem Scotus deals with by showing that there are three ways in which one could will happiness inordinately.

There are three ways, however, in which a will, able to moderate itself as regards the happiness befitting it, could fail to do so. As to intensity, it might love it more passionately than it deserves. Or through precipitance, it might want it sooner than is becoming. Or with disregard to the proper causal way to obtain it—for instance, it might want it without meriting it—or perhaps for other reasons, all of which one need not bother with here.

Probably in one of these ways, then, the will of the angel went to excess: Either by wanting happiness as a good for him rather than loving it as a good in itself—that is, wanting a good, like the beatific object, to belong exclusively to himself, rather than to be in another, such as in his God. And this would be the supreme perversity of the will, which—according to Augustine . . . —is to use as means what is to be enjoyed as an end, and treat as an end what is to be used as a means. Or the angel could have failed in the second way, wanting at once what God wished him to have after a period of probation. Or it might have been in the third way, by wanting to possess happiness by natural means rather than by earning it by grace, since God wished him to merit it.

As for the second problem—which he discusses in answer to an objection—Scotus shows how the blessed in heaven might well wish or desire happiness, not just by reason of an affection for the advantageous, but even out of an affection for justice.

To want an act to be perfect so that by means of it one may better love some object for its own sake, is something that stems from the affection for justice, for whence I love something good in itself, thence I will something in itself. And thus the good could have wanted happiness so that, by having it, they could love the highest good more perfectly. And this act of wanting happiness would have been meritorious, because they are not using what is to be enjoyed as an end, but are enjoying it, for this good that I covet for myself, I desire in order that I may love that good in itself [i.e., God].

The Latin original is a corrected text of the *Ordinatio* II, dist. 6, q. 2, supplied to the author by the courtesy of the Scotistic Commission some years ago. It may not be identical in every respect with what is eventually published in the Vatican edition, volume VIII.

30. *The sin of malice*

Scotus seems to admit that, while the elicited act of the will is always free, if it elicits an act it must elicit it in accord with one of its two inclinations. Either it wills the good as an intrinsic value in itself or it seeks the good as something advantageous for self or nature. He also admits that even when confronted with the beatific vision, the will is not necessitated in its action by reason of this particular end, and uses other ways to explain why the soul of Christ or the blessed in heaven could not sin (Prentice, 1972, pp. 328–42). Nevertheless, Scotus does seem to hold that the will is limited in some way, namely, in that if it elicits an act in regard to a good it is free only to love it or abstain from loving it, but not to hate it qua good. Similarly, in the presence of evil it is still free to hate or turn away from it or not, but it is not free to love it.

In the present question he raises the deeper issue of whether something evil can be willed for its own sake, and leaves the question open. Later in a supplement to *Ordinatio* IV, dist. 49, q. 10 (art. 2), he resolves the question. That question reads: "Is everything that is desired, desired because of happiness?" ("Utrum omnia quae appetuntur, appetantur propter beatitudinem") and was presented earlier in selection 7.

The present question is taken from the *Ordinatio* II, dist. 43, q. 2, reconstructed with the help of three manuscripts, listed by the Scotistic Commission as A, P, and S.

31. Lying

In dist. 38 of Bk. III of the supplement to the *Ordinatio*, Scotus asks: "Is every lie a sin?" He may well have been reading St. Bonaventure, who in *Sentences* III, dist. 38, q. 2 (*Opera omnia*, Quaracchi ed. III, p. 843) begins his response in almost the same way as Scotus, indicating that all the doctors concur in asserting that every lie is a sin, but it is difficult to find the reason why this is so. However, he says, we shall attempt to do so by setting forth the various theories that have been suggested. The first is identical with that mentioned by Scotus, and Bonaventure shows its inadequacy in almost the same words as the subtle Scot. He goes on to give a second view, not mentioned by Scotus, which he also refutes, namely, that in lying a lack of harmony exists between the mind and one's speech. Noting that these first two opinions center on what is extrinsic to what a lie means, Bonaventure presents the following third view as something based on what is essential to a lie:

There is still a third way of speaking, which explains evil in a twofold way: either evil stems from the generic nature of an act, insofar as it has to do with some unsuitable matter, or it stems from a bad intention. Now, when it has to do with unsuitable matter, this can be understood in two ways, either with respect to God, or with respect to creatures. If it is with respect to God, then it is evil in itself and is so intrinsically such that it in no way can become good; such, for instance, would be hatred of the highest Good or the act of blaspheming God. If it is with respect to one's neighbor, such as doing him some personal or real harm, then though evil in itself, it could still be done for some good end, because given a dispensation one could do it for a right intention. However, if something is evil because of an evil intention, then whether it be with respect to God or with respect to one's neighbor, it is simply evil, and no end for which it is done can make it good, because a fitting purpose is by stipulation wanting in such a case. Hence, to make this evil thing good means nothing more or less than making something be at once good and evil. Now, lying is this sort of thing, for a lie implies something evil not only inasmuch as the act has to do with unfitting matter, but also on account of the indirect intention, insofar as in the essence of a lie these two things concur, namely, a false statement and the intention to deceive. And the first is evil in itself, and it could become good if stated by one who unknowingly said something false. By reason of the second, however, it is evil on its own account and in no way can become good, nor could there be a dispensation from it, just as there is no way in which one can have [carnal] knowledge of another with the intention of committing adultery or for some other wicked motive. One must concede, therefore, all those reasons that show that it is essential to a lie that it be a sin and that a lie is evil in itself, as Augustine says, for the very name "lie" refers to something that includes an inordinate intention, as was shown.

Scotus may well have had this analysis of Bonaventure in mind, for though differing in details, Scotus' general discussion of this question is roughly parallel to what Bonaventure has to say on this subject. Scotus divides his treatment into two main articles. The first is a critical inquiry into the various opinions given as to why lying is sinful; the second analyzes the nature of the sin, which in turn depends on the kind of lie one tells.

In the first article he presents three views. The first coincides with Bonaventure's first view, namely, that a lie is a deliberate untruth and it necessarily turns one away from God, who is Truth, with a capital "T." Scotus refutes this in the same way as Bonaventure; a lie is opposed immediately not to God qua Truth, but rather to some specific created truth, and hence a lie cannot immediately turn one from God.

Omitting Bonaventure's second unsatisfactory view, Scotus turns rather to his third, which he splits up into two distinct opinions on the basis of the two elements Bonaventure considers to be essential to a lie. The first of these the editors of the Wadding edition ascribe to Aquinas and the second (Scotus' third view) to Bonaventure himself and Gerard Odonis.

Since Bonaventure had already sketched the main outlines of the view attributed to Aquinas, it obviously had enjoyed some considerable measure of popularity prior to St. Thomas. As Scotus describes it, this opinion states that lying is intrinsically immoral, since the primary or generic morality of an act stems from its object, and the object of speech is to convey the truth to one's fellowmen and not to mislead them. Hence, since the primary goodness or badness of an act stems from the object, an act that is bad or evil on this account cannot become morally good by reason of circumstances or the purpose for which it is done. Aquinas—we know—tended to lump together all the precepts of the natural law, whether they be of the first table or the second, as something intrinsically either good or bad and hence as something God can not dispense from without contradicting himself, as it were. Bonaventure disagreed with this, as indicated by his cryptic remark about how one could do something otherwise bad for a good intention provided God gave a dispensation from those command-ments that regard obligations to one's neighbor. Scotus agrees substan-tially with this position, but spells it out in greater detail than Bona-venture. Since the arguments given in the Pro and Con for the licitness of lying are all drawn from instances of the Old Testament where the patriarchs, or others, appeared to lie and yet seemed not to sin, Scotus sees the question of whether God dispensed from lying in the same way as he did from killing or monogamy as a real objection to Aquinas' solution.

According to the third view—which the editors of the Wadding edition rightly ascribe among others to St. Bonaventure himself—the malice of lying lies principally in the bad purpose or intention one has in not telling the truth, because bad will is essential to what is meant by the name "lie." Scotus agrees, but where Bonaventure simply states that the very name "lie" refers to something which implies an inten-tion to deceive, Scotus explains in some detail how this works where the thing named is not something that has a *per se* unity. And since he explains rather than criticizes this third view, Scotus seems to credit it with probability and adopt it as his own.

In his second article, as to what sort of sin lying represents, Scotus distinguishes between (1) the pernicious lie, which is used to inflict harm on the one lied to or lied about; (2) the officious or polite lie, which is useful to someone and harms no one; (3) the jocose lie, which is told jokingly or in a light vein so as not to be taken seriously by the auditor.

In regard to the polite and jocose lies, Scotus refers to a dispute among moral theologians involving the distinction between "perfect" and "imperfect" individuals. Some say the perfect must avoid even such lies under pain of mortal sin; others claim that no circumstance makes something venially sinful mortally so, and persons referred to as "perfect" have no more bound themselves by vow or oath to tell the truth than have other Christians. (Note that this distinction of perfect and imperfect persons is based on a gloss on Psalm 5:7 attributed to Augustine, "It does not behoove the perfect to lie, not even to save the temporal life of another. For the perfect may not speak falsely, lest for the life of another they kill their own soul" [*Glossa ordinaria*, PL 113, 851; Augustine, *Enarrationes in Psalmos*, PL 36, 85]. The *Summa fratris Alexandri* IIaIIae, inquisitio 3, tr. 1, sect. 2, q. 2, c. 5 [Quaracchi ed. III, n. 403, pp. 406–8] may have introduced this problem to the earlier Franciscan masters at Paris. Bonaventure's fourth question, for instance, asks whether every lie is a mortal sin "in viris perfectis.")

Scotus' own solution to the dispute is to distinguish two senses of "perfect." The first refers to some person exercising an exalted office, such as judging, preaching, or solemnly teaching, where the dignity of the office itself obliges the person holding it to tell the truth. The other refers to those who have bound themselves by the vows of religious life to strive for perfection in a special way.

In the case of the first, where the individuals holding the exalted offices are actually involved in the solemn exercise of such, they have a special obligation under pain of serious sin to tell the truth where to do otherwise would threaten or imperil their authority or general credibility. Scotus briefly mentions a problem, here, without attempting to solve it, namely, that while a single lapse in regard to a polite or jocose lie might not destroy one's authority, since two judicial acts according to law establish a custom, would a repeated breach of truthfulness be a serious matter? Whatever is to be said of solemn judicial utterances of this sort, says Scotus, where other acts not *ex officio* are concerned, polite or jocose lies would not be seriously sinful where scandal is excluded.

As for those who have embraced a life where "perfection is to be acquired, not exercised," says Scotus, such persons are no more obligated than others except to those aspects of perfection they have bound themselves to by vow. Hence, where scandal is excluded, polite or jocose lies would not constitute a mortal sin.

However, even where scandal might occur, one must distinguish between avoiding "scandala pusillorum" and avoiding "scandala Pharisaeorum." Even Christ could not avoid pharisaical scandal, nor can those striving for perfection after the example of his disciples. Hence, Scotus lays down some practical norms for both religious and other Christians, who are not "perfecti" in either of its two senses.

Having presented his idea of what a lie is and why it should be regarded as sinful, Scotus—in his reply to the arguments at the beginning—offers his own solution to those classic passages in the Old Testament where lying seems to have been permitted, excused, or even rewarded by God.

The text translated here is from the supplement to the *Ordinatio* III, dist. 38, revised from the Wadding edition on the basis of Codices A (ff. 180va–81va) and S (ff. 222rb–23va).

32. Perjury

The present question discusses a special kind of lie, one in which God is invoked as a witness to the truth. It is a good example of how certain specific sins involving social aspects of our behavior which normally pertain to the natural law only in the secondary sense, can be invested with an absolute malice, namely, insofar as they are reducible to what pertains to the natural law in a primary sense.

Scotus divides the question into three articles: (1) the first deals with the nature of an oath; (2) from this Scotus derives the reason for the second point he wishes to make, why perjury—where the act is done deliberately and knowingly—is always a serious or mortal sin; (3) the third article goes on to deal with special kinds of oaths and the types of sin involved if one takes them carelessly, or uses them to guarantee the truth of a deliberate lie.

The first article defines an oath in terms of St. Paul's letter to the Hebrews:

I say that an oath is an assertion that some human statement is true, and this in a final or ultimate sense, according to that text from the Epistle to the Hebrews [6:16]: "An oath confirms a statement and ends all argument." And the reason is this. Man knows he cannot trust completely his mendacious and ignorant fellowman, since he can be deceived and can deceive. Therefore, he turns to a witness who is truthful and knows the facts, one who can neither deceive nor be deceived, and he does this by taking an oath; for there he asks God, who knows the truth and cannot lie, to bear witness to what he is saying.

From this description of an oath, Scotus sets up his main thesis, namely, that perjury is a mortal sin because it violates the second commandment of the first table of the natural law in what it forbids absolutely, viz., that God be shown any irreverence. This obligation binds at all times and under all conditions, and God can never dispense from it.

From this our thesis on perjury follows. For it is an act of irreverence to call upon God as witness to the truth of a false statement; or to treat him as if he were ignorant of the truth, and hence not omniscient; or to deal with him as though he would gladly bolster a lie, and thus were not entirely truthful. All of these, however, manifest an irreverence towards God that is immediately opposed to that commandment of the first table: "You shall not take the name of the Lord, your God, in vain" [Exodus 20:7]. Hence, any deliberate instance of this would be a mortal sin.

Scotus then raises two doubtful points: First, does lack of deliberation excuse one from serious sin? Second, may one sin mortally by calling upon God to bear witness in the aforesaid way to something that is only an opinion one believes to be true, or to something which only has some plausibility, but which one is more inclined to believe false? In other words, how certain must one be of what one confirms with an oath?

In reply to the first doubt, he points out that moral theologians commonly admit that one such indeliberate instance of swearing to the truth, where the truth in question is not anything serious or anything that would cause injury to anyone, would not be seriously sinful, since to commit a grave sin one must avert to its gravity and deliberately choose to do it. However, many would claim that habitual or continued behavior of this sort, where no attempt to correct it is made, could eventually become something grave. The assumption here is that the acquired habit is a more serious matter than an individual act. Scotus disagrees with this view on the ground that if one instance is not a serious sin, neither is a second, or a third, etc. Furthermore, the gravity—in terms of sinfulness—of a habit depends not on how strong it is, but on the gravity of the individual acts from which it stems. If the acts which generate the habit are venial, then so too is the habit generated. He calls attention to another common moral principle, namely, that if by repeated acts one has acquired a formidable habit of sin—for instance, impurity, drunkenness, violent anger—and seriously repents of such, and hence is restored to grace, this does not immediately destroy the force of the acquired habit. One has to set up an equally strong counterhabit by repeated acts of virtue before the vice that has become a second nature is eventually eliminated. Hence, a sin of backsliding may actually be less grievous in such a repentant sinner than it would be in one who deliberately indulged in such.

Hence, Scotus concludes that the strength of the habit is only contingently connected with the gravity of a particular act. One must judge the act on its own merits, that is, in terms not only of its object, but of the specific circumstances that surround it. If one takes God's name in vain without due deliberation, the sin is always venial; if one knowingly and deliberately does so, then it is a mortally sinful act of irreverence against the second commandment. In regard to the necessary deliberation, however, he adds this caveat. Deliberation is not necessarily a lengthy matter. Just as one skilled in how to act in a particular instance can act prudently without a belabored reasoning process, so too one accustomed to acting imprudently could easily and instantaneously recognize that the action one is about to commit is gravely sinful, and hence the necessary deliberation for sin would be present.

Scotus' second doubt concerns taking an oath where there is no certain knowledge, but only probability. What occasioned this doubt seems to have been the custom of requiring witnesses to swear to the worthiness of candidates for certain ecclesiastical or educational offices, such as the prelacy or the office of chancellor, rector, or master, according to certain university regulations. By way of solving the problem by dispelling this doubt, Scotus appeals to how positive law or custom regards the nature of such an oath. He writes:

As for the second doubt, I say that according to positive law or custom a person swearing regards the oath in one of two ways. Either [a] it represents an unqualified assertion of the matter sworn to, or [b] it does not, but rather expresses something the person swearing regards as a probable assumption one ought to believe.

The first sort of oath would represent the type taken in a court trial where punishment (either imprisonment or the death penalty) could be meted out according to the truth or falsity of the witness's testimony. Here Scotus says that "a person sins mortally in calling on God to confirm as simply true and certain what is not simply such."

The second sort of oath is quite different, inasmuch as the witness is not called upon to testify to something unfavorable to the person whose worthiness is under consideration for some sort of favorable promotion. It suffices, says Scotus, to favor the candidate, unless one is absolutely certain of his or her unworthiness for the position. Here, the qualification "so far as human frailty permits" is either tacitly assumed or expressly stated by the witness in giving testimony about the candidate.

This distinction between the two sorts of oaths is in accord with the general principle of canon and civil law that in unfavorable matters one is presumed to be innocent of crime until proven guilty, whereas in favorable matters one is presumed to be worthy unless proven otherwise.

He concludes this second article, however, with a reiteration of the truth of his basic thesis:

Generally speaking, however, whether it be in favorable or in odious matters, a person sins mortally who swears to the opposite of what he more strongly believes to be so, or swears to something simply dubious where he has no more reason to believe in his heart that this is true rather than that. For he calls God to witness something he ought to be certain about which is in neither way certain to him.

He goes on to deal with the other aspect of his thesis, namely, that perjury is essentially a sin against a precept belonging to the first table of the law.

If you object to what was said about perjury being against a precept of the first table of the law, because it seems that according to the Master [Peter Lombard] perjury is a kind of lie and hence against that commandment of the second table, "You shall not bear false witness against your neighbor" [Exodus 20:16], one could reply that in perjury there is a double sin, namely, [i] a lie (as the material aspect) and [ii] taking God's name in vain, that is to say, not just uselessly, but irreverently, which is a sin against reverence. The first pertains to the second table, but the second pertains formally to the first table, because irreverence is prohibited there.

To show that it is the second or formal aspect (irreverence) rather than the material aspect of lying that is essential to perjury, Scotus shows how one can commit perjury without lying, namely, by swearing to something one has doubts about, for such a solemn appeal to God as an oath involves should not be made lightly, in accord with Christ's exhortation against taking an oath. Unlike the Catholic Church, certain other Christian sects have interpreted Christ's words to imply an absolute prohibition against taking an oath, even when called as a witness in a judicial court case. Agnostics and atheists may likewise object to calling God as witness. Positive law usually respects the conscientious objector in such a case by allowing him or her not to swear, e.g., on the Bible, but, at the same time, treats any lie given by such a person on the witness stand as equivalent to perjury and punishable by the same penalty.

The third article deals with various types of oaths, and what Scotus says there reflects the common juridical distinctions of his day. What he says in respect to each is clear enough, as are his replies to the initial arguments against his thesis.

The Latin original is from the supplement to the *Ordinatio* III, dist. 39, revised from the Wadding edition on the basis of Codices A (ff. 181va–82va) and S (ff. 223va–24va).

33. *The obligation to keep secrets*

The discussion of the sin of telling secrets is an excerpt from Scotus' discussion of the obligation of the priest to keep the seal of confession. This he develops in the form of five conclusions, which reveal a manifold obligation: one stemming from the law of nature itself; the second from divine positive law; the third from positive Church law, which imposed the most severe penalties upon any priest guilty of violating the seal. In his day, Scotus tells us, this entailed not only suspension from the priesthood and any office the guilty party held, but (by decree of the Lateran Council) confinement for the remainder of his life to some monastery where this was possible, and if it was not possible— says Scotus—the earlier punishment was not to be omitted, namely, that which compelled the guilty priest to wander through the Christian world as a vagabond till he died. Scotus discusses this triple obligation to keep the sacramental seal of confession inviolate in his first three conclusions. The fourth is devoted to explaining the details covered by ecclesiastical law, namely, who is obligated to keep the secret, for how long, and in regard to what details, particularly those involving other persons. Since the first conclusion Scotus draws is that the obligation also stems from natural law, no superior, not even the pope, can command a priest to reveal anyone's sin. In the fifth and final conclusion, Scotus shows how far the arguments for the natural law basis of this special sacramental obligation apply to other secrets that are revealed to some confidant. Since only the first and the initial part of the fifth conclusion—viz., the natural law obligation—are of primary philosophical interest, we have translated only what is covered under the first conclusion and, in the final paragraph, the text concerning to what extent the principles of natural law apply to secrets in general.

The text translated here is from the *Ordinatio* IV, dist. 21, q. 2; Codex A (ff. 243va–44va).

34. *The sin of enslavement*

The only question in which Scotus discusses the topic of slavery is concerned with the various impediments to a sacramental marriage recognized by canon lawyers in his day. The question reads: "Is slavery an impediment to marriage?" What occasioned the question is that canon law had a special section entitled "The Marriage of Slaves," which insisted on the legal right of slaves to contract a sacramental marriage despite the opposition of their masters. It was one of the many ways in which the Church sought to better and Christianize the institution of slavery, which in Scotus' day was still a recognized universal political and economic fact. Scotus, however, in contrast to many of his contemporaries, restricts extensively the conditions under which slavery could become legitimate and a slave bound in justice to render service to his master. To understand the context of what Scotus writes in this question, we should consider the following points.

As C. Williams notes in his article "Slavery and the Church," in the *New Catholic Encyclopedia*, vol. 13, p. 281: "The Church was born into a world in which slavery was universally accepted as a social and economic institution pertaining to the very structure of society, just as today the system of remunerated employment is taken for granted. As in modern society few would be likely to contemplate seriously the abolition of the existing system, so neither did it occur to Christians of the early Church to advocate the abolition of slavery." Nevertheless,

Christianity could not help but introduce a profound, if subtle, change in the existing attitude towards this social institution. For, in the eyes of God, all men are equal, even though by nature they are endowed with varying talents. As St. Paul put it in his letter to the Galatians (3:27): "All you who have been baptized into Christ have put on Christ. There is neither Jew nor Greek; there is neither slave nor free-man; there is neither male nor female. For you are all one in Christ Jesus" (see also 1 Cor. 12:12; Eph. 5:9; Col. 3:22–24; 1 Peter 2:28). Under the influence of this new leaven, the whole Christian attitude towards all sexual or social class differences began to change slowly but surely, and with it the meaning of "servus," which in Scotus' day could be translated as "serf" as well as "slave" or "servant."

The fact that it can have either of these last two meanings, how-ever, highlights the fact that, as the institution of slavery existed in many parts of the world, slaves were entrusted with most of the man-ual labor, the chores, and even the management of the day-to-day re-quirements of running a household or business. Aristotle, for instance, thought it beneath the station of a freeman to engage in manual labor for profit. The manual arts, we recall, were long referred to as "ser-vile," whereas the fine arts were labeled "liberal," because they re-quired the leisure characteristic of a freeman. ("School" itself—we know—is derived from the Greek term σχολή, meaning "leisure.")

With the advent of Christianity, however, this attitude towards ser-vile work changed dramatically, occasioned by the fact that Christ himself was the son of a carpenter and presumably worked at that pro-fession as well. St. Paul prided himself because he labored as a tent-maker to support himself while preaching the revelation of Christ. In-deed, the very idea of serving others became an integral part of the Christian message, for as Jesus pointed out to his disciples when he washed their feet, he came to serve, not to lord it over, others. Fur-thermore, servitude or slavery itself did not always have the odious connotation that it has today. As Williams points out, it existed in at least two distinct forms, one of which he calls "symbiotic slavery," the other "parasitic slavery." In its symbiotic form the relationship was analogous to that of an organic body. Master and slave worked to-gether for their mutual good as human beings. The slave was a part of the household and was treated as such. And just as one might hire oneself out to others to pay off a debt or in return for the means of livelihood for self and family, so one could voluntarily enter such a servile state as an indentured servant or as a slave for life. Where the institution of slavery existed—for instance, during the period of the Roman Empire—the Church insisted on the rights and duties of both masters and slaves, just as in our own times she emphasizes the mutual rights and duties of employers and employees.

But just as the symbiotic relationship between owners and workers, capital and labor, employer and employee, can degenerate into what is practically a form of slavery and a gross violation of social justice, so too with the institution of slavery. Thus we have what Williams calls "parasitic slavery," where the master or owner exploited the labor of the slave for his own private advantage and pleasure; and in this form there was inhumanity, brutality, and vice in both masters and slaves. In some cases, slaves lost all civil rights and were not permitted by law to marry lest they prejudice their owners' right to buy and sell them "like an inanimate instrument" or "an animal." From the beginning the Church condemned this degrading form of slavery and, where such *de facto* existed, continually labored to better the condition of those condemned to such an ignominious state. During the Middle Ages, with the advent of new religious orders, some—like the Mercedarians (or "Order of the Blessed Virgin Mary for the Ransom of Captives," founded in 1218 by St. Peter Nolasco)—not only specialized in working with the slaves, but added a fourth vow to the usual three of poverty, chastity, and obedience, the vow to act as captives themselves if necessary to free those Christian slaves of the Moors whose faith was in danger. Another way in which the Church sought to attack parasitic slavery was by defending the right of slaves to marry, even without the consent of their masters or owners. It is in this context that Scotus raises the question: "Is slavery an impediment to marriage?"

Scotus divides the question into two principal articles, one dealing with the origin and legality of slavery, the other with the question of whether it represents a legal impediment to a sacramental marriage.

As for the origins and legality, we might note, many political philosophers, like Aristotle, considered some form of slavery to stem from the very nature of man. Scotus alludes to this in answering an objection to his own view drawn from Aristotle's *Politics* I, ch. 5: "Those strong in mind should rule; those strong in body should serve." Advocates of this view argued that slavery or servitude could be something healthy and good for a certain class of individuals, namely, those not "naturally strong in mental ability and hence [not] naturally disposed to rule," but "more robust in body," if "less prudent in mind," and hence "naturally suited to be servants." Christian thinkers generally rejected this, but considering the fall of man from a primitive state of innocence together with the widespread existence of slavery, they generally adopted some variant of the view of Ulpian (d. 228 A.D.). This famous Roman jurist claimed that by the law of nature, or *ius naturale*, all men are born free, but slavery as a social and economic institution stems from the law of nations, or *ius gentium*. Though this latter term itself was of earlier, probably Roman, origin, and was interpreted differently, it was always distinguished from positive civil law, or *ius civile*, on the ground that it is so common as to be virtually universal, and hence is close to general precepts of natural law, written into the heart of man, if not indistinguishable from conclusions drawn from such precepts (Aquinas, *Summa theologiae* IaIIae, q. 95, art. 4). We find this theory, for instance, in St. Thomas Aquinas and his disciples. In his *Summa theologiae* IIaIIae, q. 57, art. 3, ad 2, he says: "The fact that this man is a slave rather than that man is not due to natural reason, but is so only because of some consequent usefulness, insofar as it is useful for this person to be governed by someone wiser, and for this latter person to be aided by the other. . . . And thus slavery which pertains to the law of the nations (ius gentium) is natural in the second sense [i.e., by reason of some resultant consequence], but not in the first sense [viz., absolutely]." And in the supplement to the *Summa theologiae* III, q. 51, art. 1, ad 2, we read that while servitude is against the original intention of nature, nevertheless—considering man's actual condition—"Natural reason tends to this, and nature desires the same, namely, that a given person might be good. But given the fact that someone sins, nature inclines that he be punished for his sin, and thus slavery is introduced as punishment for sin." (see also IaIIae, q. 94).

Scotus apparently makes no attempt to justify slavery in general, either as stemming from the law of nature "like the servitude or, more properly, filial subjection to the father," or as a consequence of original sin, or as having its roots in the *ius gentium*, as does Aquinas. He is concerned only with the origins of its most extreme and "damnable form," and this as a possible impediment to a sacramental marriage, for this question is the first of a series devoted to canonical marital impediments. He explains the nature of the slavery or servitude he has in mind and traces its origin simply to "positive law," which, judging from the context, he seems to understand as some particular form of civil law, namely, laws governing the punishment of certain kinds of criminal behavior or certain types of voluntary contracts, which can be entered into foolishly and may even be against the natural law, yet until proven such, could bind in justice. He is talking about the slavery or servitude described by Aristotle in Bk. I of the *Politics*, ch. 4 (1254a11–17), "according to which the master can sell the slave like an animal, for he cannot exercise acts of manly excellence, since he has to perform servile actions at the command of his master." This was precisely the sort of servitude that jeopardized the right of the slave to marry, and about which the canon law intervened to declare: "Marriage among slaves shall in no way be prohibited." Nevertheless, Scotus, in contrast to many of his medieval colleagues, seems to have had little sympathy with the whole institution of slavery, though it is clear from his answers to objections to his own views that he recognized the distinction between this most inhuman and "damnable form of servitude" and other, symbiotic forms where the relationship between master and servant was likened by those who sought to defend it, he says, to "the members of the human body, where certain parts naturally serve the main part."

Since the slavery he is speaking of has its origins in some form of positive law, this prompts the further question, "But how can such slavery be just, where a master acquires the right to buy or sell his slave, or send one to this part of the world and his mate to another?" He refers back to selection 21, as to how civil authority arises and how a state or commonwealth can pass just positive laws governing the punishment of criminals or how one can transfer property one has justly acquired by law to another person. But, as he explains later, no human person is chattel, and the "reasons for possessing gold and persons who serve you are not the same." By way of example, he goes on to say, "It would be difficult to establish the justice, by prescription, of retaining slaves of this sort, unless one assumed they became such from the outset by one or the other legitimate ways in which servitude is introduced."

And what are the possible legitimate ways in which slavery of this sort might conceivably arise? Scotus himself can think of only two. One is where slavery is inflicted as a punishment for criminals "so vicious that their liberty would harm both themselves and the public." The other is where persons voluntarily, presumably for some economic reason, enslave themselves in such a way as to cede to their masters even the right to buy or sell them at will as well as to receive service of a specified sort. But, Scotus goes on to add, anyone who knowingly and willingly binds himself in this latter way is stupid, for "talis subiectio est fatua." Not only that, he adds—it might perhaps be a violation of natural law to abdicate one's freedom in this way. His use of "forte," the Latin word for "perhaps," however, seems to indicate he is not sure this is so, and in the case of doubt the legitimacy of the civil law must be presumed. And hence such a contract voluntarily made could bind the individual in justice to render the service he has contracted for. As he explains later, in art. 2, "an obligation not of the law of nature could impede some liberty that one has in virtue of natural law." And he cites an oath of fealty or a religious vow of obedience as instances. "By the law of nature I owe you nothing; nevertheless I can vow obedience to you, and then I am bound to obey you."

In Scotus' day, when Moors commonly enslaved Christians and Christians enslaved Moors as captives of war, many attempted to justify such slavery on grounds Scotus could not accept. As he puts it:

If you insist that there is also a third legitimate reason for slavery, for instance, that if one captured in war is preserved unharmed, and thus spared from death, he may become a slave destined to serve, I doubt this—unless [playing on words] you mean by "servus" here one who is "pre*served*" [nisi dicatur "servus" ibi "servatus"]. Neither is such enslavement a clear case of justice, even if the captor, perhaps, might have otherwise killed his captive (assuming the war was a just one of self-defense and not one of invasion, and that the captive persisted in his obstinacy against the person fighting defensively). Nevertheless, given that the captive could cease to be obstinate, since he has it in his power to change his mind, it seems inhuman to inflict on him a punishment that is against the law of nature. Neither does the [other] justifying reason for enslavement apply here, since he might very well not remain rebellious or abuse his liberty, but become docile, perhaps, and use the liberty granted to him in a proper way.

Scotus then goes on to raise two objections to his position. The first is the one referred to earlier, based on Aristotle's contention that some form of slavery "is not against the law of nature," but stems from the natural differences that exist among individuals, where some are meant to rule and others to serve. Proponents of this view used the analogy of the organic character of the human body to express the symbiotic relationship. Another analogy used to prove the naturality of symbiotic slavery is that hinted at in the opening lines of Scotus' first article, namely, that many despite their age resemble more immature children than responsible adults capable of ruling themselves. If filial subjection is a natural form of servitude, other forms may also be defended as being rooted in the nature of things. Whatever is to be said of symbiotic servitude, Scotus says, this does not refer to the "slavery" that is discussed here as a possible impediment to marriage. Furthermore, what Aristotle says in *Politics* I, ch. 5, applies "only to political service, where superiors appoint inferiors, not as distributing or arranging inanimate things, but rather in the way the less gifted are assigned appropriate tasks by the more gifted."

The second objection is that if slavery is against the law of nature, how can it ever become just, for "crimes are not ratified by their longevity"? He indicates that with the exception of the two cases he has given for enslavement, slavery of any other form is not justified. How, then, will he explain St. Paul's injunction that slaves should obey their masters? To this Scotus replies that many obligations may have originally been unjustly introduced, but once they have become established they should be observed. As a general principle, what he seems

to have in mind is that often less-than-desirable customs are to be endured as the lesser of two evils if a political revolution or civil war with
all its devastating hardships becomes the only practical way to change
the positive laws governing a particular commonwealth. More specifically his idea seems to be—and he introduces the notion only to justify the words of the Apostle to the Ephesians (6:5) and the Colossians
(3:22)—is that some form of symbiotic slavery, such as was practiced
by the Romans, though "not something commendable in itself," was
something a Christian might endure in a spirit of service. For as Paul
said to the Corinthians: "Even supposing you could go free, you would
be better off making the most of your slavery." This problem of how to
correct an evil without doing more harm, we might recall, was something slave owners like Jefferson had to face. They did not regard slavery as something laudable, yet did not feel they could responsibly simply free their slaves, since they knew that the latter, like children,
could not provide for themselves here, nor could they be sent back to
the primitive tribes from which they were taken. This problem of how
to correct an evil in a legal and orderly fashion is not always easy to
solve; it is not only something legislators had to face at the time of the
American Civil War, but something that continues to plague those
charged with governing in countries where the ownership of the land
or sources of economic productivity in the hands of a few have reduced
the rest of the population to a form of labor that is equivalent to
slavery.

    In the second article, Scotus discusses whether slavery is an impedi-
ment to marriage. As we said earlier, one of the more important and
successful ways in which the Church sought to better the condition of
the slaves was to condemn the practice, common in many places, that
forbade slaves to marry lest they compromise the legal civil rights of
their masters to sell their servants to buyers from other parts of the
world. Around 1230 Pope Gregory IX, himself an accomplished can-
onist, sought to update and revise the corpus of canon law developed
by his papal predecessors. He devoted a special section to various previous papal decisions regarding the marriage of slaves, entitled "De
coniugio servorum." Since many of these dated back to a time when
slavery was an accepted social and economic institution, the popes intervened as mediators in disputes about the respective rights of Christian masters and slaves. One such intervention referred to the case
where a slave married without the consent or against the will of his
master, and the pope defended both the legitimacy of the slave's sacramental marriage and his obligation to render his master the service he
legitimately owed according to the civil laws of the state or common-

wealth. Scotus refers to this canonical decision in his own solution regarding the limited rights and obligations of a slave who marries when his master is unwilling. Generally speaking, where a sovereign city-state or commonwealth recognized some symbiotic form of slavery, the Church strove to defend both the natural rights of the slaves and the legitimate civil claims of their masters. This attempt of the Church to do justice to the rights of both masters and slaves occasioned later theologians to discuss what they considered the rationale behind the canonical legislation regarding the marriage of slaves. Though they agreed substantially as to what the rights of each might be, they gave greatly different explanations as to why a slave could marry and, in particular, how far a person could voluntarily abdicate his natural rights or by violation of just criminal law so enslave himself that he could be justly bought or sold by his master or owner. It was in this context of their common assumption that both slave and master have legitimate rights that the late thirteenth- and early fourteenth-century medieval theologians and canonists discussed the question of whether slavery is a diriment impediment to a Christian sacramental marriage. Scotus, before presenting his own views, critically reviews the opinion held by St. Thomas and others. In view of what he has said previously about natural law, in its twofold sense, the threefold aspect of a Christian marriage, the origin of positive civil law, etc., what he says both by way of criticism and by way of a positive solution should be clear enough. Where a slave marries with the consent of his master, the latter has implicitly relaxed the service he might otherwise expect of one who has no marital obligations. If he does not, "that master sins mortally and clearly needs to be corrected by the Church as well." If the slave marries without the consent of his master, however, then according to canon law the marriage is valid, but the slave is still bound in justice to give the service he has voluntarily contracted for. The difficult problem comes when two slaves marry without their masters' consent and each master, presumably for a just reason, wants to send his slave to a different land, one to Africa and the other to France. The situation is not unlike the marriage of two working persons both of whose employers discover that their respective employees need to be sent to a different and distant city by the nature of their work and neither partner can afford or is willing to give up his or her job. "Legally [the] marriage is favored," says Scotus, and both masters should be induced to preserve it intact if they can. But if for economic or other legitimate reasons they cannot afford to do so and insist on breaking up the partners, "it is not clear"—says Scotus—"how they would be acting unjustly towards their servants, granting their

servile condition." Perhaps the validity of Williams' initial analogy of
the similarity of slavery as a social and economic institution to that of
remunerative employment in our own day will not be lost on those
who deal with contemporary problems of divorce and separation. If
the economic structure of much of present-day society is not exactly
an enslavement, where both married partners feel the need or are
compelled to work, or the nature of one's employment means lengthy
separation from home and family, it often seems to have as devastating
an effect on such unwise marriages as the medieval problem discussed
by Scotus. In both cases, the basic difficulty is how to do justice to
both what one's employer and what one's marital partner have a right
to expect.

Be that as it may, Scotus, if a child of his age, still seems to have a
more sympathetic and humanistic view of the plight of the slave than
many of his medieval contemporaries. What makes his approach most
different, perhaps, is the severe limitation he puts on what might justify the sort of slavery that could make marriage a practical, if not a
legal, impossibility. As he says in answer to the initial arguments, it is
clear no slave belongs to his master in every respect. Not only does he
have a legal right to eat, drink, sleep, and engage in all activities that
do not detract from the service he owes his master, but he has the legal
right to marry. Even what Aristotle says of "that damnable form of
servitude, where the slave is like an animal," should not be interpreted
to mean that he actually is one.

Because no matter how much of a slave he might be, he is still a man and so
has free will. And on this score, it is clear what great cruelty is involved in
first imposing such servitude, for it reduces a man who is his own master and
free to act in a manly and virtuous fashion, to the status of a brute animal, as
it were, unable to choose freely or to act virtuously.

For that reason, we have placed this question in the chapter on sin,
and entitled it, for want of a better name, "The sin of enslavement."
For some sin seems involved in all three cases of slavery that existed in
Scotus' day. The common war-captive excuse for slavery Scotus rejects
as unjust. Even the just punishment for criminal behavior implies the
criminal has sinned. What of the third case, viz., voluntary contractual enslavement? True, Scotus does not absolutely condemn this,
though he regards it as "stupid," and suspects it may even be in violation of the natural law. Yet, as a bachelor theologian arguing a canonical case with his peers, he cannot deny the existence of this distressing practice, or the fact that it was condoned and legally regulated
by so many city-states and sovereignties from which his colleagues

came. Yet as he develops this canonical question as scholastic dialogue with his contemporaries and himself, one can hardly doubt where his personal sympathy lies. For he uncovers so many areas where sin could enter in as to severely limit the possibilities that even voluntary enslavement could ever be fully justified, particularly as a lifelong or ongoing commitment.

The Latin original is taken from Codex A, ff. 255vb–56va, and is considerably clearer than the version presented in the Wadding edition. We have omitted only the introductory paragraphs to the question which give a general outline of all the canonical impediments to a sacramental marriage that were recognized by the Church at his time.

Texts in Translation

PART I

The Will and Intellect

1. PRACTICAL SCIENCE
(*Lectura* prol., pars 4, qq. 1–2)

Is a science called speculative or practical because of its end?

[Preliminary Notions]

We must first consider the generally accepted fact that practical knowledge extends to practice, because knowledge that remains within the intellect alone is theoretical knowledge.

Also note that praxis or practice is [1] an act of some power or faculty other than intellect, that [2] naturally follows an act of knowledge or intellection, and [3] is suited by nature to be elicited in accord with correct knowledge if it is to be right.

To begin with, praxis or practice is the act of some faculty other than intellect, because practical knowledge "extends" to it and does not just stay with itself.

It is also naturally posterior to intellection, for it must have some relationship of order to an act of the intellect. Hence, acts of the generative or nutritive potencies, which have no such order to the intellect, are not practical, nor can they be posterior [by nature] to the act of the intellect. And hence acts of the sense powers, be they cognitive or appetitive, are not practical because they precede intellection.

Also it is suited by nature to be elicited in agreement with right knowledge for the practice to be right. Hence, VI *Ethics* says that if the choice is to be right, then both intellect and appetite must be right. And similarly Augustine wants to say that the intellect comprehends itself as well as the acts of the other powers, and that it passes judgment on their acts.

From all this it follows that nothing is formally praxis except a commanded or elicited act of the will, because no act other than that of
the will is elicited in agreement with a prior act of the intellect. For
the actions of all the other powers could precede any act of the intellect, but not so with an act of the will.

From this one draws a further conclusion. Since a commanded act
has the character of praxis only because some elicited act that could
precede it possesses such, it follows that only the will's elicited act is
primarily praxis. And because the formal meaning of praxis is to be
found primarily in an act of the will, all other actions are practice only
in virtue of some act of the will.

Furthermore, a practical act is in the power of the practitioner. But
no action is solely in our power except an act of the will and by virtue
of such. Hence, praxis or practice is primarily attributed to an act of
the will.

Also, the Philosopher in III *De anima*, in the chapter about the
sources of movement, assumes there are two such sources, because
there are appetites that run counter to one another, namely, the sense
appetite and the appetite guided by reason [i.e., the will]. If therefore
the action of the sense appetite apart from producing anything is
praxis, all the more so is the mere act of the will.

[The Opinion of Others]

[First opinion: Godfrey of Fontaines] Presupposing the above, certain persons claim the intellect is only incidentally practical, based on
an accidental difference, whereas the knowledge-habit and act are
called "practical" because of an essential difference. For intellect is
said to be practical because of the end, since the intellect first shows
the will some end, such as good health; then the will, from a desire of
this end, moves the intellect to advise it as to the means whereby this
end may be obtained; now the intellect, considering things in this
fashion because an act of the will made it do so, is practical. Hence,
the intellect is only accidentally practical, because it could have had
this act without a command of the will. The act and habit of knowledge on the other hand are said to be practical because of their object,
which assigns them their formal character.

[Scotus' refutation of this view] If the intellect is said to be practical
from the end, whereas act and habit are practical because of their object, since the intellect can consider the object of a practical habit
without having any practical end in mind, the intellect could have a
practical act and not be practical.

What is more, a similar consequence follows, namely, that the practical habit could be in a theoretical intellect, since the intellect could simply contemplate such an object without being moved to do so for some practical purpose.

Furthermore, if the intellect can be called "practical" derivatively because of an act accidental to it, *a fortiori* it can be so called because of an act that is essentially practical.

Hence, I maintain that it is in virtue of the same thing that intellect, act, and habit are called practical, but nevertheless the intellect is only accidentally such, whereas the other two [viz., the act and habit] are essentially practical. But just what it is that makes them practical will be explained later.

[Second opinion: Henry of Ghent] Therefore, others say that a habit is said to be practical because of its end, since a habit must be practical either because of its object or because of its end. But it is not so because of its object, since the same object is considered sometimes theoretically, sometimes practically, for "the intellect becomes practical by extension."

Furthermore, a practical action is good or bad by reason of what makes it practical. But goodness and badness come from the circumstances of the act, the chief of which is the purpose or end. Therefore a habit will be practical most of all because of its end.

[Refutation of this view] If a habit becomes practical, because of its extension to some end and to praxis, this is because of either an actual or an aptitudinal extension. But it is not because of an actual extension, because then a physician who does not wish to operate would not be practical. But if it is because of an aptitudinal extension, then we have this situation. There is no aptitude in this thing that is inconsistent with another thing unless it be by virtue of the nature of the things in question. And because it is in such a thing, that thing is that sort of nature. Therefore, it is not because of the extension to an end that a habit is practical.

Furthermore, if what makes a knowledge-habit practical is that it results in praxis, then this is because practice is an actual effect it elicits as an operative potency or because practice is the subject of its consideration. But it is not the former, because praxis in this sense is posterior to the knowledge-habit, and the reason or cause [the habit is practical] must be prior [to its subsequent effect]. If it is praxis as something considered and intended by practical knowledge, then praxis has the character of an object, and consequently the habit is called practical because of its object.

What is more, praxis generally is not the end result [i.e., the action commanded by the will, but the will-act itself]; therefore the habit does not become the specific thing it is because of its end. Proof of the antecedent: an imperfect act cannot be the end of a perfect act; but the act of a power that is appetitive, sensitive, and source of movement is less perfect than an act of the intellect. Therefore, [it cannot be the end of an intellectual act or habit of knowledge].

[A third opinion, also that of Godfrey] Therefore certain persons, wishing to correct this view, say that knowledge is called practical not because of its final result, which is praxis and work, but because the same intellectual potency in which the knowledge-habit resides is actually considering [praxis and work] and this act of consideration, as its proximate end, is what the habit of knowledge immediately achieves.

[Refutation] To the contrary: Why, I ask, is this consideration called practical? It is not because of the intellect, because this as such is indifferently theoretical or practical; neither is it because of the end [or subsequent results], as was proved earlier. And by the same token, there would have to be some prior cause why the habit is called practical other than this consideration. Therefore, it is by reason of its object that knowledge is called practical, which is our thesis.

[Scotus' Personal Opinion]
   Therefore we have to say a habit is called practical or theoretical by reason of its object, because the only cause prior to the habit is either the intellect or its object. But since of itself intellect is neither practical nor theoretical, intellect cannot be the reason why its knowledge is practical . . .

   Is theology a practical science?

   Some [like Henry of Ghent] say theology is not practical but theoretical, because there is a twofold act of the will, one of which regards the end and the other the means to that end. But here the principal intent is the end itself and not the means thereto. Now, the will needs no directive habit as regards the end, but merely requires that it be shown the end. It does need directives, however, regarding the means to attain such an end.

   This is also proved by a citation from [Augustine's] sermon "On Jacob and Esau," where it is said that "every action ought to be in order to cleanse the eye and see God."

   Furthermore, our theology is the same as that of the blessed [in heaven]. But theirs is not practical, because they need no directive, for then there could be error [in their knowledge of God].

   [Refutation of Henry] To the contrary: the first argument actually establishes the opposite of what they propose. For I concede the aforesaid dual act of the will. Nevertheless the will could under different circumstances have opposite acts (good or bad, intense or remiss) when the ultimate end is shown to it in particular, though not in regard to the ultimate end in general. But where some faculty is indifferent with respect to certain acts, one of which is suited to it whereas the other is not, there a directive habit is needed and required. But the end of theology is not the good in general, but this particular good [viz., God]. Hence theology is practical, directing one to a particular end.

Furthermore, a practical habit is postulated not because of the substantive character of the act, but because of the circumstances under which it is performed. For example, a moral habit directs one not in regard to the act of eating as such, but in regard to how to eat, namely, temperately. Therefore, even though the will were determined to have the substance of an act that regards the end in particular, nevertheless it requires a directive habit in regard to that act as qualified by circumstances.

Furthermore, what we want to know about most of all provided it is not knowledge for the sake of knowledge, is what we want to love the most. But God in himself is the one we want to love the most, and hence love of God is the end or object we most desire, and the knowledge we want most of all is knowledge of God. Therefore the principles here are practical; ergo, etc.

What is more, directive knowledge which is about those things conducive to the end is of the same sort as is knowledge of the end, since the cognition of the end is first and is the cause of the cognition of the means to the end. If one is practical, therefore, the other will be practical also.

As for the proof from authority, this refers to external acts commanded by the will.

Another opinion [that of Godfrey of Fontaines] claims that theology is both practical and theoretical and it does not exist as a single habit of knowledge but as two. If one were to write into a single volume bit by bit a mixture of philosophical and legal items, the resulting doctrine contained therein would pertain no less to two distinct knowledge-habits. It is that way with the Scriptures, where it is not only that one part, or one chapter, contains the theoretical and another speaks of what has to be done, but even at times one verse contains what is to be believed and the next verse what is to be done. Therefore, theology is both practical and theoretical.

They give this sort of argument. No theoretical science treats of practical things in any more detail than is necessary for knowing that theoretical science; on the other hand, neither does a practical science treat of theoretical things in any more detail than is necessary to know that practice in question. But here we have both. For the Scriptures treat of what is to be done as if it were concerned solely with this, and the same is true of theoretical items. Therefore, there are two different habits of knowledge here. This is clear from what the Philosopher says in I *Ethics* about not treating of the powers of the soul except insofar as is needed to treat of the virtues which reside therein.

[Refutation of Godfrey] Using his argument one can argue to the opposite conclusion in this way. Every science that deals with theoretical items in no greater detail than is necessary for praxis is practical and not theoretical. But any knowledge about the ultimate end and of what is conducive to attaining it is such that the more a well-disposed man knows about this, the more he is disposed to love God. Hence the blessed, who know more about him, love him more. And here on earth, the more one knows of the wonderous works of God, the more one is ordained to praise and love God.

[Scotus' Personal Opinion]

Therefore one must say that theology is purely and simply a practical habit. For it is a practical consideration that is the sort of consideration that is naturally prior to praxis, in agreement with which practice is suited by nature to be elicited in the right way. Hence, it is said in VI *Ethics*: "The end of practical knowledge is truth in agreement with right desire." There are two conditions, then, for a consideration to be practical. One is agreement with praxis, and this it has from its object, which it apprehends directly. The other is the note of priority, which it has from the intellect. Therefore the intellect apprehending an object according to rules from which praxis can be caused through the movement of the will is practical. But the intellect perfected by the habit of theology apprehends God as one who should be loved and according to rules from which praxis can be elicited. Therefore, the habit of theology is practical.

[Solution of Some Doubts]

[1] What has been said about theology's being a practical science and concerned with contingent matters raises a doubt whether it is a science at all. For if it is practical, then it has to do with contingent matters; and if it is concerned with contingencies, then it is not a science. From the outset, then, if theology is practical, it is not a science. This second implication is clear from the Philosopher's statement in the *Ethics* that science differs from deliberative knowledge because deliberative knowledge has to do with contingencies, whereas science is in the scientific portion of the intellect and not in that part that calculates or deliberates. This is also confirmed by the definition

of science or scientific knowledge in the *Posterior Analytics*, where it is said that "to know a thing scientifically is to know its causes," etc.

[2] Also, if theology is a practical habit of knowledge, then it has to do with actions or what can be done; therefore it is "a habit involving true reasoning that enables one to act well." But this is the definition of prudence, and prudence is not a science [according to the Philosopher]; therefore, it follows as before that theology is not a science.

[3] Furthermore, on the above assumption that theology is about the ultimate end, it follows that it is not practical. Proof of the implication: we show that "praxis is nothing other than the operation following choice" and choice is not about the end but about the means thereto. The assumption then is shown through what the Philosopher says in VI *Ethics*: "Choice is the principle of action, its efficient, not its final, cause." But an efficient principle precedes the effect. Also, the assumed proposition is established by reason: a practical habit is generated from praxes, and is produced by acts following choice, because according to II *Ethics* a habit is generated from similar acts and inclines one to repeat such. From such like, then, is it produced, and hence the act following choice will be praxis . . .

[To 1] To the first of these it must be said that the argument is invalid, for if it held, no science would be practical. If the contingent is the object of a practical habit of knowledge, and nothing contingent can be an object of science, it follows that no science is practical; nevertheless, philosophers distinguish between practical and theoretical science. For the Philosopher makes this point in VI *Metaphysics*: "If therefore all science is either theoretical or about acting or making," etc. And the "if" is not added to weaken the statement but only notes its implication and the Philosopher's mode of speech. In his *Metaphysics* I Avicenna makes the same distinction of sciences.

Therefore, I say there are necessary truths about contingent things, because while it is contingent that a stone fall, nevertheless there are necessary truths about its descent, such as that it seeks the center and that it descends in a straight line. Similarly, for me to love God is contingent, and nevertheless there can be a necessary truth in regard to this, such as that I should love God above all. And this can be inferred demonstratively in the following fashion. "God is that greater than which nothing can be thought"; therefore he is supremely lovable; therefore I ought to love him above all. This science, then, is truly about something contingent contained in the first object, although it is not contained there primarily, and nevertheless it is about necessary truths which can be concluded about contingent things. And when the implication is proved that "if it is about something contingent, then it is not a science according to the Philosopher in VI *Ethics*, for otherwise one would confuse a deliberative and a scientific habit of knowledge if both could be about the same contingent thing," the following needs to be said. It is true that two diverse objects could not belong to a single potency or habit (for then the habit would not be one and nevertheless it would depend completely upon each one and it would simultaneously be and not be if the other object were destroyed). Nevertheless the same object under the same aspect so far as its role as object is concerned, can pertain to two potencies, such as intellect and will, as will be explained below. Similarly, there can be two habits, although the same object can not pertain to two potencies so far as the aspects go which follow the act. Hence it is that when diverse things are included primarily in something, it can be the object of diverse habits. It would be like the two properties of a binary, one that it is an even number, the other that it is a prime number. And therefore something contingent is not excluded entirely from the object of a science. Hence even though something contingent be the object of a deliberative habit, such as prudence, as regards those conclusions one can necessarily draw about such a contingent thing, that same item is the object of a scientific habit.

[To 2] As for the other, one must admit the argument is invalid, for then prudence would be a moral habit, because it too is "a habit involving true reasoning that enables one to act well." And in such a case, one who knew moral science would necessarily be prudent, and hence would have all the virtues, which is false.

Therefore, I say that "practical reason" refers to such knowledge as is immediately and proximately practical, whereas other knowledge that precedes this [logically] is more remotely practical, such as the first principle from which one ought to begin to arrive discursively at such a conclusion or end. And a precept or dictate about such an initial principle is itself practical in the proper sense of the term. It is just that the conclusion "One should eat soberly" is more immediately conformed to praxis than is the principle "One should live uprightly," from which it is nevertheless inferred necessarily. Hence prudence is simply a habit that is more immediately directed towards practice, so that a prudent person knows immediately the means to use and does not have to reason backwards from principles to other prior principles. A science, like moral philosophy, however, is only mediately practical, because it teaches how one should behave in regard to actions through a process of reasoning. Hence, just as an artist with a knowledge of his art in mind is more remotely practical than one who knows [how to do or make something] simply from experience and not deductively from any art he possesses, so too one who knows the science of morals is more remotely practical than one who possesses prudence.

[To 3] As for the claim that [theology is not practical because it has to do with our ultimate end] we must answer that praxis is primarily concerned with the end, though choice [in the technical sense of selecting the means to attain the end] may not be involved here. Nevertheless, the praxis which has to do with means to the end is included in the praxis which has to do with the end itself.

And when it is said that, according to the Philosopher, "praxis follows the choice, which is its [efficient] principle," I say it was not the Philosopher's intent that praxis consists primarily in such acts as follow choice. One can show this as follows. There are practical principles, such as right reason and the [intellectual habit] of moral knowledge, that have a bearing on one's choice, as is clear from that same Bk. VI [of the *Ethics*]. And if the principles are practical, the conclusions that follow will be practical.—Also, the habit inclines one to repeat the same sort of acts that produced the habit to begin with; but a practical habit inclines one to make a choice, because choice is the first act elicited by the moral habit; therefore, the moral habit will be generated by this [sort of] act.

For that reason I say that the acts following choice are truly practical, though they are only accidental to practice, because the practical moral habit does not extend necessarily to external objects. For it is not required of every liberal person that he or she actually perform such executive acts as follow their choosing to be liberal, since one destitute of money could be liberal at heart, desiring to carry out such liberality through imaginary acts. And the same is true of the contingent. Hence, choice is the moving principle, because the will is its source, and it is to this [act of the will] that praxis refers primarily, and only after this [i.e., secondarily] does it refer to those other acts to which the dictum "Choice is their moving principle" applies.

As for the other point, that "a practical habit is generated from praxes," I have this to say. [a] Either this remark is not to be understood in its proper sense, since it is practical actions other than praxes that produce the practical habit [of knowledge], for "praxes" refers to acts of some potency other than the intellect. [b] Or one must say that even though the practical habit inclines one to perform actions following one's choice, it nevertheless first inclines one to make such a choice.

2. THE WILL AS A RATIONAL FACULTY
(*Questions on the Metaphysics* IX, q. 15)

Text of Aristotle: "It is clear that some potencies will be nonrational but others will be with reason. Hence, all the arts or productive sciences are potencies."

Is the difference Aristotle assigns between the rational and irrational potencies appropriate, namely, that the former are capable of contrary effects but the latter produce but one effect?

[Arguments Pro and Con]

Arguments that the distinction is inappropriate: first as to the rational potencies:

[1] Anything having a potency or power is capable of doing what is in its power; therefore, it could perform opposites [simultaneously, if it were rational].—Some try to escape this conclusion by saying, as Aristotle himself seems to say in the above text, that a rational power does not have the ability to produce contrary effects simultaneously, although it does possess simultaneously the potentiality for opposite effects. But this evasion is no good. At that moment when it has one of the contraries, I ask: Could it have the other present or not? If it could, we have what we propose, for it seems opposites are had simultaneously. If not, then this power at this precise moment is capable only of this contrary.

[2] Also there is this second argument. What is unable to do anything is certainly not a potency, but that which has to do with opposites, since it is incapable of having contrary effects at the same time, seems unable to do anything unless it is determined [by something else such as desire or election], as the argument goes in the text of ch. 4. Once determined, however, it seems able to do but one thing; therefore insofar as it is a potency it seems to be capable of but one thing.

[3] Thirdly, if the distinction were appropriate, then it would follow that the will could tend to the opposite of what its end is and could will evil under the aspect of evil just as well as it could will the opposite of such things. But the consequent is false, because, as Aristotle puts it in Bk. VIII, ch. 8: "Freedmen are not at liberty to act at random."

Aristotle's distinction is not appropriate for irrational potencies either:

[4] To begin with, the sun is capable of producing opposite effects in the terrestrial world, for it dissolves ice and dries clay; nevertheless it is an irrational power.

[5] Also, the Philosopher admits in ch. 7 that "every potency is at the same time capable of contradictory states" and declares that this holds good also for active potencies.

[6] Also, according to Aristotle, the rational is not related to both contraries *per se*, but only to the one it possesses as a habit, whereas the privation of such a habit it can only have *per accidens*. But an irrational potency is able to have contraries in this fashion, for cold is an accidental cause of heat, and throwing a ball against the wall is the cause of its rebounding. Therefore, the distinction Aristotle makes is not appropriate.

To the contrary is the Philosopher's statement in the text cited above.

[Body of the Question]

As for the question, granting the distinction to be well made, we must first see how it is to be understood and then what its rationale is.

[Article 1: How Is the Distinction to Be Understood?]

As for the first, keep in mind that any active potency whatsoever, be it a power to act in a certain way or an ability to produce something, is such that so long as its nature remains unchanged, it only does what it can do of itself. Frigidity, remaining frigidity, for example, cannot warm or draw heat from itself if it is not this sort of agent. No matter what the circumstances might be, if something associated with it peripherally, for instance, could produce heat in something, it would never be frigidity qua frigidity that would do this. When we speak of an active potency for opposites, then, be these contradictory or contrary states, it means that with no change in its nature, either falls equally under the scope of its power. But when such a potency has to do with opposite actions, it means that, keeping its unitary character, it suffices to elicit the said actions of itself. And if the action of an active potency is labelled "act" in the sense explained in the third article of the fourth question [i.e., act qua form], then all that has to do with opposite actions or action has to do with opposite acts, but not vice versa. However, this concern with opposite actions or action should be understood to include the negation of action [i.e., the ability deliberately not to act when all conditions for acting are present]. This will become clear in the second article. Now, it is not the relationship itself that we call "active potency," which relationship is listed among the number of correlatives, but an absolute nature [i.e., something nonrelative such as substance or quality], which represents the proper foundation for several relationships towards opposite effects.

[Article 2: What Is the Rationale for the Distinction?]

As for the second point, Aristotle seems to have understood the distinction to stem from the fact that a natural form is a principle for making only one of a pair of opposites, that which resembles itself naturally, just as this is this and not its opposite. But a form that is in the intellect, in the way that knowledge informs the mind, is a principle for representing opposites by an intentional likeness, just as knowledge is a virtual likeness of opposites [e.g., medical science is knowledge of both health and sickness], since one of the contraries includes the privation of the other. But the agent is active in regard to what can be modeled according to the form by which it acts. For this reason, then, Aristotle appears to have introduced the distinction.

[1. The Opinion of Others]

This argument, however, is attacked on multiple grounds:

First, because a natural form can be the originative source of virtual opposites, as it clear in the case of the sun.

Second, it seems to assume that the intellect or its knowledge is the only rational potency (which is false, as will be shown later). This assumption appears even more expressly in ch. 4 where [Aristotle] concludes that a rational power has to do with opposites and it does nothing unless it is determined to one or the other of these opposites. What determines it goes by the name of appetite [i.e., desire] or deliberate choice. This would seem to exclude desire or will from the concept of a rational potency. What follows makes this conclusion even more obvious. There Aristotle seems to say that once the rational power is determined in this way, it acts necessarily, just as the irrational power does of itself. Hence, it seems that properly speaking a rational power is not the combination of both intellect (which he assumes has to do with opposites) and the determining desire (which he requires as necessary if anything is to occur).

Thirdly, the proof that the intellect has to do with opposites only privatively appears invalid, for a contrary, though it includes the privation of the other contrary, does not include such precisely, since the other has a positive nature, and thus there is some knowledge corresponding properly to its entity that is not gained precisely through knowledge of its opposite. In fact it is known only in a qualified sense through the knowledge of its opposite.

[2. The Opinion of Scotus]

As for this second article, then, we must first investigate the distinction itself and then see what Aristotle thought about it.

[a. The Distinction Itself: Nature and Will]

As for the first, keep in mind that the primary distinction of active potencies stems from the radically different way in which they elicit their respective operations [rather than from what they are concerned with]. For if we can somehow distinguish them because one acts in regard to this, another in regard to that, such a distinction is not so immediate [i.e., radical or basic]. For a power or potency is related to the object in regard to which it acts only by means of some operation it elicits in one way or another, and there is only a twofold generic way an operation proper to a potency can be elicited. For either [1] the potency of itself is determined to act, so that so far as itself is concerned, it cannot fail to act when not impeded from without; or [2] it is not of itself so determined, but can perform either this act or its opposite, or can either act or not act at all. A potency of the first sort is commonly called "nature," whereas one of the second sort is called "will." Hence, the primary division of active potencies is into nature and will—a distinction Aristotle had in mind in II *Physics* when he assumed there were two incidental or *per accidens* efficient causes: chance, which is reducible to nature; and fortune, which involves purpose or will.

Suppose someone seeks a further reason for this distinction. Just why does nature have to do with only one sort of action? i.e., if it has to do with this or that, why is it determined of itself to cause just this effect or these effects, whatever they may be, whereas will, by contrast, has alternatives, i.e., it is not intrinsically determined to this action or its opposite, or for that matter to acting or not acting at all? One could reply to such a question that there is no further reason for this. Just as any immediate effect is related to its immediate cause primarily and *per se*, without benefit of any mediating cause—otherwise one could go on *ad infinitum* looking for reasons—so an active cause [as opposed to a material or other "cause"] seems to be immediately related to the action it elicits. One can give no other reason why it elicits its action in this way except that it is this sort of cause. Yet this is precisely what one is [foolishly] asking a reason for. Hence, just as "Heat heats" because it is heat, nor is such a proposition mediate [i.e., a conclusion], but rather it is a primary proposition in the fourth mode of *per se* predication, so also is this: "Heat is determined of itself to heat." "The will wills" and "The will does not will in a definite way by reason of some intrinsically necessary specification" would be similar sorts of statements.

[Two objections] Against this it is first objected that the proposition "The will wills" is contingent. Now, if the will were not determined of itself to will, how would any contingent proposition be immediate?

Secondly there is this objection. Why postulate this indeterminacy in the will if it cannot be proved to follow from the nature of the will? [In which case "The will wills" would be a conclusion and not a *per se* proposition of the fourth mode.]

[Solutions] The answer to the first is that the contingent does not follow from the necessary. This is clear if you consider some contingent proposition. If it is immediate, we have what we seek; if not, then there is some proposition that is intermediate; but this other premise from which it follows is also contingent; otherwise a contingent proposition could be inferred from necessary premises [which is logically impossible]. But if this intermediate premise is contingent [according to the objector], there must be some further contingent proposition from which it follows; and so *ad infinitum*, unless one stops with some proposition that is admittedly immediate [or axiomatic].

What Aristotle says near the end of the *Posterior Analytics*, Bk. I, confirms this. There his meaning is that opining occurs both as a truth that is "propter quid" (that is it is expressed in terms of a first principle or immediate proposition) and as a factual or "quia" proposition that needs further proof. And so it is with the proposition under consideration, "The will wills A." If there is no further cause or mediate reason why this is the case, then our proposal is conceded [viz., that it is a first or *per se* proposition]. If there is some reason or cause, such as "Because the will wills B," then one inquires further. Somewhere, however, you must stop. Where? Why does the will will this last? There is no other cause to be found except that the will is will. Now, if this last proposition were necessary, it could not be the sole premise from which something contingent followed.

As for the second objection [i.e., that indeterminacy must be proved from the nature of the will and hence *a priori*], the proof here is *a posteriori*, for the person who wills experiences that he could have nilled or not willed what he did, according to what has been explained more at length elsewhere about the will's liberty.

[A doubt] A further doubt arises about the aforesaid. What reduces such a potency to act, if it is of itself undetermined towards acting or not acting?

I reply: there is a certain indeterminacy of insufficiency, based on potentiality and a defect of actuality, in the way, for instance, that matter without a form would be indeterminate as regards the actuation given by the form. There is another indeterminacy, however, that of a superabundant sufficiency, based on unlimited actuality, either in an unqualified or in a qualified sense. Now, the first sort of indeterminacy is not reduced to actuality unless it first is determined to some form by something else. Something indeterminate in the second sense, however, can determine itself. If this could occur where some limited actuality exists, how much more where the actuality is unlimited! For it would lack nothing simply required for an acting principle. Otherwise God, who, in virtue of his indeterminacy of unlimited actuality, is supremely undetermined in regard to any action whatsoever, would be unable to do anything of himself, which is false. Take this example: fire has the ability to heat, neither do we seek anything extrinsic to fire itself that determines it to burn. Suppose, without losing any of its perfection as heat, it were given the perfection of coldness, why should it not be able to determine itself to heat something, as before? Nevertheless, this example is not quite similar, as will be pointed out later in answering the initial argument. But the indetermination ascribed to the will is not like that of matter, nor, insofar as it is active, is it the indeterminacy of imperfection, but rather it is the indeterminacy of surpassing perfection and power, not restricted to some specific act.

[b. What about the Mind of Aristotle?]
   But how reconcile the aforesaid interpretation with the mind of Aristotle, who distinguished, not between nature and will, but between irrational and rational potencies, understanding "rational" apparently as referring only to the intellect, as the second objection claims?
   I reply: intellect and will can be compared either with the proper act each elicits or with the acts of other subordinate powers over which they exercise a kind of causality—the intellect, by showing and directing; the will, by inclining and commanding. Of the two, the first comparison is clearly the more essential. From this standpoint the intellect falls under the heading of "nature," for it is of itself determined to understanding and does not have it in its power to both understand and not understand; or as regards propositional knowledge where contrary acts are possible, it does not have the power to both assent and dissent. If, as Aristotle seems to say, some one type of knowledge has to do with opposites, still with respect to this knowledge the intellect is not indeterminate of itself. Quite the contrary, in such a case it would elicit of necessity an act of intellection, just as it would in regard to knowledge that involves only one thing. The will, however, has the ability to elicit an act proper to itself in opposite ways, as was stated earlier. It is in this vein that we assume only two productions in the divine [namely, that of the Word and that of the Holy Spirit] and put intellect [whereby the Word is spoken] in the same class of principles as nature. Now, Aristotle apparently says nothing about this first and more essential comparison.

The second comparison or relationship seems to be accidental, as it were, for two reasons. One, because these potencies [of intellect and will] are related to the acts of the other potencies they control only by means of acts proper to themselves, since their proper acts are prior to these others. The other reason is that the intellect in particular does not have the character of an active potency properly speaking, according to [Aristotle] in Bk. VII, ch. 7. And it is of this second relationship that Aristotle appears to be speaking, and he assumes some order such that some knowledge of opposites is first required. But this initial knowledge is of itself insufficient to cause any extrinsic effect, for as Aristotle argues in ch. 4, it would then produce opposites. But this does not seem to follow unless the intellect also knows of such opposites. So far as its causality over things outside itself is concerned, the intellect is determined of itself in regard to what it directs. Hence, not only as regards its own acts is it not rational, but it is not fully rational even as regards the external acts it directs. As a matter of fact, speaking precisely, even as regards its intrinsic acts it is irrational. It is rational only in the qualified sense that it is a precondition for the act of a rational potency. A determining will follows, but not in such a way that this potency of the will is determined of itself to one alternative and hence the combination of intellect and will together has to do with one effect, as the objection above claimed. Rather the will, which is undetermined as regards its own act, elicits its act, and through its elicited act it determines the intellect insofar as the latter has a causal bearing on some external happening. Hence Aristotle says: "I call this desire or *prohaeresis*, i.e., choice." But he does not call it "will," that is to say, a potency. And so if intellect is called a "rational potency," the aforesaid distinction [between rational and nonrational] must be understood in the way explained above. For the distinction is not applicable to the intellect's own acts nor insofar as the intellect concurs with the acts of subordinate powers solely by means of its own act, for in both these ways it falls under the heading of "nature." Nevertheless it falls under the other heading [i.e., of "will"] insofar as earlier its own act is subject to acts of the will.

But if "rational" is understood to mean "with reason," then the will is properly rational, and it has to do with opposites, both as regards its own act and as regards the acts it controls. And it has to do with opposites not in the way that a nature, like the intellect, acts, which has no power to determine itself in any other way. But the will acts freely, for it has the power of self-determination. Properly speaking, however, the intellect is not a potency with regard to external things, because if it does have to do with opposites, it cannot determine itself, and unless it is determined, it is unable to do anything extra.

[3. Scotus' Reply to the Objections to Aristotle Raised in 1]

With this in mind one could answer the objections raised earlier to the way of Aristotle.

I reply to the first about the sun. A natural form, if it is not limited and is a principle of opposite effects in materials disposed to receive such, is still determined to produce these effects in the same way as a form with but one effect is determined to produce a single effect. For the sun does not have it in its power to generate an alternative to the form it produces—when the recipient of this or that form is present— any more than it would have if it could produce but one form. The will, however, is not the sort of principle that is of itself determined in regard to its action, whether the action has to do with this or that opposite, but it possesses the power to determine itself in regard to either alternative. And this makes clear why the example cited above about heat and cold being found together in the same agent is deficient. In short, there simply is no appropriate example whatsoever that could be given, because the will is an active principle distinct from the whole class of active principles which are not will, by reason of the opposite way in which it acts. It seems stupid, then, to apply general propositions about active principles to the will, since there are no instances of the way it behaves in anything other than will. For the will alone is not this other sort of thing. Hence, one should not deny that it is the sort of thing it is, just because other things are not like it. For there is nothing contradictory about a created active principle having the perfection we attribute to the will, namely, that it is not just determined to one effect or to one act, but has many things within its scope and is not determined towards any of these things that fall sufficiently within its power. For who would deny an agent is more perfect the less it is determined, dependent, and limited in its action or effect? And if one concedes this in regard to a lack of limitation as regards many contrary effects, even in a case [like the sun], where this is associated with a natural determination towards every one of them, how much more perfect would it be if we were to assume the second sort of indeterminacy [i.e., of superabundant sufficiency] to be added to the first! For this sort of contingency is more noble than necessity, as was pointed out in Bk. VII (in the question raised there about the chapter "On the Necessary," namely, how it is a matter of perfection in God that he causes nothing necessarily). Consequently, if this perfection we ascribe to the will is not opposed to the notion of a creative active principle—and the will is the highest such—then such perfection ought reasonably to be attributed to the will. And this is a better assessment of the case with the will than the earlier example about the combination of heat and cold. The reasoning that seems to underlie our opening text from Aristotle, consequently, could be treated as follows. If the selfsame knowledge enables the intellect to deal in some way with opposites, as the text indicates, then an active potency even less limited should be able to do this even better; i.e., while retaining its integrity it could determine itself to either of the alternatives shown to it. Otherwise, the initial potency for opposites would seem to have been given in vain, for without a second principle [like the will] an intelligent agent would be unable to do either. In this way, the argument would rest on the dialectical rule *a minori*, and not be an instance of reasoning from a proper cause, for knowledge is not the proper cause of the aforesaid distinction.

As for the second objection, Aristotle did not exclude the will from the rational potencies, unless you restrict the meaning of "rational potency" to what is incompletely such, namely, the knowledge of opposites. But Aristotle acknowledged that such an incomplete potency could cause something external only if it had some additional determination from another source. Now, I ask: What is the source of this determinate choice? It can only come from a potency distinct from reason that is able to choose. For reason is not a determining factor, since it has to do with opposites with respect to which it cannot determine itself, much less determine something other than itself. Or if it were to determine itself, it would be to produce opposites simultaneously, as Aristotle argued would be the case with a productive agent. Neither does this other factor [distinct from reason] determine itself necessarily to the opposite alternative, for then the intellect would not be in even remote potency to opposites. Hence, this other potency determines itself contingently, and once it has done such through its own act, as a consequence it determines the intellect. Aristotle, then, at least hinted that this other potency of itself has to do with opposites in such a way that it is self-determinative towards either alternative. And in virtue of its act already elicited determinatively, he assumes it is determined as regards the work of something exterior [viz., the intellect] which of itself had to do with opposites in such a way that it was impossible for it to determine itself. And thus by showing in the fourth chapter how this incomplete rational potency proceeds to act, Aristotle clearly seems to imply that there is another complete rational potency (in the sense of the distinction he postulates here), and that these two [potencies of intellect and will] together with their [proper] acts concur to produce the external effect. Properly speaking, the executive power is not in contradictory potency to the effect it carries out, since it is only rational by participation. But the full meaning of a potency for opposites is found formally in the will.

As for what Aristotle adds, however, about a rational potency, once it is determined [by choice or desire], being necessarily restricted to what is desired and that it must do this, one could note that the necessity in such a case is not absolute. For if the antecedent—for instance, "This is willed"—is not necessary, then neither is the consequent. If such a volition exists necessarily, then the consequent (namely, what is done externally) is also necessary. But if the necessary implication is merely "The will wills this external thing; therefore, if not impeded, it will do this," Aristotle would be saying nothing more than that nothing occurs without some prior cause being first determined to do this. The sole exception is the volition itself that follows the intellectual apprehension of the alternatives, and it is this volition that determines what takes place outside. In this way one could gloss or explain his statement at the end of the chapter: "Even if one had the will to do both at the same time, one will not do them . . . for this is not a potency for doing both contraries at the same time." Why should this not apply to the will as well? Yet he had argued earlier, at the outset of the chapter on rational potency, that its simultaneous ability to produce opposites seems to be a good basis for distinguishing it [from the non-rational], because the way it will act will be in accord with its potentiality, but it [will not act all at once] in every way it has a potency to act. Now, the potency characteristic *per se* of an incomplete rational potency, as has been said, is natural so far as opposites are concerned. Therefore, so far as itself is concerned, it will be not only simultaneously capable of opposites, but capable of producing opposites simultaneously, and therefore, if this potency were to produce them on its own [i.e., without benefit of will], it would produce them simultaneously. The situation here would resemble that of the sun, which produces opposite effects at the same time in the diverse receptive subjects that are brought near to it, and if it were related to such different effects in equal measure, and only one object, equally receptive towards such opposite effects, was placed near the sun, the latter either would do nothing to it or would produce such effects in it simultaneously.

Objection: the intellect is not equally disposed towards opposites; therefore it would act in accord with the stronger pull.

I reply: it is true that with only a single item of knowledge, representing something positive together with its privation, the intellect is not equally disposed towards both but relates towards one *per se* and the other *per accidens*. However, with positive knowledge of both alternatives [the intellect] could be the cause of opposites. Otherwise, how would [Aristotle's] inference based on inequality follow?

But it is not this way with the will. For if it has to do with opposites, only virtually does it have to do with them simultaneously. But it does not actually have to do with both at once, because it is not related to them in the manner of nature. Rather it has the potentiality to determine itself to either alternative with the other alternative before it, and therefore it will act in this way.

And in this way, perhaps, one could explain this fourth chapter, where much is said that could refer to the will, though some statements seem to militate against such an interpretation.

But then one might ask, why does he so frequently call the intellect a "rational potency" and not the will, though admittedly, from what has been said, he hints of this?

One could say that the initial act of the intellect is more common and better known to us than the act of the will. But Aristotle oftener than not speaks about the more obvious, and hence we find him saying little about the will, although some things follow from his remarks that he would have talked about later had he considered the matter.

The third objection against Aristotle does make a valid point, namely, that each contrary has a concept proper to itself which is grasped through a proper species; nevertheless discursive or inferential knowledge, where one item is naturally prior to another, can be the source of knowing something about the other. In this way one can expound the statement in I *De anima*: "By means of the straight line we know both itself and the curved." For judgment is not a function of simple apprehension, but involves a comparison of propositions. Qualified knowledge of one thing, however, can be simply apprehended through the species of another, to the extent that its privation is included, not in the essence or essential notion of the other, but concomitantly. As apprehended simply, then, formal knowledge of one contrary is virtual knowledge of the other, just as formal knowledge of principles is virtual knowledge of conclusions. And if some volition, such as choosing perhaps, first requires some judgmental knowledge about what the choices are, one of the contraries could be known through the other in this way, though at times the choice runs counter to that judgment. As for the second type [namely, discursive knowledge], the same knowledge of contraries has to do with one of them simply and with the other in a qualified sense. And this suffices for the will to select either of the contraries shown to it in this fashion, and so it can act in contrary ways. Hence it can also select contraries in a simple or unqualified sense, because they are not opposed to each other except in the sense that one is a privation of another. It is not under this privative aspect, however, that each is able to be willed, but rather inasmuch as both are something positive, it seems.

If one objects that a rational potency has opposites in its power only when it is not determined to one and that otherwise it does not, I say this is not so. If it were, there would be no difference between the opposed rational and irrational potencies in terms of their power over opposites. But according to what is said in IX *Metaphysics*, the consequent is false; therefore, the antecedent is also false. Proof of the implication: an irrational potency, whether active or passive, insofar as it is naturally prior to the act that determines it, is in potency to opposites. This is clear from Aristotle's *De interpretatione*, Bk. II, and Boethius' commentary on the same (second edition), where he gives the example of water that can either chill or warm.

Also, if it did not have opposites in its power, even when actually determined to one of them (i.e., in the very instant that it had settled upon this particular alternative), then no effect it is actualizing would be actually contingent. Now, the consequent is false; therefore, the antecedent is also. The falsity of the consequent is clear from what the Philosopher says in *De interpretatione*, Bk. I, where he speaks of the need to qualify this proposition: "That which is, must needs be when it is," because something does exist only contingently. Proof of our initial implication: an effect is not said to be potentially contingent unless its cause has the power to do the opposite. Neither, then, is an effect actually contingent, unless the cause actually causing it has the power to do the opposite at that very moment that it is causing the other, whereas your argument is that it has no power at present because it is now determined.

And if you say the effect is said to be contingent because [at a moment prior to such a decision, one could still say] it could have not happened, I object. Prior to that moment it was not a being; neither, then, was it an actually contingent effect before it existed. For we are speaking now of contingency as a mode of actual being, and about a "now" at the time it is actual.

Also, if something pertains primarily and *per se* to a subject, then its opposite does not pertain to that same subject *per se*, or even *per accidens* so long as the other remains. Otherwise, a demonstration of the reasoned fact, inferring an attribute of its subject, would not be based upon necessary premises. But to have opposites in its power is something a rational potency possesses primarily and *per se* as proper to it qua rational. For this is what distinguishes it from an irrational potency according to IX *Metaphysics*. Therefore, [it possesses power over the opposite even when the alternative choice remains].

Also, all [theologians] admit God is able not to predestine some predestined person at the moment such a one is predestined; therefore, his decision does not take away his power to do the opposite.

[Reply to the Initial Arguments]

[To 1] As for the initial argument at the beginning, it is clear that a rational potency, such as the will is said to be, does not have to perform opposites simultaneously, but can determine itself to either alternative, which is something the intellect cannot do. When it is objected that I am unable to be not seated, on the assumption I am sitting, my answer is this. A proposition about the possible would be false in the composite sense, because it would imply I could do both at once. In the divided sense, however, some would say that when the sitting occurs, this is so necessarily, according to that principle in *De interpretatione*, "That which is, must needs be when it is," and that nothing else is possible then, but only at the moment before, when the present situation could have been otherwise. And these persons see no way of saving the claim that *now* the will has a potency for the opposite of the state it is actually in. This is absurd, however, for it would mean that necessity and contingency are not properly conditions of being at the time they exist. But if that were true, necessity and contingency would never exist, for when something is nonexistent, it is neither necessary nor contingent. It would take too long, however, to explain now why the *De interpretatione* principle does not support their claims, because their argument is invalid on three counts, being an instance of the fallacy of consequent, of figure of speech, and of the simple and qualified sense. To put the matter in another way, one could say that when the will is in a certain state of volition, it is in that state contingently, and that its present volition stems from it contingently, for if it does not do so then, it will never do so, since at no other time does it proceed from the will. And just as this particular volition is contingently in the will, at that very moment the will is a potency with power over the opposite; and this holds for that moment in the divided sense. Not that it could will the opposite at the same time as it wills this, but in the sense that it has the power to will the contrary at that very instant, by not willing the other at that instant. For at this very instant it could, nevertheless, posit the other, in a divided sense, and do so not necessarily but contingently.

[To 2] As for the second argument, if it is the will one is speaking about, then I say that it is able to do what it does with no conceivable predetermination to act, so that the initial determination, both in the order of nature and in the order of time, occurs in the very placing of its act. And if one claims that at that instant it can do nothing unless first determined [by something other than itself], this is false. But if the argument refers to the intellect knowing opposites, then it is true that the intellect can accomplish nothing externally unless it be determined from some other source, because it knows contraries after the manner of nature, and is unable to determine itself towards any one of these opposites. Hence, it will either act towards both or not act at all. And if one concludes from this that the intellect does not suffice to qualify as a rational potency, it follows from what has been said that this is true. Indeed, if—to assume the impossible—the intellect and its subordinate powers alone existed, without a will, everything would occur deterministically after the manner of nature, and there would be no potency sufficient to accomplish anything to the contrary.

[To 3] As for the third, some say that the will has a choice of opposites so long as all fall within the scope of its first object, which—for the will—is assumed to be a real or an apparent good; whereas an act where evil qua evil is willed lies beyond its scope. Another assumption in regard to acts of willing and nilling is that the will can do either so long as its object contains something good or bad; but where the ultimate end is concerned, where nothing evil can be found, some assume that the will is no longer a rational potency. Others appear to hold that the will can be immobilized in regard to some things other than the ultimate end. Here, however, I omit discussing these things as well as the question of whether the will is determined to will the end, or— where evil qua evil is concerned—whether its act must be one of nolition.

[To 4] The answer to the fourth argument about the sun is evident from our response to the first objection to the way of Aristotle.

[To 6] To the fifth, one could say—in accord with the principle set forth in art. 1—that cold cannot be active as regards the essence of heat. Still, it can do something that makes another agent heat more effectively, for instance, constrict or contract a thing so that its interior heat is not dissipated but compressed to produce greater warmth. As for the bouncing ball, though reflex motion is in some sense contrary to rectilinear motion at the locus where the one motion ends and the other begins, still the contrariety is not formal, for whatever moves something violently, moves it to every possible location it can acquire through such motion. If it can move it straight ahead, it will do so; if not, it will cause it to rebound, and this will go on until the movement is proportionate to the violence of the mover. As for these and other things that resemble rational contingency, such as reflected and refracted rays, etc., none of these are assumed to require in any irrational potency the sort of indifference that exists in a rational potency.

[To 5] To the last I say that all passive potencies without exception are of themselves in contradictory potency, although if the form were necessarily a being [as in the case of the heavenly bodies], it would necessarily depend upon the matter of the composite; it would be incorruptible, and the matter would necessarily be in this form actually, but not by reason of the matter itself, but because of the form. — Active potencies, however, are in contradictory potency, as Aristotle explained, by being present or not [to the patient they act upon]. If this means that the patient is either present to the agent or not, then all active potencies whose action depends upon a patient or recipient can be in potency of contradiction, not of themselves, but from another source. If this refers to what impedes an agent, then every perishable natural agent can be impeded even by some other naturally active cause. But no natural active potency has of itself the ability to elicit contrary actions as regards the same thing, or to act or not act, in the way a rational potency has [liberty] of contrariety [i.e., acting this way or that] or of contradiction [i.e., acting or not acting]. Therefore, that proposition [that "every potency is at the same time capable of contradictory states"] does not militate against what Aristotle had in mind when he assigned the aforesaid distinction [between rational and irrational powers].

3. HOW THE WILL CONTROLS THOUGHT
(Opus oxoniense II, dist. 42, qq. 1–4; nn. 10–11)

I reply by first setting forth three propositions. The first is that for every single perfect and distinct intellection existing in the intellect, there can be many indistinct and imperfect intellections existing there. This is evident from the example of vision, the field of which extends as a conical pyramid at the lower base of which one point is seen distinctly, and yet within that same base many things are seen imperfectly and indistinctly; but of these several visions, only one is perfect, namely, that upon which the axis of the pyramid falls. If this is possible in one of the senses, all the more so is it possible in the intellect.

The second proposition is that by some intellection existing there, though not known [distinctly] qua object, the will can will and take pleasure or not take pleasure in the object of this intellection or in the intellection itself; otherwise the will could not join the parent [the mind] with its offspring [knowledge], which is against what Augustine says almost everywhere in Bk. IX of The Trinity.

The third proposition is that the will, by taking pleasure in the intellection, strengthens and intends it, whereas the intellection that is nilled or in which the will takes no pleasure is weakened and dismissed—which is explained in this way. An agent with many different operations and actions, if it acts upon one and the same object, acts more vigorously and perfectly than if it is engaged at the same time with many diverse things (for unified power is stronger and more perfect). Therefore, if the soul with all its potencies concentrates on the same thing, it acts more forcefully and perfectly than if its diverse potencies were concerned with different things. And hence, if the will turns towards the same thing as the intellect, it confirms the intellect in its action. And this argument gives us the reason why this is so. The fact that it is so, however, is certainly evident from experience, as anyone can discover for himself.

Furthermore, a lesser agent acts more perfectly when a higher agent concurs with it, even though the latter's action is not necessarily required. But the will with respect to the intellect is the superior agent, although it is not necessarily required for the action of the intellect; ergo, . . .

I say, therefore, that for one intellection that exists perfectly in the intellect, many confused and imperfect intellections can also be there, unless one is so perfect and actual that it suffers no other to coexist with it. Hence, by means of these confused and imperfect intellections present there, the will—according to the second proposition—can take complacency in any one of them, even though that intellection was not known actually as a [distinct] object, and—according to the third proposition—by taking pleasure in one, the will confirms and intends that intellection. Hence, that which was imperfect and disregarded becomes perfect and intense through this complacency, and thus the will can command thought and turn the intellect towards it. But by not willing some other intellection or taking no pleasure in it, that intellection diminishes in intensity and ceases to exist. Thus the will is said to avert the intellect from that intellection, just as the visual power, without moving and remaining within the same cone of vision, can focus on another point which it envisioned only imperfectly before, unless perhaps the earlier vision was so perfect that it allowed no other to be seen with it.

4. COERCION AND FREE WILL
(*Ordinatio* IV, dist. 29)

How can consent be forced?

I say that where man is concerned, no human act, properly speaking, can be coerced, for it is a contradiction for the will to be simply forced to will. According to Bk. III of the *Ethics*, "Violence occurs where the moving principle is outside and the person himself contributes nothing [as if he were carried along with the wind or by men who overpowered him]." Understand "the person himself contributes nothing" not simply in a negative sense, but contrariwise, that is to say, the action suffered, to which he contributes nothing, runs counter to his own inclination. Now, willing cannot exist in the will in such fashion, for then one wills who refrains from willing, which is clearly a contradiction.

Nevertheless, a voluntary agent can be forced to suffer something (for instance to remain here if tied) or perform some purely instrumental action (for example, someone striking my hand could make it fly in the air).

But only in a qualified sense can the will be forced to elicit or command an act (the only sort of act that is properly human), namely, through fear of an evil worse than the act in question. Even a virtuous man is subject to such coercion if he not merely suspects or rashly judges, but knows with such certainty as suffices, at least, for a human act, that the alternative evil is even less desirable and more to be shunned than the displeasing action before him. And right reason may well indicate that there are indeed worse evils for him, such as death, imprisonment or captivity, serious mutilation, and the like. Being master of his own will, then, he can choose something he would not otherwise will, or command some action he would not otherwise want performed, before he incurs such an evil, and all this according to right reason. Therefore, such fear may well befall a man of solid character. But no fear can lead one into mortal sin according to right reason, since no threat of evil is greater than that of a sin of this sort, for no mere pain is worse than that of mortal sin.

PART II

The Will and Its Inclinations

5. THE WILL AND ITS INCLINATIONS
(*Ordinatio* III, suppl., dist. 46)

According to Anselm, two affections may be assigned to the will, namely, the affection for justice and the affection for the advantageous. He treats of these extensively in *The Fall of the Devil*, ch. 14, and *The Harmony of God's Foreknowledge, Grace, and Predestination*, ch. 19. The affection for justice is nobler than the affection for the advantageous, understanding by "justice" not only acquired or infused justice, but also innate justice, which is the will's congenital liberty by reason of which it is able to will some good not oriented to self. According to the affection for what is advantageous, however, nothing can be willed save with reference to self. And this we would possess if only an intellectual appetite with no liberty followed upon intellectual knowledge, as sense appetite follows sense cognition. The only point I wish to make from this is the following. To love something in itself [or for its own sake] is more an act of giving or sharing and is a freer act than is desiring that object for oneself. As such it is an act more appropriate to the will, as the seat of this innate justice at least. The other act [of wanting something for oneself] pertains to the will inasmuch as it has an affection for the advantageous.

From this it follows that just as these affections are distinct in the will, so also the habits inclining one to these acts will be distinct. That is why I say that charity perfects the will insofar as it is inclined to, or subject to, the affection for justice, whereas hope perfects the will insofar as it is inclined to, or subject to, the affection for what is advantageous. And so charity and hope will be distinct virtues not only by reason of their acts, which are to love and to desire respectively, but also by reason of what receives these acts, namely, the will insofar as it has an affection both for justice and for what is advantageous.

6. NATURAL WILL AND NATURAL VOLITION
(*Ordinatio* III, dist. 17)

I say that will can be understood either properly or in the general sense of an appetite. Taken in this broader meaning, there were at least three appetites present in Christ, namely, (1) an uncreated intellectual appetite, (2) a created rational appetite, and (3) an irrational or sense appetite. Properly speaking, however, the will is more than an appetite, because it is a free appetite coupled with reason. Strictly speaking, then, there were but two wills in Christ. But according to common usage, which equates will with appetite, in Christ, as in ourselves, there were as many appetites as there are distinct powers of apprehension in us. Just as perception by sight or taste is other than that grasping a thing by touch or smell, so too is the proper appetite associated with each distinct, as is also the pleasure consequent upon each sort of apprehension—even though we commonly lump them together and speak as if there were but one sensitive appetite.

But what about natural and free will? Are these two powers? I say that a natural appetite in anything is just a general name for a thing's natural inclination towards its proper perfection. A stone is naturally inclined to the center of the earth, for example. Now, if such an inclination in the stone were some absolute thing other than its heaviness, I might then believe that man's natural inclination qua man to his proper perfection was something other than his free will. But I believe the first to be false, namely, that the inclination of the stone towards the center is something absolute in addition to its heaviness and represents another power that functions with respect to the center, as some imagine. But it would have to be a transeunt sort of action with no end point. The center is what is sought, yet the operation neither destroys nor preserves it. No one has suggested a solution as to what sort of operation is involved save that it concerns, perhaps, conservation of one's proper place. But it may well be that its presence in the center is in a continual state of becoming, like light in the intervening space. But then the action is not directed into the center, because the whereabouts or ubiety is in the subject that is in place and not in the place where it is located, and it is the center which locates the body in it. Hence, besides the heaviness there is only the relation inclining a weight towards the center as its proper perfection.

I say then that the same thing holds for the will, because the natural will is really not will at all, nor is natural volition true volition, for the term "natural" effectively cancels or negates the sense of both "will" and "volition." Nothing remains but the relationship a power has to its proper perfection. Consequently, it is the same power that is called "natural will" as regards the necessary relationship it has to its perfection as is called "free." The latter term expresses the proper and intrinsic relation that is specifically the will.

Another way in which one could speak of "natural will" would be to distinguish will from a supernatural power or will. In such a case the distinction would be between the will itself as in a purely natural state and the same will as informed by gifts of grace.

Still a third way would be to take "natural will" to mean the will insofar as it elicits an act in conformity with its natural inclination, which would always be aimed at its own advantage. The will is called free, however, insofar as it lies in its power to elicit an act opposed to this inclination, for it possesses the power to elicit or not elicit an act in conformity with this inclination.

I concede that every will is in control or master of its own act . . . I say that "natural will" as such and as natural is neither a will nor a potency, but refers to the inclination the potency has to *tend* towards its proper perfection, not the inclination to act in this way. It is imperfect unless it possesses that perfection to which this tendency inclines this power. Hence the natural will does not tend, but is the tendency itself by which the will as an absolute or nonrelative entity tends, and this it does passively, being a tendency to receive something. But there is another tendency in this same power inasmuch as it tends freely and actively to elicit an act. Thus there is a twofold tendency in the one power, one active, the other passive. Therefore, to the form [of the argument to the contrary] I say that "natural will" according to its formal meaning is neither a power nor a will, but rather an inclination of the will, being a tendency by which it tends passively to receive what perfects it.

7. HAPPINESS
(*Ordinatio* IV, suppl., dist 49, qq. 9–10)

Must happiness be desired above everything, and is it the rationale behind all willing?

I reply to this first question: There is a twofold appetite or "will": one, namely, that is natural, another that is free. For the will can be considered as a certain kind of nature insofar as it has an inclination and natural appetite for its own perfection, just as any other nature does. The first thing to consider about the will, then, has to do with its natural volition as a certain kind of nature; and then, secondly, we have to consider the will insofar as it is a free appetite with a volition that is free.

[Article 1: The Will as a Nature]

As for the initial article, we must first consider just what a natural appetite is. And I say it is not an elicited act, because the natural appetite of the will is related to the will as the natural appetite of the intellect is related to intellection. If this is not an elicited act of the intellect, then neither is the natural appetite in the will an elicited act.

Also, the natural appetite of the will is always present in the will; if it were an elicited act, then, there would be some elicited act that is perpetually in the will; but the will has no such perpetual act, for then we should have experienced it in ourselves. For it is incongruous that there should be some perpetual operation going on in us that we are ignorant of—as the Philosopher argues in regard to the incongruity of habits [being actions of ours].

Furthermore, if it were an elicited act in the will, then there would be two opposing acts in the will at the same time, because the free will can will the opposite of what the natural appetite desires. Consider St. Paul, who cried out by reason of his natural appetite: "We do not wish to be stripped naked but rather to have the heavenly dwelling envelop us" [2 Cor. 5:4], and yet, according to his free appetite he longed to be freed from this life and to be with Christ [Philippians 1:23]. Hence the natural appetite is no more an elicited act of the will than is the natural appetite in a stone.

What, then, is it? I say that it is simply the inclination the will has towards its own perfection, just as in the case of other things that lack a free appetite. In Bk. I of the *Physics*, the Philosopher refers to this appetite when he says that matter desires form as the imperfect desires its perfection.

[To the question] If it is the natural rather than the free appetite that is referred to, then the reply to the question is clear, for the will necessarily or perpetually seeks happiness, and this in regard to a particular happiness.

That it does so *necessarily*, is obvious, because a nature could not remain a nature without being inclined to its own perfection. Take away this inclination and you destroy the nature. But this natural appetite is nothing other than an inclination of this sort to its proper perfection; therefore the will as nature necessarily wills its perfection, which consists above all in happiness, and it desires such by its natural appetite.

That it seeks this in the *highest measure* is proved, because the supreme inclination of nature is towards its own perfection. For if nature desires its perfection, then it desires above all its supreme perfection. The Philosopher argues in this fashion in his preface to Bk. I of his *Metaphysics*. If "all men desire by nature to know," then they desire above all that which is the supreme science [namely, metaphysics]. But since the supreme perfection of the will is happiness, it follows that the will as nature wills this above all.—Also, if as nature it seeks happiness necessarily, then it seeks it above all. The implication follows, because if it is not in something's power to tend or not to tend, then it is not in its power to tend in a remiss fashion. Therefore, if the will as nature is determined necessarily to seek happiness, then as nature it seeks it above all.

That it seeks happiness *in particular* in this fashion, is evident, because this appetite is directed towards a perfection in which the will is really perfected; but real perfection is not something general or universal, but something singular. Therefore, it desires happiness in particular.—Furthermore, this "seeking" is not an act that follows upon knowledge, because then it would not be natural, but free. But the universal is only an object of the intellect or something consequent upon an action of the intellect; therefore, this appetite in the will refers to happiness in particular.

[Article 2: The Will as a Free Appetite]

[The view of St. Thomas and Henry of Ghent] The second article asks whether all desire happiness necessarily and in the highest measure in virtue of their free appetite. There is one opinion which claims they do so in regard to happiness in general, but not in particular. The reason they give is this. That is necessarily desired in which there is no aspect of evil or defect of good. Such is happiness in general; therefore, it follows that such is desired in the highest degree, because that which has no power to act or function also lacks the power to act intensely or remissly. But they admit it is not necessary that happiness in particular be so desired, because then no one could sin.

[Refutation of this view] Against this opinion we argued at length in Bk. I in the question as to whether one who apprehends the ultimate end necessarily enjoys it as such. As for the present, it seems to me that the following involves a contradiction: "All necessarily desire happiness in general when they apprehend it, but this is not the case when they know of happiness in particular." For if happiness known in general induces desire necessarily because it possesses every aspect of good and no evil aspect or defect of goodness, and happiness in particular possesses every aspect of good even more fully than does happiness in general, it follows that when the end or happiness in particular is known, all must seek it necessarily.

Also, the universal does not include any greater perfection than does the particular. Indeed, the particular seems rather to add perfection beyond that of the universal; therefore, happiness in general bespeaks no greater perfection than beatitude in particular. Hence, if it is impossible not to seek happiness when grasped in general because such lacks any aspect of evil, all the less could one fail to seek our particular end.

Furthermore, if the will necessarily seeks happiness in general, this necessity in the will can be presumed to stem from a natural inclination of the will to happiness. But the natural inclination of the will is towards something particular and not to something universal, as was made clear above. Therefore, all the more must one assume necessity in the will in its quest of the ultimate end.

Also, how can both these statements be true at once: "The will necessarily desires happiness known in general" and "The intellect, without a shadow of doubt, dictates that happiness is only to be found in this particular end, and nevertheless, the will need not necessarily will this particular end"? This is saying nothing less than that the will seeks the same thing necessarily and not necessarily.

[Scotus' answer to the question] I reply to this article that the will of a pilgrim in this life for the most part wants happiness, whether known in general or in particular, namely, where the intellect judges or asserts without doubt that happiness is to be found in this particular. Nevertheless, it does not of necessity will happiness either in general or in particular. The reason is this. Necessity in a superior cause cannot stem from necessity in an inferior cause, because the lesser cause cannot determine the mode of action of the superior cause any more than it can force it to act. Therefore, the superior cause, if it acts of necessity, does so because of something intrinsic to the potency and stemming from the nature of such a cause. If, then, the will were necessitated to will something, this necessity would pertain to it of its very nature and not from some other inferior cause. And then I argue further that the superior cause, if it acts necessarily, moves the inferior causes to act by the same necessity, whenever their action is required necessarily for its own function. Since the will requires apprehension in the intellect for its own act of willing, it follows that if the will necessarily wills happiness, then it necessarily forces the intellect to continually consider happiness, which is false.

I say therefore that the will contingently wills the end and happiness both in general and in particular, although in most cases it seeks happiness in general, and also in particular when the intellect has no prior doubt that happiness consists in this particular thing. Hence, if someone seeks happiness and at the same time believes that beatitude consists in the fruition of the divine essence shared by the three [divine] persons, then for that moment it wills that end. But because it has no desire to live virtuously, it does not will that end, or at least it does not will the means needed to attain such.

The reason why the will wants happiness in most cases, is that the will for the most part follows the inclination of its natural appetite. For it is impossible that the will be habituated or inclined to will something to any greater degree than it is inclined by its natural appetite. Since the will, then, can only be habituated by a habit to follow for the most part the inclination of that habit and, indeed, to take delight in acting in accord with such an inclination, all the more so will the will, for the most part, will that towards which its natural appetite inclines it. And therefore, a just person, even when blessed with a gift or habit, finds death difficult to choose, and it becomes a matter of patience for such, because it runs counter to one's natural inclination. Since all will happiness by reason of their natural appetite, as we said above, it follows that the will for the most part wills to be happy.

But is this act of the will whereby it wills happiness "natural"? I say it is not properly such, because "natural volition" refers to the will's natural inclination qua nature for happiness. But it can be called a "natural act" insofar as it is conformed to one's natural inclination. For that reason Augustine says in his *Enchiridion*: "Neither should we say the will is not free, because it so wills to be happy that it cannot will to be miserable." Hence, just as some volition is said to be virtuous, not because virtue elicited this act (for, I believe, no habit is the total elicitive principle of any act), but because it conforms to the inclination of virtue and is elicited in accordance with that inclination, so too in this case the will's volition of happiness can be called natural because it is conformed to the natural inclination of the will. Nevertheless, the act is not merely natural, but free. However, it is not the result of deliberation. For, to be deliberative, volition has to do with something like the means to an end, involving choice and known inferentially through a practical syllogism. "Happiness is a good and should be sought," however, is not a practical conclusion, but rather a practical principle.

[A doubt] But the above quotation from Augustine gives rise to a doubt. For if we cannot wish to be miserable, then I nill misery in an unqualified sense. And then this follows: "If I necessarily nill misery, then I necessarily will happiness." The implication is clear for two rea-

sons. First, because volition is no less related to happiness than nolition is to misery or evil. Second, because the act of nolition is only
possible in virtue of some volition, for—as Anselm said above—I nill
a thing only because I will something else. But a cause is more perfect
than its effect; hence I will happiness even more than I nill misery.

[Solution] I reply that neither do I will happiness necessarily, nor do
I nill misery necessarily. Hence, this does not follow: "I do not will to
be miserable, therefore I nill misery," or "I nill to be miserable." Nor
does this follow: "I cannot will to be miserable, therefore I must of
necessity nill to be miserable," for nilling is just as positive an act as
willing is, and one is as free as the other. Therefore, neither is elicited
necessarily as regards any object, and hence I can refuse to elicit an act
of nolition with respect to evil just as I can refuse to will what is good.
Nevertheless, when evil is shown to me I am able to elicit an act of
nolition only, just as when offered some good, if I elicit an act, it can
only be one of volition. And therefore, one ought to argue here in this
fashion: "I cannot will to be miserable, therefore I cannot hate to be
happy." But from this it does not follow that "therefore it is necessary
that I do not nill happiness," because no nilling is necessarily elicited
by the will, as was made clear above.

[Objection] But one may still persist in objecting that no power is
necessarily deprived of performing an act except in virtue of some determination it has towards the opposite act, just as frigidity is not taken
away from fire except by reason of its determination to heat, neither is
some color excluded from a surface except because it has been determined by another color. Therefore, in the will there is no impossibility of nilling happiness unless it be because it is necessarily determined towards the opposite act, namely, towards willing happiness.

[Answer] I reply: the reason an act of willing misery or nilling happiness is excluded from the will is that misery is not suited by nature to
be an object of volition any more than happiness is naturally suited to
be an object of nolition. Just as the eye is excluded from seeing black
through an act of vision produced by a dilation of the medium, because blackness is not suited to be such an object for that sort of visual
act, so too in the case at hand. Hence, the will is incapable of having
such an act with respect to such an object. I admit, then, that the will
is determined to will happiness and to nill misery to this extent that if
it should elicit some act with respect to these objects, it is limited and
has to elicit an act of willing in regard to happiness and an act of nilling as regards misery. Nevertheless, it is not absolutely determined to
elicit either the one act or the other.

As for the reason given to support the other view, namely, that the
will must necessarily love whatever possesses no aspect of evil or lack

of good, I say that this is false, for the will is free with respect to any act of volition or nolition, and no object necessitates it. Nevertheless, the will cannot hate or nill happiness, nor will misery. Hence, one ought to argue in this way. The will cannot recoil from that object in which there is no aspect of evil or defect of good; therefore, the will cannot hate or detest happiness—which is true. But it does not follow from this that it wills happiness necessarily.

If you object: If the will of necessity neither wills happiness nor hates or detests it, then what sort of act can the will have when the intellect shows it happiness? I grant that in most cases it will have an act of volition, but it does not necessarily have any act. Hence, when it is shown happiness, it can refrain from acting at all. In regard to any object, then, the will is able not to will or nill it, and can suspend itself from eliciting any act in particular with regard to this or that. And this is something anyone can experience in himself when someone proffers some good. Even if it is presented as something to be considered and willed, one can turn away from it and not elicit any act in its regard . . .

As for the second question [viz., is happiness the rationale for all willing?], it must be admitted that so far as its natural appetite goes, the will seeks whatever it seeks because of happiness, since according to its natural appetite it seeks only what perfects it. Whatever perfects its natural appetite, however, is a perfection ordered towards its ultimate perfection, and therefore, since by its natural appetite it seeks whatever it seeks as something ordered to the good of the seeker, which is happiness, it follows that whatever the will seeks in virtue of its natural appetite, it seeks because of happiness.

But if one asks the question about the will's appetite insofar as it is an elicited act, then I say that it is not necessary that the will seek whatever it seeks because of its ultimate end as a source of happiness. For one could fail to seek something because of happiness either negatively or contrariwise. Negatively, because one could seek something and not consider the ultimate end of happiness, and consequently at that moment the will would not seek it because of happiness, since one would not be thinking of it then. Similarly, one could seek something without ordering it to this other end, and therefore, it would not be sought because of happiness at that time. Also one could fail to seek something because of happiness in a contrary sense, if it were something contrarily opposed and not ordered to happiness. For someone having faith could conceive of happiness in particular insofar as it involves the enjoyment of the divine essence, shared by the three [divine] persons, and at the same time such a person could think of something, such as fornication, that is in no way ordered to this happiness. And if one continued to think of this fornication, which is in no way able to be ordered to happiness, one could seek such. And thus seeking fornication, one is not doing so as something ordered to happiness. Therefore, the will can seek something and not do so because of happiness.

8. SYNDERESIS AND CONSCIENCE
(*Ordinatio* II, dist. 39)

Questions are raised about conscience and synderesis in the thirty-ninth distinction [of Bk. II], and the first is this: Is synderesis in the will?

[Arguments Pro and Con]
It is:

[1] For synderesis always protests against evil, and to protest pertains to the will, therefore, etc.

[2] Furthermore, the will necessarily wills what is advantageous, according to Anselm. Hence, it also wills justice with equal necessity, for justice is a perfection suited to the will as much as is the advantageous. But that whereby man necessarily is inclined to justice is stipulated to be synderesis. Therefore, there is something in the will that is assumed to be synderesis.

[3] Also, the natural will necessarily wills that towards which it tends, according to *On the Trinity*, Bk. XIII, ch. 5, where Augustine says it is certain that all will happiness because of their natural inclination towards it. This would not be certain, however, unless the will necessarily willed it. Therefore what is willed naturally is willed necessarily. But justice is something naturally willed by the will, because it is as natural a perfection for the will as is the advantageous. Therefore, it is necessarily willed, and hence must be presumed to be in the will, for one assumes there is some principle there necessarily inclining the will towards justice. But such is synderesis, therefore, etc.

[4] Likewise, a lesser nature, such as the irrational, has a principle necessarily inclining it to what is suited to its nature according to reason. Hence, the will too will have a principle necessarily inclining it towards the justice it is suited by nature to have.

But the Master in the text [of this distinction] holds otherwise, citing Jerome's on Ezechiel to the effect that synderesis represents the higher portion of reason, and hence synderesis is in the intellect which is concerned with contemplation or the theoretical.

Secondly, I ask: Is conscience in the will?

[5] Paul, in his Epistle to the Hebrews, speaks of his "good conscience," but goodness pertains to the will, therefore conscience does likewise.

[6] If it were in the intellect, the more one knew, the more conscientious such a person would be; but the consequent is false, hence the antecedent is also false.

For the opposite view there is that text [Ecclesiastes 7:22], "In your heart you know you have spoken ill of someone." Also this is clear from the acts of conscience, which are to testify, accuse, and judge, all of which pertain to reason and intellect; therefore, etc.

[Body of the Question]

[The view of Henry of Ghent] Here it is claimed that the law of nature contains the natural principles for acting. Look it up in Henry's first *Quodlibet*. You will find it in q. 18.

[Refutation of Henry] Against this it is argued first in regard to synderesis that if this has an elicited act that necessarily tends towards good and resists evil, then there is nothing of this sort in the will. Hence, synderesis is not in the will. Proof of the assumption: In the first distinction of Bk. I it was shown that the will does not necessarily love and enjoy the end shown to it, neither is there any potency, power, or habit in the will that can be a principle of necessarily enjoying the end; therefore neither is there any necessary principle that requires it to will in accord with the practical principles derived from the nature of its end.

Furthermore, if there were some such potency, power, or part of the will, whereby it would tend to good and resist evil through an elicited act, then this would be the highest thing in the whole of the will, because it would have to do with its ultimate end, from which the first practical [moral] principles are derived. Hence, any lesser power or portion [of the soul] would be in the power of the will to such an extent that if it willed such, the lesser power or part would obey it and be moved accordingly. Therefore, it would prevent any sin in the will, because as this higher portion moved, so would the whole of the will move. For the whole would be moved in the way this higher portion moved it, and if the whole of the will were right, then there would be no sin.

Against his other position on conscience these arguments are brought to bear. First of all, conscience is not an appetitive habit generated by a single [appetitive] act, but is produced deductively by way of a practical syllogism; conscience represents an evident conclusion inferred from first practical principles and hence is not an acquired appetitive habit at all. It is also clear that it is not something innate, nor a part or power [of the soul].

Also, what is suited by nature to be produced by some [proper] cause cannot be caused by any other cause unless this virtually contains the perfection of [its proper] cause. Now, a habit of the will is suited by nature to be caused by an act of the will as its proper cause, and hence it cannot be caused by any other act unless this act contains virtually the act of the will. But an act of the intellect does not virtually contain the act of the will, because according to [Henry] the act of the will is more perfect than that of the intellect. Hence, no act of the intellect could cause such a bias in the will as would weigh upon it like a quasi-habit.

Also, either the will could refuse to receive such a weight, and then the intellect would be insufficient to cause it (for a sufficient cause is effective, above all when a suitable recipient is appropriately present), or it could not refuse to accept it. In such a case, then, given some actual consideration in the mind, the will could not throw off its weight, because reason must be no less effective in conserving than in causing this bias necessarily.

Also, either the will must needs act in accord with this weight put upon it, or not. If it has to act according to it, then it is not free, because the agent producing this weight is a natural cause, and hence its effect will be a natural form. Consequently, something acting necessarily in accord with this bias or inclination will not act freely, because it will no longer be in its power to act in this way or otherwise. But if it does not have to act accordingly—and it seems manifest it does not from that gloss upon the Apostle's letter to the Romans, "Whatever is against conscience," etc., which clearly indicates that sin is something committed contrary to one's conscience—then it follows that given a perfect conscience, the will can still will the opposite of what it dictates, and thus [according to Henry's view] one could never corrupt this habit by an act of the will, which seems absurd, assuming it is a habit of the will.

[Scotus' own opinion] I reply to these questions: If synderesis is assumed to be something having an elicited act that necessarily and at all times inclines one to act justly and resist sin, then since nothing of this sort is in the will, we cannot assume it to be there. Consequently, it is in the intellect, and it cannot be assumed to be anything other than that habitual knowledge of principles which is always right. For the intellect, in virtue of its own natural light, assents to these principles immediately on the strength of their terms. And then, insofar as it depends in part upon the intellect, the free will is apt by nature to choose in accord with these principles, though such a choice may fail to follow insofar as the other, the principal cause, freely chooses otherwise, because there is no necessitating cause involved here.

According to this line of reasoning, we can also assume that conscience is the habit of making proper practical conclusions, according to which a right choice of what is to be done is apt by nature to follow, and hence it can be called a stimulus to good, insofar as free choice, as a whole, has one partial cause [practical knowledge] disposing it correctly and a volition that is right and good will follow unless there is a defect in the other partial concurring cause needed for willing.

[Reply to the Initial Arguments]

[To 1] To the first argument I say that synderesis protests effectively because it shows what good ought to be willed, and in this it is an occasion for protesting against evil.

[To 2] To the other, I admit that the will, as a power to act freely, by its elicited act does not will necessarily what is advantageous any more than it necessarily wills what is just. But if this same power be considered insofar as it roots an inclination for the advantageous, and not insofar as it possesses an affection for justice (that is to say, if it were viewed as an appetite that is not free), then it would not have it in its power, as it does at present, to refrain from willing the advantageous, for then it would be only a natural intellective appetite just as the brute's is a natural sense appetite. I say, then, that Anselm's statement that one cannot not will the advantageous must be understood not of the volitional power as a whole, which at present can freely not will not only what is advantageous but also what is just; for it can freely not will this or that. Rather one must understand him to mean the volitional power insofar as it is the seat for the advantageous, i.e., as excluding liberty, and no act is elicited in us in this fashion. Hence, I have said in my solution to the question that synderesis is something having an elicited act.

[To 3] The same can be said in answer to the third objection. The natural will as tending necessarily to the object willed has no elicited act in its regard. It is only a certain inclination in such a nature towards the perfection most appropriate to it. This inclination necessarily exists in nature, even though an act in conformity with such an inclination and nature may not necessarily be elicited. For no act is elicited except by the free will, whether it be conformed or natural or whether it be difformed or against nature. And no matter how much it wills the opposite of that to which it is inclined, that inclination necessarily remains as long as the nature remains.

[To 4] To the last I say that this nature alone is free, having as it does a mode of action superior to any other created nature.

[To 5] As for the arguments for the second question, I say that the habits of the practical intellect are called good or bad because of suitability for the will, just as conversely the will can be said to be upright or bent down because of its suitability to a theoretical act, formally residing in the intellect, that is either right or not. Goodness, however, pertains to the will just as rectitude does to the intellect. But in a transferred sense "goodness" is more fittingly applied to the practical intellect than to the theoretical intellect.

[To 6] To the other, one can respond with that observation of the Philosopher, namely, in ch. 3 of Bk. VII of the *Ethics*, that even men under the influence of passion can recite verses from Empedocles, but such knowledge proves nothing. And thus one could concede that a person is conscientious insofar as he has practical knowledge in an unqualified sense, and is not just uttering words of that sort. And this it seems could be admitted particularly by that person whose opinion we have rejected, because according to him at the same moment of time that the will is bad, reason is blinded. And thus, even if conscience pertained to the will, one would have no less evidence of such; and hence, we have a common argument that applies to him as well as to the other side, and it can be solved in the aforesaid fashion.

PART III

Moral Goodness

9. THE NATURE OF MORAL GOODNESS
(*Ordinatio* I, dist. 17, nn. 62–67)

One could say that just as beauty is not some absolute quality in a beautiful body, but a combination of all that is in harmony with such a body (such as size, figure, and color), and a combination of all aspects (that pertain to all that is agreeable to such a body and are in harmony with one another), so the moral goodness of an act is a kind of decor it has, including a combination of due proportion to all to which it should be proportioned (such as the potency, the object, the end, the time, the place, and the manner), and this especially as right reason dictates should pertain to the act, so that we could say of all these things that it is their conformity to right reason that is essential. If this is given, then the act is good, and if this is not given, then—whatever else the act may have—it is not good. For whatever be the object, and howsoever the act has to do with it, if it is not performed according to right reason (for instance, if right reason did not actually dictate its performance), then the act is not good. The moral goodness of the act, then, consists mainly in its conformity with right reason—dictating fully just how all the circumstances should be that surround the act.

But this goodness, like any other relation, does not have an active principle all its own—especially since this respect follows from the nature of the related terms once they are given. For it is impossible that some act be given existence and right reason be present as its guide, without this conformity to right reason being also present in the act as a necessary consequence of the nature of the two related terms [i.e., the nature of the act and what right reason dictates of it]. But a relation that necessarily follows, given its terms, has no cause of its own other than the cause of its terms.

Therefore, so far as this accidental condition of the act, which is moral goodness, is concerned, there is no need that some habit play the role of a proper active principle, save insofar as it functions as a cause of the substance of an act, suited by nature to agree completely with the dictate of prudence: and some habit in virtue of its nature as a habit inclines one to this act in itself, and from this—as a consequence—it inclines the agent to an act in conformity to right reason, if right reason is at work in the agent.

And what was said of moral goodness as an act, applies analogously to the habit in question, that is to say, moral virtue does not add to the substance of the habit—insofar as that habit is a form in the category of quality—anything except this habitual conformity to right reason. For the same habit in nature, which would be generated by elicited acts of abstinence for an erroneous reason in the person eliciting such, if the habit remained after the error of judgment was corrected by right reason, would become the virtue of abstinence, whereas before that same habit was not a virtuous habit as long as the right reason for abstaining was missing. Nothing changed so far as the habit itself was concerned, but now it is conjoined with prudence, whereas before it was not.

"Joined with prudence," then, makes the habit (as a form in the category of quality) a virtue when that habit is by nature apt to be conformed to prudence—and so nothing else in the way of an absolute entity allows one to call one habit "moral virtue" and another habit of the same nature "not a moral virtue" except that prudence is missing from the latter. Consequently, there can be no other causality involved in the case of virtue than is involved in causing such a natural quality, except that what is implied by "conjoined with prudence" is suited by nature to be a second cause—directed by prudence, as it were—with respect to the common effect of both. But where it is without prudence, it can not be a second cause with respect to the same effect (just as vision in a mad person cannot be a free power by participation, because such a one has not the use of the will, which is a free potency by its essence—but in a sane person, vision has the use of free potency by participation and is as it were a second cause together with the will). But still, when it is a second cause with regard to prudence, the proper causality—pertaining to it in the order of causation—derives precisely from this that it is such a form or certain sort of quality by nature, but not because of a conformity or union with prudence, because although a second cause is conjoined to the first, so that it acts differently than it does without prudence, nevertheless the virtue does not get its proper active principle from such a union, but from the absolute nature [of its cause].

10. THE SOURCE OF MORAL GOODNESS
(*Quodlibet*, q. 18)

[Moral goodness] The moral goodness of an act consists in its having all that the agent's right reason declares must pertain to the act or the agent in acting.

This description is explained as follows: Just as the primary goodness of a being, called "essential" and consisting in the integrity and perfection of the being itself, implies positively that there is no imperfection, so that all lack or diminution of perfection is excluded, so the being's secondary goodness, which is something over and above, or "accidental," consists in its being perfectly suited to or in complete harmony with something else—something which ought to have it or which it ought to have. And these two suitabilities are commonly connected. As an example of the first, health is said to be good for man because it suits him. [As an example of the second] food is called good because it has an appropriate taste. Augustine gives an example of both. "Health without pain or fatigue is good," he says. This refers to the first type of suitability, since health is good for man because it suits him. Then Augustine adds: "Good is the face of a man with regular features, a cheerful expression, and a glowing color." This is an instance of the second, because here the face is called good for having what is appropriate to it.

There is a difference between the two. What suits someone is said to be good for him, that is, for him it is a good or a perfection, but we do not speak of it as being derivatively or actually good in itself. That to which something is appropriate, on the other hand, is called good denominatively because it has what is suited to it. In the first case, the form takes its name from the subject in which it is. As the soul is called "human," so something is called "good for man" because it is a human good. In the second case, the subject gets its designation from the form. Thus we say a man is good because of some good he has.

Now, an act by nature is apt to be in agreement with its agent as well as to have something suited to itself. On both counts, then, it can be called "good" with a goodness that is accidental. This is true in general of a natural act as well, so that this goodness, which consists in having what is appropriate to it, is not only an accidental, but also a natural, goodness.

And either this suitability stems from the nature of the terms or, if it must generally be traced back to the judgment of some intellect (since the intellect is the measure of suitability), this judgment will be that of the intellect which is the rule of the whole of nature, viz., the divine intellect. Indeed this intellect, just as it knows perfectly every being, so it knows perfectly the harmony or disagreement of one thing with another.

Furthermore, some agents without intellect and will neither judge nor can judge what is appropriate to their acts. In such a case, what is suitable is determined by natural causes alone, and they incline the agent to act. Or if in addition there be the judgment of some mind and the movement of some will, it would be that of God alone as universal director and mover of the whole of nature. Now, the goodness in the act of an agent without intellect and will is merely natural.

Over and above this general judgment [of God] about the suitability of the action (which concerns alike agents that act with and those that act without knowledge), a general judgment is involved in the case of agents with an intrinsic knowledge of their actions. Those with sense knowledge alone somehow apprehend the suitability of the object of their action. But whether or not they judge the action appropriate, the goodness of the action does not transcend the natural. Others act by virtue of intellectual knowledge, which alone is able to pass judgment, properly speaking, upon the appropriateness of the action. Such agents are suited by nature to have an intrinsic rule of rectitude for their actions. Only they can have an act whose goodness is moral.

But for this it is not enough that the agent have the ability to adjudicate the appropriateness of his acts. He must actually pass judgment upon the act and carry it out in accord with that judgment. If someone is in error and still acts in accord with the correct judgment of another, he is not acting rightly, for by his own knowledge he was meant to regulate his actions, and in this case he is acting not in accord with it but against it, and hence he does not act rightly. Similarly, such an agent elicits the sort of act that lies in his power. Now, he has in his power the sort of act he deliberately elicits, for the power of free choice consists either formally or concomitantly in knowledge and election. And so it appears clear how the moral goodness of the act lies in its suitability judged according to the agent's right reason.

We explain the added qualification "all that must pertain to the act" in this way: Every judgment begins with something certain. Now, the first judgment about the appropriateness cannot presuppose some knowledge determined by another intellect; otherwise it would not be first. Hence it presupposes something certain but judged by this intellect, namely, the nature of the agent and the power by which he acts, together with the essential notion of the act. If these three notions are given, no other knowledge is needed to judge whether or not this particular act is suited to this agent and this faculty. For instance, if someone knows what man is, what his intellectual powers are, and what an act of understanding is, then it is clear to him that it befits man to understand with his intellect. Since he knows what it means to attain knowledge, it would also be clear to him what it is not appropriate for his mind to reach. Similarly, it is evident from the notions of the nature, the potency, and the act why understanding does not befit the brute, or rather why it is not compatible with his nature. For this first judgment, based precisely on the nature of the agent, the operative power, and the act, reveals not something just ill-matched, i.e., some unbecoming or disorderly connection, but a simple inconsistency, i.e., the absolute impossibility of any such union.

What is more, from these three notions one can conclude what object is appropriate to a given act of a certain agent. Take the act of eating, for example. Food capable of restoring what man has lost would be its appropriate object, whereas a stone or something nourishing for animals but not for man would not be.

This delimitation introduced by the object first brings the act under the generic heading of moral. Not that the nature of its object determines its moral species; rather it opens it to further moral determination, for when an act has an appropriate object, it is capable of further moral specification in view of the circumstances in which it is performed. That is why an act is said to receive its generic goodness from its object, for just as genus is potential with respect to differences, so the goodness derived from its object first puts it into the generic class of moral acts. Only goodness of nature is presupposed. And once it has generic goodness, the way is open to all the additional moral specifications.

The procedure for determining specific goodness, called "goodness from circumstances," is as follows:

The first goodness comes, it seems, from the circumstance of the end, for given the nature of the agent, of the action, and of the object, one immediately concludes that such an action ought to be performed by this agent for such an end, and that it ought to be chosen and wanted for the sake of such an end. This circumstance is characteristic not precisely of the act as actually performed or not, but rather of the act as willed and as related to this end by an act of the will. Indeed, the decision to do something for a worthy purpose is no less good when the external act that ensues fails to achieve that end than when it succeeds.

The next circumstance seems to be the manner in which the action is performed. How it ought to be performed we infer from all or from some of the aforesaid considerations.

Next comes our conclusion regarding the appropriate time. For a given action done for such a purpose and in such a manner is not always befitting such an agent; it is appropriate only when the act can be directed to or can attain such an end.

Last of all is the circumstance of place. Indeed there are many acts with complete moral goodness in which place plays no part.

It is clear, then, how many conditions right reason sets down, for according to the description given above, to be perfectly good, an act must be faultless on all counts. Hence Dionysius declares: "Good requires that everything about the act be right, whereas evil stems from any single defect." "Everything," he explains, includes all the circumstances.

Objection: Circumstances are relations, whereas good is a quality, according to the *Ethics*; virtue is also a quality, according to the *Categories*.

I answer: According to the *Physics*: "All virtue and malice are relative." That acts are good or virtuous, therefore, implies one or several relations. But like "healthy" or "beautiful," "good" and "virtuous" are spoken of, and predicated, as qualities, and this commonly happens with the fourth type of quality.

[Moral badness] In view of the second part of the citation from Dionysius we ought to look into the source of moral badness in an act.

Badness can be opposed to goodness in an act either privatively or as its contrary. Man is said to be bad in this second sense if he has some vice, for though this implies a privation of a perfection that should be there, a vice is certainly a positive habit. In the other sense, man is said to be bad privatively if he lacks the goodness he ought to have, even if he does not have the contrary vice or vicious habit.

We find this distinction in Boethius where he explains the first characteristic of quality: "They say justice is not contrary to injustice, for they think injustice is a privation and not a contrary state." And he adds in refutation: "Many habits are expressed in privative terms such as 'illiberality' and 'imprudence.' These would never be contrasted with virtues, which are habits, if they themselves were not habits."

Reason also justifies this distinction. For it can happen that an act is performed under circumstances that are not all they should be [to make the act morally good], yet neither are they so improper that they ought not to be there—for instance, when an action is neither directed to an appropriate end nor directed to an inappropriate one. In such a case the act is bad only privatively, not contrarily, as it would be if it were performed for some unlawful purpose. And from many similar acts, a corresponding habit would arise, namely, one whose badness is privative rather than a positive contrary. For example, to give alms, not for a good end, such as the love of God or to help one's neighbor, but not for a bad end either, such as out of vainglory or to hurt someone, is an act of this sort that is privatively, not contrarily, bad.

It is to such privative badness that Dionysius refers when he states that the absence of any one of the required circumstances suffices to render the act bad. But for it to be bad contrarily there must be some positive circumstance present that involves some deformity.

Briefly, then, just as moral goodness is integral suitability, so moral badness is unsuitability. Privative badness is a lack of suitability, i.e., the absence of what ought to be there, whereas badness as the contrary of goodness is unsuitability as a contrary state, i.e., as some condition that is incompatible with suitability.

[Corollary] From what has been said this corollary follows. The same fundamental act can have a manifold moral goodness. It is not just that it is correct in all its circumstances (something which invests the act not with many goodnesses but with one integral goodness), but it can also have at the same time all that is needed for two distinct virtues, and thus be directed to several ends according to different dictates of perfect prudence. For example, I go to church to fulfill an obligation in justice, because of obedience or some vow. And I also go out of charity or love of God, to pray or worship him. And I also go out of fraternal charity to edify my neighbor. In short, the more morally good motives there are, the better the act is. This is true whether the goodness in question be moral goodness alone or that additional goodness we call meritorious.

In like fashion, badness multiplies if one and the same act violates several dictates of reason.

11. DEGREES OF MORAL GOODNESS AND BADNESS
(*Ordinatio* II, dist 7, nn. 28–39)

I say that besides volition's natural goodness, which pertains to it as something positive and which is characteristic of any positive thing according to the grade of entity it has (the more the entity, the more the goodness; the less the entity, the less the goodness)—in addition to this there is a threefold moral goodness according to its grade. The first of these is generic goodness; the second goodness could be called virtuous or circumstantial goodness; the third, meritorious or gratuitous goodness or goodness as ordered to a reward by reason of the divine acceptance.

The first pertains to volition because the object willed is something appropriate to this act, not merely on natural grounds, as sunlight is suited to an act of vision, but according to the dictates of right reason. This is the first moral goodness, and hence it can be called "generic" because it is as it were the material basis for all further goodness in the category of mores. For an act tending towards the object is formable, as it were, through whatever other moral circumstances there are and thus is quasi-potential—not as something lying completely outside the category of the moral (as would be an [unfree] act in the category of nature), but within the moral category, because it already has something of that genus, namely, an object appropriate to this act [of the will].

The second goodness pertains to volition on this score that the act is elicited by the will under such circumstances as right reason approves of in full. For according to Dionysius in *The Divine Names*: "Good requires that everything about the act be right." This is specific moral goodness, so to say, because it has all the moral differences that delimit or specify generic goodness.

The third goodness pertains to the act on this ground that, presupposing the aforesaid twofold goodness, the act is elicited in conformity with the principle or source of merit, which is grace or charity, or in accord with the inclination of charity.

An example of the first goodness would be to give alms; an instance of the second would be to give alms of one's own means to a needy pauper in the proper place and for the love of God. An example of the third would be to perform the aforesaid act not only because of a natural inclination (as a person in the state of innocence might have done, or as perhaps even now an unrepentant sinner moved by natural affection for his neighbor might do), but because of that charity that makes one a friend of God, insofar as God views one's works with favor.

Now, this triple goodness is so ordered that the first is presupposed by the second, but not vice versa; and the second by the third, but not the other way round.

Opposed to this threefold goodness is a threefold badness. The first is generic, namely, when an act with only the natural goodness [of freedom] that would put it into the moral order is bad because its object is inappropriate, for instance, an act of hatred directed to God. The second is badness that stems from some circumstance that makes the act inordinate, even though it is directed towards an object right reason approves of. The third is the badness that results in demerit.

Each form of badness can occur either as a contrary or as a privation of its corresponding goodness. As a privation, it is merely the lack of such goodness. As a contrary, it has in addition to this absence something that is positively inconsistent with this goodness. Boethius makes this distinction clear in the chapter "On Quality" in his work *On the Categories*, where he deals with justice. But where generic badness is concerned, badness taken contrarily and privatively are convertible in the sense of being extentionally equivalent. Hence there is no middle ground between lacking goodness and having goodness, so that generic goodness and badness are immediate contraries. And the reason why is that there can be no act that is not directed to some object, and this object has to be either appropriate or inappropriate to the act in question. And so a worthy object makes the act necessarily good generically, whereas an unworthy object makes it generically bad.

But the privative and contrary forms of badness understood in the second way are not equivalent. For some act can lack some circumstance needed for it to be virtuous and yet not be performed in such a way as to become vicious. For example, if someone gives alms to the poor without a good reason, because he does it without considering why he does it, or gives alms when the circumstances required to make it virtuous are not present, such an act is not morally good or virtuous because of the circumstances, and yet it is not contrarily bad, since it is not done for an unworthy purpose such as would be the case where a person gave alms to the poor out of vainglory or for some other unbecoming reason.

The contrary and privative forms of the third type of badness are not extentionally equivalent either, because an act can be privatively bad in the sense that it does not proceed from grace, and nevertheless it need not be demeritorious. This is clear from what was said of the second type, since an act that is only morally good is not meritorious, and nevertheless not every such act is demeritorious. And so it seems there can be indifferent acts in the second way as well as in this third way—acts, namely, which are bad privatively though not contrarily, because they are indifferent. And we shall speak about this indifference elsewhere [namely, in dist. 41]. But it is not only because of its neutrality at the second level that an act is neither good nor bad in the third way, but it could have neither merit nor demerit insofar as these are contraries, because of the state the agent is in—for instance, someone in a state of innocence, without grace, could have acted rightly, and such an act would have been perfectly good in the second way, but not in the third, because the person did not have the principle of meriting, and nevertheless such a one would not be contrarily bad.

But perhaps in our present state there is no act that is neutral in the third way, except in the one case where an act is good by reason of some circumstance to which [supernatural grace or] charity does not incline one. The reason is that everyone is either in a state of grace or in a state of sin. If one is in the state of grace and performs an act that is morally good in the second way [i.e., circumstantially], then grace inclines one to do this, and thus it is meritorious. On the other hand, if the act is morally bad in the second way, it is clearly demeritorious (for the prior badness always includes the second, but not the converse, and the second implies the third, but not vice versa). But if a bad person has an act that is bad in the second way, such a one sins by such an act. But if a bad person has an act that is good in the second way, such a one is neither good nor bad in the third way, and therefore is neutral [as to merit and demerit], but is not neutral speaking of the second type [of moral goodness].

12. DOES THE END ALONE JUSTIFY ACTIONS?
(*Ordinatio* II, dist. 40)

As for the fortieth distinction [of Bk. II], I ask: Is every act good by reason of its end?

[Arguments Pro and Con]

For the affirmative there is Augustine's citation in the text [of Peter Lombard] that "it is the intention that makes the work good."

Furthermore, an act of understanding is true by reason of a principle; but the end here functions as a principle does there.

To the contrary, there is Augustine's statement in his work *Against Lying*, also cited in the text [of Peter Lombard] to the effect that there are many acts that cannot be good even though they are done for a good end.

[Body of the Question]

I reply that we must first look at natural goodness and then at moral goodness.

[Natural goodness] As for the first, I say that natural goodness is like beauty of body, which results from a combination of all that is internally harmonious and is becoming to the body, such as size, color, and figure (as Augustine wants to say of a good face in Bk. VIII of *The Trinity*: "Good is the face of a man with regular features, a cheerful expression, and a glowing color"). And this natural goodness is not that which is coextensive with being, but that which is opposed to evil and is a second perfection of a thing, in which we find united all that is becoming to it and is internally harmonious. And where all these concur there is perfect goodness according to that statement of Dionysius: "The good stems from a cause that is perfect and whole." Should there be a nature in which all those things are missing which it ought to have, then it would be completely bad. If only certain things are lacking, it is bad but not completely so, like a body in which there is both beauty and ugliness. Now, an action is naturally suited to be in accord with its efficient cause, its object, its purpose, and its form. It is naturally good when it has all that becomes it insofar as these things are concerned that are suited by nature to concur in constituting it naturally.

[Moral goodness] As for the second, I say that the goodness of a moral act is a combination of all that becomes the act, not in an absolute sense, as if it were constitutive of its very nature as an act, but in the sense that according to right reason it is becoming to the act. Now, since right reason dictates that an act agree with a certain object and do so in a specific way—and so with the other circumstances— complete goodness is not the result of the intention alone. Now, the first reason for its goodness is its appropriateness to the agent in question, namely, because the act is free it is said to be moral. And this is something a morally good and a morally bad act have in common, for if an act is not from the will, then it is neither praiseworthy nor reprehensible.

The second condition has to do with the object. If this is something appropriate, then the act is good generically, because it is still in- different to the further aspects of goodness that arise because of the special circumstances, just as the genus is indifferent with respect to the many differences.

After this the first circumstance is that of the end itself. But this does not suffice apart from the other circumstances, such as the cir- cumstance of its form, for example, that it take place in a becoming fashion, a point pertaining to the fourth circumstance, after which come the more extrinsic circumstances, such as time and place and the like. It is clear, therefore, that the goodness of the purpose alone, even when intended according to right reason, does not suffice to make the act good, but the other circumstances according to the aforesaid order are required that goodness be there.

[Reply to the Initial Arguments]

How the text from Augustine should be interpreted is clear from his citations for the opposite, for if the end is the main condition for goodness in the act, it is not simply sufficient in an unqualified sense. In like fashion, speaking of the goodness of merit, which adds some- thing to moral goodness, we can say this derives principally from the end, since what meritorious goodness adds to complete moral goodness arises from the appropriate way the act is related to the end. This appropriate relationship stems from the fact that the act is elicited by charity. One can explain the authorities cited in this way, namely, meritorious goodness does stem from the end.

As for the second, I say that so far as an act of understanding goes, the effective cause, inasmuch as it is a function of the intellect or a habit of the intellect, is a cause that acts naturally [and not freely]. Neither can it act otherwise than the object allows, and that is why it always acts correctly. But the will does not always act in such a way that it is conformed to the object, because it is a free agent and not a natural cause. Consequently, when there is rectitude on the part of the principal portion of the moving cause [which is the will] the whole action becomes righteous, but this is not something that is here because of the intention.

As for the third objection, I say that while this one goodness does unite in itself all that is becoming to the act, it does not stem from any one thing, any more than in the case of bodily beauty.

13. MORALLY INDIFFERENT ACTS
(*Ordinatio* II, dist. 41)

As for the forty-first distinction [of Bk. II], this question is raised: Could any act of ours be indifferent?

[Arguments Pro and Con]

For the negative: between possession and privation there is no medium; good and evil are privatively opposed; therefore, etc. The major is evident from Bk. V of the *Metaphysics*, where the point is made that privative opposites are contradictorily opposed in something which is suited by nature to have one of them. But between contradictories there is no medium, according to Bk. IV of the *Metaphysics*.

Furthermore, habits result from actions. If there were some midpoint between good and evil, there would be some habit that is neither good nor evil.

To the contrary is Ambrose's statement cited in the text [of Peter Lombard]: "It is your motive which gives the name to your work." If there were no act that was of itself indifferent, it could not become good *per se* by one act and bad *per se* by another.

[Body of the Question]

[St. Bonaventure's opinion] Here it is claimed that while no particular act is indifferent, acts in general are indifferent. Look it up in Bonaventure.

[Scotus' own view] One could say that the case is different where moral goodness or evil and where meritorious good or demeritorious evil are concerned.

[Moral goodness] As for the first type of goodness or badness, comparing it to a natural act, one could, it seems, find an indifferent act, namely, when—in relation to all its causes—it is of a determinate species in the category of nature, it could still be indifferently related to moral goodness or evil. This is proved first from the Philosopher in II *Ethics*: "The habit of justice is not produced by doing what the just do, but by doing such things in the way that the just do them." The first sort of act is not morally good, because it does not proceed from virtue. The same would hold even for acts elicited after virtue is acquired, for just because the will possesses a virtue this does not mean it must necessarily use it at all times, but it may be used only when passion becomes so violent that it would subvert reason if one did not make use of the virtue.

[Meritorious goodness] Speaking of this second type of goodness or evil, it seems there could also be something in between a good and a bad act. For given the existence of moral goodness, as was pointed out in the preceding question, merit seems to be a relationship to an end that ought to be there, a relationship that stems from the existence of charity in the agent. Now, an act can be referred through charity to its end in three ways: (1) Actually, as is the case where one is actually thinking of the end and loving it. (2) Virtually, which is the case when from a knowledge and love of the end one has come to will this means to that end—for example, from a knowledge and love of God in the higher portion of the soul, the lower portion considers doing some act, for instance, of penance, and afterwards carries out such an act voluntarily, but does not refer it to the end because at that time one is not actually thinking of or loving the end. (3) Habitually—for instance, every act, able to be referred to the end so long as charity (which is the basis for the referral) remains, may be said to be habitually referred to the end.

Also there are three ways in which we may say an act is not referred to its end. [4] One would be in an absolutely negative way, because it is not referred either actually or virtually. [5] Another way is privatively, because it is not suited by nature to be referred, as would be the case with a venial sin, for though it could coexist with charity, it is not suited by nature to be referred to such an end by means of charity. [6] A third way would be contrarily, namely, where the act destroys the principle of reference, namely, charity, as would be the case where the act is mortally sinful.

In the last two cases, namely, of venial and mortal sin, it is certain that the act in question is evil. As for the first two cases [of actual and virtual reference], it is certain that the first is meritorious and sufficiently probable that the second is also. As for the two middle types, namely, where the act is referred to the end only habitually or not at all, it is doubtful whether such an act is meritorious or venially sinful (for it cannot be mortally sinful) or whether such an act is just indifferent. If one claims it is either of the first two alternatives, it would seem that a man continually in the state of grace would either continually merit or continually sin either mortally or at least venially, since there are many such acts which he elicits continually and which are neither actually nor virtually referred in the aforesaid way.

For that reason it seems probable that we should assume such acts to be indifferent because they do not seem to be sufficiently malicious to be venial sins, since it is possible that there is nothing disorderly about them to make them sins. For man is not bound, either under pain of mortal sin or under pain of the lesser venial sin, to always refer his action to God either actually or virtually, because God does not oblige us to do this. But neither does there seem to be sufficient goodness in these acts for them to be meritorious, since it seems unlikely that any relation less than a virtual reference would suffice for merit.

There are many indifferent acts, therefore, which are such not merely because of the being they have as a specific nature, but also according to the being they have as something moral. And there are also acts that are indifferent as regards the goodness that is meritorious or the evil that is demeritorious, for one individual good can be of this sort and another of that sort. Many individual elicited acts can also be indifferent, because they are neither the meritorious sort nor the other, and we are not speaking here of nonhuman acts, such as stroking the beard or brushing off a bit of straw and suchlike, acts which originate with the sense imagination and not from any free impulse, for freely elicited acts may also be indifferent.

[Reply to the Initial Arguments]

As for the first argument, I say that where moral goodness and badness or meritorious goodness and demeritorious badness are concerned, you do not have the privative opposition between acts. For an act is not evil solely because it lacks this or that goodness, but only if it lacks some goodness that it should have. Not every act, however, is required to have such moral or meritorious goodness.

As for the other, I grant that similar acts give rise to a corresponding habit, and that many indifferent acts can produce a habit that inclines one to perform similar indifferent actions; but it does not incline one to them insofar as they are either good or bad, just as it in itself is neither good nor bad, as it was not produced by acts that were good or bad. And so this incongruity that is brought up turns out to be no inconvenience at all, but a truth that must be admitted.

14. IS MORAL GOODNESS CONFORMITY TO GOD'S WILL?
(*Ordinatio* I, dist. 48)

In regard to dist. 48 [of Bk. I], I ask whether the human will, or more generally, whether a created will is morally good whenever it is conformed to the uncreated will.

[Arguments Pro and Con]
That it is:
When the created intellect is conformed to the uncreated intellect it possesses truth. It is the same, then, where the created will is concerned. It is good when it is conformed to the uncreated will.
To the contrary:
The Jews willed that Christ suffer and die, something which Christ also willed; and still they sinned ("Forgive them, Father," he said, "for they know not what they do"); therefore, etc.

[To the Question]
I reply: according to Dionysius *On the Divine Names*, ch. 4, good stems from a cause that is good in every respect, and the Philosopher in Bk. II of the *Ethics* indicates that if an act is to be morally good, it must be so in all its circumstances. A defect in any one suffices to make the act morally bad.

Suppose the created intellect is in substance conformed to the divine will, be this conformity one of substance together with any one circumstance or one involving all circumstances having a bearing on moral goodness. Even if the created will were conformed in every respect, so that the two wills willed the same thing and in the same manner, and so with all the other circumstances, the created will would still not have to be good in the way the uncreated will is good, because where the agents are basically different, the circumstances proper to their respective actions are not the same. A created will is not suited to love a good as intensely as does the uncreated will. There is indeed a great difference in the intensity of the acts whereby a created and an uncreated agent regard an object. And whatever is to be said of a conformity in every respect between a created and an uncreated will, at least the goodness of act and object is not sufficient conformity, because it still allows for possible difformity in regard to the other circumstances required for the goodness of an act of the will.

[Reply to the Initial Argument]

As for the argument for the opposite view, I say the situation is not similar, for truth of intellect depends solely on the object's being such as it is understood to be. Goodness, however, depends not solely on the object, but on all the other circumstances as well, particularly upon the end. For that reason, notice, all our volition is especially oriented towards that ultimate end which is both *Alpha and Omega, beginning and end*, to whom *be all honor and glory, world without end.* Amen.

PART IV

God and the Moral Law

15. GOD'S JUSTICE
(*Ordinatio* IV, dist. 46)

Because the forty-sixth distinction [of Bk. IV] treats of how both justice and the mercy of God concur in the punishment of the evildoers, therefore four questions are raised here: first, whether there is justice in God; second, whether there is mercy in God; third, whether in God justice is distinct from mercy; and fourth, whether in his punishment of evildoers justice and mercy concur on God's part.

[Arguments Pro and Con]
To the first question it is argued that there is no justice in God:

[Arg. 1] According to Bk. V of the *Ethics*, ch. 6, there is no justice where lord and servant are concerned, because of a lack of equality. All the more so is this true of the God-creature relationship or the creature-God relationship, since what Paul says in 1 Corinthians 4:[7]: "Name something you have not received," could be uttered even more forcefully by God.

[Arg. 2] Furthermore, Bk. X of the *Ethics* [ch. 8] says it is tasteless and injudicious to praise the separate substances [or gods] for acts of virtue, particularly justice. And [Aristotle] confirms this using an analogous argument about why it is meaningless to speak of their temperance and, by the same token, to speak of their justice.

[Arg. 3] Furthermore, justice inclines a person to render others what is their due; but God is a debtor to no one.

To the contrary is that passage from Psalm [48:11]: "Of justice your right hand is full."

[Body of the Question]

[Definition of justice] To begin here with a definition of justice: Anselm in his *De veritate* gives the most general notion: "Justice is rectitude of will *served for its own sake.*" The Philosopher in V *Ethics* makes this specific with the addition: "it has to do with another."

It is clear that God has justice in both senses: the first, because he has rectitude of will—indeed, a will that cannot be gainsaid, because it is the first rule or norm, and is "served for its own sake." Not that "served" here implies any submission or acceptance on the part of the one ob*serving* it, but rather it is "served for its own sake" in the sense that it is always spontaneously pre*served*. It is clear he also has justice in the second sense, because he is upright to others, and therefore, in all his actions towards others there is rectitude.

[Justice towards another] This second sort of justice is subdivided, because either [a] it is quasi-universal with respect to others, for instance, to the legislator and to the law, insofar as the law is a certain general regulation determined by the legislator, and some call this "legal justice"; or [b] it is particular, for instance, uprightness to another in some specific aspect pertaining to law.

And this second is subdivided, because it can be toward another in an unqualified sense, or to oneself as quasi-other. (This second member of the division is illustrated from what was said about penance, namely, that this sort of punitive justice regards not only others in an unqualified sense, but also oneself as quasi-other, because it is granted to individual persons, as ministers of the judge [God], to punish themselves as guilty.)

Now, the first of these, namely, legal justice, could be postulated of God if there were some other law antecedent to any decision of his will, with which "law and its legislator" as other his own will could rightly agree. Now, there is indeed this law, "God should be loved"— if one ought to call it a "law" rather than a practical principle of law; and in any case it is a practical truth that is prior to any decision on the part of the divine will. As for particular justice, however, it would be the second sort that is in him, namely, that which has to do with oneself as quasi-other, since his will is determined by its very rectitude to will what is becoming to his goodness. And this is a quasi-rendering to himself and his goodness what is due to it as other—if one could call such justice "particular," because it is in some way universal, at least virtually.

And these two kinds of justice, namely, legal justice and particular justice to oneself as quasi-other, are the same thing, as it were, in God, because they are identical with the rectitude of the divine will with respect to his goodness.

[Commutative and distributive justice] If one speaks about the other type of particular justice, which has to do simply with neighbor, this is divided into commutative and distributive; and in this way we distinguish justice in ourselves, as is clear from V *Ethics*. In distributive justice equality of proportion is required; in commutative justice, some require quantitative equality, not only proportional equity. These are explained in that book.

As to whether these are in God, commutative justice properly speaking has to do with punishment and reward, namely, in exchange for merits, as it were, rewards are rendered, and for sins punishments. Distributive justice has to do with natures and their additional perfections, which are bestowed on them, as it were, in proportion to their essential perfection. Just as distributive justice in our republic bestows on persons of various gradated stations in life the goods that pertain to their station, so too in the hierarchy of nature as a whole our princely God distributes to the more noble natures those greater perfections suited to them, whereas the less noble natures receive lesser perfections.

Now, the first of these [i.e., commutative justice] cannot be in God in an unqualified sense where creatures are concerned, since there is no simple equality there, but there can be something akin to it such as obtains between a master and a servant. For a generous or liberal master may fittingly give a greater reward than the servant could merit, and still there could be some proportionality as to what is given in exchange, so that if the servant does what he should, he is rewarded accordingly. In the same way, such a master may punish delinquent servants to a lesser degree than they merit.

But the second [viz., distributive justice] could be present in God in an unqualified sense, because he could give natures the perfections that are their due or are suited to their degree of excellence.

Thus the whole definition of justice, then, insofar as it is applicable to God, could be reduced to two sorts, the first of which would be called rectitude of will with respect to what is due to divine goodness; the other, rectitude of will with respect to what the exigencies of the creature demand. And we find this distinction in Anslem's *Proslogion*, ch. 10, where he says of God: "When you punish the wicked, it is just, because punishment corresponds to their merits"—so far as the second member goes. He adds immediately: "When you spare the wicked, however, it is just, not because it corresponds to their merits, but because it befits your goodness." This last clause refers to the first member of the division [i.e., what is due to the divine goodness]. And such is the distinction between these two kinds of justice that God cannot operate against or beyond the first justice [viz., what is due to his goodness], but he can go beyond what the second requires, but not in all matters, for he cannot damn the just or the blessed.

[Objections to this view] One may object that in God the first sort of justice cannot be other than the second sort, because then there would be one that is the rule, namely, the first sort of justice, and an-other that is regulated, namely, the second sort of justice; but in the divine will there cannot be rectitude that is the result of regulation, and this is proved as follows. In us the same virtue inclines us to our proper end and to those things which are means to that end precisely qua means; therefore, if that virtue which inclines us to our end were simply perfect, it would incline us to the means to that end in a simple unqualified manner, as is clear from the way the virtue of charity func-tions in the case of the blessed in heaven. Now, the first sort of divine justice is simply perfect; therefore, in the divine will nothing more is required.

However, what is said about the inability of the divine will at times to act against the second sort of justice does not seem probable, for whatever does not include a contradiction, the divine will could do, and therefore could will. But it could not will something that it could not will rightly, because God's will is the first rule or regulation; there-fore, whatever does not include a contradiction, God can will and do so rightly, and therefore, he could act contrary to this second justice.

Perhaps some would concede the first of these points, namely, that in God there is not a double justice, but only one, which has, how-ever, two different effects, as it were, namely, insofar as God could will some things as due to his goodness and will other things in accord with the exigencies of the creature.

However, it seems clear that the second argument implies that to whatever the first justice inclines the divine will the second justice does likewise, since it inclines that will definitely after the manner of nature [and hence not freely]; thus it leaves no room for the possibility of the will acting against or beyond what the second justice requires, and so there will be no distinction between those matters where the will could act beyond justice and those where it could not.

[Scotus' own view] Not by way of disparaging these distinctions, I reply with greater brevity to the question that in God there is but one justice, both conceptually and in reality, although by stretching the meaning of "justice" one could say that in addition to the aforesaid justice there is some justice, or rather something just, about the way he deals with creatures.

To explain the first: justice properly speaking represents a habitual state of rectitude of will, and hence as a habit it inclines one in a quasi-natural manner to another or to oneself as quasi-other. Now, the divine will does not have any rectitude that would incline it deterministically to anything other than its own goodness as a quasi-other (recall that the divine will is related to any other object only contingently, so that as will it has the capacity to will either this or its opposite). From this it follows that there is no justice in God except that which inclines him to render to his own goodness what is its due.

Thus there is also but one act, conceptually and in reality, to which this habit of justice inclines this will. Nevertheless this will-act, in terms of what follows from it, has to do with many secondary objects in the same way as we explained (in Bk. I, dist. 35) that the divine intellect, in addition to its one primary object and act, regards a multiplicity of secondary objects. There is a difference, however, between the intellect there and the will here, because the divine intellect of necessity regards these secondary objects, whereas here the will regards its secondary objects only in a contingent manner. And hence not only is it the case that both there and here neither act depends upon its respective secondary objects, but here the will is not necessarily related to its secondary objects in the way the intellect necessarily knows its secondary objects.

But if we wish to distinguish this one real will-act into many conceptually distinct acts, just as there we distinguish one real intellection into many conceptually distinct acts of knowledge insofar as it has to do with a multiplicity of secondary objects, I say that where the will-act is concerned one cannot even speak of conceptually quasi-distinct "justices." In fact we cannot even speak of one justice as regards these multiple secondary objects, howsoever that justice might be distinct or indistinct. The reason is that a habit inclines after the manner of nature and thus limits the respective faculty to but one mode of action, so that it would be repugnant for a potency having such a habit to tend towards the opposite. But there is nothing in the divine will that inclines it specifically to any secondary object in such a way that it would be impossible for it justly to incline towards its opposite. For without contradiction the will could will the opposite, and thus it could justly will such; otherwise it could will something absolutely [i.e., by its absolute power] and not do so justly, which seems incongruous.

And this is what Anselm says in ch. 11 of his *Proslogion*: "Only what you will is just, and only what you do not will is not just." As such, if one postulates in the divine intellect some intellective habit with respect to oneself and to others, one could make a stronger case for a conceptual distinction than in the case at hand, because there the intellect is deterministically inclined to each of the secondary objects, but that is not the case here with the will. Nevertheless, one could say that this single justice, which determinately inclines the divine will to its first act, modifies each of these secondary acts, although not in a necessary manner, as though it could not also modify the opposite of each. Neither does this justice precede the will, as it were, inclining it after the manner of nature to some secondary act; but the will first determines itself in regard to each secondary object. And by this very fact this act is modified by that first justice, because that act is in harmony with the will to which it is conformed as if the rectitude inclining it this way were the first justice itself.

In this second way God is said to do what is right in a creature from the way he makes one created thing correspond to another (just as we say it is just on the part of the creature that fire be hot and water cold, that fire rise and water descend, and so on), because this created nature demands this as something suited to it—just as we could say in politics that while justice exists as such only in the ruler himself, we could still speak of him as being somehow just in the things he ordains, namely, to the extent that he arranges things in such and such a way, since this is something demanded by the things themselves insofar as they are destined by nature for the use of the citizens.

However, the primary justice intrinsic to God does not determine him to be just in this second way in the same manner that it determines him in regard to his first act, because this primary act [of justice towards himself] does not look to any [created] object or secondary act, because insofar as it looks to such his justice does not incline his will in any necessary manner, as was said.

[Objections] against this:

[1] To begin with, justice can only exist in a will if it inclines the will according to some dictate of prudence, which is the conclusion of a practical syllogism; now, the divine intellect does not reason syllogistically, since it does not think step by step.

[2] Also, the divine intellect first knows of a possible action before the will can will it, and the will cannot disagree with the intellect understanding it; but the intellect apprehends the possible action in a definite way, so that it does not grasp it as an indefinite either/or; therefore the will definitely wills this action in such a way that it cannot will the opposite if it is to will rightly.

[3] Also, if it is just to save Peter, and God justly wills this, then it is

unjust to damn Peter, and thus if God can will to do so, he can will something that is unjust.

[Solutions] To the first, I say that if in us there can be another moral virtue inclining the will in accordance with the conclusion of a practical syllogism, all the more so is there in us a practical appetite which inclines in accord with the first practical principle, because this principle is more true, and consequently more correct [than a conclusion therefrom]. Justice, however, which in God is one, both conceptually and in reality, as we said, inclines the will in accord with the first practical principle, namely, "God ought to be loved." But if you want to insist that, strictly speaking, what does not incline in accord with the conclusion of a practical syllogism is not some special virtue, I concede that this justice which God has is only a quasi-universal and root sort of "virtue," from which all particular sorts of rectitude or justice spring, although not in a necessary manner.

To the second, I say that the intellect grasps or knows of some possible action before the will can will it, but it does not apprehend it as something definite that must be done, as if "to apprehend" meant "to dictate." Indeed it is offered to the will as something neutral; after the will makes a definite decision that this is to be done, the intellect consequently grasps as true that this is to be done, as was said in the matter about future contingents in Bk. I, dist. 39, q. 1.

Granted that before the will wills something, the intellect apprehends that it should be done (e.g., "God must be loved") and the will cannot disagree, it still does not follow, however, that it is by natural necessity that the will wills this. For while it cannot disagree about the object, namely, as regards willing or nilling what is shown to it as something it ought to will, the way each tends to that object disagrees, or rather should properly be distinguished. For the intellect tends to it in its way, namely, naturally, whereas the will tends in its own way, namely, freely. And these powers are always in harmony because they always tend to the same object according to their respective manner of doing this, just as the imagination and the intellect do not disagree if the former tends to the object qua singular and the latter to that same object qua universal.

To the third, I say the legislator in matters of state regards something as simply just if it is right for the public good, whereas he regards other, partial rights always in the qualified sense that they do not militate against this unqualified right of the community at large, and therefore in certain cases he sees it is right not to observe just laws concerning these partial rights, namely, when their observation would be detrimental to what is just publicly, namely, to what is in the best interests of the state. In a similar fashion God is determined to do what is just publicly as something right and becoming to his goodness, and to do this not for a group that is just an aggregation of citizens, but rather for a community whose members are knit together in a far more excellent way. But everything other than what is right for this community is only a partial right that may be just in this case but not in that, depending on how it is ordered to or in harmony with that more basic right.

I say therefore that God could will that Peter be damned and be right to will such, because this particular instance of what is just, viz., "Peter is saved," is not necessarily required for what is just for the community in the sense that its opposite could not also be ordered to that same end, namely, what is just for the community as befitting divine goodness. For the attainment of this end, indeed, no being represents a definitely necessary requirement.

[Reply to the Initial Arguments]

To the first argument at the beginning I admit there is no simple equality except in God with respect to himself, and hence there is no justice in an unqualified sense except with respect to himself. Therefore, neither is there any unqualified justice with respect to himself as quasi-other. As for the latter, however, there can be a sort of equality such as obtains between a master and a servant whose respective stations differ exceedingly.

To the second I grant that no virtues that imply any imperfection exist there, but only such as can exist without imperfection. This is clear from the example of temperance, since this requires the nature it tempers to be capable of taking immoderate delight in something, and this represents an imperfection. For that reason one could more properly assume that justice is there, because this does not require some passionate excess or some such imperfection, in the way that temperance does. But it is questionable whether [a] justice as it exists in God is a virtue under this precise aspect that it is something formally distinct from the will that plays a quasi-regulatory function or whether [b] it merely represents the will as determining itself according to some first rule [such as "God should be loved"]. For if the second be the case, then it is easier to answer the argument, because then justice is not present in God precisely as a moral virtue.

To the third, I say that God is no debtor in any unqualified sense save with respect to his own goodness, namely, that he love it. But where creatures are concerned he is debtor rather to his generosity, in the sense that he gives creatures what their nature demands, which exigency in them is set down as something just, a kind of secondary object of this justice, as it were. But in truth nothing outside of God can be said to be definitely just without this added qualification. In an unqualified sense where a creature is concerned, God is just only in relationship to his first justice, namely, because such a creature has been actually willed by the divine will.

16. GOD'S ABSOLUTE AND ORDAINED POWER
(*Ordinatio* I, dist. 44)

In this forty-fourth distinction—where the Master [Peter Lombard] asks whether God could have made things better than he did—I raise this question: Could God have made things otherwise than he has ordered them to be made?

[Arguments Pro and Con]
It seems not:
For then he could have made things inordinately. The consequent is false, therefore the antecedent is also false.
On the contrary:
That things could have been made otherwise is not self-contradictory, neither is the world necessary; therefore, etc.

[To the Question]
I reply:
In every agent acting intelligently and voluntarily that can act in conformity with an upright or just law but does not have to do so of necessity, one can distinguish between its ordained power and its absolute power. The reason is that either it can act in conformity with some right and just law, and then it is acting according to its ordained power (for it is ordained insofar as it is a principle for doing something in conformity with a right or just law), or else it can act beyond or against such a law, and in this case its absolute power exceeds its ordained power. And therefore it is not only in God, but in every free agent that can either act in accord with the dictates of a just law or go beyond or against that law, that one distinguishes between absolute and ordained power; therefore, the jurists say that someone can act *de facto*, that is, according to his absolute power, or *de jure*, that is, according to his ordained legal power.
But when that upright law—according to which an agent must act in order to act ordinately—is not in the power of that agent, then its absolute power cannot exceed its ordained power in regard to any object without it acting disorderly or inordinately. For, as regards such an agent, the law must remain in force, but an action that is not in con-

formity with this right and just law will be neither right nor ordinate, because the agent is bound to act in accord with that regulation to which it is subject. Hence all who are subject to a divine law, if they do not act according to it, act inordinately.

But whenever the law and its rectitude are in the power of the agent, so that the law is right only because it has been established, then the agent can freely order things otherwise than this right law dictates and still can act orderly, because he can establish another right or just law according to which he may act orderly. In such a case it is not simply necessary that his absolute power exceed his ordered power, because his action might still be ordered according to another law just as it had been earlier, but he would still exceed his ordained power according to the prior law if he acted beyond or against such. This could be illustrated in the case of a ruler and his subjects in regard to a positive law.

Applying this to the issue at hand, I say that there are some general laws, ordering things rightly, that have been set up beforehand by the divine will and not by the divine intellect, as something antecedent to any act of the divine will, as was said in dist. 38. But when the intellect presents such a law to the divine will, for instance, "Everyone to be glorified must first be in a state of grace," if it pleases his free will, then it becomes a right or just law, and so too with other laws.

God, therefore, insofar as he is able to act in accord with those right laws he set up previously, is said to act according to his ordained power; but insofar as he is able to do many things that are not in accord with, but go beyond, these preestablished laws, God is said to act according to his absolute power. For God can do anything that is not self-contradictory or act in any way that does not include a contradiction (and there are many such ways he could act); and then he is said to be acting according to his absolute power.

Hence, I say that many other things can be done orderly; and many things that do not include a contradiction other than those that conform to present laws can occur in an ordained way when the rectitude of such law—according to which one acts rightly and orderly—lies in the power of the agent himself. And therefore such an agent can act otherwise, so that he establishes another upright law, which, if it were set up by God, would be right, because no law is right except insofar as the divine will accepts it as established. And in such a case the absolute power of the agent in regard to something would not extend to anything other than what might happen ordinately if it occurred, not indeed ordainedly with respect to this present order, but ordinately with reference to some other order that the divine will could set up if it were able to act in such a way.

Keep in mind also that what is ordained and happens regularly can occur in two ways:

One way is with reference to a universal order. This would involve common law, like the common law that ordains that "every impenitent sinner must be damned" (as if a king were to establish the law that every murderer is to die). The second way is with reference to a particular order. This involves a particular judgment or decision that does not pertain to a universal law, since a law has to do with cases in general, whereas in a singular case what is involved is not a general law, but rather a decision according to law about something that is against the law (for instance, a decision that this murderer is to die).

I say, therefore, that God can act otherwise than is prescribed not only by a particular order, but also by a universal order or law of justice, and in so doing he could still act ordainedly, because what God could do by his absolute power that is either beyond or runs counter to the present order, he could do ordainedly.

But we speak of ordained power in reference only to an order established by a universal law, and not to that which rightly holds by law for a particular case. This is clear from the fact that it is possible for God to save one whom he does not actually save, a living sinner who will die, however, without repenting and will be damned. Admittedly, however, God could not in the same way save Judas, who is already damned. (But for God's absolute power not even this is impossible, since it does not include a contradiction.) It is impossible, therefore, to save Judas in the same way it is possible to save this other sinner, since it is true that the latter could be saved by God's ordained power, whereas Judas could not. And God could save the sinner not just by a particular order (which is concerned, as it were, with only this specific action and particular operation), but by one that is universal, because if he were to save this sinner, he could still do so within the framework of his preestablished just and right laws about the salvation and damnation of individuals. For the salvation of such a sinner is still consistent with the decree "One who remains evil to the end, will be damned" (which is a preestablished law about those who will be damned). The reason is that this sinner has not yet died in sin, and can still cease to be a sinner (especially while still in this life). By his grace God could prevent him from dying impenitent—like a king who prevents someone from killing, and then if he does not condemn the man, he is not violating his universal law against homicide. But it is not consistent with the particular law he did establish that he could save Judas. God could foresee that Judas could be saved by his ordained power—not what is now his ordained power, for at present

Judas could only be saved by God's absolute power; but Judas's salvation could have been accomplished by God's ordained power in another order he might have set up.

The sort of possibility the divine will still retains with regard to particulars and to what has been instituted according to just and right laws, without God actually willing the opposite of what he now wills, is explained in dist. 39.

[Reply to Both Arguments at the Beginning]

To the initial argument, it is clear that the implication does not hold, because to make something in another way than is presently ordained is not by that very fact to act inordinately, because other laws could be set up according to which he would be acting ordinately.

To the argument for the opposite I concede that it proves God has absolute power; but if his power were to become a principle or cause of anything, it would by that very fact be ordained, but not according to that same preestablished order he had before.

PART V

The Moral Law in General

17. NATURAL LAW AND DIVINE POSITIVE LAW
(*Ordinatio* IV, dist. 17)

By what precept is one obliged to confess sins to a priest?

As for the sort of obligation involved here we could find no precept obliging one to confession were it not of natural law, or divine or ecclesiastical positive law.

[Re natural law] Now, a practical truth of natural law is either one whose truth value can be ascertained from its terms (in which case it is a principle of natural law, even as in theoretical matters a principle is known from its terms) or else one that follows from the knowledge of such truths (in which case it is a demonstrated conclusion in the practical order). And strictly speaking, nothing pertains to the law of nature except a principle or a conclusion demonstrated in this fashion.

Nevertheless, something is said in an extended sense to pertain to the law of nature if it is a practical truth that is immediately recognized by all to be in accord with such a law.

From this it is clear that Gratian does not speak correctly about the law of nature when he has in mind to include all that is in the Old and New Testament Scriptures under the law of nature, because not all of this represents practical principles known from their terms or practical demonstrated conclusions, or even truths that are evidently in accord with such. One should interpret him, then, as extending "law of nature" to the positive law of the author of nature, namely, as distinct from such positive law as stems from one who is not nature's author.

[Re divine positive law] This clarifies, secondly, the notion of divine positive law as well. Whatever law the Scriptures contain for the dura-

tion for which it obliges that is not known from the terms, nor immediately known to accord with such, pertains purely to divine positive law. Such would be all the Jewish ceremonies during the period
that law obtained, or the Christian ceremonies at the time of our
present law. For it is not known from the terms of the law that God
ought to be worshiped by the animal sacrifices of the Old Testament,
and that for all times, or by our ceremonies, for instance, the eucha-
ristic oblation or chanting the psalms, even though these may be consonant with the law of nature in the sense that they are not opposed
to it.

This is also clear from the fact that whatever pertains to the law of
nature, either properly or extensively, is uniform, whereas these ceremonies are not so, being different during the span of the other law's
jurisdiction.

[Re positive Church law] The third source [from which the obligation of confession could arise] is also evident, because in addition
to the divine positive law contained in Sacred Scripture, the Church
has established many things that moral observance be more upright
and that the sacraments be received and administered with greater
reverence.

[Scotus' reply to the question] To the question at issue, then, I say
that no one is obliged to confess his or her sins by any precept of natural law—which is the question we set out to answer. The reason is that
if it were a matter of natural law, the obligation would have held for
any state of law—which is false. For no such obligation existed in the
state of innocence or during the tenure of the Mosaic law.

[Objections to this solution] You may protest—on the basis of the
gloss on Genesis 3: "Adam, where are you?"—that after the Fall, the
law of nature did require confession. For the gloss says: "The voice is
one of rebuke and is asking for a confession," etc.

Similarly, we read [in Scripture] that Aaron and his sons must confess all the sins of the people of Israel [Leviticus 16:20], and elsewhere,
that a person who has sinned against the law should confess his sins
and offer such and such a sacrifice.

Many authorities in the Old Testament confirm the need for confessing. See what is said about this text: "A person is regarded as just
before his accuser cross-examines him" [Proverbs 18:17].

Any conclusion that is based upon the principle of natural law is
obviously proved as follows. Every guilty person, we know, must be
judged; and no one ought to be a judge in his own case; therefore, the
guilty party must be judged by another. Now, no one can be judged by
another unless the other person accuses him; and—if his sin is se-

cret—he can be accused only by himself; therefore, he is obliged to accuse himself to that person who will judge him. And it is more in line with reason that his accusation be private than that it be public. Indeed, it may even be sufficiently known to natural reason that if the sin is secret, the accusation must also be private. From these propositions, then, known to be of the law of nature, or at least very much in accord with it, it follows that private confession of personal sins must be made to some other person, and to no one more reasonably, then, than to a priest.

[Scotus' reply to the objections] I reply to the first: Adam ought not to have hid his sin, for the judge was none other than the one to whom all sin is manifest, and before whom every sinner is obliged to acknowledge his sin. It was this confession that God required of him. Not only did Adam not make it, but he excused his fault by blaming it on the woman, saying: "The woman you gave me [as my companion offered me the fruit, and I ate it" (Genesis 3:12)]. But this does not entail that according to the law at that time, confession must be made to another human being, although there would have been an obligation to do so to God, who asked for it.

As for the second objection [about the time when the Mosaic law was in force], there is no instance of the sort of confession we speak of, but only of confessions of secret sins to God. Where certain faults were public, involving legal observances, the confession occurred when a sacrifice was offered in atonement for the same, and there was the general confession of the priests—"We have sinned and have acted unjustly!" This public confession by the priest was a quasi-disposition, begging God's mercy on the people, just as it is in the Church at present. But the sort of confession we are inquiring about is one where we admit we have sinned and we ask mercy for ourselves and all the people.

As for the third, I maintain that all the instances cited from the Old Testament to prove the existence of this sort of confession refer to one that is merely vocal and not judicial. To what kind of confession, then, do these texts refer? I claim it is that general sort of confession such as the priests, Daniel, and many other holy Jews made, or the confession of public violations of those legal observances that made them unclean or irregular before the law.

As for the supporting argument from reason, I grant that we know by the natural light of the mind that a guilty person must be judged, or at least we recognize that this is highly in accord with a proposition that is known in this way. For no sin should be left unpunished anywhere if there is one ruler of the universe and he is just—something we know naturally or recognize as exceedingly in harmony with what we do know in this way. I even concede further what is said about the necessity of another as judge. But just who is this other? From what is known by natural reason, or from what is consonant with this, such a judge would be God alone, the one who rewards merit and punishes sin. As for the additional claim that this other party cannot judge unless there be an accusation, we deny this to be the case, because God knows sins even prior to their occurrence even without any self-accusation. But let us grant it to be in accord with what is known from reason that a person ought to accuse himself of his sin before this judge, since only he knows of it. But from all this it follows only that sin should be confessed to God. Now, I admit that this sort of confession pertains to the law of nature, that is to say, it is consonant with truths that pertain to the law of nature and hold good in every state after the Fall, for just men who believed in God as a ruler of the world who punishes justly, would have behaved as follows. After they had sinned, they would confess their sins to God, begging his pardon, knowing full well that without such remission, he as a just judge will avenge such sin.

But if you argue that one person must accuse himself to another person who is his judge, this is something that cannot be proved from what is known of the law of nature or from what is evidently in harmony with that law, since no sinner can be judge of a man's sin unless he be the minister of the Supreme Judge. For this function of being ministers of that Judge in avenging and punishing what has been committed is something conceded rather to oneself than to any one individual with respect to another. For God commits to each person the role of being God's minister in punishing his own sins, in evoking sorrow and displeasure because of his sin. But it is not known that God has given to anyone the commission of carrying out judgment against any other person because of his sin.

And if you argue that in a human state or republic one person is judge of another, I reply: This is true only of such matters of public knowledge as can be brought before a civil tribunal.

18. THE DECALOGUE AND THE LAW OF NATURE
(*Ordinatio* III, suppl., dist. 37)

In regard to the thirty-seventh distinction [of Bk. III] I ask: Do all of the commandments of the decalogue belong to the law of nature?

[*Arguments Pro and Con*]

For the negative view:

[1] In those things which pertain to the law of nature it does not seem God can dispense; but he has done so in some matters that run counter to precepts of the decalogue; therefore, etc. Proof of the major premise: What pertains to the law of nature is either a practical principle known immediately from its terms or necessary conclusions that follow from such principles. In either case they possess necessary truth. Therefore, God cannot make them false. Hence, he cannot make what they say is good to be anything but good, or what they say must be avoided to be anything but evil, and thus he cannot make what is illicit licit. Proof of the minor premise: To kill, to steal, to commit adultery, are against the precepts of the decalogue, as is clear from Exodus [20:13]: "You shall not kill" [etc.]. Yet God seems to have dispensed from these. This is clear in regard to homicide from Genesis 22, regarding Abraham and the son he was about to sacrifice; or for theft from Exodus 11:[2] and [12:35] where he ordered the sons of Israel to despoil the Egyptians, which despoilment is taking what belongs to another without the owner's consent, which is the definition of theft. As for the third, there is Hosea 1: "Make children of fornications."

[2] Furthermore, the Apostle says to the Romans 7:[7]: "It was only through the law that I came to know sin. I should never have known what evil desire was unless the law had said: 'You shall not covet.'" But what is known from the law of nature is recognized as something to be done or not to be done, even though it is not written, just as what is known naturally in theoretical matters would still be known naturally, even if it were not revealed.

[3] Besides, the law of nature is obligatory for every state in which man finds himself, because it is known what such a nature must do and must not do. But the decalogue was not obligatory in every state, for instance, in the state of innocence, for the law had not yet been promulgated, nor did it seem to oblige before it was given.

For the opposite view:

In the beginning of the *Decrees* [*of Gratian*, in dist. 6], the first gloss "Illis omnino."

And look in the canonical epistle of John, ch. 2 [vv. 3–7]: "The way we can be sure of our knowledge of him is to keep his commandments, because whoever keeps his word, truly has the love of God been made perfect in him. The man who claims, 'I have known him,' without keeping his commandments is a liar. It is no new commandment I write to you, but an old one which you had from the start." This for the negative view.

[Body of the Question]

[View of others] One view here claims that the whole decalogue pertains to the law of nature and explains it in some such way as this. The law of nature is a law proceeding from first principles known to hold for actions; these are seminal practical principles known from their terms. The intellect is naturally inclined to their truth because of their terms, and the will is naturally inclined to assent to what they dictate. From such principles everything in the decalogue follows either mediately or immediately. For all that is commanded there has a formal goodness whereby it is essentially ordered to man's ultimate end, so that through it a man is directed towards his end. Similarly everything prohibited there has a formal evil which turns one from the ultimate end. Hence, what is commanded there is not good merely because it is commanded, but commanded because it is good in itself. Likewise, what is prohibited there is not evil merely because it is prohibited, but forbidden because it is evil. On this view, then, it seems the reply to the first argument should be that God simply cannot dispense from such cases, for what is unlawful of itself cannot, it seems, become licit through any will. For instance, killing is an evil act, from the fact that it is directed against such and such a person, for instance, a neighbor. Then given this situation, it will always be evil, and so no willing extrinsic to what are the circumstances of the case can make killing good. And then one would have to explain away those texts where God seems to have given a dispensation. One way of doing this is to claim that though a dispensation could be granted to an act that falls under a generic description [like killing in general], it could never be given insofar as it is prohibited according to the intention of the commandment [e.g., killing an innocent neighbor], and hence [killing an unjust aggressor, for example] would not be against the prohibition. Put another way, an act that is inordinate cannot become well ordered, but an act insofar as it violates a prohibition is inordinate. Therefore, it cannot be subject to dispensation insofar as it is against a prohibition.

[Refutation of this view] But these explanations, which come down to the same thing, do not seem to save what they were intended to save. For to dispense does not consist in letting the precept stand and permitting one to act against it. To dispense, on the contrary, is to revoke the precept or declare how it is to be understood. For there are two kinds of dispensations—one revokes the law, the other clarifies it.

My question then is this. Granted that all the circumstances are the same in regard to this act of killing a man except the circumstances of its being prohibited in one case and not prohibited in another, could

God cause that act which is circumstantially the same, but performed by different individuals, to be prohibited and illicit in one case and not prohibited but licit in the other? If so, then he can dispense unconditionally, just as he changed the old law when he gave a new law. And he did this in regard to the ceremonial functions he required, not by letting the ceremonial precepts stand, but not requiring them to be observed, but rather by letting an act remain the same [e.g., eating only kosher food], but not requiring anyone to do this as he did before. This is also the way any legislator dispenses unconditionally when he revokes a precept of positive law made by himself. He does not allow the prohibited act or precept to remain as before, but removes the prohibition or makes what was formerly illicit now licit. But if God cannot cause this act [of killing], which under such and such circumstances was formerly prohibited, to be no longer prohibited, even under the same circumstances, then he can not make killing licit—but that he did so is clear in the case of Abraham and in many other instances.

Also, those propositions which are true by reason of their terms, whether they be immediately so or conclusions therefrom, have their truth value prior to any act of the will, or at least they would be true even if, to assume the impossible, no act of willing existed. Therefore, if those precepts of the decalogue or the practical propositions that could be formed from them possessed such necessity (e.g., if these were necessary: "No neighbor should be hated or killed," "Theft should never be committed," and the like), it would follow that apart from all volition the divine intellect would see such propositions as true of themselves, and then the divine will would necessarily agree with them or it would not be right, and thus one would have to assume God has practical knowledge [as regards creatures], which was denied in the first book in the question about praxis. It would also be necessary to assume that his will is necessarily determined in an unqualified sense in regard to willing things other than himself, the opposite of which was asserted to be the case also in the first book, dist. 2, where we discussed the fact that his will tends to nothing other than himself except contingently.

And even if you say that a created will must necessarily be conformed to these truths if it is to be right, this still does not say that the divine will wills in accord with them; rather because it wills accordingly, therefore they are true.

The proponent of this first view replies to the question [I raise] that reason proves the opposite [namely, that God cannot make an act with the same circumstances licit at one time but not at another], for when the divine intellect apprehends these terms [of the propositions in question] and can understand from them that the propositions are true, a truth they possess prior to any act of his will in regard to them, then in the second sign of nature, namely, when the will does act in regard to them, it has to will necessarily in conformity to that dictate and hence cannot will the opposite.

[Scotus' own opinion] To the question, then, I say that some things can be said to belong to the law of nature in two ways:

[1] One way is as first practical principles known from their terms or as conclusions necessarily entailed by them. These are said to belong to the natural law in the strictest sense, and there can be no dispensation in their regard, as the argument for the first opinion proves. It is to these that the canon of the *Decrees of Gratian* refers, where it is said that "the natural law begins from the very beginnings of rational creatures, nor does time change it, but it is immutably permanent"—and this I concede.

But this is not the case when we speak in general of all the precepts of the second table [of the decalogue]. For the reasons behind the commands and prohibitions there are not practical principles that are necessary in an unqualified sense, nor are they simply necessary conclusions from such. For they contain no goodness such as is necessarily prescribed for attaining the goodness of the ultimate end, nor in what is forbidden is there such malice as would turn one away necessarily from the last end, for even if the good found in these maxims were not commanded, the last end [of man as union with God] could still be loved and attained, whereas if the evil proscribed by them were not forbidden, it would still be consistent with the acquisition of the ultimate end.

But it is different with the precepts of the first table, because these regard God immediately as object. Indeed the first two, if they be understood in a purely negative sense—i.e., "You shall not have other gods before me" and "You shall not take the name of the Lord, your God, in vain," i.e., "You should show no irreverence to God"—belong to the natural law, taking law of nature strictly, for this follows necessarily: "If God exists, then he alone must be loved as God." It likewise follows that nothing else must be worshiped as God, nor must any irreverence be shown to him. Consequently, God could not dispense in regard to these so that someone could do the opposite of what this or that prohibits. (In support of this put the two authorities here that are found in Richard, ch. 5.)

The third commandment of the first table is that which concerns the observance of the Sabbath. It is affirmative insofar as it prescribes that some worship be given to God at a specific time, but so far as the specification to this or that time goes, it does not pertain to the law of nature strictly speaking. Similarly with the negative portion included therein, which forbids servile work for a definite time that would interfere with the worship to be shown to him. For such work is only prohibited because it impedes or keeps one from the cult that is commanded.

[A doubt] But there is some doubt whether this precept of observing the Sabbath pertains to the natural law strictly to the extent that it requires that at some definite time worship be shown to God. For if it does not, then God could dispense from it absolutely, so that a man for the entire duration of his life would never have to manifest any affection or love for God. This does not seem probable, for without some act of goodwill or love towards God as the ultimate end, one could not do anything simply good that would be needed to attain that end, and thus this person would never be bound to will anything that is simply good in an unqualified sense. For the same reason that excludes from strict natural law the need to show worship to God now, holds also for then [i.e., the Sabbath] and, by the same token, for any specific time. Therefore, strictly speaking, it is not clear how one could infer that a person is bound then or now to worship God and, by the same reasoning, how anyone is bound at some undefined time to do so, for no one is obliged to perform at some undefined time an act which he is not obligated to perform at some definite time when some opportunities for doing so present themselves.

But if this is strictly of the natural law, so that "God must be loved" follows necessarily from "God must not be hated" or some other such precept, then this argument from singular instances to a universal statement does not hold, but represents a fallacy of a figure of speech, even as does the converse, where one argues from several determinate instances to one indeterminate one. But if this third commandment is not strictly a matter of natural law, then it must be judged like the precepts of the second table of the decalogue.

[2] The other way in which things belong to the law of nature is because they are exceedingly in harmony with that law, even though they do not follow necessarily from those first practical principles known from their terms, principles which are necessarily grasped by any intellect understanding those terms. Now, it is certain that all the precepts of the second table also belong to the natural law in this way, since their rightness is very much in harmony with the first practical principles that are known of necessity. And in this way one has to understand that statement in the *Decrees of Gratian*, dist. 6, canon 3: "The moral precepts pertain to the natural law, and therefore they show no evidence of having undergone any change." Note the gloss

which says: "The law concerns change not as regards moral matters but only as regards those pertaining to ritual."

This distinction can be made clear by an example. Given the principle of positive law that life in a community or state ought to be peaceful, it does not follow from this necessarily that everyone ought to have possessions distinct from those of another, for peace could reign in a group or among those living together, even if everything was common property. Not even in the case of the infirm is private possession an absolute necessity; nevertheless, that such persons have their own possessions is exceedingly consonant with peaceful living, for the infirm care more about goods of their own than they do about common property, and would prefer rather that the common goods be assigned to them than that they be given to the community and its custodians for the common good, and so strife and disorder could occur. And it is this way, perhaps, with all positive laws, for although there is some one principle which serves as the basis for establishing these laws, still positive laws do not follow with simple [logical] necessity from the principle in question or explicate it as regards certain particular cases. Nevertheless, these explications are greatly in harmony with the first universal principle they clarify.

To put all we have said together, first we deny that all the commandments of the second table pertain strictly to the law of nature; second, we admit that the first two commandments belong strictly to the law of nature; third, there is some doubt about the third commandment of the first table; fourth, we concede that all the commandments fall under the law of nature, speaking broadly.

[An objection] Against the first of these, I argue: According to the Apostle to the Romans [13:9]: "The commandments, 'You shall not commit adultery; you shall not murder . . .' and if there be any other commandments, they may all be summed up in this: 'You shall love your neighbor as yourself.'" Therefore, in this precept, "Love your neighbor," etc., are included the precepts of the second table. For the Apostle appears to prove this point expressly and thus seems to conclude "Whoever loves his neighbor fulfills the law." What the Savior says also proves this, for the major [of the argument] is found in Matthew 22:[40]: "On this depends the whole law and the prophets." But the love of neighbor follows necessarily from this necessary principle: "God must be loved." Therefore, all the precepts of the second table, from first to last, follow from the precepts of the first table. Hence, if those of the first table pertain strictly to the law of nature, because they are included in the first precept or principle, which does belong to the natural law in an unqualified sense, it follows that the precepts of the second table also belong strictly to that law, even though they are conclusions drawn from the same principle. —Proof of the assumption [that love of neighbor follows from love of God]: This is clear from what was said in dist. 28 of this third book, where it was proved in two ways. The perfect love of God is a well-ordered love and cannot be jealous, in the sense of being appropriated [to oneself alone], because love of the good of all as something belonging to oneself alone is inordinate. Now, the love of someone who does not want the beloved [i.e., God] to be loved by others is inordinate and imperfect. Hence, it follows that if God is to be loved perfectly and orderly, then the one loving God must will that his neighbor also love God; but in so willing, he is loving his neighbor. Indeed this is the only way in which our neighbor is loved out of [supernatural] charity, as is pointed out in the *Glosses*, therefore, etc.

[Solution] To this one can reply in three ways:

First, the precept "Love the Lord, your God," etc., is not simply of the natural law insofar as it is affirmative. However, insofar as it is negative, prohibiting the opposite, namely, "Do not hate God," it does pertain strictly to the natural law. Just when one is required to love God is not clear, however, as was pointed out in discussing the third commandment. Now, from the negative precept, it does not follow that one must want his neighbor to love God, although this would follow from the affirmative formulation, which is not clearly something belonging to the natural law strictly.

Second, one could reply that from this precept, "Love the Lord, your God," it does not follow that I ought to want my neighbor to love God. And when one insists that a perfect and well-ordered love is not a jealous one, I reply that I do not have to will that the common good pertain to another in such a way that [God] has to be loved by this other. For it is not necessary that I will this good for another, if God does not want to be the good of such [e.g., for one who dies hating God], as when he destines one [viz., the saint] and not the other [viz., the sinner], wishing to be the good of the former but not of the latter. The same argument holds for the maxim "Whoever loves perfectly, wishes the beloved to be loved," namely, by one whose friendship pleases the beloved. It is not certain from the law of nature that everyone is such that his love is accepted by the God who is loved or should be loved.

The third way of answering the objection is that even if it were strictly a matter of the natural law that our neighbor be loved in the way this was explained above, namely, that one must want the neighbor himself to love God, because this is what it means to love one's neighbor, the precepts of the second table still do not follow [logically] from this. For instance, that one must not kill him, so far as the good of his person is concerned; or that one must not want him to commit adultery, so far as the good of his partner is concerned; or that one must not want him to steal, so far as the goods of fortune that he uses are concerned; or that one must want him to show reverence to his parents, which consists not just in honoring them but also in supporting them. For it is possible for me to will that my neighbor love God and nevertheless not will that he preserve corporeal life or conjugal fidelity, and so on with the other precepts. Consequently, these two can coexist, viz., that I want my neighbor to love God as I ought to love him (which would be a kind of necessary conclusion from the practical principles) and still do not will him this or that good pertaining to the second table, since the latter is not a necessary truth.

And then one could say to the quotations from Paul and Christ that God has now explained [in the Scriptures] a higher love of neighbor that transcends that which is included in, or follows from, the principles of the law of nature. In other words, although the love of neighbor that can be inferred from principles of the law of nature only requires that we love him in himself, still the love of neighbor as explained [by Christ and Paul] includes willing him these other goods, or at least not wishing him the opposite evils, such as not wanting him to be deprived unjustly of corporeal life, or conjugal fidelity, or temporal goods, and the like. Hence it is true that love of neighbor fulfills the law, viz., in the way it has been explained that this law of love must be observed, although not in the way that love of neighbor follows from the first principles of natural law. In a similar fashion, the whole law— so far as the second table and the prophets are concerned—depends on this commandment: "Love your neighbor as yourself," again understanding this not as something that follows of necessity from the first practical principles of the law of nature, but as the Lawgiver intended the love of neighbor to be observed according to the precepts of the second table.

[Reply to the Initial Arguments]

[To 1] As for the initial arguments, the first is in my favor, for it proves that the precepts of the second table are not part of the natural law strictly speaking.

[To 2] To the second, I say that although God's existence could have been inferred by natural reason from principles known in themselves, nevertheless, for the ignorant people unskilled in intellectual matters, it would be known only from revealed law. Hence the Apostle to the Hebrews 11:[6] says: "Anyone who comes to God must believe that he exists"—understanding this to mean, if he neither had nor could have any other knowledge of God. Thus, even if some sin could be inferred to be against the law of nature, nevertheless to corrupt men it might not be known that their lusts were against the natural law, and therefore, it would have been necessary to explain—either by the law that was given, or in some other way—that such sins of lust are prohibited by the second table. One could concede that such things are not known *per se*.

[To 3] To the other, I say that in every state all the commandments have been observed and should be observed. In the state of beatitude, indeed, there will be the highest observance of the affirmative precepts and of the negative ones as well, except perhaps that alone of honoring parents, not because there will be any wish not to honor them, but because in heaven there will be no necessity of performing actions, at least so far as "honor" includes providing them with what is necessary to sustain life, for there no one will need such help. In the state of innocence also all were bound by these precepts, which were either prescribed interiorly in the heart of everyone or perhaps by some teaching given exteriorly by God and passed on by parents to their children, even though at that time nothing would have been written in a book. Nor need it have been, because they would have easily remembered it, and the people of those times had longer lives and were better endowed naturally than the people of a later age, at which time the weakness of the people required that the law be given and written down.

As to the point touched upon in the first argument about the children of Israel despoiling the Egyptians, it could be said that in this case God did not dispense them from the law "Do not steal," for they did not simply take away a thing belonging to another. Since God was the higher owner, he could have transferred the ownership of these things, even if the lower "owners" were unwilling. In this way Christ did not sin in allowing the demons to enter the pigs, which were immediately thrown into the sea; for he did not unjustly deprive their owner of his pigs. Another explanation could be this: the sons of Israel, by serving the Egyptians, deserved the things they took as wages, even though the Egyptians unjustly were unwilling to give them up. In such a case the superior judge could have compelled the Egyptians to do so, and since the Jews accepted these things which should have been theirs by permission of the same higher judge, they licitly and justly appropriated them.

As for the argument for the opposite viewpoint, the canon in question has to be understood of the law taken in a broad sense, and in this case it extends to the precepts of the second table.

19. ON MARRIAGE AND BIGAMY
(*Ordinatio* IV, dist. 33, q. 1)

In regard to the thirty-third distinction [of Bk. IV] I raise a question first about bigamy and then about divorcing one's wife. On the first subject I ask, so far as the Mosaic law or the law of nature is concerned, was bigamy ever licit, or were the patriarchs of old allowed to have several wives joined in the bonds of matrimony?

[Arguments Pro and Con]

[For the negative view]:

[Arg. 1] To the first question, it is argued that bigamy was not permitted, because it is against the law of nature. Proof of this is found [a] in those words of Genesis 2:24: "They shall be two in one flesh," which express the law of nature about matrimony; hence there cannot be more than two; [b] in one of the interlinear glosses on Genesis 4:19 about Lamech, "who took two wives," etc., where he is presented as the first to introduce bigamy and as doing so in violation of the law of nature.

[Arg. 2] What is more, a woman is never allowed to have two husbands; neither, then, is it lawful for a man to have two wives. The entailment is proved from the fact that so far as the conjugal debt is concerned, each spouse has equal rights according to Paul's first Epistle to the Corinthians, ch. 7 [vv. 2–5].

[For the positive view]:

Against this view is the fact that Abraham had Sara, Agar, and Keturah (Genesis, chs. 16 and 25); Jacob had two wives (chs. 29 and 30); and David had many wives and concubines, according to 2 Kings 5 [i.e., 2 Samuel 5:13–16]. Now, it is hardly probable that these holy patriarchs were doing anything wrong in entering into these unions. Therefore, etc.—Also, there is that text from Augustine's *Good of Marriage*, near the end [i.e., ch. 25], where he explains that "the just patriarchs did not make sinful use of their many wives, nor did they sin against nature, but did what they did for the sake of progeny; nor was there anything contrary to the law or to mores, for at that time there was no law prohibiting polygamy."

[Body of the Question]

Here we must see: (1) what strict commutative justice demands of the marriage contract, and this [a] on the part of those entering into the contract and [b] further on the part of the superior [or lawgiver]; (2) what suffices after the Fall so far as this matter is concerned. And here the question is asked, what is needed to make [bigamy or polygamy] completely just?

[Article 1: What Commutative Justice Requires of the Marriage Contract]

About the first, I say that in every exchange on the part of those who make the exchange and from the standpoint of what they exchange, strict justice requires that, as far as possible, what is exchanged be of equal value in terms of the purpose for making the exchange. In the case of the matrimonial contract, there are two reasons for the exchange: one, the procreation of offspring; the other, a remedy against fornication. As regards the first purpose, the male body is of more value than the female, for the same man could fecundate several women during the time it takes for the same woman to conceive through men.

Therefore, so far as strict justice in regard to this end goes, bigamy would seem to be licit, so that a man could make a bodily exchange with as many women as could be fecundated in the way it is possible for a man to do so. Hence, it would not be a violation of nature if, in certain other situations, one male had several females; but this was not the case in the state of innocence, where matrimony was and would have been strictly a duty of one's state, and when to have several wives would have been bigamous. For a man had no need to share his body with several women to procreate many children. The simple exchange between one man and one woman would have sufficed for reproduction, since neither man nor woman would have been sterile then.

As for the second purpose, which only held good for the state of fallen nature, namely, to avoid fornication, the bodies of man and woman are of equal value. Therefore, so far as strict justice in the state of fallen nature goes, this contract, if both ends are considered, demands a one-to-one exchange of bodies. I add that there is complete justice in this exchange of rights only because of the authority of the superior who instituted or approved of such and such an exchange. Although some things belong to their owners, still what determines whether such and such an exchange is licit depends on the legislator, and this is true even more so as regards the mutual bodily exchange in the presence of a legislator who is God. But he has ordained as the rule both for the state of innocence and for that of fallen nature that this bodily exchange be one-for-one, and therefore it is only in such a way that justice in full is to be found.

[Article 2: How Is Justice Preserved If Bigamy Is Permitted?]

About the second article, I say that a dispensation is either a clarification of the law or a revoking of the law. For God could have either clarified his law concerning this exchange or revoked it in a particular case, and he could have done so reasonably where a greater good would result from its revocation than from its observance. But at a time when members of the human race needed to be multiplied either in an unqualified sense or with reference to divine cult, since there were few who worshiped God, it was necessary that those who did so, beget as much as they could, since only in their progeny would faith and divine worship continue to exist. At such a time, then, God reasonably gave a dispensation so that one man might share his body with those of several women to increase the number of those who worshiped God, something which would not have occurred otherwise. Now, Abraham and certain other patriarchs, presumably, were dispensed in this way.

How justice is preserved here, so far as the contracting parties go, is explained in this way. When there are two reasons why something is ordered, one the principal purpose, the other a less important end, it is reasonable to make use of such in a manner that favors the chief end, even if this militates to some extent against the less important purpose. Food, for example, contributes to both pleasure (which is less important) and nutrition (which is more important). According to right reason, then, food should be used in such a way as to serve the interests of nutrition, even though this should produce less pleasure.

Now, this marriage contract to render the carnal debt has as its main purpose the good of having offspring and as its less important end the avoidance of fornication. Right reason, then, dictates that those who enter into such a contract do so in such a way that the primary interests of procreation are given greater value even if rendering the debt when desired is given lesser value. But this takes place in a contractual exchange involving the body of one man and those of several women. Just as this is what ought to be done, absolutely speaking, so too in cases of necessity. That is to say, when it is extremely necessary that the primary end be attained, this must be done, in which case the secondary end should be neglected, as it were. And so it is clear how there is justice for both parties to the marital contract, because each ought to be willing, according to right reason, to surrender something he or she has a right to as regards the less important end in view of the fact that each receives an equal good as regards the more important end—an end that should be desired more, even if one party should have to sacrifice something in exchange to obtain it. And at times it would be necessary to do so, namely, when one is obligated to make such a sacrifice. And this would be completely licit and it ought to be done when this has been ordered by one's superior [i.e., God, the lawgiver]. This is evident from Genesis 16, for Sara, as it were, forced Abraham to have intercourse with Agar, her handmaid, that he might have a son by her servant, which he could not have from Sara herself.

If you object that in our own day this would be bigamy and would be illicit, I reply: It would be unlawful now, as there is no present dispensation by the lawgiver. Indeed, that law of nature, "They shall be two in one flesh," was restored through Christ (Matthew 19). Nevertheless, the reason it is not licit, speaking of justice on the part of the contract and contracting parties, stems from the fact that the principal end does not require it at present, since, of the faithful, many are dispensed from procreating entirely, and all the children of the faithful are schooled in the worship of God and receive a religious education. Therefore, without such a polygamous contract the faith is increased. But now, since the need to sacrifice the secondary end for the sake of the primary end no longer exists, the marital contract must be observed in such a way that justice is preserved as regards both ends, and this is best done when one man marries one woman.

But in case a multitude of men fell through war, the sword, or pestilence, while a multitude of women remained, bigamy could become licit even now, if one considers only precise justice on the part of the contract and contracting parties. And also women in contracting with men ought to be willing to give more in return for less as regards the secondary end for the sake of receiving equal for equal as regards the primary end. And in such a case according to right reason a woman should be willing that her man be joined to another woman that childbearing may occur. All that would be wanting for complete justice would be divine approbation, which perhaps would then occur and be revealed in a special way to the Church.

[Reply to the Initial Arguments]

To the arguments [for the negative view]:

To the first I say (as I pointed out above in dist. 17) that something is said to be of the natural law in two ways, viz., first, what is simply a practical truth known by the natural light of reason alone. Here a practical principle known from its terms represents the strongest form of such a law of nature, only second to which are those conclusions demonstrated from such primary principles. What pertains secondarily to the law of nature, however, is anything that as a general rule is in harmony with a law of nature in the previous sense. There is no dispensation as regards the first class, and therefore anything opposed to such would always seem to be a mortal sin. But for the secondary type, dispensation occurs in a situation where the opposite seems to be generally more in harmony with the primary law of nature. And it is just in this secondary sense of natural that monogamy pertains to the law of nature and bigamy is opposed to such, and hence I concede the validity of the proofs from Genesis 2 and from the *Ordinary Glosses* on Genesis 4. But from this it does not follow that in a special case the opposite could not be licit, or even in some cases necessary. In such a case, however, there would be justice on the part of the parties entering marriage as well as in regard to what they gave to each other, for right reason would dictate that their contractual exchange take place in a different way, and in addition the divine precept to enter such a contract would also be there. {[In the other "Ordinatio" the answer is put this way]: I say that this authority, "They shall be two in one flesh," must be understood in this fashion. They are one by reason of the offspring begotten by both parents, and hence having several wives does not militate against the way marriage was initially instituted.} As for Lamech, however, one could admit that he did sin mortally, because he acted contrary to the law of nature in the secondary sense. He sinned, I say, by contracting with several women where neither right reason dictated this law had to be revoked, nor was he dispensed from the law by his superior [God]. In short, he had neither excuse to fall back on.

To the second I say that there never was a just contract between those who made a marital exchange of such a sort, namely, where the secondary end was favored at the expense of the primary purpose, since they should have wanted the latter more than the former. But biandry [or polyandry] would serve the interests of the secondary end, and far less the primary purpose, because the same woman during the same period of time could not be impregnated by more than one man.

[To the initial argument for the positive view]:

To the initial argument to the contrary, I say that although one may presume some of the holy patriarchs did not sin in contracting bigamous unions, because both of the aforesaid conditions for such occurred in their case, namely, there was a need for polygamy and it was approved and prescribed by divine authority, nevertheless, if some of them did not have such an excuse or lacked either one or the other ground for validating such marital unions, I would not argue against those who maintained that they may have sinned grievously, since I do not think they were confirmed in grace.

20. DIVORCE AND THE MOSAIC LAW
(*Ordinatio* IV, dist. 33, q. 3)

Regarding divorce, I ask: Under the Mosaic law was it licit for a man to repudiate his wife?

[*Arguments Pro and Con*]

For the affirmative:

Deuteronomy 24:1: "When a man has taken a wife, and she finds no

favor in his eyes because of something indecent, let him write out a
bill of divorce and give it to her, and dismiss her from his house."

Also, Malachi 2:16: "When you shall hate your wife, put her away,
says the Lord God of Israel."

Furthermore, there is that rule of canon law: "Everything which is
born of certain causes, can be dissolved by the same causes" [*Decretum
Gratiani* II, causa 27, q. 2]; but marriage is born of mutual consent,
therefore it can be dissolved by mutual consent.

Also, [ibid., I, canon 11], dist. 34, "Si cuius," it says: "If it be established of a married cleric that the wife has committed adultery, she
ought to be given a bill of divorce and sent away"; therefore, divorce is
licit also under the Gospel law.

For the negative:

On the contrary, divorce seems to be against the law of nature that
Adam promulgated in the words: "A man shall cleave to his wife"
(Genesis 2), from which Christ concluded: "Therefore, what God has
joined together, let no man put asunder" [Matthew 19:6]. {In the
other translation it reads thus: It is against the law of nature that man
separate those who are joined by God, as Christ assumed in the Gospel
when he said: "What God has joined," etc.}

Also, the marriage contract is essentially an irrevocable gift of the
power of one's body to another for that of the other; therefore, no ac-
commodation or gift for a time only can be matrimony. But if divorce
were licit, there would be at most a gift for a time, because if it were
perpetual, the woman divorced would remain one's wife, and therefore it would be illicit to send her away. It follows, then, that under
the Mosaic law no matrimony would exist if divorce were licit there.

Also, it was never licit for a woman to divorce her husband; therefore, neither was it licit for a man to divorce his wife, since so far as
they are marriage partners, they may be judged equal.

[Body of the Question]

[One view] Here it is claimed that under the Mosaic law it was unlawful to divorce one's wife, and any man who took a divorced woman
to wife sinned mortally, because she was unclean, for she had apparently been put away because she was impure. But her sin was not punished according to the law, but separation was permitted to prevent
husbands killing their wives, and therefore, to avoid a greater evil the
law permitted this lesser evil.

[Arg. 1] The first proof of this is found in the citation of Christ re-
proving divorce (Matthew 19:9): "I say to you, whoever puts away his

wife, except for immorality, commits adultery, and he who marries a woman who has been put away commits adultery."

[Arg. 2] It is proved also by the reason Christ gave for this, which is that from the beginning God joined male and female in marriage, as is clear from Adam's words, and he added: "Therefore, what God has joined together, let no man put asunder."

[Arg. 3] It is also proved, thirdly, from Christ's reply to the question of the Pharisees when they objected: "Then why did Moses command divorce and the promulgation of a divorce decree?" He said to them: "Because Moses, by reason of the hardness of your heart, permitted you to put away your wives; but it was not so from the beginning." And the marginal gloss on this says: "Moses permitted this, not God." And the Master [Peter Lombard], on this distinction, ch. 2, says: "This was permitted by Moses, not to concede divorce, but to prevent homicide." And Augustine in *The Lord's Sermon on the Mount* says: "By commanding that a written notice of dismissal be given he did not thereby command that the wife be put away. But in order that a careful consideration of the written notice might moderate the rash anger of the man who is casting out his wife, he said: 'Whoever puts her away, let him give her a written notice of dismissal.'" One can understand this from what Ambrose commanded the emperor Theodosius because of the cruelty of a certain law he had impetuously passed. Ambrose wanted him to issue a law that the minister would not carry out this cruel precept except after thirty days had passed, so that during that time, his anger would have cooled, perhaps, and he would temper his sentence. Hence, Plato also said to someone, as Jerome recounts: "I would punish if I were not angry." And Augustine adds, in the aforesaid work, "By seeking a delay of the dismissal of the wife, he made it known he did not wish a marriage to be dissolved, insofar as he could make this known to obdurate men."

[Arg. 4] Also, the canon on divorce in the [*Decretales Gregorii IX* IV, tit. 19, c. 8], says the truth of the Gospel has condemned divorce.

[Another view] Another opinion says that giving a bill of divorce and putting away one's wife was licit under the law of Moses, because Moses promulgated the law of God, and therefore those whom he joined and pronounced married as legislator, God himself joined, and those whom he separated, God separated, because God could divorce those who were married.

Furthermore, according to Augustine in his first letter to Jerome, which is cited in canon law [*Decretum Gratiani* I, c. 7], dist. 9: "If we once admit that in the Holy Scriptures there could be even a polite lie, what will remain of their authority?"—as if he were to say:

"Nothing would be left." And the reason is that whatever authoritative text is adduced to repel heresy one will reply that this too is the word of a jocose or polite liar, just as the other text is. And the same with the counsels—if Scripture presents some counsel as salutary and useful to observe, the observance of such will have no backing in Scripture; and similarly, if some concession in Scripture is given in regard to something otherwise illicit, it will follow that there will be no unqualified authority that such is licit. For the same holds for concessions as to what is licit as holds for commandments as to what must be done and for admonitions or counsels as to what is useful. For just as a precept is not about something which it is necessary to perform, so neither is a concession about something one can do licitly.

Also, a just law would not directly give one an occasion to sin mortally, but this concession seems to give the Jews directly an occasion to put aside their wives; for if this were not written, they would have no more reason for divorce than the patriarchs had before the law of Moses; therefore either divorce is not a mortal sin, or the law permitting it was not just.

[Defense of this second opinion] The way in which one could suitably explain the second opinion is this. Complete justice does not pertain to this matrimonial contract or exchange except by divine ratification, although prior to this there is sufficient equity in the contract and for the parties entering into it, and when such justice can be found in the exchange, it is reasonable that God should ratify it. [As we saw earlier] the exchange of the body of one man for those of several women is just when such an exchange is necessary for the procreation of children, and hence God justly dispensed from monogamy and, what is more, approved of bigamy, because a greater good would come of it than would be possible if but one woman contracted with one man; what is more, those marrying under such conditions ought to wish to marry in this way according to right reason. Now, the case is similar here. To avoid an evil which outweighs the good of wedlock's indissolubility, God can dispense from it so that the marriage holds good until such a time as the woman may come to displease her husband. And in such a contract justice is preserved to some extent. For not only to obtain a greater good, but also to avoid a greater evil, the parties marrying may want to give themselves to each other in this fashion. Now, uxoricide is a greater evil than indissolubility is a good, because it includes not only the serious evil suffered by the woman killed but also the grave evil of the guilty killer. Uxoricide would also be a serious evil for the whole country, because it would be an occasion of continual discord and fighting by reason of the ire of the wife's parents towards her murderer; and this would tend to break down the family, because if the man were killed by his adversaries or by the law, it would destroy his family and the education of his child.

Thus it could be said that just as God had given a dispensation in regard to bigamy for the sake of a greater good, so too he dispensed that race to avoid a greater evil. {In the other version this reads: And according to this it could be said that since indissolubility and a perpetual obligation represents one of the goods of marriage, no marriage of the Jews was perfect, because the matrimonial contract was always entered into under the condition that it could be dissolved by a bill of divorce. But in marriage under the new law there is not only this good of indissolubility but also another, namely, the fact that marriage is a sign of the union of Christ and the Church, which is a one-to-one relationship. But in marriage under the law of nature, which held, for instance, in the case of Abraham, the first requirement or good, namely, indissolubility, was present, but not the second, which was that a man have but one wife. But in the Mosaic law, when divorce was allowed and one man could have several wives, neither requirement was characteristic of marriage, because neither was it a one-to-one relationship, nor was the union simply indissoluble. But this had to occur by divine dispensation.}

[To the arguments for the first opinion] If one holds this view, one could answer the arguments for the other in this way.

[Re 1] Christ made his promulgation for the duration of his law, namely, that of the Gospel, in such a way that it would have the status it had under the law of nature, where it held between one man and one woman. However, since under the Mosaic law, bigamy was licit, he also returned marriage to an unqualified state of perfection, namely, as indissoluble as it was under the law of nature. And so he invalidated for the duration of his law that contract which had been licit under the Mosaic law, which was a temporary use of their bodies for reproduction until a woman ceased to be pleasing in the eyes of her husband. This, like other imperfections licit under the law of Moses, Christ removed, and those which were more permanent he brought to perfection. And hence after the time the Gospel was promulgated, to have several wives or to divorce one and marry another became damnable. But before that time, this was not condemned in the way those who hold the first opinion claim. And according to this second opinion, Jews, from the promulgation of the Gospel, are obliged to have, not two wives, but only one wife, and they are not in any way to divorce her.

[Re 2] As for Christ's proof, what he said obviously refers to the law of nature, and to refute the Pharisees it was enough to point out that they were not observing even the law of nature in regard to marriage, and he showed he was reasonable in establishing inseparability according to his law, something that was consonant with the first of these marital goods present in the law of nature.

[Re 3] As for the added argument based on Christ's reply to the Pharisees, namely, "God permitted this because of the hardness of your hearts," note that many consider this to be a genuine permission and not just a concession, since Christ said specifically "he permitted this." By these words he meant that Moses did not command this, or counsel this, or approve of this. Moses simply did not prohibit it, since he regarded it as something licit because of a certain need. This permission was not a case of dissimulation about something illicit, for such an interpretation implies that Moses only permitted them to be damned by not pointing out to them specifically that this was the way to damnation, thus suggesting the opposite. No just lawgiver, however, where human laws are concerned, can prevent many evils from remaining unpunished, according to what Augustine says in his work *On Free Choice* I, ch. 5. If a lawgiver does not punish every evil, and thus only permits some inasmuch as he does not expressly punish them, then it does not follow that he concedes such things. Hence a human law could still be just which would state that something could occur which is against that law.

What is added there as to "the hardness of your hearts," etc., does not imply that what is referred to is illicit; for frequently the obduracy of the subjects is the reason why some restrictions of law are relaxed that would otherwise not be relaxed, and which it would be useful not to relax in their case if they were more tractable. For instance, a college president, seeing that his group is prone to the opposite of what it would be more righteous to observe, although he could order the opposite advantageously if only his subjects were more amenable, can refrain from establishing such rules, or if they are already in force, he can in all honesty relax them lest their enforcement lead to a multiplicity of sins.

As for the arguments from the *Ordinary Glosses* it seems that the first could be denied, because Moses as legislator was only God's mouthpiece. If one wished to gloss the text, however, one could say that it was Moses, not God, who permitted this. In other words, God did not give this precept immediately to Moses in the way that he gave him the other commandments. That is why nowhere in the first four books of the law do we find God commanding this of Moses or of others. Therefore, this, more than the other things God spoke to Moses, is attributed precisely to Moses, as are all the other things that occur only in Deuteronomy. And there was a fitting reason for this, since God wished the relaxations resulting from human industry to appear as though they came not from himself but rather from his servants. Hence to lighten the labor of Moses, who sat through the whole day judging the people, God expressed this not immediately through himself, but to Jethro, his relative, indicating it was of human industry.

As for the other gloss, it is easy to see that it says nothing against this view. For it is true that God did not give the command to divorce, but only commanded that if one did divorce, a bill of divorce should be given. This was a human counsel, however, though not of human origin, inasmuch as the man was speaking for God.

As for the citation from Augustine I concede that the delay which writing the bill entailed does suggest that God was displeased with this dismissal; and that it was not merely that it would be better not to dissolve the marriage, but that it was bad to do so, but not so bad that one would sin gravely against marriage in the way one would if this were not licensed by law.

[Re 4] As for what canon law says about divorce, the answer is clear from what was said about the first argument; it is true that Christ condemned divorce for the duration of his law.

[Reply to the Initial Arguments]

To the arguments at the beginning:

As for the first, the answer is clear from the solution to the question. And when it is said that it is against the law of nature which says: "What God has joined together," etc., I say that it is not against the law of nature in the strict sense, because it is not against any self-evident principles that pertain to the law of nature nor against any conclusion that follows immediately from such principles that a contract hold for only a time, according to this second view, nor does it run contrary to the education of the children, for God could have arranged another plan for the education of children, but one not as convenient as this is, and then even though one of the goods of marriage is in harmony with the law of nature, namely, indissolubility, God could have dispensed with this in order to avoid a greater evil.

To the second argument, I grant that matrimony is, simply speaking, a perpetual obligation; but a marriage could be a firm obligation for a period of time that is not forever, and hence I concede that marriage under the Mosaic law was not marriage in an unqualified sense, except perhaps where some individuals wished to oblige themselves forever beyond what the law required, something they were not required to do by that law. Or one could say that if matrimony was simply perfect under the law and thus an indissoluble union, this was true, unless the legislator [God] revoked the contract or dispensed from such, and that he did dispense when a woman displeased her husband to such an extent that uxoricide was feared. Such a dispensation would be similar to that which occurs when a religious who is in a nonconsummated marriage is dispensed because of solemn religious vows, where the marriage is one in an unqualified sense and not just one that holds for a time, but the legislator in such a case dispenses because of a greater good, whereas in the other case it is to avoid a greater evil.

To the third argument, I deny the analogy, because the grounds for dispensation are not similar. Where the woman hates the man there is not as great a danger as where the man hates the woman, since the sex difference prevents the woman from taking such vengeance as a man is wont to do.

For just as one could concede that one man could have several women for the purpose of reproduction, something that is not conceded to a woman, so it would be against the marital good of having children if one woman had several husbands, and thus in neither case is the situation the same for a woman as for a man.

If one wished to hold the first opinion, however, one could easily reply to the arguments against it. As for the authorities from Deuteronomy and Malachi, they are permissions involving a lesser evil. However, the actions they permit are still mortally sinful but are allowed only to prevent an even graver mortal sin happening.

As for the second, that legal rule refers just to what can be dissolved, which is not the case with the marital obligation. Also one could say to the minor premise that this marital obligation is born of the mutual consent of the contracting parties acting only as instrumental causes, but the principal cause is the divine approbation; and this rule of law does not hold for instrumental causes. Hence, from the principal cause [Christ] inferred that marriage is indissoluble, saying, according to Matthew [19:6]: "Therefore, what God has joined together, let no man put asunder."

21. POSITIVE LAW AND CIVIL AUTHORITY
(*Ordinatio* IV, dist. 15, q. 2)

I ask: What is the source of distinct ownership such that this may be called "mine" and that "yours"? For all injustice through misappropriation derives from this as well as all justice through restitution . . .

[First conclusion] As for this question, the first conclusion is this: "In the state of innocence neither divine nor natural law provided for distinct ownership of property; on the contrary everything was common."

Proof is found in [Gratian's] *Decrees*, dist. 7, ch. 1: "By the law of nature all things were common," where he cites Augustine's commentary on John: "By what law do you defend the real estate of the Church? Is it divine or human? The first is found in the divine Scriptures; the human we have from the law of kings. Is it not by human law that we possess what we do? By divine law 'the earth and the fulness thereof is the Lord's.' And is not the reason the earth bears both poor and rich the will of man? This house, this farm, this servant is called mine, therefore, by human law." Again in the same place: "Remove the Emperor's laws and who will dare say: 'This is my farm'?" And later: "By the king's laws we own our possessions." And in causa 12, q. 1, "All men ought to have the common use of everything on earth."

The rationale for this is twofold. According to right reason men should have the use of things in such a way as, first, to contribute to a peaceful and decent life, and [second] to provide needed sustenance. But in the state of innocence common use with no distinct ownership would have been more conducive to this than individual ownership, for no one would have taken what another needed, nor would the latter have had to wrest it by force from others. Each would have taken what first came to hand as he needed it. Thus a greater sufficiency for sustenance would have obtained than if one had precluded another's use of a thing because he had appropriated it for himself.

[Second conclusion] Our second conclusion is that after the Fall of man, this law of nature of holding all things in common was revoked.

This also was reasonable, for two reasons. First of all, communality of property would have militated against the peaceful life; the evil or covetous man would take more than he needed. And to do so, he would also use violence against others who wished to use these common goods for their own needs, as we read [in Genesis] of Nemroth [the first potentate]: "He was a mighty hunter before the Lord!"—that is to say, he was an oppressor of men. The original law would also have failed to ensure the necessary sustenance of mankind, for the stronger warriors would have deprived the others of necessities. Therefore, the city-state of Aristotle (*Politics* II [ch. 5]), wherein all things were not held in common, was much better than that of Socrates, which Aristotle rejected because of the condition in which he found man to exist.

[Third conclusion] The third conclusion is this: "Once this natural law precept of having all in common was revoked, and thus permission was given to appropriate and divide up what had been common, there was still no actual division imposed by either divine or natural law."

Not by divine law, certainly, as the aforesaid citation from Augustine proves—"By what law?" and so on. Not by a law of nature, in all probability, for nothing indicates that the original law was reversed rather than revoked (and the original determination of the law was that all things be common), unless we take the proposition in the *Institutions of Justinian* to be natural law: "Goods belonging to nobody go to the first tenant." For even though it seems clear that, in all probability, a division took place once natural reason grasped that goods should be divided, it seems more plausible to say this was effected by positive law rather than the law of nature. It would follow from this that the first division of property was brought about by some positive legislation. To see why this division was just, therefore, we must look at why such a positive law would be just.

[Fourth conclusion] Hence, we have this fourth conclusion: "What a just positive law requires of its legislator is prudence and authority."

Prudence, that he might dictate what ought to be established for the community according to practical right reason. Authority, because "law" is derived from a verb that means "to bind," and not every judgment of a prudent man binds the community, or binds any person if the man is head of nothing. It is clear enough how prudence could have been operative in figuring out just laws. But what of the just authority required if the law is to be just?

[Fifth conclusion, about the origin of civil authority] A fifth conclusion follows: "Authority or rulership takes two forms, paternal and political. And political authority is twofold, that vested in one person and that vested in a group." The first, namely, paternal authority, is just by natural law in virtue of which children are bound to obey their parents. Neither was this revoked by any positive Mosaic or Gospel law, but rather it was confirmed. Political authority, however, which is exercised over those outside [the family], whether it resides in one person or in a community, can be just by common consent and election on the part of the community. The first [or parental sort of] authority regards natural descendants, even though they do not dwell in the same city, whereas the second has to do with those who live together, even though there is no consanguinity or close relationship between them. Thus, if some outsiders banded together to build a city or live in one, seeing that they could not be well governed without some form of authority, they could have amicably agreed to commit their commu-

nity to one person or to a group, and if to one person, to him alone
and to a successor who would be chosen as he was, or to him and his
posterity. And both of these forms of political authority are just, because one person can justly submit himself to another or to a community in those things which are not against the law of God and as regards which he can be guided better by the person or persons to whom
he has submitted or subjected himself than he could by himself. Hence,
we have here all that is required to pass a just law, because it would be
promulgated by one who possesses prudence either in himself or in his
counselors and enjoys authority in one of the several ways mentioned
in this conclusion.

[Sixth conclusion] From this the sixth conclusion follows: "The first
division of ownership could have been just by reason of some just
positive law passed by the father or the regent ruling justly or by a
community ruling or regulating justly, and this is probably how it was
done."

For after the flood, Noah divided the earth among his sons, each of
which occupied a portion for himself and did the same for his sons and
posterity, or else the latter divided it further by common agreement, as
we read in Genesis 13 about Abraham and Lot, for Abraham gave Lot
his choice and took what remained for himself. Or a law could have
been promulgated by a father or by someone elected as ruler or by a
group to whom the community gave this authority. This law, I say, was
or could have been that anything unclaimed would go to the first oc-
cupant, and then they split up and fanned out over the face of the
earth, one occupying this area, another that.

[Transfer of ownership] As for the second article, I say that the
transfer of property to another can be either [a] by way of ownership—
where a thing passes from one owner to another—or [b] by way of
simple use, where the ownership is retained, but another is given the
right to use the property in question. And justice or injustice in trans-
ferring the simple use involves different rules than does a just transfer
of ownership. And a transfer of ownership can take place by the public
authority or that of a ruler, or by the authority of law, or by private
authority of the owner who possesses it immediately . . . [Scotus then
discusses in detail the specific laws governing the transfer and acquisition of property.]

PART VI

The Intellectual and Moral Virtues

22. THE WILL AS THE SEAT OF THE MORAL VIRTUES
(*Ordinatio* III, suppl., dist. 33)

Regarding the thirty-second and thirty-third distinctions [of Bk. III] I ask: Are the moral virtues in the will as their subject?

[Arguments Pro and Con]

For the negative:

In Bk. I of the *Ethics*, the Philosopher says that they are in the irrational part of the soul and the Commentator explains that they are in that which is intermediate between the vegetative and the rational parts; but this is not the will but rather the sense appetite.

Furthermore, in Bk. III of the *Ethics* the Philosopher places fortitude and temperance in the appetite of the sensitive portion of the soul.

Also, look up the seventh comment on Bk. VI of the *Ethics*, which explains what prudence is.

Furthermore, according to Bk. I of the *Politics*, ch. 3, reason rules the inferior appetite with a despotic rule, but the higher appetite with a political, i.e., civil, rule, so that the appetite can be countermoved; therefore, in order that it may be moved delightfully by right reason it will be necessary to posit some virtues in it.

Also, fortitude and temperance are said to be in the irascible and concupiscible portion; these are not distinguished in the will, however, but only in the sense appetite, because the conditions in the object which they are concerned with, namely, the arduous and delectable good respectively, do not alter the object of the will *per se*, but only the sensible good which confronts the sense appetite.

For the positive:

Virtues are habits of choice, from their definition in II *Ethics*; but election is an act of the will or of reason according to the Philosopher in VI *Ethics*, for it is a deliberative appetite. But this pertains to the will, which presupposes rational knowledge for its operation. Now, a habit is in that potency to which that operation pertains *per se*; therefore, the moral habit pertains *per se* to the will itself.

Besides, virtue has the honorable good [*bonum honestum*] as its *per se* object; but this is the *per se* object of the will; therefore, etc.

Furthermore, virtue is the principle or source of a praiseworthy act according to II *Ethics*; but nothing is worthy of praise unless an action of the will is involved; therefore, virtue pertains to the faculty that acts freely of itself and is the reason why a person acts laudably, and that is the will.

[Body of the Question]
[A. The Opinion of Others]

Some claim that the Philosopher's sentiment was negative, or otherwise he expressed himself insufficiently concerning the moral virtues. For wherever he speaks of them he seems to say they are in the sensitive part, and nowhere, apparently, except in speaking of justice in Bk. V of the *Ethics*, does he admit they are in the intellective part.

Arguments are presented for this view, the first of which is this. The will is of itself determined to what is simply good in an unqualified sense, for this—in contrast to the good of nature, which is the object of the sense appetite—is its proper object. Or if the will could tend towards a good of nature, it would be sufficiently determined to tend or not tend towards such accordingly as reason reveals the good to it, for it seems that the object insofar as it is apprehended moves the will, and therefore there is no need to postulate a habit in the will, but it is enough that the intellect be perfected so that it will show the good correctly.

The second argument is based on the liberty of the will, for as free the will can sufficiently determine itself, and needs no habit to determine it. Or the argument could also be put as follows: if the will acts freely of itself, then anything that would determine it, in such a way as to incline it to act, would be repugnant to it. But virtue acts after the fashion of nature, and therefore, virtue is repugnant to the very way the will acts and hence is not to be found in it.

A third argument is this. Where there are extremes there is a middle ground; where there are extremes of passion therefore there is virtue which moderates the passions. Now, the passions are in the sense appetite and not in the will; therefore, etc.

Fourthly, I argue in this way. If virtue could be produced in the will by righteous actions other than acts of the sense appetite, then an angel could acquire virtues by performing such righteous acts of the will as pertain to the moral virtues. But the consequent is incongruous and clearly is contrary to what the Philosopher says in Bk. X of the *Ethics*, where he denies moral virtues in such [pure spirits].

[Refutation of This Opinion]

This view can be refuted by arguments similar to those presented in its favor.

[1. Arguments from authority] The first is based on the authority of Aristotle, for in the *Politics* I, he admits it is necessary for the regent to possess virtue in order to rule rightly, and this is even more necessary for him than for the servant to be rightly submissive, and he draws an analogy there with the higher and lower portions of the soul.

Furthermore, those who hold this other view concede that justice is in the will; therefore, arguments based on what holds commonly for both the will and the moral virtues are not conclusive. Nor should the authority of what the Philosopher says in *Ethics* I about those portions of the soul that can obey the rational principle be applied only to the sense appetite, because if that is the only part he understands to be obedient to reason, then he has not covered the divisions of the soul adequately insofar as it is capable of moral virtue. And insofar as he had no intention of treating this subject adequately, it follows also that he had no intention of covering its divisions sufficiently either. For he treats of the soul insofar as it is subject to moral virtue, such as justice, at least, which resides neither in the reason as such nor in that portion which obeys reason, as he understands these two terms.

Furthermore, before defining virtue in terms of a mean [between two extremes] the Philosopher, wishing to investigate the character of happiness [as an activity in accord with virtue], says in *Ethics* I that apart from the nutritive part of the soul, what comes next is the sensitive part, which seems to be common to all animals. What remains is a certain operative part of the soul, which indeed can be persuaded by reason, and this insofar as it is intelligent and willing. From this text it is clear that he first excludes the sensitive portion, because in it there is no distinctive operation of man qua human, such as that which is in accord with the moral virtues. Consequently, these virtues were not to be located mainly in that part; therefore, that which remains, namely, the operative part possessing [such virtues], is that portion of the soul that excels *per se* the entire sensitive portion, and he divides this part into what is intelligent and what is readily persuasible by reason. Hence, by "persuasible by reason" he there understands the will, because by "intelligent" he certainly refers to the intellect. Thus it seems we can infer expressly from his own words that he sometimes speaks of the will as able to obey reason, whereas at other times he speaks of the sense appetite as such, as at the end of the first book. Now, just as he takes "able to obey reason" in a twofold sense, so he also gives "rational" a twofold meaning. One sense is strict and primary, and refers only to the intellect; the other is neither strict nor primary, but is still properly called "rational" in an unqualified sense, and this is applicable to the will. The third sense, however, is not proper, but is taken broadly as referring to the sense appetite. Hence, the will, which is in the middle, is at times called "rational" in comparison to one of the extremes [the irrational appetite], and at other times called "able to obey reason" in comparison to the other extreme [or intellect]. For taking reason strictly, it is "persuasible by reason," whereas taking "reason" not properly, but broadly as anything pertaining to the mind, the will is rational. The sensitive appetite is not only persuasible but able to obey, and one could well ponder these words, for what is truly free is persuasible, but the sense appetite is not properly persuasible, but is able to obey, because it is subject to the command of the will.

Furthermore, there are many authorities for what we say, one of which is Augustine in *The Morals of the Church*, ch. 15, where he wants to point out that the four moral virtues are nothing more than well-ordered love or various orderly loves. Look it up. And also what Augustine says at some length in *The City of God*, Bk. XIV, chs. 5 and 6, is also to the point. Look for it there. And Avicenna also has something about this in the last chapter of Bk. IX of his *Metaphysics*.

[2. Arguments from reason] Furthermore the reasons cited for this other opinion can be turned in favor of the opposite view.

[As for the first] Take the first argument, about the will being undetermined as regards opposites. Now, it is such not only as regards opposite objects but also as regards opposite ways of acting, namely, rightly and not rightly; therefore it needs something which inclines it specifically to act rightly, and this will be a virtue. The implication is clear, for the sole reason for postulating virtues in the powers is to regulate what of itself could act either rightly or not rightly. Proof of the antecedent: the will can choose whatever is shown to it in which it sees some aspect of its first object, but in choosing such it can act in a way that is not right.

If you claim it is enough that reason presents the object correctly and hence reason requires the virtue, not the will, this is not true. If it were, reason would have to make a mistake in revealing the object before the will could make a bad choice, and thus there would be an error in the intellect before the first sin is in the will, which is irrational, for then the punishment [i.e., a darkening of the intellect] would precede the fault.

Furthermore, even granting the will could be sufficiently determined by the intellect to choose rightly, it would not follow that no habit is produced in the will. Since the intellect, insofar as it has an operation that precedes the act of the will and acts in a purely natural fashion, is more determined to judge correctly, one would not deny that a habit, such as prudence, is produced there by its frequent acts of correct judgment. Since the will, then, is not a potency that is of itself more determined to one way of acting than the intellect, by its frequently elicited acts, the will can produce a certain correct aptitude inclining it towards similar acts, and that aptitude is what I call a virtue.

Furthermore, a habit is postulated not only that powers may act rightly, but that they may act promptly and with delight. Now, even though the will would be able to choose correctly on the basis of reason, it would not do so delightfully or promptly without a habit of its own. Proof: if a man with a previous vice were recently called to act rightly in the opposite way, and right reason dictates that something opposed to his vice should be chosen, even though he chooses this, he would not do so delightfully. For his first righteous act does not immediately destroy the entire vicious habit he had acquired previously; indeed it makes little or no inroad against it. This is clear from experience, for the newly converted chooses what is good only with difficulty and would find it delightful rather to choose in his earlier customary way. If the will is to follow the dictates of reason with delight, it needs a habit to choose the sort of act that conforms to that habit.

To this first argument, then, I reply that it is based on an equivocation as to what constitutes "good" in an unqualified sense. For this can be understood in contrast either to an apparent good or to good in particular. If it is taken in the first sense, then an unqualified good is not an adequate object of the will, because then the will could not choose an apparent good, for no potency can have an act in regard to something in which there is not some aspect of its first object; and thus the will of any pilgrim by virtue of its object would be confirmed [in grace] already in this life and prevented from sinning. Understood in the second way, one could concede that good under the aspect of good in general is an object that can be sought by the will with its proper cognitive power [i.e., the intellect]. The sense, according to the common dictum, knows the singular and the intellect the universal. Therefore, the sense appetite could have as its object the good as now present, that is, the singular good with all its individuating conditions, whereas the will has as its object the good as revealed to it by the intellect, which is the universal good and is simply good without qualification. Also the addition to the argument that reason by showing what is right suffices [to determine the will to tend to the good] is against that erroneous article about the will being unable to choose the opposite of a universal or particular good [condemned in 1277, viz., " 'If reason is right, the will is right' is an error"].

[To the second argument] The second reason given also can be used to prove the opposite. For an agent needs a disposition even more for some action in its power than for anything else, for if it does not have this in its power, then it will not be credited with any praise or blame when it acts or in regard to the way it acts. But because the will has it in its power to act in a praiseworthy or blameworthy manner, it needs a principle that will enable it to act laudably, and virtue is just such a principle. Also it would seem strange if that for which a man's actions are praised is located precisely in that portion of his soul that is common to him and the brute. Nor is it valid to argue here that a natural agent is determined to acting, therefore the will is also, since it is a kind of naturally active agent, for all agree no habit is needed for agents acting in a purely natural manner, because they are inclined to do so in the highest way. But they do not deny a habit in the intellect, although it acts in a more natural way than does the will, because it is not of itself inclined in the highest degree. Neither does this indetermination [of the will] stem from an imperfection in the agent, but from its [superabundant] lack of limitation, which is a perfection in the agent. For other merely naturally acting agents are limited to one action, so that they cannot perform the contrary or even [refrain from acting when all external conditions for acting are present]; but the will is not thus limited, as was said in dist. 25 of Bk. II.

As for these two proofs, then, I say to the first that although the will by reason of its liberty could determine itself to act, nevertheless in virtue of its action it receives an aptitude that directly inclines it to a similar act. For this unique determination of the will is not the sort of natural form that one finds in fire, for instance, as regards the way it behaves, but it comes from a free action stemming from a potency that is undetermined, and it is in this way that it is determinable by a habit. The answer to the second proof is clear from what was said in dist. 17 of the first book and dist. 25 of the second about how a secondary cause acting naturally can concur with a primary free cause to produce a free act, and how the effect is called free because of the freedom of the primary cause. Now, a habit, if it is a cause, is a secondary one where the will is involved.

[To the third argument] The third reason, about moderating the passions, actually proves the opposite, both because there are passions in the will, according to Augustine (*The City of God*, Bk. XIV, chs. 5 and 6), and also because moderation of a passion can be understood in two ways. Either it is an existing passion or it is one in the future. [1] An existing passion can be moderated in one of two ways: either [a] there is a diminution of a passion for an object which is apt by nature to delight the sense appetite immoderately if left to itself, or [b] the moderation consists in referring this delight to an end that according to right reason is appropriate, an end, namely, to which, considered simply as an object of the sense appetite, it would not otherwise be referred. [2] A passion that might develop in the future is moderated either by avoiding the object apt to delight it immoderately or by directing the sense appetite only to such objects as are apt to delight it in a moderate way, and then the passion is not itself moderated but is simply prevented from occurring.

But howsoever this moderation of a passion is to be understood, it pertains more to the will than to the sense appetite, because, properly speaking, the will is the rational appetite, and to refer a passion to some appropriate end is an action not of the sense appetite but of the will. For "to refer" is not a function one attributes properly to the sense appetite in the way one ascribes it to the intellect and will. And if one understands "passion" to be something one should avoid if immoderate or should indulge in if moderate, it seems sufficiently clear that as regards such future action it is the will rather than the sense appetite that can do what is right, because the source of the will's knowledge is not the senses but reason, whose role it is to counsel one about future things.

If we consider these arguments which are adduced to support the other opinion, it is clear how they prove the opposite, [first] because the will is not of itself righteous and is able to be rectified as regards that action that is properly its own; [second] because the will is no less undetermined and determinable than is the intellect to which one attributes virtue; [third] because it is also inclined by nature to delight in its own way in that action that is properly its own, and so it ought to have a habit whereby it can act in a way that gives it delight; [fourth] because it is the principal agent in performing actions that are distinctively human, inasmuch as they are free, and because human actions, if they are to be praiseworthy, require in the principal agent a virtue deserving of praise; [fifth] because the will, if it possesses virtues, can more readily moderate the passions in a fitting way than the sense appetite can.

[3. Other arguments] In addition to these reasons, one argues against the individual who holds the opposite opinion in this way. If in the state of innocence there were not present in the sense appetite some passions opposing right reason, there would be no necessity of assigning any virtue to that sense appetite, and still virtues would have been present in that state, because they would have made man perfect, according to the Master. There is also the authority of Augustine for this, first in his thirty-fifth or thirty-sixth *Letter*, and also in his *Soliloquies*, where he says: "This is truly perfect virtue, reason arriving at its end." Also, ch. 15 of *The City of God*, Bk. I. The Master, also, in the text of this distinction assigns [moral virtues] to acts that could remain [with the soul] in heaven.

[B. Scotus' Own Opinion]

One could say to the question that the will on its own without a habit could perform an act that is right and morally good—nor is this true only of the will, for the intellect also could perform a correct judgment without an intellectual habit; for the first act of a correct intellect and a will that is right precedes the habit in whatsoever degree such exists, for from such acts is generated whatever is first present in a habit. Nevertheless, just as in the intellect, either through its first act or through frequently elicited acts, the habit of prudence is generated, so also with the first correct choice consonant with the dictates of right reason, or through many such correct choices, there is generated in the will a proper virtue which inclines the will to choose rightly.

What proves this is the fact that the will's act of choice is naturally prior to any command that it or reason gives to the sense appetite. For reason does not seem to reach the sense appetite except by way of the will, which is properly speaking the rational appetite. Also the will first wills something in itself before it commands any act of an inferior potency in regard to such, for it is not because it commands the inferior potency that it wills such a thing, but vice versa. Therefore, in that prior state, the will by its right choices—since it is just as indeterminate and able to be determined as is the intellect—generates in itself a habit inclining it to choose rightly, and this habit will most properly be called a virtue, because it is the elective habit that most properly inclines the will to act in the way it was generated, by making right choices.

One can concede, however, that if the will by willing can command the sense appetite (by moderating either its passion or the way it goes after or flees from a thing, if this be an act of the sense appetite), it can also leave behind in the sense appetite by such correct commands some habit that inclines that appetite to move more readily towards sensibles in the way the will commands. And this habit that is left there, although it is not properly a virtue, because it is not an elective habit, nor does it incline one to make choices, can in some sense be conceded to be a virtue, since it inclines one to such things as are in accord with right reason.

[Some Objections]

[1] Against the first part [of my thesis, namely, that virtues, properly speaking, are only in the higher portion of the soul] it is objected that on this view moral virtues could exist in an angel. I prove this because the angel can elicit a correct act of the will in regard to something towards which the sense appetite can be passionately attached, and so from many such righteous acts a virtue will be generated in the angel.—What confirms this is that right choices are appropriate not only in regard to passions existing in the sensitive part of the soul but also in regard to passions that are revealed to a person by the intellect, even if they never were nor ever have been actually present there, as was pointed out in the question about practical knowledge in the prologue to the first book. By such choices, then, virtue may be generated in the will with nothing accompanying it in the sense appetite.

[2] Furthermore, if moral virtue were in the will, then such a virtue would be more noble than prudence, because the more noble the subject it perfects, the more noble will the perfection be. But the consequent contradicts what the Philosopher says in Bk. VI of the *Ethics*; therefore, the antecedent does likewise.

[3] Against the second part [as to what is produced in the sensitive appetite] it is argued that if it is only because the sense appetite is moved by a command of the will that a certain quality is produced there which inclines it towards similar acts, and this is a virtue, then by the same token, a moral habit can be generated in that part of the body that is frequently moved at the command of the will, and not only this, but the same thing can happen in inanimate and nonrational things which the will uses.

[Solution to the Objections]

[To 1] To the first it can be granted that if an angel were created in a purely natural state with no moral virtues in the will, then these could be generated in it by many correct choices, not indeed as regards nonexistent passions of the sense appetite, which neither could be nor were nor would have been in the angel, but only as regards such passions revealed to it in general by its intellect, because assuming the intellect shows such to it and dictates to it what choices a person able to have such passions ought to make, the angel's will, by agreeing to such dictates through many elicited acts, could have a moral habit.

And this is evident because every will, if it necessarily lacks the perfection appropriate to the will, is suited to have any perfection of the will whatsoever. But to will what is good as regards actions that can be performed not only by oneself but by others (and this not merely as ordered to the divine good, but insofar as it is good for the agent) represents a certain perfection of the will, and the will of an angel is not necessarily imperfect; therefore, it can have a habit by reason of which it wishes me to have the good that is temperance insofar as such a good is suited to me. And this habit cannot be called "charity," because—as was pointed out—the habit of charity is not just something good that helps us to love God but something that helps us to do so in a special way according to that aspect of his goodness that is proper to him. But if it is not charity, neither is it something other than temperance, because the formal object of a habit does not vary in me and you. Therefore, just as I choose for myself this formal good by reason of the habit of temperance, so also by the same sort of habit everyone else wishes that I have this good, and therefore, in the angel there will be temperance in virtue of which it wishes me this good.

In this way, consequently, one could also postulate moral virtue in God, just as one admits charity in him without its accidentality. And thus the argument about the angel raised against our thesis can provide a reason in favor of it, for the will of the angel can will that good to me, which is properly the habit of temperance insofar as it is the sort of good that it is. And hence it can will this from a habit of temperance, as we have argued, and in this way temperance will exist in the angel, though not in a sense part.

And if one objects that this contradicts the Philosopher, who denies the gods have moral virtues in *Ethics*, Bk. IV, I reply: Perhaps one would deny them all accidental habits if one assumed as some do that they are naturally happy.

Otherwise, if one does not care to postulate moral virtues in them, one could simply deny the implication of this argument against us. This could be done in either of two ways: first, because virtue is not concerned with just any good, but with something difficult. But the good which is assumed to be the object of the will is difficult only for one with a sense appetite, who is apt by nature to be pulled towards the opposite of this good, at least under certain circumstances, and from the fact that the sense appetite is so inclined, the will is apt by nature to take delight in the same thing, and hence it is difficult for the will to tend to good under fitting circumstances. But since the angel has no sense appetite, its will is not inclined by nature to share the delight of such a habit or appetite, and therefore, without difficulty it can tend to what is morally good, and this under such circumstances as reason dictates. —The other way to deny the implication is to say that volition is twofold: one simple, which is a kind of pleasure or satisfaction taken in some object; the other efficacious, by which the person willing, if not impeded, goes after the object wanted. Only the second represents a choice as the Philosopher understands this term in III *Ethics* where he says: "We may wish for the impossible, but no one chooses such," that is to say, no one wills such efficaciously in the sense of going after it as the result of such a volition. By an act of simple satisfaction, however, one could wish for what is impossible, as happened perhaps in the case of the first angel, who sinned or could have sinned by willing such, namely, equality with God. Hence one could say that in those who have a sensitive appetite, the will could be a principle of many choices in regard to moral good, and this efficacious volition is what we call "choosing." This alone is suited by nature to produce the sort of habit which, though prior to any habit in the sense appetite, is nevertheless suited to be a principle for commanding such an appetite. In the angel, however, there is simple volition, but this is not suited by nature to command anything.

[To 2] As for the second, though one could say that while not every perfection in a more noble subject need be more noble, if there is some perfection there that is less noble than a kindred perfection in a less noble subject, that perfection in the highest of all noble subjects would still have to exceed the highest perfection of that sort among less noble things. But moral virtue is not the highest perfection in the will, nor is prudence the highest in the intellect; charity is the most noble perfection of the will as faith is of the intellect, and charity seems to surpass faith. Still, this answer does not seem to suffice, because with respect to the same object the more noble potency seems to have the more noble act when both act to their utmost, because in such a case there is no excess on the part of the object, which is the same, but only on the part of the potency, and to that extent the more noble excels. Therefore, if there be an act of the practical intellect and an act of the will in regard to the same object, such as a moral good, if both act perfectly, one dictating, the other choosing, then the right choice will be simply more noble than the right dictate, and consequently the habit generated by choices of this sort will be simply more perfect than those produced by correct judgments, which I grant.

As for the Philosopher preferring prudence, I reply that prudence is somehow related to the other virtues, insofar as it and its act preceded the generation of either an act or a habit of moral virtue, and because of this priority a moral act and habit is conformed to it as prior and not vice versa. And such priority according to the Philosopher implies that prudence functions as a rule and a measure, and it is in this that its dignity consists, but not in an unqualified sense.

[To 3] As for the third, it is conceded that there could be a virtue and habit in a part of the body, as is clear from the hand of a writer or painter. For my hand is not skilled in those abilities needed to play the cither. But by practice it becomes such, and this aptitude inheres in the hand and is presumed and conceded to be a kind of virtue, because it is a certain aptitude for performing a work of moral virtue. We also grant what was said further about nonrational beings, such as the horse, which can be trained to perform such acts as are customary for it. In purely inanimate things, however, we do not find such an aptitude, for a stone does not rise more easily because it is thrown repeatedly.

[Reply to the Initial Arguments]

To the arguments at the beginning, I concede the point made by all the authorities quoted, namely, that there is a certain quality in the sense appetite that could be called a virtue, but that it possesses the character of a virtue less perfectly than does that quality in the will which inclines it to choose [rightly].

As for the last argument, about the irascible and concupiscible parts of the soul, I say that such a distinction exists not only in the sense appetite but also in the will. And when it is objected that the irascible and concupiscible has to do with arduous and delectable objects—whether this is a distinction of objects or not is discussed in the following question—the point is that this distinction can be found on the part of objects in relation to the will as well as in relation to the sense appetite.—As for the further claim that the will is sufficiently perfected by a theological virtue, I reply that this is true as regards the divine good, but this virtue has to do with no other good unless it be as ordered to loving God, so that no act is elicited by charity unless God be the object aimed at, even though it be by way of other objects that serve as means towards this. But not only can I will myself a good that is well ordered, because I willed this out of love for God, but I can also will this same good insofar as it possesses in itself a proper goodness becoming to me, and to will this good under the latter aspect pertains to a habit other than charity.—And if you object that this other habit, since it does not contain a reference to God, will not be a righteous act, because it seems one is enjoying [instead of using] a created good, I reply that the lesser habit does not include in itself the act of a higher habit. Now, charity, which is the higher habit, has of itself the function of referring this other habit immediately to God. No other habit of itself, therefore, has this proper referral function, but rather has of itself as its proper act to love this good, which good ought to be referred to God through charity. From this it does not follow, however, that the inferior habit is evil, nor that it is a principle of fruition or enjoying this created good as one's ultimate end. For though, in a negative sense, this inferior habit does not refer this act to the fruition of God, it does not, however, fail to refer it in a contrary sense, namely, in a way that is opposed to right reason. For to enjoy something [created] as an end not only implies that in a negative sense there is no referral of the act to God, but implies something contrarily opposed to just using it, as was pointed out in the first distinction of Bk. I about fruition.

[Henry of Ghent's solution] to what was said in the *Politics* about reason ruling the sense appetite with a despotic power is this. He says that Aristotle thought the condition of corrupt [or fallen] human nature was the state in which it was instituted. (However, I have explained this in a different way in Bk. II, how the lower appetite is by nature to have its pleasure and how it could have been moved harmoniously by the will.) In my way also some virtue could have been postulated in both appetites, unless perhaps original justice gave the will a more perfect dominion over the sense appetite, so that it could use it immediately in a servile way. But this does not seem to save the situation, for no matter how much the will would dominate the sense appetite this would not seem to account for any delightful submission on its part, unless in that appetite there were some habit inclining it to obey such a mover. [And in such a case there would be a virtue in the will as well]; remember that if I will you to choose rightly regarding some passion, I could generate a moral habit in myself by so doing. Now, by holding this view, then, that [virtues are in the will, Henry] goes on to distinguish between the will [a] as nature, [b] as free, and [c] as deliberative. He denies there is virtue in the will in the first way, because it tends naturally either to its end as such or to any good shown to it in which some aspect of its end is displayed; and because of such a determination virtue is not required in it as nature. Neither is it required in it as free, because virtue inclines after the manner of nature, and the will as free is not suited to be moved naturally; for if it could be naturally inclined, then it could be necessitated as free. Therefore, only in the third way, as deliberative (not indeed as regards the end, but with respect to the means toward that end), will a moral habit be present in the will. He adds also that virtue moves after the manner of nature, because it acts suddenly; hence according to the Philosopher in III *Ethics:* "It is thought the mark of a braver man to be fearless and undisturbed in sudden alarms."

[Refutation of Henry] What I have said in dist. 15 of this third book contradicts his first point, because the will, as nature, elicits no act whatsoever; therefore, as nature it does not tend to any object, be it the end or something else, by an elicited act, but only by way of a natural inclination, as a heavy object is said to tend downward even though it is at rest in some high place.

Against the second two divisions he gives of will, one seems to include the other, for insofar as the will is deliberative, it is free. For it is deliberative either in the sense of commanding one to deliberate or insofar as it chooses in accord with some previous deliberation. And either way, deliberation is something pertaining to the will insofar as it is free, since it freely commands that choice. From this it follows that to deny that virtue is in the will as free, and to concede virtue is in it only as deliberative, is a contradiction. Also his proof that virtue is not in it as free, for then it would necessitate the will, does not hold up, because a superior agent, in whose power the action of the inferior agent rests, cannot be necessitated by the lesser agent. But virtue, if it is somehow an agent of the act, is only an inferior agent, as was pointed out in dist. 17 of Bk. I. And there it was also explained why there is no contradiction about the will acting freely and the habit nevertheless acting after the manner of nature with respect to their common effect.

In like fashion one could also prove that virtue is not in the will as deliberative, if it is true that virtue acts suddenly, anticipating deliberation, for the will as deliberative does not seem to act suddenly and to precede any deliberation. However, it is not necessary to ascribe such action to it, because that text has to be glossed. No virtue acts with absolutely no deliberation. For just as no one acts in a fully human way unless that person acts intelligently, so—as regards those things that pertain to the end—no one acts in a human fashion without understanding the reason for acting, and this understanding is what deliberation means. Hence no one acts virtuously by acting suddenly without deliberation in the way nature acts according to II *Physics.*

Hence, that dictum of the Philosopher should be understood in this way. Just as the virtuous person is inclined to choose rightly by reason of a correct habit, so too he has been conditioned by prudence to make at once a correct judgment as to what should be chosen, and to deliberate imperceptibly, as it were, because of the rapidity with which the practical inference is made. Another, imperfect individual, however, syllogizes practically only with difficulty and delay. And if at last he chooses correctly, he is said to act not suddenly but sullenly, whereas another, perfect person as it were acts quickly with respect to that thing, since the time it takes him to act is imperceptibly short.

23. MORAL VIRTUE AND THE GIFTS AND FRUITS OF THE SPIRIT
(*Ordinatio* III, suppl., dist. 34)

In regard to dist. 34 [of Bk. III] I ask: Do the virtues, gifts, beatitudes, and fruits make up the same habit?

[*Arguments Pro and Con*]

For the affirmative:

Gregory the Great; look up his exposition of Job [1:2]: "Seven sons and three daughters were born to him."

Furthermore, if these were different from one another, then their classifications would not overlap. But the consequent is false, because fortitude is a gift and also a virtue. And against the claim that the two represent different sorts of fortitude is the fact that their action is identical.

For the negative:

The number of gifts and beatitudes is not the same; also what is enumerated there clearly does not coincide, for there is a beatitude that is not a gift and a gift that is not a virtue, and the same with the fruits.

[*Body of the Question*]
[*A. The Views of Others*]

[1. Henry of Ghent] In q. 23 of *Quodlibet* IV, Henry gives this answer to the question. Just as one can react to intense delight in three ways, namely, humanly, superhumanly, and inhumanly, so one can react to inordinately sad situations in a human way when one bears such terrible things in a fitting fashion, and the acquired or infused moral virtue serves this purpose, but it does not do away with sorrow, according to Aristotle (III *Ethics*) and Augustine (XIII *On the Trinity*, ch. 7). Superhuman behavior is to face the terrible with joy, as some of the martyrs did. A nonhuman, and quasi-godlike, way is not only to accept death with joy but to look forward to it eagerly, as Paul did when he wrote [in Philippians 1:23]: "I long to be freed from this life and to be with Christ." Augustine proves that this is not human in his first homily on John, where, referring to 1 Corinthians 1:10: "Since there is schism among you, are you not behaving like men?" he says, "Paul wished them to be gods, as is said in the Psalm [82:6]: 'I said, You are gods.'" This third mode corresponds to the heroic virtue of *Ethics* III, which the Philosopher thought was opposed to bestiality, or an in-human indulgence in vicious pleasures. Virtues, it is said, perfect a person humanly; gifts, superhumanly; beatitudes, heroically.

[Refutation of Henry] The first objection to this is that charity is the most excellent of the gifts of God, according to Augustine in Bk. XV of *The Trinity*, ch. 17, n. 29, and even more, according to the Apostle in 1 Corinthians, ch. 13: "If I have fortitude and hand over my body to be burned"—which seems to be nonhuman or godlike, because one seeks to burn for God—"but have not charity, I gain nothing"; there-fore it does not seem that any gift perfects one more than even the first degree of charity, which is a virtue.

Furthermore, the habit of fortitude enables the human will to rightly steer a mean course in the face of terrors, and hence to act even more rightly, or with the highest degree of rectitude possible for such a nature. But if that is possible, then the identical habit of fortitude, while remaining specifically the same, can develop in strength, the de-gree of which does not vary its species; therefore, the same specific habit can dispose one to face something terrible with a minimum of courage or most perfectly.

You may claim that fortitude in the two cases is not the same, and that the habit which disposes one to bear up with only a minimum of courage is necessarily imperfect as to its act and object, since in the face of the terrible it cannot make one more perfect, and to act per-fectly under such circumstances, another species of habit is needed. But several species should not be postulated without manifest neces-sity, namely, that one species is not enough, which is clearly not the case here.

Furthermore, Christ suffered in his passion, as we have pointed out in dist. 15 of this third book, and generally every martyr, left to him-self without miraculous intervention, howsoever much he suffers vol-untarily, does not endure such suffering without sorrow. This is clear from that passage of Augustine, in ch. 7 of Bk. XIII of *The City of God*, where he challenges the philosophers who say they are happy because they have whatever they want, for if good things happen, they are pleased with that, and if adverse things occur, they are also pleased with that, because they bear these patiently. He argues against them that in adversities they did not have what they want, because so far as the event itself goes, they did not wish for it to occur, and if it happened by accident, they wished patiently to put up with it, lest, by losing their patience, they become even more miserable. And this argument is generally persuasive, for patience cannot have to do with something desirable in itself. That is why the martyrs by sustaining adverse things in this life faced a situation they did not entirely want, because the object of their patience was not something absolutely desirable or capable of being willed or desired absolutely, but rather something to be put up with for the sake of God.

Furthermore, the same agent is not simultaneously able to perform some act humanly, superhumanly, and inhumanly; for then a virtue previously acquired or infused in baptism would be rendered null by an acquired gift, or if it did remain, it would be unable to go into action, or it would no longer be necessary, because its function would be replaced by the more perfect gift. In the same way the beatitudes would obviate the need for both the virtues and the gifts, which seems incongruous, especially if we are speaking about the theological virtues, because in heaven charity will not pass away, nor will faith and hope in this life.

Furthermore, "superhuman" and "nonhuman" are metaphorical terms, for every act of man is properly speaking human. For just as it is necessary for a right act to be in harmony with its object, end, and other circumstances, so it is also necessary that it be suited to the agent performing it; for it does not suit me to behave like a king, and much less to act like an angel. Therefore, to perform a right act a man must necessarily act in a human way; whatever habit, then, disposes a man to act in a simply human way in performing some action, disposes him in an unqualified sense to perform such in regard to this.

Furthermore, if someone were always at prayer and were given the gift of understanding, but had never studied about matters of belief, such a one would not act in a human way about such beliefs, because acquired faith would be lacking, without which infused faith is inoperable. However, according to you, he could still operate superhumanly because he would have the gift of understanding, and hence could act in a more excellent way in regard to matters of belief than another skilled in Sacred Scripture, which we do not find to be the case. Indeed every such person will perhaps err more easily in regard to such matters than one well acquainted with the Scriptures.

Also, there are as many things apt to be ordered humanly as there are things apt to be ordered superhumanly or nonhumanly; therefore, they will be ordered by the same sort of habit in each case. Otherwise, true blessedness in heaven would be the act of some beatitude as a quasi-supreme habit, [rather than the virtue of charity].

[2. The view of St. Bonaventure] Another explanation is that the virtues enable one to act rightly; the gifts, to act perfectly; and the beatitudes, to act quickly.

On the contrary: by the same virtue I act rightly (because virtue is rectitude in the faculty) and quickly (because virtue is a habit making the operation quick and easy) and perfectly (because virtue is a perfection in the one who has it and is that whereby the action is rendered perfect).

[3. The view of Richard of Mediavilla] Another says that something is necessary to dispose the will so that it is able to be moved by right reason, and that is virtue. But something else is needed so that the Holy Spirit can move it, and that is the gift; and these two are postulated as moving the will.

To the contrary: this view is false, to begin with, because it falsely assumes that reason causes the will's movement, so that virtue is nothing more than a mobile disposition of that faculty. Secondly, it fails to distinguish the beatitudes from the gifts and virtues. And thirdly, since God gave the will this habit, he continues to assist both will and habit to act accordingly, just as after miraculously curing the blind man, he continued to assist him so that his eyes could be moved to see. The same habit, then, disposes the will to be moved in both the first and the second way, for though the habit disposes the will to move itself, it also disposes it to be moved by the Holy Spirit as the other mover; but this is no reason why other habits need to be postulated here.

[B. Scotus' Own View]

One could say to this question, without asserting it categorically, that the only virtues necessary in this life are the moral virtues, the intellectual virtues, and the theological virtues. This is shown in the following way. For natural reason infers the necessity of the intellectual habits perfecting the intellect in regard to theoretical matters and the intellectual habit perfecting the intellect in practical matters, and so we have the habits covering theoretical and practical knowledge. Similarly natural reason infers the necessity of a habit perfecting the appetite in regard to what is desirable for oneself and what one can seek in relationship to others, and so we have the first distinction of appetitive virtues ordering those habits to self and others.

Although one may conclude perhaps by natural reason that man is not sufficiently perfected by these habits (as the solution to the first question of the first book does), other information is required to indicate just what additional cognitive and appetitive habits are needed, for natural reason alone does not show clearly enough what intellectual and what appetitive virtues there are other than these. But one may reasonably hold, according to the persuasive arguments presented in the second question of the first book, that besides these there is a necessity for that cognitive habit and that appetitive habit which the Catholic Church says is necessary, and by faith we hold that three theological virtues are necessary and that they perfect the soul immediately with respect to the uncreated object [God].

[1. *The Virtues*]

[Enumeration of the virtues] And from this I argue as follows. We ought to postulate only such habits in a person in the present life as perfect such a one in regard to every object that one can be perfected by at present. Such are the seven virtues in general [i.e., prudence and the three moral virtues and three theological virtues]—I am not concerned here with the acquired theoretical virtues. Apart from such acquired theoretical sciences, then, no habit ought to be assumed in the pilgrim besides these seven. Proof of the major. God and creatures are the only objects one can be perfected by. Where God is concerned, the three theological virtues perfect one sufficiently in his regard, and if these three habits are most perfect, they do so in the highest measure in which it is possible to perfect a pilgrim. Where creatures are concerned (and I am not speaking of the theoretical sciences) the intellect is perfected most perfectly by prudence, if that virtue is most perfect. For then one would have the most perfect practical knowledge about every possible action and under every possible circumstance. In a similar fashion the three moral virtues perfect the appetitive part in the highest measure, if they are most perfect, because they have to do with all that can be sought for others as well as what is needed and is desirable for oneself. And they do this either primarily and directly, or secondarily, as means for attaining the primary goals. And when I speak of the four cardinal virtues, I do not understand each of these four to be a numerically single habit in anyone, as if there were a universal temperance or a universal justice which extended to everything. Rather there are single species of justice in an individual, each concerned with its own proper subject matter.

Through these three theological virtues, however, the pilgrim is sufficiently perfected immediately as regards God, because in regard to understanding him, faith is adequate perfection for this life, because we cannot have any knowledge of him except that of faith, as was said above in [dist. 24 of] this third book; therefore, etc. Charity sufficiently perfects me regarding God as lovable in himself, and hope does the same regarding God as a desirable good for me. But there are no other orderly acts it is fitting for me as a pilgrim to have towards God than to love him in himself and to seek him for myself as my good;

therefore, etc. Similarly in regard to any good object other than God the pilgrim is sufficiently perfected when he or she is perfected by intellectual and appetitive habits towards these things. But all such intellective habits as suffice to perfect the intellect are what we call intellectual virtues, for such virtues sufficiently perfect the pilgrim insofar as considering things and reasoning about them practically are concerned. Also the appetitive habits are also virtues of the appetite that sufficiently perfect it when it seeks or loves self and others. Hence, a man perfected by reason of the three theological virtues, the speculative and practical virtues, and the moral virtues that concern self and others is perfected as far as a pilgrim can be appropriately, and therefore there seems to be no need to assume any other habits than the theological, intellectual, and moral virtues.

[Generic virtues] Note further that just as habit in the category of quality represents a certain intermediate genus, so it has under it many intermediate genera before one comes to the most special species. For it may first be divided into the intellectual and appetitive, as seems probable, and the intellectual is further divided into the acquired and infused, and the appetitive similarly into acquired and infused. Or one may divide habits first into acquired and infused and both members into intellectual and appetitive, and the acquired intellectual at least can be further divided into speculative and practical, and the acquired appetitive into that which is ordered to self and that which is ordered to another. But the acquired speculative habit is divided further into real and rational, depending on whether it is concerned with real beings or those of the mind. That dealing with real being is divided according to the division proposed in VI *Metaphysics*, which is into Physics, Mathematics, and the Divine Science [or Metaphysics], and each of these, perhaps, can be further divided by many subdivisions before one comes to the most special species. But the acquired practical habit is divided into that which has to do with acting and that which has to do with making, and that which has to do with making has a number of divisions before one comes to the most special species, one of which is the practical habit concerned with this specific sort of activity, such as building. And the practical habit concerned with acting is also divided by a multiple division, as is clear from the [next] question on the connection of the virtues. For whether it be practical science or practical prudence, insofar as it deals with all that can be done, prudence is not just a single science, as will be explained in that question.

[Intellective virtues] The whole of this numerical division of intellective habits is taken over under the single infused virtue, which is faith. And there is a kind of intermediate genus with respect to many practical acquired virtues which is called "prudence." And if one also enumerates together species that are sufficiently common, there can be three such general virtues—faith, speculative science, and prudence. Nevertheless speculative science does not perfect a man in acting well morally, and therefore it is not enumerated among the moral virtues, for it is less necessary for man to live rightly than is prudence, and is also less necessary than is faith for a person to live rightly in the Church as a polity.

[Appetitive virtues] Under infused and acquired appetitive appetites, as their first species, are two infused and two acquired habits. First, under the infused are hope and charity; and under the acquired is the virtue disposing the appetite towards oneself and that disposing it toward another, and the latter goes by the common name of justice. The one towards self has no common name, and one descends to its subdivisions. Perhaps that is why it is not enumerated under the cardinal virtues, which include other, less generic virtues that fall under it [viz., temperance and fortitude].

[Virtues of the concupiscible and irascible appetites] Under the desirables for oneself are listed those which can be sought as such, namely, those which are suited immediately to agree with one, and others which are primarily to be avoided, namely, which are apt immediately to be disagreeable. Other things are not primarily desirables or avoidables, but are such secondarily, as it were, because of what is primarily sought or avoided. And the common virtue which disposes a person in regard to the first is temperance, and in regard to the second, is fortitude. Indeed the first appetibles pertain to the concupiscible appetite and the second to the irascible.

[Digression on anger and the irascible] Looking at this distinction in general, we should note that the concupiscible has to do with something agreeable or disagreeable of itself, so that on its part nothing more than apprehending such is required for an act of delight or sadness, or pursuit or flight, to follow. But the irascible does not have such things as its object. For the act of the irascible is to be angry. But to be angry, according to the Philosopher in Bk. II of the *Rhetoric*, is to seek vengeance in a conspicuous way for a conspicuous slight. Therefore, the object of anger is revenge, and more truly, if this is its act, then its object is what can be avenged. It could be called the "irascitive," or in more customary terms, "something offensive." What offends is not immediately disagreeable to the concupiscible, but it is something that impedes what is primarily agreeable, for instance, if food is what is first attractive to the taste of a bird, and therefore it desires it, and it is kept from this food or the food is removed, this offends the bird that wants it. This offensive incident is the irascible object, and the irascible appetite bears a certain nolition towards it— not indeed by turning away or shunning it, properly speaking, as the concupiscible appetite flees what it dislikes, but rather by spitting at it or repelling it. For the irascible appetite repels what it dislikes, not by desiring that the impediment be removed, but by removing it and, further, punishing it. See dist. 26 of this third book, supra.

Because the irascible appetite's act is this will to be angry or vengeful, or this nolition, where the object nilled that one seeks to avenge is not present, its anger is always tempered with grief or pain—not, however, the grief associated with the concupiscible, but that associated with the irascible, and only for that moment or time when the irascible acts not with the sort of nolition it desires, but such as it has when it has not yet avenged itself and desires to do so. Once it has actually taken revenge, however, its act is perfect and is similar to fruition on the part of the concupiscible appetite, for then the irascible appetite's anger is no longer tinged with grief or pain, but associated with a great satisfaction peculiar to itself. For as Aristotle puts it in the *Rhetoric*: "A man's anger is like honey."

[Virtues of the irascible appetite] Just as the concupiscible needs to be moderated by right reason lest it seek the things it desires inordinately, so too the irascible appetite requires a tempering habit on two counts: first, lest it punish immoderately and ward off what needs repelling in an unbridled way; or second, lest it angrily put off what should be endured or put up with. The first of these habits has no name, but it could be called "a fighting attitude" or something like that. The second is known as patience. And because it is more difficult not to thrust off in anger what offends one, patience is the most noble form of fortitude, according to the poetic saying: "Patience is the noble way to vanquish," for the patient person will conquer. The irascible, then, does not have as its object the arduous, as the concupiscible has the appetible, for its object is the offensive, so that its adequate act is to will to vindicate or nill the offensive, a nilling that is, as it were, imperfect so long as the anger is sustained before the offensive object is repelled. This phase is similar to desire on the part of the concupiscible appetite, whereas the perfected act of nolition, when with moderation it repels what is nilled or patiently puts up with it, resembles enjoyment in the concupiscible appetite.

And if you object that to nill one opposite is to will the other, and it is the function of the concupiscible to will one opposite, therefore it is the role of the irascible to nill the other, I give this reply. When the irascible functions there are two things nilled, one by the concupiscible appetite and the other by the irascible. This is clear from the example cited above, for what is nilled by the concupiscible appetite is the lack of food, and from this nolition sorrow follows, whereby it eschews what it nills as it were but does not spit at it. For another event is nilled, the removal of food, and this is what the irascible appetite nills, not by eschewing it but by an act of repulsion. And so long as it does not actually vent its anger or express this repulsion, it suffers the pain or grief proper to the irascible appetite.

It is clear however that this grief or pain of the irascible and concupiscible are not the same, because if each is faced with something offensive that is impossible to throw off, the greater suffering is in the concupiscible appetite, and yet it does not turn into anger. The most fearful person is not angry, according to the Philosopher in II *Rhetoric*, and nevertheless the more one fears the more the concupiscible appetite suffers and turns from what it fears. Though the irascible at times suffers pain when it cannot vent its anger, namely, when it has no power to vindicate itself, it suffers in another way than does the concupiscible, namely, by lacking some object it desires. But the pain of both the concupiscible and the irascible appetite is accompanied by an organic change in the sensitive part of the soul. Look this up. In the concupiscible the organs are restricted, just as they are expanded with the opposite delight. But the pain of the irascible makes one hot when the blood courses to the heart. And from this it follows that the concupiscible and sensitive parts of the soul have different organs, because the same organ could not be simultaneously moved in contrary ways.

In the rational portion of the soul there is a distinction of objects similar to that in the sensitive, because something is primarily delightful to the will, for example, some good or what suits the will itself or also what suits it according to the senses, if indeed the will is apt to share in the delight of the sense appetite joined to it in the same subject. The will can also face an offending object in a way that is either against or in accord with right reason, and it can regard it as offensive and nill it by an act that is repulsive and imperious. But there is not the same sort of distinction there as in the sense appetite, because the will is not an organic faculty, nor is it necessary to speak of its other aspect as a distinct power or another potency. The distinction is similar to the distinction of reason into a higher and a lower portion as regards its different objects, which yet form one and the same power in an unqualified sense.

As for calling one part of this "force," I don't know what needs to be said, for the term is superfluous. For there is simply the same mode of operation in regard to these distinct higher and lower objects, as we have said in dist. 24 of Bk. II. And the same can be said of the first and second types of delightful and painful objects here. The functioning element is completely one and the same, an active potency operating by the same power or force, for the same faculty that is potent is also forceful. In spiritual things the potency and its strength are the same. Neither is there reason for distinguishing the potency on the basis of the objects towards which it tends, any more than we do in speaking of the intellect as tending to know principles in one way and conclusions in another way by means of principles. No one because of this distinction thinks of distinguishing the intellect into potency and forces.

[Conclusion] Presupposing these things, then, about the irascible and concupiscible, I return now to the virtues and declare that the proper habit perfecting the concupiscible appetite is called temperance and that perfecting the irascible is called fortitude, and I speak both of the acquired and of the infused habits. However, both infused virtues [i.e., hope and charity] perfect the concupiscible, because God, which they have as their object, cannot be nilled. Although both these species, namely, fortitude and temperance, can be commonly subdivided, nevertheless in the enumeration of cardinal virtues they remain undivided. According to this enumeration, then, there are three theological and four cardinal virtues. In 1 Corinthians, ch. 13, the Apostle refers to the theological virtues, while Wisdom, ch. 8, speaks of the moral virtues: "Wisdom teaches moderation and prudence, justice and fortitude, and nothing in life is more useful than these."

This sevenfold number of virtues, then, perfects the pilgrim in this life in an unqualified sense, so that to the degree he possesses each of these in its species he is perfect, for accordingly as these are more or less intense, not in themselves but in their capacity, he is more or less perfect, and if these virtues are as intense as they can be in this life, then man is simply as perfect as he can be here below. I am not concerned at present about the perfection we have through the speculative acquired virtues, which were earlier excluded from the present discussion. These seven virtues, then (considered both in themselves and in their necessary species, of which we shall speak later), provided they are most perfect in themselves, suffice to make man most perfect in an unqualified sense as regards God in himself and all things other than God. As intelligibles of practical reason and as things desirable either for self or for others, the appetitive virtues are suited to attain such in themselves or in relation to man's ultimate end, which is in the power of the acquired virtues when they are joined to charity.

[2. How the Generic Virtues, Gifts, etc., Are Interrelated]

We need to investigate further the interrelationship of the virtues, gifts, beatitudes, and fruits.

[a. The three generic moral virtues] Note that the three acquired moral virtues of justice, fortitude, and temperance represent intermediate genera, for the first desirables seem to be divided into two, namely, honor and delights in the strict sense. For everything that is a primary good, that is, agrees with one, is either an honorable good or something delectable. For the useful is not a primary motive of desire, because it is desired only in reference to something else. The authority of the canonical epistle of John [2:16] also implies as much: "All that is in the world is the concupiscence of the flesh, and the concupiscence of the eyes and the pride of life." For the concupiscence of the eyes, which looks to riches, cannot be first, speaking of riches insofar as they represent a useful good and not something delectable. If one may speak of them as delectables insofar as they are beautiful, then they can be desired primarily like any other visible beauty. Therefore, the first things desirable to a rational nature are, as we said, honor and delight in the strict sense. Hence, the first species of temperance, which moderates the desirable for oneself, will be twofold; that which moderates the desire for honors is called humility, whereas that which moderates the desire for delight retains the general name of temperance, and there can be as many species of it as there are distinct pleasures to which the will inclines one, for instance, one species of temperance regarding the delights of taste, another that of touch— and not only sensitive pleasures, which delight the will joined to the body, but also those pleasures proper to the will as will. And hence the will of an angel can in some manner desire delectable goods, though it has no sense appetite as a pure spirit.

And that these temperances are distinguished is proved from the fact that in one there can be the highest delight and in another none. For a man can be temperate in regard to venereal pleasure, and not want to use any but his wife for sex, or refrain from such pleasure completely and still be intemperate in regard to taste, wishing to eat what he should not or not wanting to eat what he ought. One can also be temperate regarding sensibles and intemperate regarding theoretical pursuits—for instance, if the will takes the highest delight when the intellect pursues such speculative interests as are not as useful in themselves as others, and where this delight in itself is immoderate and should be tempered, since it is inordinate in itself.

It is unnecessary for our purpose to explain the species of fortitude in detail, because in treating the other topics, fortitude is only touched on in general or as patience. Patience, as we said above, is the most noble form of fortitude, because it does not throw off what one would tend to repel, so that to be patient is a sort of permitting. And if you will admit that permitting is a positive act of willing or nilling, or perhaps willing not to impede, then you can say this is the sort of act the will has in regard to bearing adversities patiently.

Justice, however, is subdivided with a view to what follows. Know that in regard to another, one can act rightly either by giving oneself to another insofar as one can or by giving him something else that belongs to him. The virtue inclining one to the first is friendship, by which one gives oneself to one's neighbor insofar as one can and one's neighbor can have one; and this is the most perfect of the moral virtues, because justice as a whole is more perfect than virtues that are directed to oneself, and this is the most perfect form of justice. If however one gives something else to another, either it is an extrinsic good or it is an intrinsic one; an intrinsic good would be one pertaining to what is necessary for human life. What concerns extrinsic goods men need to exchange is called commutative justice, and this justice is frequently called equity, where for so much, one gives something equivalent. But if one communicates something else that is necessary to man, either this is governance (and this species of justice has no name, but could be called "presidency" or "just domination"), or if what is given is just subjection, this is called "obedience."

[b. The beatitudes] On this understanding, then, I say that the beatitudes which our Savior speaks of in Matthew 5 are the same habits that make up the virtues, although at times they name more specific species of the seven virtues previously enumerated. The Savior enumerates among his beatitudes two that are species of temperance. One is humility, which moderates our quest of honor, the first of the desirables, and he expresses this there with the words: "Blessed are the poor in spirit," of whom Augustine says, "They are rightly understood to be poor in spirit and God-fearing, who do not have an inflated spirit." The other species, moderating delights in general, the Savior expresses as "Blessed are the pure of heart"; for purity of heart is the immunity the will has against all inordinate delight, both in regard to itself and by reason of the sense appetites to which it is joined.

He also speaks there of fortitude in its most perfect species: "Blessed are those who suffer persecution for the sake of justice."

The Savior expresses three species of justice: one indeed, which is the sharing of oneself in friendship, and this he indicates when he says: "Blessed are the meek," for though friendship implies more than benevolence, according to the Philosopher in Bk. VIII of the *Ethics* (for there is a recognized reciprocation and well-wishing that is more than meekness, because the meek are those who do not offend nor resist when evil besets them), nevertheless this is as it were the minimum requirement for friendship and expresses that whereby one shares oneself with one's neighbor. The other species, namely, that divided into just rule and obedience, is expressed by "Blessed are the peacemakers." For peace is served where the ruler governs justly and the subject obeys correctly. The third species of justice, which has to do with extrinsic goods, is indicated there in the words "Blessed are the merciful"; for there is no other way in which one can be disposed to give such things to one's neighbor than by being merciful. Though a person who is liberal will share with a friend, this is a lesser form of generosity than is mercy, and hence liberality is a less perfect form of justice than mercy is. God expresses this sort of justice in regard to temporal goods most specifically, in those words of Luke [14:12–14]: "When you give a dinner . . . invite beggars and the crippled and the lame . . . they cannot repay you." And so we have the three moral virtues expressed either as such or in one of their species. And the Savior also indicates two of the theological virtues there, [the first] in the words "Blessed are they who hunger and thirst after justice." For hunger is not present without some wretchedness, but the habit whereby it is elicited is charity; for charity is most properly the habit whereby in this life we hunger for justice and love God in himself, which is truly justice. The second, which is hope, is expressed when he says: "Blessed are they who mourn, for they shall be comforted." For mourning is the habit of desiring such.

And so in the eight beatitudes are expressed the two infused appetitive virtues and the three acquired moral virtues, fortitude in itself and temperance in two of its species, justice in three species. But the two intellectual virtues, one acquired, which is prudence, and the other infused, which is faith, are not expressed either as such or in their species, but they are sufficiently presupposed by the appetitive virtues, because the will is not best disposed without a corresponding virtue in the intellect.

[c. The gifts of the Holy Spirit] As for the gifts, I say that the four cardinal virtues are enumerated there. Prudence is expressed by "the spirit of counsel," for prudence is properly speaking a counseling habit, because it is a habit concerned with practical reasoning, and to reason in this way is to give counsel. Hence the habit whereby someone is counseled is prudence. Fortitude is expressed among the gifts under its own name. Fear of the Lord is a species of temperance, because it corresponds to humility, although it goes by a different name. This is clear from Augustine's explanation of Matthew 5, "Blessed are the poor in spirit." Hence, Scripture frequently commends such fear, as in Proverbs 1:7: "Fear of the Lord is the beginning of wisdom"; for nothing other than humility is the beginning of virtue; therefore something accompanies it in the intellect, and this is fear of the Lord. When it is said that such is "always blessed," this refers to what is the fond hope of the future, as is frequently indicated elsewhere in Scripture: "Blessed is he who has regard for the lowly and the poor" [Ps. 41:2], and "Blessed is the man who endures temptation" [James 1:12], and similar texts. Some wish to hold that someone is blessed who has some habit called "beatitude," because by means of its action a person merits happiness in heaven. When piety is included among the gifts this refers to what the Savior calls mercy, and it is a species of justice.

Thus among the gifts the four cardinal virtues and two infused virtues are expressed. The cardinal virtues are: prudence as counsel, and fortitude under its own name; the two others are not under their aspect as intermediate species, but rather as certain subspecies under these. Temperance, for instance, occurs as fear and justice as charity. The two infused virtues enumerated there are charity and faith. Charity is called the "spirit of wisdom." For generally when the Scriptures praise wisdom, as in this and other passages like: "Blessed is the man who finds wisdom" [Proverbs 3:13], "wisdom" is taken for charity and wisdom is charity, for it is the habit whereby the one possessing it savors that object that is to be savored in itself, namely, that good which pleases me in itself and also insofar as I wish to have it. Through the other two gifts, namely, understanding and knowledge, infused faith is expressed, not that these two are circumlocutions for two habits as "wisdom" or "sapience" for charity and "fear of the Lord" for humility, but "knowledge" and "understanding" are circumlocutions for the same habit possessed in an imperfect and a perfect manner, and both can be given from above; the first indeed without the second but not vice versa. And one can understand "understanding" as imperfect faith, which is a knowledge of the primary articles of faith, and "knowledge" or science as perfect faith, which represents an explicit knowledge of what these articles imply, just as in the case of what is known naturally, "understanding" refers to the principles and "science" or "knowledge" to the explicit knowledge of conclusions that follow from such principles. Hope here is not enumerated explicitly but is implied through the presence of charity, which is the sapience whereby I savor God both in himself and also as a good for me. For whoever savors in this sense, and approves of this taste he has in himself, desires such for himself.

[d. The fruits of the Spirit] As for the fruits, I say certain of these are virtues falling under our sevenfold classification; others are species of those listed there; and still others are neither the one nor the other, but rather delights that follow as a consequence of virtuous acts. For example, charity and faith are expressed there under their proper names, but hope is called "long-suffering." Hence, we read of the patriarchs that they were long-suffering in hope, eagerly expectant for a long while, as it were.

The moral virtues are also expressed there: fortitude, in the form called "patience," justice, in its specific form of mercy (which is here called "goodness," in the sense that one is commonly called "good" who shares himself with his neighbor), and in its other species, namely, friendship (which here is expressed as "benignity," which is a quasi benevolence and "being on fire with good"), and also in its first or third species, which has to do with ruling and being a good subject (which is here called "mildness" or specifically "obedience," for a person is mild who carries out injunctions without a murmur). Temperance is expressed in two of its species, namely, continence and chastity. If one cares to, one can say that chastity is concerned with venereal pleasure and continence with other pleasures, or one can understand both as a single species concerned with any pleasure whatsoever, as the Philosopher does in Bk. VII of the *Ethics*, where he refers to chastity as one of the degrees that can be present in any virtue. Prudence is expressed there as modesty, for one is modest who maintains a right and appropriate way of acting, and the task of prudence is to find a suitable way to act, to see how it ends, and to come to a decision about it.

Thus we have three theological virtues, as well as fortitude in the form of patience; justice in its three species; temperance in one or two species; prudence in one species; and thus all the virtues both intellectual and moral. The other things enumerated there are delights that either coincide with or follow the virtuous action, like joy and peace. For joy is properly speaking a delight in the will, and peace in the same faculty is the assurance of having possession of the object without opposition.

[To the question] And thus it is clear how, by holding that the seven virtues, either in themselves or in their species, suffice to perfect man in this life, we eliminate the need for any habits that are not these or species thereof, for neither among the beatitudes nor among the fruits and gifts are other virtues enumerated. And although the number of gifts and the number of beatitudes do not explicitly coincide, this is because some species of the seven virtues are expressed in one list but not in the other. It is not because they are other habits that are not species of these virtues. Also if we were only to consider what Scripture had said about this distinction, for in one place it lists eight, in another seven, it would be necessary to distinguish these; and then why not also distinguish the ninefold habits mentioned in the second epistle of Peter [1:5]: "Minister in your faith, virtue," etc.? Scripture frequently, then, expresses the same reality in different words, now omitting one thing, and elsewhere explaining what it omitted there.

[To the Opposing Arguments]

The answer to the initial argument for the opposite is clear enough, because although the numbers are not the same, this is not because one habit is other than these seven habits, but either because they are intermediate species falling under one of the seven, or because some of these are omitted. Everything that is listed, however, whether here or there, falls under the same seven virtues we have stated.

To the argument for the first opinion based on what the Philosopher says of heroic virtue, I say that he assigns four grades in each of the specific habits he mentions, namely, endurance, continence, temperance, and the heroic. The most perfect degree in any species is the heroic, and thus some speak of it metaphorically as perfecting man in an inhuman or nonhuman way, because everyone does not generally attain that degree in any species. And what he adduces about it being opposed to bestiality can be similarly explained as referring to an excess in the same species of vice. But bestiality could be better explained as belonging to something specifically different, because it has to do with a different object; but from this his proposal does not follow, because one could err and act in a vicelike way and nevertheless in some other matter act in a way that is perfectly right in all its circumstances. Therefore, although bestiality is a habit other than that common to human vice, because it has to do with another object, it does not follow that heroic virtue is of another species, because such virtue refers to the same object, but in a more excellent way; nor is it manifest that this excellence cannot be another degree of the same species.

24. ARE THE MORAL VIRTUES CONNECTED?
(*Ordinatio* III, suppl., dist. 26)

As for dist. 36 I ask: Are the moral virtues connected?

[Arguments Pro and Con]

For the negative:

[First], someone can be naturally inclined by temperament to perform acts of one virtue rather than those of another; thus one by nature may be readily incited to vent his anger who is nevertheless not disposed by temperament to acts of self-indulgence; therefore, such a person might practice control of temper rather than acts of temperance. Another, on the other hand, might practice only such acts towards which he is inclined and not those opposed to his bent, and so would have a virtuous habit in regard to the former and not the latter, towards which he is disinclined.

Second, in accord with one's inclination, one may have matter for practicing acts of one virtue rather than those of another, for instance, a religious could have occasion for restraining his passions, but not for confronting or sustaining the terrors of war; therefore he would develop temperance but not fortitude.

Third, because of erroneous knowledge, the will could elicit an act against one's erroneous judgment, and yet actually make the right choice one ought to make; therefore by frequently making such choices a moral habit could be generated in the will, and yet prudence not be generated in the intellect, because it did not dictate correctly; thus moral virtue could exist without prudence.

Fourth, conversely the intellect might give the right dictate but the will not choose what it dictates but rather the opposite; by frequently dictating correctly, the intellect could develop a habit of prudence, whereas the will generates in itself, not a moral virtue, but rather a vice; wherefore, etc.

Fifth, an act of despising all things for the sake of God is arduous and yet consonant with right reason; therefore, there can be a virtue which inclines a pauper to such an act; therefore, the pauper seems to have the virtue which inclines him thus, but such a person could not have the virtue of generosity or liberality, because—it seems—he does not have the wherewithal for such a virtue, since he has nothing he could give. Similarly, many who are not paupers have other virtues [that a pauper has].

Sixth, conjugal continence seems to be a virtue, for it is a certain type of chastity, and nevertheless it exists without virginity, which also seems to be a virtue.

Seventh, magnanimity is a virtue, which seems to be opposed to humility, because the magnanimous adorns himself with great honors, whereas the humble person adorns himself with few honors, because they have little value in his eyes.

For the opposite, the affirmative view, there are the texts from Bk. VI of the *Ethics* and from the *Trinity*, Bk. VI, ch. 4, of Augustine.

[Body of the Question]

[Division of the question] In this question there are many articles, the first of which concerns the interconnection of the specific moral virtues among themselves on the basis of whether they are species of the same or different genera; the second article treats of the connection of each of the moral virtues with prudence; the third, of the link between the moral and the theological virtues; and the fourth article, of the nexus between the theological virtues themselves.

[Article 1: On the Interconnection of the Moral Virtues Themselves]
[A. The Views of Others]

[1. The opinion of Henry of Ghent] As for the first it is said that the Philosopher in the first chapter of VII *Ethics* distinguishes four stages in every category of goodness or evil, of which the first is endurance, the second is continence, the third is temperance, the fourth is heroic virtue. In the first two stages there is no virtue as such, but only a certain imperfect disposition suited by nature to be followed by perfect virtue. The third stage represents what is commonly called virtue, but the fourth is that surpassing degree of virtue that is characteristic of a most excellent [or godlike] person. Now, [Henry] concedes that in the first two stages there is no connection, for where virtuous habits are concerned, someone can be practiced in acts of one virtue and not another and thus can have acquired both endurance and continence, and also one but not the other. At the third stage, a distinction is made, because virtue can exist there in three degrees: either in an inchoate or in a mediocre or in a perfect form; and there need be no connection of virtues in the first two degrees, for the same reason as before, for someone can be practiced to such a degree in acts of one virtue but not necessarily to that same degree in another. But in the third degree of this third stage, and even more so at the fourth stage, there is a connection between virtues. This is proved in many ways.

[1] The first is this. No perfect and true virtue is deficient or twisted to what is opposed to a person's end, according to what Augustine says in a sermon on the works of mercy: "Charity that can be deserted never was true charity." But if a single moral virtue could exist without the others, one could be turned from one's end, and therefore it would not be true virtue. Proof of the minor: since one virtue strengthens the will only in regard to such desirables as it regards *per se*, the will can turn away from other desirable things presented to it if it has no virtue in regard to such. But in so doing it can turn away from the object of some particular virtue; therefore, etc. An example clarifies this. One who has fortitude but not temperance is not strengthened against overindulgence in delightful things, even as another who has temperance but not fortitude is not strengthened against terrorizing incidents; therefore, the second, if confronted with choosing something

terrible, like undergoing death, or something delectable, like fornication, can be turned away from facing what is terrible and as a consequence turned towards things involving temperance, for he prefers not
to face death, rather than not to fornicate, since he is not fortified
against such great suffering.

[2] A second argument for the same goes this way. To function with
delight is characteristic of a virtue according to II *Ethics*; but one virtue without the other is not a principle of functioning delightfully, as
is apparent from the aforesaid example, for one who is tempted to
overindulgence, if he is not brave, will not flee those things that involve intemperance and as a consequence is not perfectly temperate
unless he is also brave. In the same way one could cite the example
of the miser, who chooses to hoard money rather than use it with
moderation.

[3] Furthermore, thirdly, there is this argument: Perfect virtue leads
to the end of virtue, for perfection in the moral virtues leads to one's
end; but one virtue without the other does not of itself lead one to this
end, nor does it make a man a good citizen; therefore, etc.

[Confirmation from authorities] This is confirmed by Gregory in his
Moralia, Bk. XX, ch. 1: "Whoever believes he is strong in one virtue,
is truly strong, when he is not subject for the rest to any vices," and
again in ch. 3 of Bk. XIX: "One virtue without the other is not perfect
virtue or amounts to nothing."—And the Commentator at the beginning of Bk. VI of the *Ethics* asks, "if temperance is not there, what sort
of justice is there?"—implying there is nothing there. And there is
also his comment: "We call by the name of temperance what preserves
prudence, for the virtues are sisters to one another," etc. Look for it
there.—This is also proved by the gloss on that text of the Apocalypse
21:16: "The city was square." Look for it there.

[Refutation of Henry's view] Against this it is argued in many ways,
the first of which is this. According to you virtues are not connected
in the first two stages, namely, of endurance and continence, and similarly they are not connected in the first two degrees of the third stage,
namely, when virtue is imperfect and mediocre. One can argue in the
same way about the third grade, because one could have virtue according to the first two grades of the third stage, and by continual practice
achieve the third grade of one virtue and not the other; for a person
with a habit for functioning in regard to that object is no less disposed
than another having no such habit; therefore if someone at the outset
was able to become practiced in regard to the object of one virtue and
not another, all the more so, when he has developed the habit of that

one virtue as far as the first two degrees of the third stage, will he continue to exercise himself in regard to the object of the one virtue and
not the other, and thus achieve perfect virtue as regards that virtue
and not the other. This is confirmed because it could happen that he
had no opportunity to act in the matter of the other virtue so as to
become inclined towards this in the way he did with the matter to
which he became habituated.

If one objects that although there was no external occasion to face
the matter of the other virtue, a person's imagination would bring the
matter before him and he would have to choose correctly and acquire
the virtue to some degree, this will not save one's case. For it is possible that the intellect does not consider this other, but only that to
which the habit of virtue inclines one, because the intellect cannot
deal simultaneously with more than one distinct object according to
what is commonly said, or if other things occurred which pertained to
another virtue, the will could not choose them, neither the good nor
the bad, but will command that these things be not considered but
rather that the other things which pertain to the virtue which one has
be considered, and thus what I propose stands.

[2. The opinion of St. Thomas] Another and better view says that it
is possible to acquire any habit to any degree of perfection in the category of nature by frequently elicited acts in regard to the object of one
virtue without the acquisition of the other virtue. But this habit, no
matter how intense, does not have the character of virtue unless it is
conformed to other acquired virtues, and therefore such a habit is not
a virtue, because the accord one habit has to another is necessary in
any habit if it is to have the character of a virtue.

[Refutation of this opinion] This statement could be easily refuted if
a moral virtue were a *per se* thing or something one *per se* in the category of quality, but because I do not believe this to be true, as will be
treated later, therefore I argue otherwise in this way.

[1] Virtue, with all that pertains to its essential character, is generated by acts conformable to right reason, which is evident from the
second book of the *Ethics*: "Virtue is a habit concerned with choice,
lying in a mean, relative to us, this being determined as a man with
practical wisdom would determine it." But both an act and a habit can
be conformed to right reason as a guide to one's choice without any
accord with other concurring virtues in the same agent. The assumption is evident, because one does not choose correctly about a matter
of temperance unless there be a prior judgment and dictate of right
reason as to the choice in question. But one can have a correct judgment about some matter pertaining to one virtue without any dictate
of reason as to matters pertaining to any other virtue. Therefore, etc.

[2] Furthermore, it follows secondly from that statement [of Aquinas] that each virtue will be the essential reason why another is a virtue; but the consequent is false; so too, then, is the antecedent. Proof of the implication: If this habit of temperance is a virtue only because another virtue, say fortitude, accompanies it, then fortitude, insofar as it accompanies temperance, will be the essential reason why temperance is a virtue; and by the same token, temperance, insofar as it accompanies fortitude, will be the reason why the latter is a virtue; and every habit will be the reason why another habit is a virtue; the consequence is false, because it would follow from this that something is a virtue before it is a virtue and thus no virtue will be first. Proof of these points: Let us take a habit in the category of quality that ought to be temperance. Now, if this cannot be a virtue unless accompanied by another virtue, which is fortitude, then fortitude must first be a virtue before temperance is a virtue, and it cannot be a virtue unless accompanied by the virtue of temperance, on this hypothesis. Therefore, fortitude will be a virtue before it is a virtue. This same situation implies that no virtue will be first. For temperance is not the first virtue, because it cannot be a virtue, on this hypothesis, without the concomitance of all the other virtues in their character as virtues, and no one of these others will be first, because none of them can be a virtue unless accompanied by temperance as a virtue.

But one may object with some probability that one habit can be a virtue inasmuch as all the other virtues accompany it, and although one precedes the other inasmuch as it is a habit, none is prior to another as a virtue, but all the habits, whether they were generated earlier or later, take on the character of virtues by reason of their essential nature as habits and the fact that they are mutually concomitant. I argue against this, because it would follow that one act will make all the moral virtues become virtues, which seems incongruous. Proof of the implication: Assume some habit, say temperance, is generated first and after this the habit of fortitude to a similar degree, still neither of these will be a virtue until every other habit exists in that degree required for virtue; therefore either every habit is a virtue before the other, or it is not such. If it is, then we have what I propose, namely, that one virtuous habit can exist without the other, and thus there is no necessary connection among virtues. If not, then by one act all the habits become virtues in essence, which seems incongruous, because that act seems to be an act of a single virtue, and just as it would pertain to only one virtue, if such were generated, so also as a cause it would be generative of but one virtue, and therefore not of all.

[3] Also, thirdly, it seems more reasonable that specific moral virtues of the same genus would be more likely to be connected than vir-

tues which pertain to two different genera, because a person is more inclined to be related in an orderly way to matters closely related to some virtue he has than to more remote matters. Matters pertaining to specific virtues of the same genus, however, are more closely connected than matters pertaining to virtues that are generically different; but specifically different virtues of the same genus, such as virginity and conjugal chastity, are not connected; therefore, etc.

[B. Scotus' Own Opinion]

As for this article, I concede there is no connection either of the generically different moral virtues, commonly referred to as justice, fortitude, and temperance, or of the even more general types I distinguished earlier, namely, those disposing one's affects towards self and others respectively.

For this opinion one can argue persuasively as follows. While virtue is a perfection of man, it does not represent complete perfection, for then one moral virtue would suffice. But when something has several partial perfections, it can be simply perfect according to one perfection and simply imperfect according to another, as is apparent in the case of man, who has many organic perfections, and can have one in the highest degree, and not have another. For example, someone may be disposed in the highest way as to sight and touch but lack any hearing. Someone can possess the highest degree of perfection in matters of temperance and not have the perfection required as regards another perfection, and consequently can be simply temperate also in regard to any act of temperance, although he is not brave. But one is not simply a moral person without all the virtues, just as one is not simply sentient without all one's senses. But this does not make one less perfectly temperate because one is less perfectly moral, just as one's vision or hearing is no less acute because one is less perfectly sentient in other ways.

[Solution to Henry's arguments: To 1] And this will also explain something [Henry] brought up in support of the first argument, about virtue being twisted [to what is contrary to one's end], for it is false that virtue can be so twisted. Nevertheless, one who has one virtue but lacks another can be turned away from his end because of the virtue he lacks. But this does not mean the virtue a man has is imperfect because it does not direct him as regards everything, but only as regards its proper object, just as someone is not more deaf because he cannot see than he would be if he could see, but such a one is still deprived of what can be sensed. If one argues against this as follows: "Such a habit is easily lost, therefore it is not virtue," I deny the antecedent. Quite the contrary, even though one act may be performed against his inclination, his good disposition is not destroyed except by many sins or vices or a few great ones.

[To 2] And this also answers the point raised about functioning delightfully, for one does act delightfully as regards the precise subject matter of the virtue. For instance, someone may delight in abstaining from something intemperate, but not find pleasure in facing terrible things, because he is not steeled against such; therefore, such a one will sadly commit an act of intemperance, because it goes against his habit, but because he would be even sadder if he had to undergo something terrible, he will flee what pains him and be less unwilling, as it were, to choose what gives him lesser rather than greater sorrow. Therefore I concede that such a person is imperfect and acts sadly. He is not imperfect, however, nor does he act with sorrow in a matter concerned with his virtue, except where such is accidentally associated with something with regard to which he is not habitually disposed to act in a delightful or virtuous way.

[To 3] My argument also answers his other objection about the moral virtue directing a person to his end, because one virtue does not lead one perfectly to one's end, just as one sense does not lead a man perfectly to the perfect act of sensation, but each virtue does lead in that direction insofar as it is itself concerned, but all virtues are required to bring one fully there in a virtuous and delightful way. Therefore, I concede that one virtue does not adequately lead one to one's end, but so far as itself is concerned it does lead one sufficiently towards it, namely, insofar as the perfection of such a virtue suffices to do so.

[To the authorities Henry cites] To the text adduced in the first argument from St. Augustine, I say that the Philosopher in Bk. I of the *Categories* says not that a habit cannot be lost, but only that it is difficult to lose it; therefore, even though virtue could be lost and one who had it could be turned [from his end], it is not virtue itself that is turned away, but who has it withdraws from the heights of virtue. But it does not follow that this was not also perfect virtue as a habit, because it was not incapable of being lost, but only that it would be difficult to lose it. What Augustine says about charity, then, needs to be glossed in this way. Someone truly possessed charity, who afterwards sinned mortally, however, but that was not the charity that truly joins one to his end, namely, beatitude [of heaven].—As to the citation from Gregory, one could say that he is speaking there of the principles of [supernatural] merit; and in this sense it is true that one moral virtue without the other is not [supernatural] virtue, because one does not merit with one if it is not accompanied by the other, for one who has the moral virtue of temperance does not merit [grace and glory] if humility does not accompany it, or at least if the opposite vice [of pride] is not in that person. —The same for the gloss on the words of Revelation. —And also for what the Commentator says about Bk. VI of the *Ethics* as to the virtues being "sisters." I grant they are sisters, and although they help one another to live, one is not the other, nor does one essentially perfect the other. And to the extent that these virtues do indeed aid one another, each helping to preserve the other, one can understand that saying that one is not whole without the other, because one cannot well be saved without the other. For if a man is exposed to many temptations regarding different matters, imperfection in one matter can be the occasion of acting imperfectly in regard to some other matter, whereas a perfect disposition in acting about one is a help to acting correctly about another matter; therefore, the two [virtues] assist each other like sisters, but neither is essentially required for the perfection of the other, just as one sister is born before the other; and this is always the case if both cannot be procreated simultaneously. But it is not possible to have simultaneously the two perfect acts needed to produce the two virtues, because one perfect act in one potency would impede at that time the act of the other potency needed for the two virtues to be generated simultaneously.

[Article 2: The Connection of the Moral Virtues with Prudence]

As for the second article, about the connection of moral virtues with prudence, there are two doubtful points to be cleared up. One has to do with an individual virtue's relation to some proper aspect of prudence, and the other with the relationship of prudence as a whole with each of the moral virtues.

[Part I: How Is Each Virtue Connected with Some Aspect of Prudence?]
[A. The Opinion of Others]

[The view of Godfrey of Fontaines and Henry of Ghent] As for the first, it seems this connection is a necessary one.

[Arguments] Proof is from the Philosopher in Bk. VII of the *Ethics*, ch. 3. His view there is that if the will chooses badly, it is because the intellect was at fault. Henry cites other texts there to the same effect. Look them up. The Philosopher says at the end of ch. 6 that evil makes the intellect lie and err about practical principles and thus destroys prudence.

Also, it is impossible that a prudent person should not be good and that a good person should not be prudent . . .

{[Addition] Also, I presuppose two points, one that the intellect could not understand several things perfectly at the same time, and secondly, that the will could not will something under the aspect of evil. Then I argue as follows: assume the judgment stands that something evil should be avoided; now the will either flees such evil or not. If it does, then the will cannot be evil. But suppose badness is presented correctly; now if the will could choose it, then it could tend to evil under the aspect of evil or as something not thought of. To this I reply that the first supposition, about the two entirely disparate objects that are opposed to one another immediately, is false. This is clear if we consider the individual parts, because one correlative cannot be known without the other. Neither can one know an act without knowing its subject. Still less can one know a privation without knowing the subject apt to have such, since a privation presupposes a subject together with an aptitude to have some form it lacks. Therefore, the intellect cannot know the privation alone, as the argument supposes, but can only know it as in a subject, and one in the last analysis that is suited by nature to have what is lacking. Neither can one know one correlative alone without the other or know an act without a subject. Therefore, if someone understands that evil must be avoided and presents this fact to the will, his will can elicit an act which avoids looking at the evil, though the evil is there as a quasi-necessary concomitant, and in this case the will still does not shun the evil. And even if the intellect could grasp the subject without the privation, it could not grasp the privation without a subject, because privative opposites are immediate so far as their natural subject is concerned.}

Also, *On the Movement of Animals:* "If the major premise is proposed by the practical intellect and the minor is taken from something known to the senses or imagination, the conclusion will be an operation," so that according to [Aristotle] it is necessary to act if one is not impeded. But according to him there is no operation that is completely counter to what reason dictates. Augustine also confirms this in what he says about that verse from Psalm 2: "He shall speak to them in his anger"—that "a twisting or darkening of the mind will follow those who sin against the law of God."

In support of this there is also that dictum of Dionysius in *The Divine Names:* "No one does anything considering it as evil," and that passage from III *Ethics,* ch. 3: "Every wicked man is ignorant of what he ought to do and what he ought to abstain from, and it is by reason of error of this kind that men become unjust and in general bad." And Wisdom 2:21 agrees with this: "Their malice has blinded them." As for the way in which this argument is presented see q. 17 of Henry's *Quodlibet* V.—And if one brings up that article condemned at Paris that says: "So long as general and particular knowledge of anything remains, the will cannot will the opposite: an error," Henry replies in *Quodlibet* X, q. 10, that the proposition "So long as knowledge remains, etc., the will cannot will the opposite" must be distinguished according to composition and division. In the divided sense it is false, because it signifies that the will never has the power of willing the opposite, which is false; in the combined sense one must distinguish further, because the ablative absolute can mean either "if" or "because" or "while." If it is taken as meaning "because" or "if," it is false; and it is true that this is an error, for it means that correct knowledge or understanding is the cause of rectitude in the will. But if one explains it in the sense of "while," so that it signifies not causality but simply the fact that [error in the intellect] follows or accompanies [error in the will], then one can give the aforesaid proposition a true sense and it is neither an error nor condemned. It must be so understood, however, that one does not assert that by priority of nature an intellectual error has to occur before the will can err; for it is only that error is present in both faculties simultaneously. But error in the will is prior by nature to that of the intellect, so that if one considers the intellect only insofar as it is prior by nature to the will, the intellect is correct, but the will, by freely choosing to err, blinds the intellect, and this blindness occurs at the same time as the will errs, even though by nature it is posterior [because it is caused by the will].—For this interpretation I argue in this way. If the first choice of the will did not blind the intellect, then neither did any other, for the first could be just as evil as any other, and if no act blinded it, then no matter what the actual evil in the will might be, it would never blind the intellect, and thus one could become evil to any degree whatsoever without there being any error in the intellect, which seems to contradict several authorities.

[Authorities against this view] Against this view, to begin with, there are these arguments from authority:

One is Augustine's comment on Psalm [124:2]: "Perhaps they would have swallowed us up alive," where he explains: "They are swallowed up alive who know what evil is and consent to it, or perhaps die." And there is his other comment on Psalm [69:23]: "Let their table become a snare," viz., "What is more vicious than knowingly to consent to vices one should not consent to? Behold, they know the mousetrap and put their foot in it." And again, re Psalm [119:20]: "My soul has desired . . . ," he says: "The intellect precedes, but the affections follow slowly or not at all."

The argument and authority of the Philosopher in II *Ethics* also supports this. First he says that "as a condition for virtue knowledge or reason has little weight"; but if correctness of intellect in its considerations is accompanied by right volition, since knowledge contributes much to a correct evaluation of actions, consequently it will also do much for willing rightly. Indeed, if this were not so it would follow that one ought to persuade another not that he should not follow vice but that he should simply consider things according to right reason, for according to you, by considering things rightly according to a habit of knowledge, the will could not help but be right at the same time and, therefore, there is no need to persuade anyone to will rightly but only to consider things rightly.

[Six arguments from reason] There are also these arguments from reason:

[1] Given the fact that the intellect dictates correctly, the will can make no choice, since what the intellect dictates is not a matter of choice, and the intellect is not moved simultaneously from this and from that. If the will makes no choice, however, it generates no virtue in itself. But according to you, prudence is generated by right dictates; therefore, prudence will be produced without any other moral virtue.

[2] Also, a bad choice cannot blind the intellect so that it errs in its judgment about what can be done. Proof: terms of a proposition are the total cause of knowledge of first principles, whether these be practical or theoretical, according to Bk. I of the *Posterior Analytics*; and the syllogistic form is evident to every intellect, as is clear from the definition of the perfect syllogism in Bk. I of the *Prior Analytics*; therefore, once the meaning of the terms is grasped and put into propositions and a syllogistic deduction is made, it is necessary that the intellect assent to the conclusion, whose knowledge depends precisely on a knowledge of the terms of the principles and knowledge of the syllogistic deduction; therefore it is impossible that the will should make the intellect, considering principles through a syllogistic deduction, err about the conclusion, and much less err about the principles themselves, and therefore there is no way in which the intellect can be blinded so that it errs.—If you grant this conclusion and say that therefore the will blinds the intellect by turning it away from considering something rightly, I say: No. To turn the intellect away is not to blind it; even if it could be turned away in this fashion, prudence would still remain; for a prudent person need not be considering always what is prudent, but may at times be willingly concerned with other things.

[3] Before the will can turn away the mind, it needs some coexistent knowledge as a naturally prior condition for so willing. Now, either [a] this dictate, by which the will wills to turn away the intellect, is a

dictate that stands with right reason, and then it follows that it is no sin to will to turn away the mind, according to you, because the will to do so coexists with a correct dictate, or [b] this act of knowledge, prior to the volition to avert, is something other than a right dictate, and then there are two alternatives. If it is right, then it follows as before, namely, that the will to avert is not a sin, and thus no blinding follows as a consequence. But if this act prior to willing to avert is not right, there will still be no blinding of the intellect that follows from the actual willing to avert, because that act precedes this willing.

[4] Also, either the will chooses badly despite the right dictate given it, and then you admit my position, or else it chooses badly without the right dictate present. Now, to choose, the will needs some knowledge or act of the intellect, and this act is not right, because—according to you—if it were right, there would be no sin. Therefore, this other act that is not right will be prior to the bad will itself. And the reason why it is not right can only be some other evil will, and—since there can be no circularity here, since it would imply an infinite sequence of causes and effects—my proposal would follow [namely, that the will chooses badly despite a right dictate], and consequently the will does not blind the intellect so that it dictates badly—a blinding that you claim follows from this bad will.

[5] Also, no one in this life is completely incorrigible; therefore, no one can be entirely in error about first principles. Proof of the implication. One who would err regarding first practical principles would have nothing which could recall him to what is good. For whatever one assumes might persuade him to return will be denied, for no assumption of this sort could be more knowable than a first practical principle.

[6] Also, the damned would not agree that the proposition "God must be hated" is true, for then they would not have the worm referred to in that last verse of Isaiah: "Their worm shall not die nor their fire be extinguished, and they shall be abhorrent to all mankind"; for they take unqualified delight in hating God remorselessly; therefore [they know God should be loved and their reason is not blinded].

[B. Scotus' Own Opinion]

As for this article, it could be said that the intellect can have a dictate that is right in an unqualified sense without the will having to choose in conformity to that dictate. And since a single right act of dictating what should be done generates prudence, prudence will exist in the intellect without any moral habit in the will. But if this is so, then one can ask: How does evil blind the intellect, as the authorities claim? To this one can say it blinds in two ways, one privatively, the other positively. Privatively, because it turns the intellect away from the consideration of what is right; for the will by choosing the opposite of what right reason dictates does not allow the intellect to remain thinking for long about its right dictate, but turns its consideration to probable or sophistical reasons for the opposite, if such can be found; or at least it turns it to some other irrelevant matter, lest that actual displeasure remain that consists in the remorse for choosing the opposite of what one knows to be right.—Positively, however, it blinds it in this way. Just as the will in rightly choosing the end commands the intellect to consider those things which are necessary to attain that end, and the intellect, by thus considering the means ordered to attaining that right end, generates in itself a habit of prudence, so the will in choosing a bad end for itself (it can indeed prescribe that bad end for itself, as was said in dist. 1 of the first book) commands the intellect to consider the means necessary to attain such. Augustine has a good description of this in the final chapter of Bk. XIV of *The City of God.* For the will has its virtues, as he discusses them in that book, but what he implies here is that the will, by setting before itself an evil end, commands the intellect to find the means and set forth the ways needed to attain its delights and forestall any terrible consequences. And just as prudence is the habit generated in the intellect at the command of the will once it has chosen well—a command, namely, to dictate suitable means for attaining its well-chosen end—so also the habit acquired by the intellect (when it carries out the will's command to dictate means needed to attain the evil end it has chosen) represents an error, and a habit of knowledge directly opposed to prudence. One could call it "imprudence" or [as Augustine implies in the aforesaid chapter] "stupidity"—not however in a privative sense, but rather in a positive and contrary sense. For just as a prudent person has a habit whereby he quickly chooses the right means for a good and fitting purpose, so this person has a habit by which he quickly and correctly chooses those means ordained to achieve the bad end the will has prescribed for itself. And since this habit was generated under a command of the will, to that extent it is the evil will that blinds, not indeed by making the intellect err regarding some proposition, but by forcing it to perform an act and develop a habit of considering some means for attaining a bad end; and this habit as a whole represents an error regarding actions, though it is not an error theoretically speaking.

[A doubt and its solution] Another doubt could arise here. If a correct intellectual habit and a good appetitive habit need not be simultaneously generated, because it could happen that one dictates well regarding this matter but the other does not act well in its regard, two questions arise: Is the intellectual habit generated without the moral virtue prudence? and vice versa, Is the habit generated in the appetite without this understanding [or that in the intellect] a moral virtue?

[One answer to the first question] To this first question about prudence one could say that strictly speaking prudence is never without moral virtue, because according to the definition in VI *Ethics*, ch. 2, prudence is a correct judgment "in agreement with right desire"; but the appetite is not right without moral virtue. Now, if this be true, then [not only] could the first dictates about practical principles be right without being the result of prudence (though they are a sort of seedbed of prudence), but also right dictates about the means necessary to attain some end prescribed by the will could be a habit dictating correctly, yet not one called prudence.

Thus there could be two correct intellective habits in regard to actions neither of which would be prudence. One is that which would precede correct choice of a particular end, and this would not be prudence, because it is not concerned about the means to an end, whereas [prudence] is a consultive habit, and counsel is not about the end but about the means to the end. Prudence is also discursive, because it is consultive, and thus has to do with things one treats discursively. But once a good end has been chosen, not only in general but also in particular, such as to live chastely, there can be some directive intellection as to the means for achieving such an end, but it is not actually accompanied by a right choice. Now, this would be prudence, so far as the object is concerned, for it is right judgment about means to an end, but the other condition is lacking, namely, it is not accompanied by a righteous desire regarding the same object.

According to this way it must be said that any habit generated in the intellect, although it is practical and correct as regards a particular or universal end, or in regard to the means necessary to attain the particular end chosen, if it is not accompanied by a right choice of the will in regard to the same, is not prudence.

[Objection] And if one argues against this as was done in the preceding article about the connection of moral virtues, namely, that it would follow that by reason of this accord, prudence constitutes the moral virtue and vice versa; and thus one act in the last analysis suffices to generate both habits, namely, prudence and the moral virtue; but this act cannot be one of both the intellect and the will; therefore, it is an act of one or the other, and hence it could not generate both habits—[Solution] it could be said that what is necessary is not conformity of one moral virtue with another, because no one is the rule for the other, but conformity of each moral virtue to prudence, because a defining characteristic of virtue is that it is an elective habit in accord with right reason; and therefore, a habit could be constituted also in its moral being by the presence of prudence as a concomitant condition, and vice versa, prudence could be constituted by moral virtue as a concomitant condition; but one moral virtue does not constitute another in this way. And then one could grant that one habit that is prudence and another that is moral virtue could be generated simultaneously, and that this effect is produced by one act or one habit which ultimately generates either the moral virtue or the corresponding habit of prudence. For while it is incongruous that one act generate two moral virtues, it is not incongruous that such should occur with prudence and temperance, because this act which generates prudence in its regulative role, also generates temperance in a regulative role. But since temperance does not have its character as a virtue except by reason of this regulative role, this act or habit also generates it in its character as a virtue. But one cannot say this about temperance as regards fortitude, because fortitude does not exercise a regulative function in regard to temperance.—Hence one would not claim that prudence and moral virtue constitute themselves as virtues according to any priority, as though one were a virtue before the other was, but by a simultaneity of nature there is the intellectual habit of prudence and corresponding to it a moral virtue.

And if one asks: By what are these two habits produced in their perfection? I concede it is by one act, whether that act be a right choice (for without a right choice of the end there is no appetitive habit in accord with right reason, and therefore, neither is there prudence) or an act pertaining to the intellect (for without a right dictate of the intellect there is no choice in accord with right reason, and hence nothing virtuous or productive of moral virtue). Therefore, either the act of the intellect or the act of the will, by generating something *per se* in its natural being, can concomitantly give both it and, what is more, its correlative their respective regulative characters, and thus one act can generate by a simultaneity of nature both the moral virtue and the prudence that corresponds to it.

According to this it may be said that both habits preceding a righteous choice would indeed be habits of moral science or of special moral knowledge. For just as in making art products the artist is directed by experience, because the artist knows the reason why, but the one with experience knows how to do it, according to Bk. I of the *Metaphysics*, and also the artist is not prompt in acting, whereas one with experience is (ibid.), so too it is in morals. One who has only a right habit of practical principles or conclusions, but is not experienced in acting or in loving or in ordering or in directing in such matters, although he may have a habit that is remotely directive (which can be called understanding or moral science)—such a one, I say, does not have a proximate directive habit, such as prudence, which is like the habit of one experienced in making things.

[A more probable answer] Although the above may seem a probable solution to the distinction of practical knowledge and prudence, prudence is concerned not only with means ordered to attaining one's ultimate end, but also with directing one to an end, at least to a particular end, such as chastity. This is proved first in the following way. For, according to a certain order of nature, moral virtue always follows some form of prudence; but by choosing a particular end such as chastity, a moral virtue is generated; therefore some prudence precedes this choice. Therefore, it seems that prudence should not be restricted solely to the habit for dictating the specific means which are ordered to a particular chosen end, but should also be concerned with that end properly and *per se*.

This is proved secondly because otherwise one specific prudence would not correspond to one moral virtue, for such a virtue is unified by reason of the choice of its end, and to this it principally inclines one. But if prudence dictated nothing about that end but only about the means thereto, there would be no object from which this prudential direction would get its unity, but there would be many "prudences" concerned with the many dictates directed to that end, and yet there would be but one moral virtue derived from the unity of its end. Hence, both because of the natural priority of prudence to moral virtue as well as for the sake of giving unity to the prudential knowledge involved with one moral virtue, it seems one ought to concede that this practical act that directs one rightly to a particular end is properly speaking prudence.

It is no objection to say that prudence is called a consultive habit, and so has to do with the means to an end and reasons to these, for concerning proper ends or those proper to moral virtues it dictates by reasoning from a first practical principle taken from some universal end particularly applied, and this discourse represents a first consultation, although more commonly counsel refers to the means for attaining virtues.

The other point that is added, about prudence being conformed to a righteous appetite, does not shake this position, for what is naturally prior does not seem to derive anything of its essential being from what is posterior. But prudence qua prudence seems to be naturally prior to moral virtue because it defines it. What therefore is said about a conformity there, must be understood in the way explained in our first question, about practical and theoretical theology, namely, it is conformed to right practice itself, i.e., the knowledge must be such that so far as it itself is concerned right practice must be conformed with it. But knowledge is of this sort whether or not it is followed by a right choice on the part of the one who has such.

Hence one could give another answer, that this habit, generated by correct judgments, whether about the means to an end or about the ends themselves (at least certain particular ones which are properly speaking the ends of distinct moral virtues and where perhaps there is no other judgmental habit about such ends), is prudence, even though a correct choice does not follow. And then it would not be always necessary that a corresponding moral virtue be connected to a prudential judgment about some moral matter. But the converse relationship is different, for no choice can be morally right unless it is conformed to some rule or measure, which is a correct dictate. Such a right dictate, however, is suited by nature to generate prudence, even though this prudence refers only to this particular matter. Therefore, one can concede the existence of the converse connection, since a moral virtue cannot exist without there being a prudential habit concerned with its respective matter.

To the reason and authorities cited for the opposite view one can find answers. Look them up in Henry's *Quodlibet* XIV or V, q. 3.

[Part II: The Connection of All the Moral Virtues in One Prudential Habit]

[The views of others] As for the other part of this article, namely, the connection of all moral virtues in one habit of prudence, it seems that the Philosopher says they are connected in Bk. VI of his *Ethics*, ch. [13]: "For with the presence of the one quality, prudence, will be given all the virtues." Look up the Commentator's remarks on this text.

As to how one can make a case for one virtue of prudence in regard to all *moralia*, even as one assumes one habit of science, look up the opinion of Henry and my critique of it in the first question on Bk. VI of the *Metaphysics*.

[Scotus' own view] As for this article, one can say that just as art regards all makable things, so prudence regards all possible actions, neither is there any greater connection of possible actions with regard to one habit than there is among makables; therefore just as diverse artifacts require their own proper arts, so diverse actions require their proper prudences; and just as one's affects towards some actions may be good and one's affects towards others bad, so also in dictating what should be done, one can be habituated to judge rightly regarding some actions but not regarding others, but right dictates about the former are neither guiding principles nor conclusions about the latter.

How all these "prudences" form one habit and how all habits of geometry pertain to one universal science has been explained in my first question on Bk. VI of the *Metaphysics*, for one should understand this not as a formal but as a virtual unity. Just as a habit which is about a first subject is formally one by reason of that subject, and is virtually concerned with all those things contained in that first subject, though it is not formally about them, so this habit, which is formally about some end of certain actions, is virtually, but not formally, concerned with all of these possible actions, the practical knowledge of which is virtually included in that end. And so, by extending the name "prudence" to that habit which is an understanding of first practical principles, that prudence, which is formally one in itself, is virtually concerned with all the virtues.

[Reply to the authorities for the other opinion] According to this, one can explain that authoritative citation of VI *Ethics*, "For with the presence of the one quality, prudence, will be given all the virtues." For either he speaks of one virtue formally, and then one must understand that all virtues will be there where one prudence exists perfectly, not merely intensively but extensively, for prudence is never as perfect extensively as it could be unless it is perfect in regard to all to which it could extend, and this area represents all the objects pertaining to all the moral virtues whatsoever.—The other way this citation could be glossed is that it is referring not to formal unity, but to a generic unity. For just as temperance, according to the Philosopher, is said to be one virtue, formally other than fortitude, yet each of these virtues represents a sort of intermediate genus with many species under it, as was said earlier, so prudence also, according to this classification of intermediate genera, could be called one by reason of its unity as an intermediate genus. For even though it contains under itself many species, prudence can still be one by a generic unity. And understanding the unity of prudence in this way, it is the case that all the moral virtues are connected under one habit of prudence insofar as to each of its species some virtue is connected, and this presupposing what was said in the preceding part of this second article about the connection of each virtue to its own prudence, whether the interrelationship between the two is mutual or nonmutual.

[*Article 3: The Connection of the Moral and Theological Virtues*]

As for the third article, Augustine says in his work *Against Julian*, Bk. IV, ch. 3, that there are no true or perfect virtues without charity, and he proves this because such are not perfectly glorified in God.

Against this is what Augustine says in his sermon on patience . . .

[To the question] It can be said that no virtues incline a person to his ultimate end except through the mediacy of that which regards the ultimate end *per se*; and thus, if only charity immediately regards the ultimate end, the other virtues do not order one to that end except by means of charity. However, in so far as the virtues are certain instruments perfecting man, they must also be instruments for ordering him to the ultimate end in which his supreme perfection lies, and therefore they are imperfect without charity, to which end they cannot otherwise be ordained. However, since this imperfection is not something that pertains to them by virtue of their specific nature, therefore each of the other virtues in their own nature can be perfect without such a virtue. Inasmuch, then, as they are without charity they are said to be "unformed," and they are "formed" through charity in the sense that charity orders these and their respective ends to the ultimate end, in which ordination they achieve their true and highest extrinsic perfection.

This answers the various authorities cited above. Take those of Augustine, for instance. It is true to say virtues are not truly such without charity, because they do not lead to beatitude if it is missing.

On the other hand, there is some doubt whether the theological virtues presuppose the moral virtues. So far as their acts go, it is manifest they do not. For if someone who had been living a life of vice is suddenly converted, he has all the theological virtues from the beginning of his conversion, but not the moral virtues, at least not those that are acquired. For he does not act with delight regarding all those things to which virtuous habits incline one. Quite the contrary, it would be more delightful for him to act according to the old habits of vice he had previously acquired than to act otherwise.

But you may object that in the sacrament of penance all the virtues are infused in such a person in a way similar to that of the infant in baptism, and in this manner the connection is preserved, because if one does not possess the virtues innately, at least one has them by infusion. Proof of this is the fact that one will have them in heaven, according to Augustine, whom the Master quotes in the text of this distinction. But it does not seem probable that anyone would have them in heaven if he had not already acquired them on earth, since he may die suddenly.

Although much might be said about these infused moral virtues, namely, that they seem necessary because of the manner or the medium or the end, nevertheless (inasmuch as every end which they cannot have of their specific nature, is sufficiently specified by the inclination of charity, whereas the mode and the medium are specified by infused faith) it does not seem necessary to postulate infused moral virtues. Now, acquired virtues are enough in those persons who have acquired them or can have them; nor do these virtues seem necessary in those who have not acquired such, when there is no more pressing reason why they should be infused here if they are not infused in those who have acquired them.

And then there are several answers we can suggest in the case of infants: One is that there is no need to assume they have the moral virtues in heaven, but it suffices that they are well disposed towards what is desirable by charity. Charity indeed disposes one in regard to all objects that could be willed under one aspect [viz., love of God], but it is not necessary that one have knowledge of all such objects in their proper nature. It suffices to know them in the Word, which is perfect knowledge.

Or secondly, if they do possess such, one could say these virtues are infused in them at the instant they are beatified. For there is no greater need that those things which pertain to the pilgrim be thus given in baptism, when the infant is a future pilgrim, than that those things which pertain to the beatified state be given at the instant one is beatified. Indeed, there is less rationale for the former than there is for the latter.

Or one could say, thirdly, that if those virtues pertain to some perfection of one who has gained heaven, and are not given at the instant of their beatification, they could still have been acquired by their actions in heaven, for just as there appears no reason why one could not learn about some previously unknown things directly from those things themselves, so here there seems no apparent reason why one could not make good choices about some desirable things that are conducive to one's end, and this, not merely by willing them for the sake of God himself, but because they are something good for oneself, and thus one beatified could acquire a moral habit inclining him to such desirables for what they are in themselves and thus acquire moral virtue.

[Conclusion] To this article, then, I say, as I said before, that the moral virtues do not require the theological virtues in order to be perfect as regards their own specific nature, though without such, they do not have that further extrinsic perfection they could have. And neither is it necessary, conversely, that the theological virtues have the moral virtues, either in this life or in heaven.

[Article 4: The Interconnection of the Theological Virtues Themselves]

As for the fourth article, about the connection of the theological virtues [of faith, hope, and charity] among themselves, I say that they are not necessarily connected, as is apparent in heaven, where the habits and acts of charity exist without the habits and acts of faith and hope. This lack of connection is also clear in this life, where faith and hope remain in the sinner without charity. Therefore, as to their existence, there is no necessary connection among them.

But what of their infusion or coming into existence? Are they connected here? I reply that whatever can be separated in existence such that one can be without the other, God can also separate from one another in their coming to be or their infusion. Hence, in their infusion they are connected not of themselves by necessity, but only by God's generosity, since he perfects man as a whole, for according to Augustine in *True and False Penitence*: "It is impious to hope for half a pardon from God." Just as no one is healed bodily unless he is perfectly healed, so also spiritually one is not healed save perfectly. But perfect health is present if one has faith in the intellect and hope and charity in the will.

But if one asks whether faith and hope without charity would be virtues, one can say, as was said of the virtues, that in their own nature they could be perfect insofar as they are principles of their own acts with respect to their proper objects; but without charity it is impossible to have that final perfection that comes of attaining the end to which they are ordered by charity. And this indeed is perfection, both in morals and in these *supernaturalia*. However, it is commonly said that in attaining the end through some elicited operation, because of some order these or those acts have towards our end, we can say, speaking precisely, that insofar as these acts are accepted by God, they are ordered to beatitude. And thus indeed no moral or infused virtue or moral act is accepted without charity, which alone divides the children of the kingdom from those of perdition.

As for the intellectual habits, there is no need to tarry, for they have no necessary connection with one another, unless some are subordinate habits, such as the habit of understanding principles and that of knowledge of conclusions, and in such cases the prior can be without the posterior, but not vice versa.

[Reply to the Initial Arguments]

As for the arguments at the beginning, I accept the first two, because they are included in what was said in the first article.

To the third, I say that although by frequently acting [against his erroneous judgment] a person does generate a certain quality, which is suited by its nature to be in accord with right reason and which would be a virtue if it were accompanied by right reason in the person so acting, nevertheless this quality that is produced is not a habit of correct choice, and hence is not a virtue. For inasmuch as such a person lacks the right judgment, he has no correct rule for acting as he does, and therefore his choice, though apt by nature to be righteous, is not right for the simple reason that it does not follow a correct rule.

I grant the fourth argument, because its conclusion agrees with what was said in the second article about the connection of the moral virtues with prudence.

As for the other following arguments, about the incompatibility of certain virtues, I concede that, although one could say that no virtue, even taken specifically, is incompatible with another, insofar as they support my position, they prove that diverse species of the same generic moral virtue or those of different genera are not necessarily connected, as we have admitted in the first article.

PART VII

The Love of God, Self, and Neighbor

25. THE INFUSED VIRTUE OF CHARITY
(*Ordinatio* III, suppl., dist. 27)

Regarding dist. 17 [of Bk. III] I ask: Is there some theological virtue inclining one to love God above all?

[Arguments Pro and Con]

For the negative:

[1] If there were such, it would be a certain kind of friendship, which is clear from its corresponding act, which is to love. But according to the Philosopher in VIII *Ethics*, ch. 7, there is no friendship towards God because God excels beyond any proportion, and such an excess prohibits any friendship towards him, because friendship is among equals in some sense.

[2] Also, no virtue moves one to an act that is impossible, but it is impossible for us to love God above all. This is proved in two ways: first, because the marks of friendship are measured by one's relationship to oneself, according to the *Ethics* IX, ch. 9; but what is measured does not exceed the measure in the perfection of qualities measured; therefore, love for oneself exceeds that which one has for another. Second, because friendship is based on how much another is one with us; but it is impossible that anything be more one with me than myself.

[3] Also, thirdly, to the main issue, someone without virtue can love God above all; therefore no theological virtue is necessary for this. Proof of the antecedent: First, because if one can do something with a habit, it is also possible to do such without a habit, because the habit

does not give one, in an unqualified sense, this ability to act, for then it would be a potency [and not a habit] for such, and second, because one could, by one's natural endowments alone, enjoy something as an end, and not necessarily inordinately; but there is no ordinate enjoyment or fruition of any object other than God; therefore, etc.

[4] Furthermore, from frequent acts of loving God above all, a habit could be acquired similar to that of charity whereby we love God above all; therefore charity cannot coexist with one who has such a habit, because if it could, two habits of the same species would be in the same subject, which seems incongruous. The antecedent is evident, since—from the preceding argument—God can be loved above all by purely natural endowments, and hence nature is capable of acting repeatedly in this way and thus generating a habit of this sort. Nor can one object that these two habits are compatible because, having different efficient causes, they are of different species. For the efficient cause alone does not suffice to distinguish the effect specifically, as is clear from Augustine in *On the Trinity* III, ch. 9, and also Ambrose, *On the Incarnation*, who insists that differences in origin do not make for different species. He makes the same point clear in the case of man produced by creation as compared to production by generation, because Adam was of the same species as myself; therefore, etc.

Against this we have the statements of the Master in the text of this distinction as well as Augustine in *Christian Doctrine*, 4 and 5, whom he quotes. Look it up in his *Sentences*.

[Body of the Question]

In this question there are three points to be investigated: (1) Since habits are revealed by their acts, we must first see whether this act of loving God above all is something morally right, so that there could be a virtue corresponding to it. (2) What is the formal object or objective basis of this act and of the habit that inclines one to that act? (3) Can nature without an infused habit perform such an act?

[Article 1: Is It Morally Right to Love God Above All?]

As for the first, I say that to love God above all is an act conformed to natural right reason, which dictates that what is best must be loved most; and hence such an act is right of itself; indeed, as a first practical principle of action, this is something known *per se*, and hence its rectitude is self-evident. For something must be loved most of all, and it is none other than the highest good, even as this good is recognized by the intellect as that to which we must adhere the most.

A confirming argument: Since the moral principles are of the law of nature, "Love the Lord, your God," etc., is also, and therefore such an act of love is known to be right. From this it follows that there can be a virtue inclining one naturally towards such an act. Now, this virtue is theological, because it is directed immediately to a theological object, viz., God. Nor is this all, for this virtue is based immediately upon the first rule of human action, and it had to be infused by God, since this sort of virtue is made to perfect the highest portion of the soul, which cannot be perfected in the best possible way except immediately by God.

This virtue is distinct from faith, because its act is one neither of belief nor of understanding. It is also distinct from hope, because its act does not desire the good of the lover insofar as it benefits the lover, but is an act that tends to the object for its own sake, and would do so even if, to assume the impossible, all benefit for the lover were excluded. This virtue which thus perfects the will insofar as it has an affection for justice, I call "charity."

[Article 2: What Is the Formal Object of Charity?]

As for this article, I say the "objective basis" of an act or habit of charity can be understood in three ways: the first meaning would be that which is suited by its very nature [as something absolute] to be the essential reason why an act tends towards it and rests with attaining it; a second meaning would be some [relative] aspect of the object, prior to the act, which makes it appropriate for an act to be directed towards that object; a third meaning would be something which only accompanies, or even follows, the elicited act as a kind of consequence.

Only in the first sense, and no other, is anything, properly speaking, an objective basis for an act or habit. And in this sense, God himself, as this individual essence, is the objective ground or object of charity. For the formal object or end towards which every theological act or habit inclines us is his unique essence, as was pointed out earlier in the question on the subject of theology in the prologue of Bk. I. And a brief proof is this. A power that regards something as an adequate motive or terminal object can only be perfectly satisfied in something in which that common feature is most perfectly realized. Now, every intellective or volitional power has as its motive and terminal adequate object the whole of being. In no being, then, whether created or uncreated, can such a power be satisfied save in that in which the aspect of "being" is to be found most perfectly. But only this First Being is this sort of thing.

According to the second meaning of the term, something relational can be called in some sense an objective basis precisely for being loved, for it is also in some sense suited by nature to be loved. And in the case of God, it is this relative aspect of his unique nature as a good, sharing itself with one who loves it. For just as in our case someone is first loved honestly, that is, primarily because of himself or herself, and only secondarily because such a one returns our love, so that this reciprocal love in such a person is a special reason of amiability over and above the objective goodness such a person possesses, so too in God. Not only does God's infinite goodness, or his nature as this unique nature in its uniqueness, draw us to love such, but because this "Goodness" loves me, sharing itself with me, therefore I elicit an act of love towards it. And under this second aspect of amiability, one can include everything about God that proves his love for us, whether it be creation or redemption or preparing us for beatitude in heaven, but in such a way that among these manifestations of his love no distinction is made. For charity does not look more to the last, nor regard the second more than the first, but all of these reasons are combined, as it were, into the one notion that God is worthy of love not only for what he is in himself, but also because he shares himself and is our good as well; hence he deserves to be loved in return, according to that text from John: "Let us love God because he has first loved us."

The third meaning refers to the satisfying happiness God gives as our ultimate end, although this is not properly speaking a formal objective reason, since it is a natural consequence of the elicited act of loving him. Nevertheless, inasmuch as this satiety inevitably accompanies this act of love, it could serve as a kind of object. And in this sense God is loved inasmuch as he is that good object that makes us completely happy, and he is said to be loved in this way insofar as he is loved supremely, that is, not qua formal object, but under an aspect in the object that accompanies the act of loving it.

An example of this triple distinction: Suppose, first of all, in the nature of things there is one that is most beautiful to the eye; secondly, assume this beautiful object also gave the eye its power to see; thirdly, assume, if vision could be said to love such visual beauty, that in seeing this object the eye's love of seeing was satisfied to the full. The first of these represents visual beauty, as the adequate object of the power of vision, embodied in an object in all the perfection it is possible to have in beauty of this sort. The second represents an additional reason for loving such, inasmuch as it shares itself with the eye by giving the latter the power to see it. The third is something that accompanies an act in which the desire for visual beauty as a good in itself is perfectly satisfied. Therefore, the primary reason for vision, or love in vision, if vision could love, would be the nature itself of this most beautiful thing; whereas the least and most improper reason would be the fact that it is reached through a visual act. From this it follows that they speak most improperly who claim that God is the object of charity insofar as he is the beatific object, if they understand by "beatific" an actual relationship, viz., insofar as he is the actual terminus of the beatific act. But if they refer to an aptitudinal relation, then, as we have argued, it is only by reason of his nature that God functions as a beatific term or object.

[Article 3: Does Nature Suffice to Love God Above All?]
[1. The Opinion of Others]

[First opinion] Regarding the third article, one view assumes that nature is not sufficient for this act of love without an infused habit:

First, because nature is determined to one action. But according to Bk. II of *On Generation*, nature is determined to seek its own being or existence, and therefore it cannot seek its nonbeing, and this no matter how it is proposed, unless one says it is determined to seek its being only conditionally, which does not seem probable. Every intellectual nature, then, is more determined to its own being than desiring that God be, if both could not coexist. For it is determined to seek its own being as its one natural desire, and no condition one assumes it bears towards anything else will incline it otherwise, for then it would only seek its own being conditionally.

Furthermore, a natural appetite, it seems, does not regard anything other than what is advantageous for its subject, and consequently its primary regard is the one for whom it seeks this advantage, which is none other than the loving subject itself. But if this is its primary regard, then it cannot have a greater regard for something other than itself.

[Second opinion] Another argues against this for the following reasons:

First, the part loves the whole more than itself. The macrocosm and microcosm illustrate this. In the macrocosm water rises lest there be a vacuum in the universe. This is clear from many experiments such as in an inverted vessel when a candle is burnt within it, and in many other instances. Now, this behavior is contrary to the natural inclination of water's particular nature, since it is naturally heavy and hence tends to descend, but the universal inclination overcomes this. For in this way the good of the universe as a whole is preserved, namely, its continuity and the contiguity of its parts. To this good—as in the present example—water is more inclined, wanting, as it does, the universal rather than the particular good. This is also apparent in the microcosm, for the hand exposes itself to save the head as naturally desiring more the safety of the head than of any other part, including itself;

for the safety of the head preserves the health of all the other members so far as function of life and vital influences are concerned. From this, he argues further that since each creature is a kind of sharing in the divine goodness, it will seek more the divine good or the existence of the divine good than its own good or existence, and consequently, a rational creature will be able with its natural resources to love the divine good more than any other good, including itself as well.

Furthermore, a rational nature loves beatitude above all, as one gathers from Augustine in XIII *On the Trinity*, ch. 5. But the beatific object is loved no less than beatitude itself; therefore, a rational nature loves the beatific object above all else and hence above itself. —This is confirmed from the case of a person who kills himself in despair. He hates his existence but does not hate happiness, because he seeks it, if he could have it; therefore, he loves happiness more than himself, and consequently he loves the beatific object more than himself.

[Refutation of these arguments] These reasons are not cogent:

The first is not, because these examples do not establish his thesis, for they only show that the whole loves itself more than it loves a part, or a more important part loves itself more than a less important one. This is clear from the first example of water. For it is impossible that water should move itself upward for any good of the universe as a whole. Because it has a natural form that is determined to one action, so long as that form remains the same numerically, it can never be the formal reason for acting in the opposite way. Therefore water itself does not move itself upward, but is only moved in this way by something moving it extrinsically. To this upward movement its nature contributes nothing, and in consequence it is moved violently in comparison with its own nature as water. This part, therefore, does not love the whole nor seek to preserve it out of love, but rather the whole, or the ruling power in the whole [i.e., God], to whom all the powers of the universe are attributed, moves each part of the universe in such a way as is suited to the well-being of the whole. What we gather from this, therefore, is that the whole universe loves the well-being of the whole more than it does the proper welfare of this part. The same point we glean from the other example. The hand does not of its own desire expose itself for the good of the universe. Rather it is man, having these parts, one as more important, another as less important, who exposes one less important part that could be lost without danger to the whole in order to save the whole or to save some part that could not be lost without damage to the whole and to the universe. And so too with what he proposes. Any argument he gives only proves that God loves the good of the universe or its well-being more than that of one part, or that God loves the more important part more than the less important part. But the argument cannot be made to prove that some part loves the being of God or that of the universe more than its own existence. In those examples he presents, a part, left to itself and considered according to its own inclination, never exposes itself to nonexistence for another. In other respects his simile limps, for while what he says about the parts may be true— namely, that these parts are something of the whole in reality and by saving the whole they save themselves insofar as they have existence in the whole—a creature is not something pertaining to God as if it were a part of God, though it is something that belongs to God as an effect of his or a participation of him.

The second reason, from beatitude, is also inconclusive, because it is based only on the affection for the advantageous. Among the things desired for the lover himself beatitude or happiness is that which is desired most, but it is not that which is loved most of all, in the way the end is loved more than those things which contribute to that end. Likewise, the assumption about beatitude is not true unless one speaks of it in general, not specifying what it consists in. For in general one cannot love some other thing more than oneself, for this "thing" other than the lover has not been specified as that in which beatitude consists.

[Scotus' own arguments] Hence, I do not rest content with these reasons but propose two other reasons of my own for the main conclusion:

The first is this. Natural reason reveals to an intellectual creature that something must be loved in the highest measure, because among all objects, acts, and habits that are essentially ordered to one another, there is something supreme, and thus there is some love that is highest and also some object that is supremely lovable. But natural reason reveals nothing other than infinite good to be such, for if it did, charity would then incline one to the opposite of what right reason dictates, and thus charity would not be a virtue. Therefore, natural reason dictates that the infinite good be loved above all. Consequently, the will can do this by its purely natural endowments, for the intellect could not rightly dictate something to the will that the natural will could not tend towards or carry out naturally. If it could do so, then the will would be naturally bad, or at least it would not be free to tend towards everything according to that aspect of good revealed to it by the intellect. This is what is said particularly about the angels [whom we suppose were created in a natural] state of innocence. For in that state they would not have been unjust and could not have had an act that was unrighteous, but only an elicited act that was right. Now, presupposing that they did act in some way, that act would have to be right,

and it could only have been right if God were loved above all; therefore, [in their natural state of innocence the angels could have had an
act whereby they loved God above all].

The second reason is this. The Philosopher, according to III *Ethics*,
thinks the brave citizen ought to expose himself to death for the good
and utility of the state. But the Philosopher did not assume such a
person will receive his reward in the afterlife, as is clear from many
passages where he expresses his doubts about whether the soul is immortal or mortal, and more often inclines towards its mortality. Now, if
indeed someone, following natural reason, doubts about the existence
of a future life, no one—because he is doubtful—is obligated to expose
himself to a certain loss of a good and civic virtue. Therefore, apart from
any future reward, every brave citizen ought to will his nonexistence
lest the good of the state perish. According to right reason, then, the
divine good and the good of the state must be loved more than the good
of some individual. Therefore, everyone according to right reason
should be willing to cease to exist for the sake of a divine good.

[An objection and its solution] Here it is claimed that the brave
citizen in exposing himself to death for virtue's sake is experiencing
the greatest good that virtue can bring, together with the greatest delight. It is because of this good—brief though it be—that one ought to
choose and love such an act in preference to an ignominious life, for
according to IX *Ethics*, ch. 8, one intense act is to be preferred to any
number of desultory actions. In this case the brave citizen is choosing
not his nonexistence, but rather his finest hour from a virtuous viewpoint, because right reason dictates that he should not forego this act
of virtue with its many other advantages.—On the contrary, here I
simply love more what I want to save and shield from evil. I am willing
to lose something else rather than this other, for whose sake I am willing to surrender my very existence. But brave persons of this sort are
willing that both themselves and their act of virtue should cease to
exist rather than that evil befall their state or country. Therefore, they
simply love the public good, which they wish to preserve, more than
they love themselves or love to have this act of virtue. Hence they
expose themselves to death, not for the sake of such virtue, but rather
to save their country—and thus my argument stands.

A third reason is added, which is a kind of theological persuasive
argument. If no one could have a virtuous act of loving God above all
by purely natural means, then whoever would find himself performing
such an act in this life would know that he possesses charity [and
supernatural grace] because without charity, he would have no inclination to love God above all. But the consequent is false; hence the
antecedent is also.

[2. Scotus' Solution to the Question]

As for this article, because of these two reasons—conformity of the will to right reason and the case of the brave citizen—I concede the conclusion that by purely natural means any will could love God above all, at least as human nature existed in the state in which it was instituted. To clarify this, then, I explain first how "above all" is to be understood; then, second, to what extent a rational creature is bound to such love; and third, why, despite this natural capacity, the habit of charity is still necessary.

[A. How Is "Above All" to Be Understood?]

As for the first, "above all" can be understood either extensively or intensively. Extensively, namely, when one loves God more than everything else, for instance, when someone out of affection for him would will more readily that all else should cease to be rather than that God not exist. Intensively, for instance, because one wills God well with a greater measure of affection than one has for any other person's welfare. As for the first, it is commonly conceded that nothing other than God, nor all other things combined, can be as valuable as God.

[Opinion of others] As for the second, a distinction of this sort is introduced. One love may exceed another because it is more fervent or tender, or because it is stronger and firmer; and these loves are said to exceed one another in the way a mother loves her son more fervently and tenderly, whereas a father loves him with a love that is stronger and firmer, because he will expose himself to greater danger out of love for his son.

And it is said that the love of God above all ought to be of this latter sort in strength, lest something other than God be able to turn one away from him. But it is not necessary that he be loved above all as to tenderness and fervor and sweetness, because at times a person finds himself loving a creature more fervently than God is sometimes loved, as is clear in the case of a jealous person.

And this is confirmed, because if one could love God above all in both of these intensive ways, then one could fulfill that precept of Deuteronomy 6:[5]: "Love the Lord your God with all your heart, and with all your soul, and with all your strength." But the opposite is true, according to Anselm, Augustine, and the Master in the text of this distinction. They do not wish to make this a precept that one is obliged to fulfill, but consider it rather as an ideal towards which we ought to strive.

[Refutation of this view] We argue against this distinction, because only one who loves more firmly loves more. For I love this more to which I will less evil and for the preservation of whose good I put myself out to a greater extent, for readiness to put oneself out for someone is a consequence of love of that person. And I am speaking here about that love which is an act of the will, and not about that which is a feeling in the sense appetite. And although some others are said to love more fervently and tenderly who do not love firmly, this is not from some excess in them of that higher understanding-love, but perhaps results from some feeling of sensitive-love, as some who are said to be devout feel at times some greater sweetness than others who are much more solid and firm in their love of God, and are a hundred times more ready to sustain martyrdom for him than these others. But such sweetness is not an act elicited by the will, but a certain rewarding feeling associated with the will-act whereby God nourishes his little ones and draws them to himself lest they fall by the way.

[Scotus' view] I say, then, that this "above all" must be understood in both ways, extensively and intensively, for just as I am held to love God above all extensively, so I am held to love him also intensively with a greater affection than simply anything else. I say "greater affection" because it is more opposed to anything incompatible with it, in the sense that one could more easily be turned against loving anything else than turned against loving God. As for what is added about that commandment, this is not valid. For it would be equivalent to giving a precept about the beatific vision, not as something we should fulfill, but as something we know we ought to tend towards. It is clear the opposite is the case with the commandment to love God above all.

[B. How Does This Precept Oblige?]

I say therefore that this precept, both extensively and intensively according to the aforesaid way, can be fulfilled in this life, but not as to all the conditions which are implied by the words "with your whole heart, your whole soul," etc., because in this life there cannot be that recollection of our faculties with all impediments removed, so that the will could exert the sort of effort it could if our powers were all united and recollected and all impediments were removed. And it is in regard to such intensity, when all impediments are removed and our faculties are recollected, that one must understand the dictum of Augustine and the Master that this precept is not fulfilled in this life, for the propensity of the inferior powers in the present state impedes the superior powers from acting perfectly.

As to this I say that the affirmative precept of Deuteronomy 6 and Matthew 22: "Love the Lord, your God, with your whole heart," etc., not only always obliges us to refrain from the opposite, viz., an act of hatred, but also obliges us to elicit an act that is directed to [God] as our end, from whose goodness stems the moral goodness of any act that is a means to that end. Just as man, then, is sometimes required to perform some virtuous act, so he is held sometimes to have at some time an action in accord with this commandment about gratuitously loving the end. But when this is to be, perhaps has been determined by that divine precept: "Keep holy the Sabbath and let every one remain recollected and raise his heart to his God." And the Church has specified that mass be heard on Sunday in canon [64, part 3, dist. 1, of the *Decretum Gratiani*]. Nor is the law of love of neighbor similar in this respect, as will become clear in the following questions.

[C. Why the Habit of Charity Is Necessary]

As for the third point of this article, namely, the need for a habit of charity, I reply as I did in that seventeenth distinction [q. 3] of the first book, namely, that this habit adds to the substantial intensity of the act a further intensity, which the will alone could also have given to the act by exerting an equal effort. And the more perfect the created power is, so much more imperfect would it be (speaking arithmetically, for geometrically the imperfection would be equal) if it did not have created charity corresponding to it proportionately. For as much as a lesser will is deficient if it does not have charity proportionate to itself, so much the greater would the will seem to be deficient geometrically if it did not have the charity proportionate to it. As for this added circumstance, that the act has the special character of being accepted by God, this is something due principally to charity and less so to the will. Briefly, then, I say, as I said there, the reason habits are needed because of acts, especially the habit of charity, is due to something that is a circumstance of the act. As for the substance of the act, however, I maintain what I said there, that the habit is not required.

Also as to the condition of the habit, namely, that it be infused, I say—as I did above about faith and hope—that one cannot prove by natural reason that such habits are infused, but this is only held on faith. A good argument from congruity would be that it does not seem probable that for acts that have to be elicited immediately about God, the highest part of the soul could be perfected most perfectly except immediately by God.

[Reply to the Opposing Arguments of This Question]

[To 1] As for the initial arguments, I concede the first, that charity can be properly called friendship. I do not take it entirely in the strict sense in which the Philosopher uses the term when he speaks of it. If we somehow extend the meaning he had in mind so that it applies to God, we can say that charity is something more excellent than friendship. For this excess in the object does not take away anything of perfection in it, but only removes what is imperfection. Therefore this excess does not invalidate our proposal. Uprightness indeed in what is lovable and a return of love in the beloved are *per se* conditions in the lovable object. But equality in these things is only a concomitant condition, and not a matter of perfection. Indeed, charity is not more perfect if it is only a return of love. God, however, has both grounds for being loved, namely, the fact that he returns our love as well as that more excellent amiability or goodness in itself, and with him there can be a friendship that is called "superfriendship." And if one argues that equality is also a basis for friendship, this is true, but it always presupposes some honorable good that deserves to be loved for its own sake, and this is the primary reason why something is amiable. Equality is a basis for friendship strictly speaking, but excellence is an even greater reason for a similar or even more perfect habit than friendship, and here I call such a habit "charity."

[To 2] To the second, I say that God can be loved above all not only by charity, but also by one's natural endowments, at least in the state in which nature was instituted. And as to the principle of the Philosopher in IX *Ethics*, I say that this citation ought to be understood about our recognition of friendship. For friendship for another becomes known when I desire things for another similar to what I desire for myself. It is not to be understood as its essential characteristic, however, as if there were no other sort of friendship, unless one is speaking strictly of that which holds between equals (for there indeed love for oneself is a measure of love for another, and not vice versa).—And when one argues there about unity, I say that there are two concurrent conditions in the lovable object, namely, goodness and oneness with it, and though at times unity [with oneself] surpasses unity [with the beloved], the goodness of the latter may make up for this.

[To 3] To the third, I concede the conclusion, but this still does not make charity superfluous, as we have said.

[To 4] As to the fourth, I say that one cannot acquire by one's own acts a habit of the same species as charity. However, one could acquire some habit of friendship that tends to God under the same objective aspect and by a similar act, because by loving him above all, a habit of this sort can be acquired by way of repeated acts. Any two natures that cannot stem from an efficient cause of the same species are specifically different, because effects of the same species can only be from causes similar in kind, and therefore the sort of charity that can only be infused cannot be of the same species as this other friendship that can be acquired by actions.

[To the arguments in art. 2] I reply to the two arguments for the other member in the article about the formal object of charity. To the first I say that this assumption of two gods destroys the nature of charity. For any habit of itself tends to but one thing. To assume that it tends to several is to assume we are no longer dealing with the same habit. Take a similar case. If there is a habit proper to first principles alone, to assume some other habit of first principles is to assume that this first habit does not pertain to this as its proper object. And so I say that to assume there are several gods implies on the one hand that each should be loved by charity, and on the other that none can be so loved.

To the other I say that where one is dealing with some extrinsic agent operating in regard to what is in that order, the relationship to what is more or less may be unlike the relationship to what is supreme in that order. For some operation to be most perfect may require something that is supreme, and still not require the other things pertaining to that order. Take the example of colors. The most perfect vision can only be that of the most perfect color, and one can have such without any proportionately perfect vision of the next-most-perfect color. The reason for this is that the ability of the most perfect color to satisfy the eye includes, as it were, whatever lesser satisfying capacities other colors may have. And although in the question at hand, one thing may excel another in goodness, none of these other things contain anything that is necessary for complete satisfaction, although the potency we have here is naturally free to love these others. The infinite good, and that alone, will quiet or satisfy the will, and it will do so insofar as it is infinite good. The will has no need, then, to be satisfied more or less by any finite good according to its degree of goodness, for such degrees of goodness are only accidental as regards what quiets the will extrinsically.

26. LOVE OF GOD AND NEIGHBOR
(*Ordinatio* III, suppl., dist. 28)

In regard to dist. 28 [of Bk. III] I ask: Is it by the same habit by which we love God that we are bound to love our neighbor?

[Arguments Pro and Con]
For the negative:
Each habit has but one formal object; but the goodness of God and the goodness of our neighbor represent distinct formal objects; therefore, etc.

Also, the habit whereby God is loved is a theological habit; therefore, it has as its formal object God alone and not something created. —In answer to this it is said that this is true of its main object;

nevertheless it still regards others, but only insofar as they are ascribed to God himself. Against this evasion, it is objected that if this ascription alone sufficed, then there would be but one intellectual habit for everything as well as one appetitive habit, because all that can be understood by the mind is attributed to one [source]; similarly all moral virtues have but one aim, namely, felicity, which all moral virtues seek *per se*.

Furthermore, to the main question there is this argument. A habit concerned with a principle is other than that concerned with a conclusion; similarly, then, the appetitive habit concerned with the end is other than that which is concerned with means to that end. But charity is concerned with our end; therefore, etc.

For the affirmative:

There is that text from the first epistle of St. John [4:21: "The commandment we have from him is this: Whoever loves God must also love his brother"].

[Body of the Question]

There are [two] points to investigate in this question: First, how does this habit whereby God is loved refer to our neighbor as an object of love? and second, who is this neighbor of ours?

[Article 1: How Does Charity towards God Refer to Neighbor?]

To the first I say, as in dist. 17 of the first book, that charity is defined as the habit by which we hold God to be dear. Now, it could be that someone is considered dear because of some private love where the lover wants no co-lovers, as is exemplified in the case of jealous men having an excessive love of their wives. But this sort of habit would not be orderly or perfect. Not orderly, I say, because God, the good of all, does not want to be the private or proper good of any person exclusively, nor would right reason have someone appropriate this common good to himself. Hence, such a love or habit, inclining him to this good as exclusive to himself and not to be loved or had by another, would be an inordinate love. Neither would it be perfect, because one who loves perfectly wants the beloved to be loved by others, as is clear from Richard [of St. Victor, cited] in dist. 13, Bk. I. Therefore, God, in infusing the love by which all tend towards him in a perfect and orderly way, gives this habit by which he is held dear as a good that is to be loved by others as well. Thus this habit which regards God in himself, inclines also to this, that he be loved by another, at least by anyone whose friendship he is pleased to have, or whose friendship is pleasing to him at present or at some time when it is pleasing to him. Just as this habit, then, inclines one to a perfect and orderly love of God, so too does it incline one to want him to be loved by himself and by anyone whomsoever whose friendship he is pleased to have.

From this it is clear how the habit of charity is one, because it does not refer to a plurality of objects, but regards as its primary object God alone insofar as he is good and is the first good. Secondarily, it wills that God be loved by anyone whose love is perfect and directed to loving him as he is in himself, for this is what perfect and orderly love of God means. And in so loving, I love both myself and my neighbor out of charity, viz., by willing that both of us love God in himself. And this is something that is simply good and an act of justice. Thus the first object of charity is only God in himself; all the others, however, are certain intermediate objects. They are objects of quasi-reflex acts by means of which one tends to the infinite good, who is God. It is the same habit, however, that has to do with both direct and reflex acts.

[Objection] Against this the objection is raised that it is not the same intellectual habit whereby I know God on the one hand and whereby I know another knows God on the other; therefore, by the same token it is not the same habit whereby I wish God well and wish that another wish him well.

To this I reply: the act on which I reflect can be designated by a noun, and then it refers to the essence of the act, or it can be designated by a verb, and then it refers to the act as it is in some subject, or concerned with some subject. In the first way generally there can be a reflection upon a direct act by the same habit that can elicit that act itself. This is true not only of intellectual but also of appetitive habits. By the same habit whereby I understand something I also know I understand it; this would be true if I were able to know something by an intellection inhering in another just as it is true of my knowledge that inheres in myself. The second way of referring to the act is by the infinitive of the verb, and the infinitive mode, as when I use "to know," "to will," and similar verbs. And if these are compared with willing, they do not necessarily refer to the present. For I could wish that you run, not now, but some other time. But if you compare "to know" with knowing, we have this situation. Since knowledge is only with respect to what is true, and I know of something acting only when it is actually going on in such a subject, knowing is known by reflecting on the act signified by the verb only when that act is something presently going on in the knower. And because it is possible that in me knowledge can coexist with a reflex act itself, it is not necessary that this act be present in anything other than myself. Therefore, my reflex act is not about the act itself as designated by a verb, but about it as asserted of some subject [designated by a noun].

Hence it is clear that although it is not by the same habit that I know God and I know you know God, nevertheless it is by the same habit that I want God and want that you also want God; and in this I want you to use your will in such a way that justice exists in you. This means that our neighbor is assigned not as a kind of secondary object of charity, but rather as something that is entirely an incidental object, as it were, because it enables me to want the beloved to be loved perfectly and orderly, and enables me to love him in such a way that he be loved by others. In this, I love the other incidentally, as it were—not for his or her sake, but because of the object I want him or her to love, and in willing that [God] be loved by such a person, I want something that is good for that individual in an unqualified sense, because it is a good that pertains to justice . . .

[Article 2: Who Is My Neighbor?]

As for the other point, I say that my neighbor is anyone whose friendship is pleasing to the beloved, namely, anyone by whom God would want to be loved. But I am not obligated rationally to want that the one loved above all be loved also by one by whom he does not care to be loved, or whose love is not pleasing to him. Since it is certain that the love of the blessed in heaven is pleasing to him, however, it follows that I must want God to be loved by them in an unqualified sense. Since in this life, however, there is some doubt as to any specific individual, I ought to want such to love God conditionally, namely, if it pleases God to be loved by him or to be loved now or whenever it pleases God to be so loved. As for pilgrims in this life in general, since one must always presuppose there are some whose love is pleasing to God, or not displeasing to him, one can will absolutely that God be loved by them also. I ought not will that God be loved by the damned, the devils, or also those displeasing men who are blind to him.

[Reply to the Initial Arguments]

To the first argument at the beginning, it is evident how there is but one object involved. And when you prove that the goodness proper to God is different from that proper to one's neighbor, I say that the goodness proper to neighbor does not function as the terminal object of an act of charity, but it is only the divine goodness that plays such a role. For even though one intends the goodness of this neighbor, it is only by way of a reflex act, which always implies some further direct act that tends to the object [which is the divine goodness itself], as was explained earlier.

To the second, the same notion applies, because this virtue only has God as the object that satisfies it *per se*. For the immediate object of its reflex act, however, it can have something created. Perhaps in this way the vision had in heaven could also have something created as an object, not as something standing there on its own, but as pointing to God.

To the third, I say that the habit of principles is directed towards a principle according to the truth proper to it, which it has by reason of its terms. The habit whereby I know a conclusion, however, is directed to the conclusion according to the truth proper to it, which is something other than the truth a principle has. But that is not the case here, for there is but one goodness towards which charity is directed, and that is God in himself and neighbor as turned towards God in love. For the goodness of the neighbor does not move me more than if a straw could love God. But if I love God perfectly, then I love him to be loved by all who are able to love him in a way that is not inordinate, and whose love is pleasing to him. This same situation does not hold universally in regard to objects shown to us by the intellect and in regard to objects that are attractive to the will.

27. LOVE OF GOD AND SELF
(*Ordinatio* III, suppl., dist. 29)

In regard to dist. 29 [of Bk. III] I ask: Is everyone bound to love self most after God?

[Arguments Pro and Con]
For the negative:
Bk. IX of the *Ethics* censures the self-lover, and there are many other passages that do the same.

Furthermore, Gregory, commenting on that passage in Luke, "He sent them two by two," etc., says: "No one properly speaking is said to have charity towards himself, but rather he is said to have charity who reaches out to another in love. Truly charity is this love of another."

For the affirmative:
The measure is more perfect than the measured; but love of self is the measure of love of neighbor, according to Matthew 22:39: "You shall love your neighbor as yourself."

[Body of the Question]
From what was said in the preceding question, viz., about how charity has reference to neighbor, the solution of this question is clear. For insofar as charity is the principle of tending directly towards God

by a direct act, it is also the principle for reflecting on those acts whereby one tends to God; and on this account, as was pointed out there, it is the principle for wanting everyone able to love God to do so. This is the principle for loving a neighbor whose love is pleasing, or not displeasing, to God. Among all the acts of the same nature, however, the principle of tending to God is also the principle of reflecting most directly upon the act one elicits; this is the act by which one having charity loves God. Therefore, most directly after loving God, charity inclines a person to love that by which he tends to God, or by which he wants himself to love God. In wanting himself to love God, he loves himself out of charity, because he wills for himself a just and honorable good. Therefore, immediately after love of God, he loves himself out of charity.

This is also confirmed, because weighing the reasons of goodness and unity, which are grounds for love, and primarily love of the infinite good, in which the aspect of goodness is most perfect, one sees in oneself the next greatest reason, viz., that unity which is perfect identity. Hence, everyone is naturally inclined to love himself most after the infinite good. Now, a natural inclination is always right; therefore, etc.

[Reply to the Initial Arguments]

To the first argument, I say that what the Philosopher is explaining there is how despicable is an immoderate love of self, but not a self-love that is moderate.

To the second, I say that everyone who loves out of charity, loves himself in reference to the infinite good, because he loves that act or habit whereby he tends to that good; and it is in this way that his love is directed to another. For God is the principal object of his act, and then he has charity for himself not as the ultimate end, but as a proximate object that is ordered to the first and ultimate end distinct from himself.

PART VIII

Sin

28. IS THE POWER TO SIN FROM GOD?
(*Ordinatio* II, dist. 44)

In connection with the forty-fourth distinction [of Bk. II] I ask: "Is the power to sin from God?"

[Arguments Pro and Con]

According to Anselm in *Freedom of Choice*, ch. 1: "To be able to sin is not liberty or any part of liberty"; therefore, insofar as free choice is from God, it is not the power to sin. But the ability to sin is not from God for any reason other than that free choice comes from God. Therefore, the ability or power to sin is in no way from God.

To the contrary: the Master cites authorities in the text affirming that the ability to sin is from God.

[Body of the Question]

I reply: The power to sin either expresses the immediate order of potentiality to the act of sinning or else refers to the foundation of such a potentiality, by virtue of which the one having such is said to be able to sin.

If it be taken in the first sense, then the order is either to the act that is the basis for sin or else to the deformity that is present in the sinful act. If the first is meant, then this order is from God, just as are both members of the ordered pair, and God has power also over that act which underlies or is the basis for sin, and not just the created will, according to one opinion. If the second is meant, then there is no such ordering to sin, even as the term [i.e., the deformity or lack of goodness] is nothing, and hence is not from God.

If one is speaking of the basis or foundation of this order, however, I say that something positive lies at the root of this order in both senses [i.e., something positive underlies both the act that is the basis of sin and the deformity itself]. For as is the case of passive or receptive potencies, where the same subject can either have something or be deprived of it, so too where the subject is a power that is free to act deficiently. Such a power is the immediate basis or source of its opposite states by either acting or being deficient. By acting it is a power for righteousness, by being deficient it is a power to sin. And this absolute entity [i.e., the will] is the proper power for both in the respective way that there can be a power for both [righteousness and sin], namely, by the power being either effective or defective. And in this sense the power to sin is from God, i.e., God is the source of that nature which enables its possessor to commit sin by using its powers not effectively but defectively, of which deficient usage, however, this positive entity is the proximate ground.

And if one objects that the will is always deficient inasmuch as it is created from nothing and not because of anything positive that it contains, I answer: To be defectible in the sense of being able to return to nothingness is a consequence of every creature coming from nothing. But to be defectible in this sense of being able to sin is a property peculiar to this nature and is a consequence of its being the specific sort of nature that it is, namely, with a principle of action that can function in opposite ways, acting properly or defectively.

[Reply to the Initial Arguments]

To Anselm I say that liberty is a pure perfection. Hence he assumes it to be in God. Liberty in us is limited, but it can be considered according to its formal nature without that limitation, and then it is not a limited perfection but a pure perfection. For example, wisdom is a pure perfection, and according to its nature, considered absolutely, it is also found in us; but not only is it in us, but it exists there only with limitations, and hence our wisdom includes two things, one of which is pure perfection; the other [i.e., perfection qua limited or finite] is not pure perfection as such, but it includes pure perfection as part of what it is. And so I say that although the species of will that is in us includes that liberty which is pure perfection, it not only includes that, but also includes it as limited, which limitation is not pure perfection. The ability to sin does not pertain to it by reason of its pure perfection, nor is this the proximate foundation of this order to being actually deficient. Rather it is the second [i.e., the limitation of this perfection].

We can explain Anselm, then, in this way: the capacity to sin does not pertain to liberty as a pure perfection, nor does his argument that this capacity is not in God prove anything more. But if we are talking about created liberty and its capacity to choose badly, then this is only a part of what pertains to the perfection of the will, whereas the basis for choice itself [namely, the freedom to act in diverse ways] is a matter of perfection purely and simply, for this power is a positive reality and thus is in God, from whom and in whom and through whom all things exist, to him be honor and glory. Amen.

29. THE SIN OF LUCIFER
(*Ordinatio* II, dist. 6, q. 2)

First we must examine the order that exists among the acts of the will. And here I say there is a twofold act of the will, namely, to like and to dislike, for dislike is a positive act of the will whereby it turns away from the distasteful and shuns the inconvenient, whereas to like or love is the act whereby it accepts some appropriate or suitable object. Furthermore, there is a twofold like or love, one which can be called the love of friendship [or benevolence], another called the love of desiring or wanting or coveting. Friendship or benevolent love concerns an object of well-wishing, whereas the love of desire concerns some object I want for some other beloved.

The order among these acts is clear, for every dislike presupposes some liking, for I turn away from something only because it is inconsistent with something I regard as suitable; and this is the point of Anselm's example of the miser who gives up his money to buy bread (*The Fall of the Devil*, ch. 3). And the order that exists among the two forms of love is also evident, because the coveting presupposes the other love of friendship. For, with respect to what is desired, the one befriended becomes a quasi-end for the sake of whom I want this good (since it is for the sake of the beloved that I desire the good I wish that person to have). And since the end has the distinction of being the first object willed, it is clear that friendship or benevolent love precedes the love of desire or coveting.

And it follows further, from what has been proved, that there is a similar process in disorderly acts, for the first inordinate act can never be one of dislike, since it is only in virtue of something liked or loved that an act of dislike is possible. And if the love is orderly as to its object and all the circumstances, then the dislike that is a consequence of such a love would also be in order. By the same token, if the friendship-love would not be inordinate, the consequent love of desire would also be ordinate. For if that for which I desire some good is loved ordinately, then the will whereby I desire something for the one I wish well will also be in order.

It follows, then, that [Lucifer's] very first inordinate act of will was the first benevolent love he had towards one to whom he wished well. But this object was not God, for God could not have been loved inordinately, speaking intensively of friendship-love. God is so lovable solely by reason of the object he is, that he renders the most intensive act of love completely good. Neither is it likely that something other than oneself could have been loved too much by an act of friendship-love, first because a natural inclination tends more towards self than towards any other creature, and also because friendship, according to Bk. VIII of the *Ethics*, is based on oneness, and (from Bk. IX) what is amicable for others has its roots in what is amicable for oneself. The first inordinate act, therefore, was one of benevolence towards himself.

And this is what Augustine says in *The City of God*, Bk. XIV: "Two loves created two cities; the love of God to the contempt of self created the city of God and the love of self to the contempt of God created the city of the devil." The first source from which the city of the devil stems, then, is inordinate friendship-love, which root germinates until it yields contempt of God, in which malice reaches its peak. It is clear, then, that the initial disorder in an unqualified sense consists in that inordinate love that was simply first.

What remains to be seen is what the initial disorder was in regard to the love called desire. And here it seems we have to say that [Lucifer] first coveted happiness immoderately. The proofs are these:

First, the initial inordinate desire did not proceed from an affection for justice, as no sin proceeds from such. Hence, it must have come from an affection for the advantageous, because every act elicited by the will stems from an affection either for justice or for the advantageous, according to Anselm. And a will that fails to follow the rule of justice will seek most of all what is most advantageous, and thus it will seek such first, for nothing else rules that unrighteous will but an inordinate, immoderate appetite for that greatest beneficial good, namely, perfect happiness.—And this reason can be gleaned from what Anselm says in ch. 4 of *The Fall of the Devil*. Look for it there.

The second proof is this. The first sin of covetousness will be one of love or desire (for nothing is shunned to avoid disaster except it be that one desires the opposite of such a calamity). And this first love called "desire" is either just, utilitarian, or hedonistic (for nothing is loved save in one of these three ways). But it was not a just or honorable love, for then the angel would not have sinned; neither is it utilitarian, for this is never first (inasmuch as this regards someone for whom it is useful, and no one covets the useful first, but rather that for which it is useful). Hence he first sinned by loving something excessively as his supreme delight. What is supremely delightful, however, is the honorable good and as such is beatitude itself [viz., God].—And this argument is based on what the Philosopher says in Bk. VIII of the *Ethics* and the commonly accepted distinction of good into what is useful, delightful, and honorable.

Third, there is this persuasive argument. Every appetite whose act presupposes some antecedent awareness first craves that delectable most in harmony with its associated cognitive power, or the delight that comes from having such, because this most satisfies its hunger. This is clear in the parallel instances of taste, hearing, and touch, where the associated appetite triggered by these senses craves the most perfect object of which they are actually aware. A will unassociated with any sense appetite, then, first seeks what is most agreeable to the intellect or the delight that comes from such an object in harmony with the mind, for desire follows from such knowledge. Hence the will first wants such happiness as comes from knowing and delighting in the knowledge of such an object.

A fourth persuasive argument is this. If justice did not regulate it, what the will would want first is something it would want if such alone existed and in the absence of which nothing else would be wanted. Now, delight is such a thing. For if one were sad, what one would want would be not some excellence or any other such thing, but happiness or something like it.

As for the angel's first sin of desire, then, he would apparently have first coveted happiness.

For just as the first sin of the visual appetite would be coveting a vision of what is most beautiful to the eye (which would most perfectly delight and satisfy it), to a will joined to a sense appetite, but unchecked by right reason or justice, the first appeal would appear to be something most inviting to the sense appetite with which the will was most in harmony at the time it acted. And so in men the dominance of sense appetites is in accord with their varied dispositions. For if each cognitive power has its corresponding appetite, and, according to the different ways they are disposed, various cognitive powers and appetites may predominate, still I say in each case, the will is most inclined towards that action dictated by the predominant sense appetite. Thus anyone who follows his first inclination unchecked by any rule of justice will in one case be first inclined to lust; in another, to pride; in a third, to something else.

A will unassociated with any sense appetite, then, and consequently not attracted to anything by the inclination of such an appetite, if deserted by justice, follows that inclination the will has in itself as will.

For what perfects the intellect most, perfects the appetite corresponding to this cognitive power. Hence, [the angel's first sin of covetousness] was an immoderate desire for happiness, for happiness is the object of the will.

Against this you may raise these objections:

First, happiness is wanted by everyone, according to Augustine in ch. 5 of Bk. XIII of *The Trinity*. But what is found uniformly in all would seem natural. Therefore, happiness is wanted naturally. But a natural appetite is always right, because it comes from God. Hence, a will conformed to this is always right, because it is conformed to what is right. Therefore, in seeking happiness no one sins.

Furthermore, no intellect errs in regard to first principles, according to *Metaphysics*, Bk. II. Therefore, neither does the will err as regards its ultimate end. The validity of the inference is proved from the Philosopher's analogy that as the principle functions in theory, so the end functions in practice (*Ethics*, Bk. VII, and *Physics*, Bk. II).

A third objection, also, is that the good would have an affection for the advantageous just as well as the evil. But according to Anselm in *The Harmony between Foreknowledge and Free Will*, the will is unable not to will the beneficial; hence the good will the beneficial good just as the evil do. Therefore, all would have sinned equally, if they sinned because of the affection for the advantageous.

To the first:

In order to understand the solution to these objections, I first distinguish ways in which these affections for justice and the beneficial that Anselm speaks of in ch. 4 of *The Fall of the Devil* might be understood.

Justice can be understood to be either infused (which is called gratuitous or grace), or acquired (which is called moral), or innate (which is the will's liberty itself). For if one were to think, according to that fictitious situation Anselm postulates in *The Fall of the Devil*, that there was an angel with an affection for the beneficial, but without an affection for justice (i.e., one that had a purely intellectual appetite as such and not one that was free), such an angel would be unable not to will what is beneficial, and unable not to covet such above all. But this would not be imputed to it as sin, because this appetite would be related to intellect as the visual appetite is now related to sight, necessarily following what is shown to it by that cognitive power, and being inclined to seek the very best revealed by such a power, for it would have nothing to restrain it. Therefore, this affection for justice, which is the first checkrein on the affection for the beneficial, inasmuch as we need not actually seek that towards which the latter affection inclines us, nor must we seek it above all else (namely, to the extent to which we are inclined by this affection for the advantageous)—this affection for what is just, I say, is the liberty innate to the will, since it represents the first checkrein on this affection for the advantageous.

Anselm may often be speaking not just of the actual justice which is acquired, but of infused justice, because he says it is lost through mortal sin, something true only of infused justice. Nevertheless by distinguishing from the nature of the thing the two primary characteristics of this twofold affection (one inclining the will above all to the advantageous, the other moderating it, as it were, lest the will in eliciting an act should have to follow its inclination), he makes these aspects out to be nothing other than the will itself insofar as it is an intellective appetite and insofar as it is free. For, as has been said, qua pure intellective appetite, the will would be actually inclined to the optimum intelligible (as sight is to what is best visible), whereas qua free, it could restrain itself in eliciting its act from following this natural inclination, as to either the substance of the act or its intensity.

But if some power were exclusively appetitive, following its inclination in acting as the visual appetite follows the visual inclination of the eye (though I admit it could only want what is intelligible, as the visual appetite can only seek what is visible), that power still could not sin in seeking such, for it would be powerless to seek anything other than what the intellect would show it or in any way other than the cognition would incline it. But this same power, having been made free (because we have nothing more here than one thing which includes virtually several perfectional aspects, which it would not include if it lacked that of liberty)—this power, I say, through its liberty could moderate itself in willing. It could do so as regards that volition towards which it is inclined by the affection for the advantageous, even though it might be most inclined to will the advantageous. And from the fact that it could moderate this, it is bound to do so according to the rule of justice it has received from a higher will. It is clear, then, from this that a free will is not bound in every way to seek happiness (in the way a will that was only an intellective appetite without liberty would seek it). Rather it is bound, in eliciting its act, to moderate the appetite qua intellective, which means to moderate the affection for the advantageous, namely, lest it will immoderately.

There are three ways, however, in which a will, able to moderate itself as regards the happiness befitting it, could fail to do so. As to intensity, it might love it more passionately than it deserves. Or through precipitance, it might want it sooner than is becoming. Or with disregard to the proper causal way to obtain it—for instance, it might want it without meriting it—or perhaps for other reasons, all of which one need not bother with here.

Probably in one of these ways, then, the will of the angel went to

excess: Either by wanting happiness as a good for him rather than loving it as a good in itself—that is, wanting a good, like the beatific
object, to belong exclusively to himself, rather than to be in another,
such as in his God. And this would be the supreme perversity of the
will, which—according to Augustine (*Eighty-three Different Questions*,
q. 30)—is to use as means what is to be enjoyed as an end, and treat as
an end what is to be used as a means. Or the angel could have failed in
the second way, wanting at once what God wished him to have after a
period of probation. Or it might have been in the third way, by wanting to possess happiness by natural means rather than by earning it by
grace, since God wished him to merit it.

His free will, then, should have moderated his desire in such ways as
right reason had revealed to him. For happiness should have been
wanted less for his sake than for the sake of God, and he should have
wanted it at the time God intended and on the basis of merit, as God
planned. If in some such fashion, then, he yielded to this affection
for the advantageous, not moderating it through justice, be it infused
(if the angel had such), or acquired, or innate (which is liberty itself),
then he sinned.

With this in mind, then, consider the objections.

As for the first, the natural will is not of itself immoderate, since it
inclines only after the manner of nature—and in this it is not immoderate, for it inclines as it was made to do, nor has it power to do otherwise. But to be so inclined or less inclined is in the power of the will as
free, through an elicited act.

When the natural will is taken to be orientated towards happiness, I
grant this. But this will is not actually immoderate through an elicited
act. For the inclination of a natural appetite is not an elicited act, but
resembles the first perfection [i.e., something identical with the substance or being of the will]. And this is no more immoderate than is
the nature to which it belongs. However, that nature is so inclined
towards its object by this affection for the advantageous that if it had
of itself an elicited act, it could not help eliciting it with no moderation in the most forceful way possible. But the natural will, as having
only the affection for the beneficial, is not the cause of any elicited
act; only the will as free can cause such, and therefore, qua eliciting an
act, the will does have what is required to moderate passion.

As for the assumption, then, that a will conformed to a natural will
[or appetite] is always right, because what is natural is always right, I
reply by saying this. If in eliciting its act, the will behaves as it would if
it were acting solely on its own, then it is not right, for it has another
rule for acting than it would have if it were to act solely on its own.
For it is bound to follow a higher will [viz., that of its Creator], from

whom it was given the power to moderate or not moderate this natural inclination, for it has the power not to act in the most passionate and forceful way that it could.

My reply to the second objection is the same. It is not in the intellect's power to temper its assent to the truth it apprehends. For when it is shown the truth of principles in the very meaning of their terms, or that of conclusions as contained in their principles or premises, it must assent, for it lacks the freedom to do otherwise. But the will—both in itself and in the powers under its control—can be moderated so that no act is elicited, or if one is, it is not completely dominated by this inclination [for the beneficial]. For the will can turn away the intellect, lest it think about such things as it is inclined to do, and the will is bound to do so, if such thoughts would represent in the intellect matter for sin, or lead to formal sin in the will. On the other hand, the will has an obligation to moderate its own inclination towards its ultimate end, lest it will this immoderately, or want to possess it in an unbecoming way, or want it only for self rather than as something good in itself.

Another answer to this objection would be that just as an act of the intellect considering a principle in itself cannot be false, so an act of the will loving the end in itself cannot be evil. But the act in this case is an act of friendship and not one of covetousness. But just as the act of an intellect could be false in ascribing the truth that some first cause exists to some created principle to which it does not belong, so an act of the will can be bad by wanting the goodness of the ultimate end to pertain to something other than the ultimate end, in a way unfitting to any other.

To the third, I say there was a natural inclination towards happiness in the good [angels] as well as in the bad—in fact, a greater inclination if their natural endowments were greater, for this inclination increases in proportion to the perfection of one's natural gifts. But in eliciting an act the good did not use the will as a mere intellective appetite, by wanting happiness in the way such an appetite would want it, but made use of the will's more perfect aspect (which is liberty), by acting in a way befitting a free agent as acting freely. But this means they acted in a manner ordained by a higher will, and hence they acted justly.

As for the claim that it is impossible not to will the beneficial, I reply: The good neither were able, nor wished, to dislike having happiness, or to have no desire for it. But they did not want it more than they wanted God to have everything good; rather they wished for happiness less than they wished God well, for they could moderate this desire through their liberty.

And if you object: Then the good really did not pursue happiness very well, but only did well to moderate this desire, I reply:

To want an act to be perfect so that by means of it one may better love some object for its own sake, is something that stems from the affection for justice, for whence I love something good in itself, thence I will something in itself. And thus the good could have wanted happiness so that, by having it, they could love the highest good more perfectly. And this act of wanting happiness would have been meritorious, because they are not using what is to be enjoyed as an end, but are enjoying it, for this good that I covet for myself, I desire in order that I may love that good in itself [i.e., God].

Seeing what the angel initially desired inordinately, we can assume he went on to covet for himself some further good, such as superiority over others. Or he could have had an inordinate dislike, such as hating anything opposed to what he wanted, for instance, he could have been unwilling to have happiness in a lesser degree than God himself, or disliked the very existence of God. Or he might have been unwilling to postpone his happiness to the end of his period of probation, or to earn it through merits. Consequently, he was unwilling to submit to God, and to that extent, did not want God to exist. In this his malice appears to have reached its peak, for just as no act is better formally than to love God, so no act is formally worse than to hate God.

30. THE SIN OF MALICE
(*Opus oxoniense* II, dist. 43, q. 2)

In reference to dist. 44 [of Bk. II] the question is raised: Can the created will sin out of malice by willing something that does not have the characteristic of a true (i.e., unqualified) good or apparent (or qualified) good?

[Arguments Pro and Con]

Here it is claimed on the authority of Dionysius in *The Divine Names* that "no one acts with an eye for evil."

But this does not seem to be so, because then the created will could not tend towards an object under any aspect other than what the divine will could, for the divine will can tend towards every good underlying that deformity [that is evil], even though the divine will cannot will the evil aspect that accompanies it.

[Body of the Question: Two Opinions]

If it be conceded that everything capable of being willed by one will is also able to be willed by the other, since the object of either will is equally extensive, it still does not follow that what is willed orderly by

the other, because a well-ordered volition de-
bject, but on whether the act and its object
culty. For an act towards some object may
one will [i.e., the divine] but not for the

, however, because hatred of God is con-
er that is not in error, and hence is pre-
of good but of evil. Now, if the will can
erthesis is proved, because there is no
the act of willing itself. For if one may
e act itself of the will, this is not some-
prior to the act, but something conse-
. If one cannot will this obvious evil
ood and not evil, it follows that either
se there is a blinding of reason, which
that argument in Bk. VII of the *Ethics*
premise, and not the particular [when

one holds on this question that it is
n it is easy to distinguish a sin against
or the will, because it is joined to the
n in its delight, and so if one sins,
ion of the sense appetite towards its
f passion, a sin of infirmity or impo-
ainst the Father, to whom power is
es intellectual knowledge to act, and
s not will rightly, and its sin of error
ainst the Son, to whom wisdom is
f the will on its own, not influenced
mind, but out of sheer liberty, and
nd appropriately described as being
oodness is appropriated.
that a created will could will evil
still assign a sin of certain malice
z., when the will, without passion
mind, freely sins. Now, here is the
thing other than the will attract-
t of pure malice. Here is as com-
be in a sin, since with full liberty
occasion, the sinner chooses for
malice is not such that the will
something evil.

der, and
aham to
vas com-
uld come
in mind;
inned in
d him.
other ex-
id he was

ing to his
g the op-
et he had
ivination.
e who ob-

eferred to
account in
the camel
xcused her-
" [Genesis
n they said
it does not
d dealt well
ld not have

ter sin than
than words,
lameworthy
ter pretense
lie or simu-
case of King
he feigned
u pretended
roy [2 Kings
ather he was
Baal.

31. LYING
(*Ordinatio* III, suppl., dist. 38)

Regarding dist. 38 [of Bk. III] I ask: Is every lie a sin?

[*Arguments Pro and Con*]
[Arg. 1] Genesis 22:[4]: "The boy and I will go on over yo
after we have worshiped, we will come back to you" [said Al
his servants], but he intended to kill the boy, because he
manded to do so; therefore he did not intend that the boy wc
back with him; hence he said the opposite of what he had
therefore, he lied. But it does not seem probable that he
carrying out this act of obedience for which God commend

[Arg. 2] Furthermore, the same point is proved by many
amples, as is clear from Genesis 22:[19] about Jacob, who s
the firstborn, though he knew this was false.

[Arg. 3] Also, in Genesis 42 and 44 we read of Joseph sa
brothers: "As Pharaoh lives, you are spies" [42:16], knowi
posite to be true. Also, frightening his brothers with the go
hidden in Benjamin's sack, he said he used this goblet for
He was not an augur, however, for it was not licit for tho
served the law of God to practice augury.

[Arg. 4] Furthermore, Rahab lied about those spies
in Joshua [2 and 6:25]; Judith also lied, according to the
Judith [10:12–13], and so did Rachael, when, sitting or
cushion under which her father's idols were hidden, she
self from rising, saying: "A woman's period is upon m
31:35]. The midwives also lied, according to Exodus 1, wh
the Hebrew women have the art of midwifery [v. 19]. Now
seem that they sinned, nor is it said that they did, for G
with them and built up their families [v. 20]; but God wo
rewarded them with good for doing evil; therefore, etc.

[Arg. 5] Furthermore, simulation in words is not a gre
simulation by actions, because actions speak more clearly
so that where falsity is found in both, actions seem more
than words, because falsity in deed represents an even gre
of what is in one's mind than does falsity in speech. Now,
lation in deed is not always a sin, as is clear from the
David, namely, when, in the presence of King Achis
madness when he was not mad [1 Samuel 21:14]. Also, J
to worship Baal, whose worshipers he wished to des
10:18–19]; neither was he blamed for his ruse, but
praised, because he seemed to have zeal for God agains

For the contrary view, we have Augustine's frequent remarks in his book *On Lies* and the citations from him in the text [of the Master].

Furthermore, every lie is a mortal sin; I prove this because it is against the commandment and law of nature: "Do not do to others what you do not want them to do to you" [Matt. 7:12]; for no one wants to be deceived by his neighbor when his neighbor ought to say what he has in mind; therefore, he should not act otherwise in his regard.

Furthermore, whatever is against some virtue or some act necessary for some virtue is a mortal sin; a lie is this sort of thing, because it is against truth or veracity, which is a virtue that falls under justice. For a truthful person communicates to his neighbor whatever he has conceived in his heart that should be shared with him. But one who lies does not communicate, but rather removes from his speech what ought to be shared, because he speaks for the purpose of communicating his ideas, and by lying he does not express these but asserts the opposite.

Furthermore, to lie is to abuse speech; for as Plato says in the *Timaeus*: "Words were instituted and imposed that they might become present indices of what we have in mind"; but liars do not use words as indices of such, but of the very opposite; therefore, etc.

Furthermore, the citations from Augustine in the aforementioned books seem to assert this. Look them up.

[Body of the Question]

In this question, all commonly hold the conclusion that a lie is a sin, a persuasive argument for which is the reason Augustine gives in his book *Against Lying*, that it is foolish to believe a person for whom lying is permitted. But one must believe many things, otherwise there would be no sharing of concepts and affections of the mind, and social life among human beings would be destroyed; therefore, in these things which need to be believed, it is not licit to lie.

But different persons give different reasons why lying is illicit.

[Article 1: Various Opinions Why Lying Is Sinful]

[The first view] Some say that a lie is necessarily a sin, because it necessarily turns one away from God, who is truth, and a lie is opposed to truth.

But against this is the fact that a lie is opposed not immediately to the first truth [i.e., God], but to the truth of some particular thing one is talking about. Therefore, just as badness opposed to some created good does not necessarily turn one away from the first uncreated good, so neither does the falsity opposed to some truth that has no relationship to the first truth turn one away from that first truth.

[The second view] Another explanation is that an act is said to be good or evil by reason of its object, which puts it into the generic category of the moral, hence an act's genus is derived from what is potential with respect to its differences. But what first constitutes the generic character of an act as moral, so that it can be further determined by other circumstances as quasi-differences, is the object of the act. For beyond the natural goodness an act has by reason of what it is, what first determines it as potential ethical material is its object. To the issue, then, it is said that an act that is generically bad never can be good, because no circumstance accruing to it can remove the badness which it has *per se* by reason of its object, for every circumstance presupposes the object. But to lie is an act that is generically bad, because it deals with matter that is inconsistent with the act in question, for matter suited to the act of speaking should be true or what is believed to be true. The subject matter of a lie, however, is opposed to this.

Refutation of this view. False beliefs are no more inappropriate or illicit matter for speech than is the innocent killing of a human being for the benefit of the state. But granted that all the conditions are the same which make this an illicit matter, namely, killing an innocent person, the act of killing can become licit, for example, if God revokes this precept: "You shall not kill," as was said in the previous question [about the natural law]. In such a case it may be not only licit but meritorious, for instance, if God were to command one to kill, as he commanded Abraham to kill Isaac. Therefore, by the same token, or by the dialectical rule that what holds good for a lesser excusing reason holds good for a greater, it could also become licit to speak what one believes to be false if the precept of not deceiving one's neighbor were revoked. For the precept of not deceiving is not more binding than the precept of not killing—indeed one's neighbor loses less if occasionally given a false view or if deprived of our true opinion than he would if deprived of bodily life; in fact there is no comparison here.

This is confirmed, because if to lie had the malice necessary to make it become the sort of subject matter [that averts one from God], it would not be prohibited by a precept of the second table, because the second table of the law prohibits only what is bad for our neighbor. But according to you this is not just an evil that harms our neighbor, because then, as the argument puts it, since it is a lesser evil than killing, it too could fail to be evil, just as killing might be. Would it more possibly be a violation of a precept of the first table? This does not seem probable, because it does not immediately turn one from God, just as the opposite action [i.e., telling the truth] about some indifferent matter does not have to do with God as its immediate object.

Furthermore, if one who said "He is running" were deceived, so that he believed this to be true, his statement would have to do with the same subject matter as it would were he not deceived, but believed what he said to be false. But one who mistakenly believes he is telling the truth does not sin; therefore, there is no evil here that stems from the very nature of the object.

[The third view] A third explanation says that to lie by its very nature implies a bad intention, because a lie is intended to deceive, and although some acts which do not include a bad intention could be good by reason of some good circumstance, nevertheless an act that includes a bad intention could never be good, because it formally includes bad will; and so it is in the present case.

This can be explained as follows. Although the positive act and its malice do not represent anything that is one *per se*, a name can still be imposed which signifies not just the act or its deformity, but the whole combination at once. The name "adultery" is imposed to signify not just the natural act of copulation, but also the impropriety that it is not done with one's own spouse. The name "theft" has been imposed to signify not just the taking of this thing, but also the illegal appropriation of what belongs to another against his will or that of any higher owner. It does not seem that the sort of combinations signified by such names could possibly be good, though it is possible for the underlying act to exist without the deformity, for instance, the act of intercourse or that of appropriating such a thing. Such is the case here. Although the utterance of such and such words with or without such signification could be sinless, nevertheless, to utter them knowing the opposite to be the case, and hence with the intention of deceiving, could not occur without sin, because it implies that in addition to the underlying act there are such circumstances as necessarily deform it. The assumption is evident, because Christ uttered the words "I know him not" without asserting them when he said: "If I were to say: 'I know him not,' I would be like you a liar" [John 8:55]. Also a Greek could utter any Latin words, no matter how false, without committing a sin.

[Article 2: What Sort of Sin Is Lying?]

Secondly, we must see what kind of sin a lie is, and though lies can be distinguished in many ways, for our purpose the distinction of the pernicious, the officious, and the jocose lie suffices.

1. The *pernicious* lie is one which harms the one lied to or lied about, and if it harms such so far as the Christian religion is concerned, for instance, in faith or morals, etc., then it is a mortal sin. However, if it injures one bodily or keeps one from observing conjugal fidelity or separates one from a child or person in any way connected

with one, or harms one to a greater or lesser degree regarding any other temporal good, the gravity of the lie is weighed according to the good lost, so that it is more or less grave on this score, and generally every such lie that deliberately asserts what is not known to be such or the opposite of what is known to be true is a mortal sin. It is simply forbidden by the precept: "Do not bear false witness against your neighbor." This refers not just to testimony in court, but to any deliberate assertion of something that is not known or is the opposite of what is known. Hence, whoever says the opposite of what he or she knows to be true with the intention of deceiving the person spoken to or of giving misinformation about the person spoken of, and by so speaking injures the one addressed or spoken about, is bearing false witness against a neighbor. Whether lack of deliberation excuses one from guilt will be treated in the following question.

2. An *officious* or polite lie is one that is useful for someone and hurts no one.

3. A *jocose* lie is a story which all hearers know is not true; neither is it told as something true, nor are those who hear it deceived; neither does the speaker intend to deceive, nor are the words he uses of themselves deceptive, because it is not the sort of tale that is apt to be believed by those who hear it, but rather it is recognized as something told without the purpose of convincing one of its verity. Similarly a lie is jocose when someone jokingly intends to deceive in such a way that the victim is truly deceived but not as regards something that would inflict any great harm and where those who play the joke know him to be deceived. And one can be formally joking, as Augustine says was the case with the lie of Joseph, who truly wished to deceive his brothers in saying: "You are spies," etc., though he himself, because he knew the truth, could have been joking about the deception and fear which they suffered; and others also, if they had known the truth and finally recognized that this was not said seriously, they too could have joked about this.

As for these two lies, namely, the polite and jocose, it is commonly conceded that neither sort is a mortal sin in imperfect men, because neither of itself violates charity, nor do they militate against anything necessary to the status of the persons who tell such lies.

[Re states of perfection] But some claim both of these lies are mortal sins in the perfect [i.e., those who are in an exalted position or state of perfection], because they destroy the authority such are entitled to, and they demean their status itself as well as scandalizing those who hear them tell such lies.

But against this, others argue that no circumstance makes something that is venial for one a mortal sin in another unless the one is necessarily obliged to something the other is not. But persons in such an exalted state, by vow or oath, have no more bound themselves than other Christians to tell the truth; therefore, the circumstance of being that specific sort of person—though not specially obligated—does not turn a venial matter into a mortal sin.

[Scotus' opinion] One can admit this provided one distinguishes what is meant by a person in such a perfect state. One sense refers to a person exercising some exalted office, like a prelate; another refers to one striving for perfection, such as a religious.

[Re 1] As for the first, one can concede that in the act of exercising some function that pertains to such a state of perfection, such as teaching, judging, or preaching, either sort of lie would be a mortal sin, because it destroys the authority and utility of the message being preached, according to the principle Augustine laid down in his third letter to Jerome: "If lies, no matter how jocose, are to be admitted in the Holy Scriptures, they will retain nothing of their authority." If, in preaching, for example, a prelate were to mix in the jocose lie, his message would lack any solid authority, because one could doubt the truth of what he says just as one could question the word of anyone else. The same reason for not assenting to his jocose lie would apply equally to whatever else he says, and so the authority of a Doctor of the Church in teaching would perish and any utility for the listening audience would likewise be lost.

The same would be true of a solemn judgment or solemn teaching. (I am thinking of the case, of course, where the lie in question is not recognized as distinct from the act of judging or teaching. For one sitting in judgment may introduce something in a lighter vein which is recognized from the manner of speaking as not pertaining to the judicial decision as such.)

[But there is a problem here.] For it seems that while one jocose or polite lie would not destroy the authority of a judge or teacher, it would, however, where this sort of lie is frequent or customary, but then, since two judicial acts according to law establish a custom, it follows that the second such act would be a sin, though the first would not, even though the second seems to be entirely similar in circumstances to the first. Whatever is to be said of one or more such lies in teaching or judging, at least where other acts are concerned such a lie would not seem to constitute a mortal sin, where scandal is excluded.

[Re 2] But if one speaks of a person in a state where perfection is to be acquired, not exercised, it seems one must judge otherwise. Such an individual does not seem to be more obligated than others are, except to those things of perfection he has vowed. For as a religious, one does not assume the pastoral office of care of souls, and hence, is not charged with acts pertaining to such. If such persons, then, are not exercising some exalted function, such as teaching, preaching, or the like, it does not seem they, any more than other Christians, sin mortally by a polite or jocose lie, except perhaps where scandal would arise. For those who have not entered such a state of perfection could be scandalized by the lie of such persons more than they would by that of an ordinary individual. Still, deeds cannot be evaluated simply on the basis of such scandal as may or may not accompany them. For generally speaking according to the Gospel law, the scandal of the little ones should be avoided, according to that text of Matthew [18:7]: "Woe to that man through whom scandal comes!" But this does not apply to the case of pharisaical scandal, according to what the Savior said in Matthew [15:12–14]. When the disciples asked him: "Do you realize the Pharisees were scandalized when they heard your pronouncement?" Christ replied: "Let them go their way; they are blind leaders of the blind." Therefore, whether it is actions that are indifferent in themselves (such as eating meat, which the Apostle speaks of in his first letter to the Corinthians [ch. 8]: "Therefore, if food causes my brother to sin I will never eat meat again") or deeds that are venially sinful, but are apt by their nature to occasionally scandalize little ones who happen or chance to be present, such should be avoided because of scandal. Still, the scandal they may give is not the basis for judging what sort of sin a lie would be by reason of its nature.

As for the nature of a jocose or polite lie in the case of those in a state for acquiring perfection, it does not seem they are obligated by their profession to avoid such lies by some special reason or restriction that other Christians do not have. Nevertheless, if right reason dictates that a single act or frequent acts of lying give scandal to those who hear it, where they would not do so where another person telling such was concerned, then such persons are bound by charity or the welfare of their neighbor to avoid scandal. In accord with that precept regarding flight in the face of persecution, the shepherd is bound at times not to flee, according to what is said in John [10:12]: "The hired hand—who is no shepherd—sees the wolf coming and runs away," etc. Augustine has a good treatment of this text in one of his letters. Look up Henry [of Ghent]'s reference to it in his *Quodlibet* XV, q. 10 or 16. Others, however, who have not entered a state for acquiring perfection and are not pastors, while they are not bound of necessity not to flee if they can act otherwise, are still bound not to scandalize their neighbor by fleeing, for at times their flight would give scandal when the flight of those weak in faith would not give scandal. For their neighbors might judge from the flight of those who have chosen such a strict form of life that they would not risk their life to defend their faith, because they do not think life worth jeopardizing for such a reason, or that faith should be taken so seriously.

[Reply to the Initial Arguments]

To the arguments at the beginning of this question:

[To 1] To the first I say that Abraham did not say something that he did not believe in his own mind. For Josephus in his book of *Antiquities* [I, ch. 22] gives this account. When he went apart with his son, leaving his servants, he informed his son of how he had been miraculously conceived and how, if he were sacrificed, God would miraculously restore him to life. Abraham firmly believed this would happen, because he did not doubt the promise of God [in Genesis 21:12]: "It is through Isaac that descendants shall bear your name." Hence, even though he intended to sacrifice Isaac, nevertheless he also had in mind that God would miraculously restore him to life and he would return with him. Hence, when he said to his servants: "We will come back to you," he said what he believed in his heart. Neither would Abraham, whose life was so exemplary, be easily accused of telling a lie.

[To 2] As for Jacob's lie, although some have tried hard to excuse him and other patriarchs of the Old Testament from the charge of lying, since in other matters it is conceded that they had a law that was imperfect and a modicum of grace, whereas we by contrast have a perfect law and an abundance of grace, and still there is no denying our people at times lie and have been deceitful, it does not seem very reasonable to deny that at times the patriarchs lied or could have lied. And if this be so, even though they are praised for their good deeds, and we take them as examples in this but not in what they did badly, we do not obstinately defend them or excuse them. Nevertheless, such tales as are told of them could be understood figuratively, or given another meaning than what the words seem at first reading to express. But there is no need to dwell further on such interpretations.

[To 3] In the case of Joseph, however, because he was a perfect observer of the divine law, one could say his lie to his brothers was only jocose, which is clear from what happened afterwards. For in the end he revealed the truth to them, and if he instilled fear into them for a time, he only punished them according to their deserts. For their treachery in selling their brother into Egyptian slavery, they not only deserved to be frightened, but merited a much greater punishment.

[To 4] As for the other arguments, about Rahab, the midwives, and Rachael, there is no need to excuse them; neither does Scripture commend their deeds insofar as their lies went. It rather praises the prudence of Rahab, whereby she saved herself and her family.

As for the statement about God building up the families of the midwives there are various opinions, as the Master of History [Peter
Comester] indicates in his exposition on this passage; and perhaps the
more probable view is that which states that they had a good motive of
charity, and it was for this that God gave them a temporal reward,
since they did not deserve an eternal one, because of the sin connected with their action. Or even more probably, one could say that
theirs was a polite or white lie, because it was useful in saving the Jewish children and harmed no one. Therefore God would have rewarded
their motives and good will and would still not have denied them eternal life, since their sin was only venial.

But then this question arises. Should one, because of a powerful
motive of charity, choose to tell such a lie and commit a venial sin, or
should one refrain from both the lie and the act of charity it represents? That one should never choose to sin venially seems to prove the
case of the second alternative, whereas in favor of the first is the fact
that this state of venial sin will not remain forever and will be expiated
either in this life or the next, whereas the magnanimous act of charity
on the other hand will merit a reward great, because eternal, or at
least the degree to which it will be rewarded will be eternal. Since
such an evil is of itself not eternal but temporal, it does not seem one
ought to omit something which of itself is the cause in some way of an
eternal good. Though I will put off discussing this question here, this
much can be said in reply to the present objection that the midwives
only sinned venially, because their lie was an officious or polite one.
And their charitable motive—were anything else required for it to be
meritorious—was of such great value that it would have merited eternal life as well as a reward in this life, because in that age God did
bestow some temporal goods on his worshipers.

To the argument from Judith it is said that she did not sin, because
the additional words said in the presence of Holofernes, she did not
mean to direct to him but to God. Now, it is necessary that words said
aloud be intended to convey not what the hearer has in mind, but
what was intended by the speaker. But in speaking to a ruler, to whom
one is bound to reply in good faith, some declare one is obliged to
answer according to the mind of the inquirer, so that here—by using
words that would be false if they were directed to the authority, but
true if addressed to God—she does not speak truthfully, because in
such a case one is not allowed to be addressing God. For if this were
permitted, nothing would seem to be certain where human speech is
concerned, nor would anyone seem to have any certainty about words
one's neighbor spoke. At least no one would appear to lie no matter

what he might say to a second person, provided it would be true if addressed to God.—But if you are bound to answer truthfully only your ruler, though not someone else, and by not telling him the truth, you could be disobedient or lying, whereas you would not be disobedient or lying in not speaking the truth to someone else, it is still not clear how you are lying more by not speaking the truth to the one than to the other.—If therefore those words, which were said there and which seem excessive, cannot be excused in some way, it does not seem to be a great inconvenience to admit that she was speaking a white or polite lie to her own people but perniciously to him, whose death she intended. Nevertheless, her lie in the first case is preferable to her perniciousness, because the good of the state, especially one worshiping God, is preferable to the temporal good of a private person, especially an infidel.

Some may object to this that even in warfare it is necessary to keep faith, so that the lack of faith or the lie of any Christian in war, even against the infidel, is condemned. If some subterfuge or deception not repugnant to truth is permitted in war, it would not include lying.

Also if she adorned herself with the intention of seducing Holofernes by her looks, and in this sinned mortally by wanting him to will to sin mortally with her, then it does not seem entirely certain that she avoided all mortal sin, and thus her exploit is narrated in Scripture and recited in the Church as something laudable only insofar as it manifested religious devotion, though some of the other circumstances connected with this deed are neither praiseworthy nor licit.

[To 5] To the last, about dissimulation, I say that one could do so in several ways: [1] a person could pretend some good was in him by using some probable signs or arguments. For example, through genuflections and adorations one could pretend devotion was present where there was none, and such simulation is hypocrisy and a mortal sin. [2] In another way, a person could pretend evil is not in him by showing signs to the opposite effect, or [3] he could simply conceal it by not manifesting signs that commonly reveal it. And the first of these would seem to pertain to hypocrisy, for instance, if some lustful man, hearing talk about women, were to spit and swear as a sign of chasteness, though he had opposite sentiments in his heart. The second is not an evil for someone who perceives such simulation. Indeed simulation of this sort can be something praiseworthy in an evil person, because it is shameful to parade one's sin, according to that dictum [of Isaiah 3:9]: "They declare their sin and hide it not." For though evil be in the heart, to add an external sign of it is to add evil to evil. But in indifferent matters [4] someone can perform some actions which of their nature are signs of something amiss; [5] someone else can do some things which are not signs of their nature, but know also that they can be perceived by those present as signs of something wrong. For example, to perspire is a natural sign of fatigue or of some bodily weakness; but to spit so that saliva runs down the beard is not of its nature a sign of mental illness, although from the circumstances one could judge this to be a sign of madness or insanity—if, for instance, in that locality, it was customary to regard it as such.

Generally speaking, then, I say the first and second types of simulation are sins and frequently mortal sins, because this is hypocrisy. The third type, provided no other evil accompany it, is laudable, in that a man does not reveal one evil by means of another. In indifferent matters the first kind of simulation, in regard to certain things, would perhaps be evil, but not a grave matter; for instance, if someone could make himself perspire, but had not labored, as certain pranksters move their bodies in such a way as to signify certain dispositions not in them or certain actions they had never performed. But the other simulation, which is the second in indifferent matters, is no sin and it is the sort that David performed. But Jehu's simulation must not be excused. For besides the simulation that perhaps could be excused he added a lie: "I have a great sacrifice to offer Baal." This lie—though from his intention it was a kind of officious lie, because it was destructive of the worship of Baal—was of itself pernicious, not just because it procured the death of others, but also insofar as it was of itself provocative of [i.e., it tended to provoke] the worship of Baal. Although he was commended because of his detestation of the cult of Baal, and his prosecution of such, nevertheless he was blamed because he did not withdraw from the golden calves of Ieroboam, nor was he a true worshiper of God.

32. PERJURY
(*Ordinatio* III, suppl., dist. 39)

Regarding this thirty-ninth distinction [of Bk. III] I ask: Is every perjury a mortal sin?

[Arguments Pro and Con]
For the negative view:
[Arg. 1] Sometimes an oath is taken which it is not licit to fulfill; but what is illicit *per se* does not become licit just because one swears under oath to do it; therefore, it still remains illicit after the oath is taken, and hence one sins mortally in fulfilling what is sworn to. But according to Christian law, one is never faced with the quandary of

sinning mortally whether one does something or omits doing it—
which seems to apply here. Nevertheless one would commit perjury by
not fulfilling what one swore to do; hence to commit perjury is not a
mortal sin.

[Arg. 2] Also, it is more serious to swear by God than by the Gospel
according to [canon law; see *Decretum Gratiani*, ibid., c. 6] ("Si aliqua
causa fuerit"), just as it is more serious to swear by the author than to
swear by a work of his, or by the temple than by the gold of the
temple, because it is the temple that makes the gold sacred; and the
same evaluation applies to reverence [due to God]; therefore, if it is a
mortal sin to perjure oneself, the most serious perjury is one based on
swearing by God; consequently, ordinary persons would be sinning
mortally all through the day, because they consider it as nothing to
swear "By God," even when asserting something false, or promising
something difficult, which they are not sure of doing—which seems to
be too harsh an interpretation.

[Arg. 3] Also, every promissory oath necessarily obliges according
to [canon law; see *Decretum Gratiani*, ibid.], causa 22, q. 4: "It is
better not to fulfill a foolish promise than to commit a crime." Proof of
the antecedent is found in the canon about a forced oath (look for it in
the [*Decretales Gregorii IX* II, tit. 24, c. 15, Verum]); and also in the
case of the deceitful oath, it is clear that the one swearing does not
intend to oblige himself; for no one is obligated unless he intends to
obligate himself (see the [*Decretales*, ibid.] in the *Glosses* on "De
iureiurando," where it says, "If someone swears five times," etc.). The
antecedent is also proved in the case of an incautious or rash oath,
because if a person fulfills it, "he will come to a worse end," according
to the [*Decretum Gratiani* II], causa 22, q. 4, "Si aliquid." Therefore, it
would be a greater evil to fulfill the oath. Proof of this in the case of
these two oaths, namely, the deceitful and the forced oath, is found in
the analogy with marriage, for a forced or deceitful oath, that is, one
that is simulated, does not bind persons to matrimony; see the [*Decretales Gregorii IX*], "Concerning Those Things Which Happen because
of Force or Fear"; and [ibid.] "Concerning Espousals and Marriage" . . .

To the contrary: Exodus 20:7 [and Matthew 5:33]: "Do not take a
false oath; rather make good to the Lord all your pledges"; and in
Psalm [76:12]: "Make vows to the Lord, your God, and fulfill them."

[Body of the Question]

In this question we must first examine the nature of an oath; and,
second, see from this why perjury is a mortal sin; and third, distinguish
special kinds of oaths and see what sort of sin each is.

[Article 1: The Nature of an Oath]

As for the first, I say that an oath is an assertion that some human statement is true, and this in a final or ultimate sense, according to that text from the Epistle to the Hebrews [6:16]: "An oath confirms a statement and ends all argument." And the reason is this. Man knows he cannot trust completely his mendacious and ignorant fellowman, since he can be deceived and can deceive. Therefore, he turns to a witness who is truthful and knows the facts, one who can neither deceive nor be deceived, and he does this by taking an oath; for there he asks God, who knows the truth and cannot lie, to bear witness to what he is saying.

[Article 2: Perjury as a Mortal Sin]

From this our thesis on perjury follows. For it is an act of irreverence to call upon God as witness to the truth of a false statement; or to treat him as if he were ignorant of the truth, and hence not omniscient; or to deal with him as though he would gladly bolster a lie, and thus were not entirely truthful. All of these, however, manifest an irreverence towards God that is immediately opposed to that commandment of the first table: "You shall not take the name of the Lord, your God, in vain" [Exodus 20:7]. Hence, any deliberate instance of this would be a mortal sin.

[Two doubtful points] But here two doubts arise: First, does lack of deliberation excuse one from serious sin? Second, may one sin mortally by calling upon God to bear witness in the aforesaid way to some opinion one believes to be true, although it is not true, or to something which has some plausibility, but one is more inclined to think it false?

[Re 1] As for the first, it is commonly conceded that a single indeliberate instance of perjury in a light matter would not be mortally sinful, but where this becomes customary or habitual the perjury would be a mortal sin, because habits generated by many acts incline one to a more serious act than those which preceded.

But this is not so. If the first act of perjury was not a mortal sin, then neither is any other, even if it results from habit, for the habitual inclination cannot increase the seriousness of the act. If someone through repeated acts has acquired a formidable habit of impurity and shortly after repenting is moved impurely to do something towards which the strong habit inclines him, he does not sin mortally; indeed his sin is not more notably serious than such an act would be in another who had no such habit.

Confirmation of this. If we can speak of the gravity of a habit at all, it cannot be graver than the acts by which it is acquired, since to be exact, it has no culpable gravity apart from those acts. But since the acts whereby it is engendered are themselves only venial, the habit itself will not give acts elicited by force of habit some mortal gravity.

Hence it seems one could maintain that habit or custom is completely irrelevant. Perjury with full consent, however, is against a precept of the first table [of the natural law] and hence turns one immediately from one's ultimate end. Consequently there is nothing to keep it from being a mortal sin. But if the perjury is not deliberate, then no matter how often it occurs one could never say it is mortally sinful. To be meritorious an act must be fully human and thus done with full deliberation. Now, no less is required for demerit, for God is not more inclined to condemn a sinner than to spare such. Consequently one could claim that this indeliberate perjury, no matter how often it is repeated, is never a mortal sin.

What must be kept in mind, however, as was noted earlier in speaking of the virtues, is the fact that the deliberation required for a virtuous act may be so short as to be imperceptible, because one's prudence may be so great that one deliberates almost instantaneously. So too a person habitually imprudent could acquire the facility of deliberating so quickly that it seems but an instant. And this sort of deliberation would suffice for sin just as it does for merit.

That is why, in regard to its seriousness, I distinguish not as to the rarity or frequency of the perjury, but only whether there is deliberation or lack of it. Where deliberation is present, the perjury is mortally sinful, whether it be committed once or many times. Similarly, indeliberation excuses, whether it be a first or repeated offense.

[Re 2] As for the second doubt, I say that according to positive law or custom a person swearing regards the oath in one of two ways. Either [a] it represents an unqualified assertion of the matter sworn to or [b] it does not, but rather expresses something the person swearing regards as a probable assumption one ought to believe.

[Re a] Now, if one swears in the first way to something in any way doubtful, i.e., something that one has not yet determined is certain and true, I say that such a person sins mortally in calling on God to confirm as simply true and certain what is not simply such.

In this way one should understand the oaths of all who testify in court, where it is customary to pass some sort of sentence that would not be passed if the fact sworn to were not simply certain, for example, where the death penalty would not be imposed except for a certain crime. To swear to something criminal a witness is uncertain about, no matter how probable that person might think it to be, and to do so in a forum of justice, where by positive law or custom condemnation to death follows, would be to sin mortally. The same holds true of any forum where someone, through perjured testimony, is condemned as guilty or is declared to be infamous by law. For here there is not only irreverence to God's name, in violation of a commandment of the first table of the law, but a lie that is pernicious because it harms one's neighbor.

And if you object that it is in the interest of the state, because otherwise evil would be multiplied exceedingly, God himself replies: "Justice and justice alone shall be your aim" [Deuteronomy 16:20]. For there are certain evils that should not be punished by man but left to divine justice. Such, for example, are all cases where man as man must lack sufficient knowledge, and concerning those things about which one cannot adequately learn the truth needed to pass a just punitive sentence. Nor is it only the witnesses that are guilty in such judgments, but the judge as well. For if the judge knows from past experience that the witnesses are not testifying under oath to anything more than what they suspect might be true, then he must not pass the sort of sentence he would if guilt were proven to him in an unqualified fashion. For he knows from experience that guilt has not been proven sufficiently to justify such punishment.

[Re b] But if from custom or positive law it is clear that the person is not swearing to his certainty in the matter but only to what he believes to be true, provided he has more probable indications that such is the case rather than anything else, then he does not sin, according to the [Decretales Gregorii IX I, tit. 12], ch. 1, regarding the scrutiny required for those taking Holy Orders: "The Lord Pope replies that so far as human frailty permits one to know, he knows and testifies that the person is qualified for the burden of such an office, and the Pope goes on to say that we do not believe that a person sins in giving such testimony, provided he does not speak against his conscience. For he is asserting not that the candidate is worthy in an unqualified sense, but only that he should be considered as worthy insofar as he is not known to be unworthy."

In promoting candidates to Orders or to certain elected offices of dignity (such as a mastership in certain colleges, e.g., in universities, or in religious orders to the prelacy, or to other functions of this sort), if it be the approved custom that such replies be made under oath, either as to carrying out one's duties faithfully or as to promising obedience, all such oaths should customarily be understood to refer only to what the witness believes, viz., so far as human frailty permits him to know, the respondent believes a candidate to be worthy whom he does not know to be unworthy. All such replies should be understood according to common custom. Neither does the one testifying sin, even though the candidate for promotion is not worthy, although it would be safer for the witness there not to give a simple answer but to add some qualification, like that mentioned in the aforesaid decretal, namely, "so far as human frailty permits one to know." And in such cases the judge promoting such a candidate does not sin, since the custom is such that it suffices that the witness testify as to his belief. Here, then, that legal maxim applies: "The favorable is to be interpreted broadly, whereas the odious is to be interpreted strictly." The reason is that where matters of possible condemnation are concerned a witness under oath must tell the strict truth, and only about what he is sure of, for were it not for his testimony no sentence of condemnation would be passed. Confirmation of this rule: in favorable matters an oath concerning what the witness believes to be true suffices, especially where such is the custom, or where the positive law in a college requires one to state only what he believes, since the president can promote one to such an academic degree on the testimony of what the witness believes to be true.

Generally speaking, however, whether it be in favorable or in odious matters, a person sins mortally who swears to the opposite of what he more strongly believes to be so, or swears to something simply dubious where he has no more reason to believe in his heart that this is true rather than that. For he calls God to witness something he ought to be certain about which is in neither way certain to him.

If you object to what was said about perjury being against a precept of the first table of the law, because it seems that according to the Master [Peter Lombard] perjury is a kind of lie and hence against that commandment of the second table, "You shall not bear false witness against your neighbor" [Exodus 20:16], one could reply that in perjury there is a double sin, namely, [i] a lie (as the material aspect) and [ii] taking God's name in vain, that is to say, not just uselessly, but irreverently, which is a sin against reverence. The first pertains to the second table, but the second pertains formally to the first table, because irreverence is prohibited there. One can also commit perjury without lying—for instance, if someone swears to something he has some doubts about, one might perhaps claim he was not lying, since he did not believe the opposite to be true—or at least in those cases where one taking an oath has to be certain, a person commits perjury if he is not certain, and nevertheless if he were to assert such without an oath, because he believed this rather than its opposite, he would not be lying. Hence it is dangerous to frequently utter oaths in speaking, for many statements where no oath was taken would not be sinful, whereas they would be if an oath were added, and indeed, gravely sinful if the oath were fully deliberate. Hence, our Savior's counsel in Matthew 5:[37] is useful: "Let your speech be, 'Yes, yes'; 'No, no.'"

[Article 3: Concerning Special Kinds of Oaths]

As for the third article [about the kinds of oaths and the sort of sin each is] I say that human statements are either about the present and the past, where the truth is determinate, or about the future, the truth of which is uncertain and indeterminate. In the first case the statements are said to be "assertive," where the term is applied broadly to both affirmations and negations. But those about the future are called "promissory," because they are in the power of the one swearing or making the promise. And according to this, since an oath is an assertion of either of these statements, there are two forms of oaths, the assertive and the promissory, and they both are obligatory. The assertive is such because it obliges the person swearing to tell the truth, thus inducing such a witness to confirm what he says. The promissory is such because it obliges the one swearing to express his true intentions. But since the assertive oath obliges one only at the time of utterance, the promissory oath alone is called an "obligation," namely, in regard to the future. Hence, only the promissory oath is appropriately called "obligatory," because it obliges one to carry out something one swears to do in the future. And these two species of oaths resemble the two species of obligations used in sophistical disputations, namely, position and petition. Position obliges the disputant to uphold a postulate as true, and petition obliges the disputant to follow out the consequences of what is postulated.

But a doubt arises here. In a promissory oath is the swearer's quality [or constancy of purpose] presupposed, and, this having been weighed, a fitting witness [God] is called upon to confirm that the man is speaking his mind? Or is the veracity of the witness presupposed in order to consider secondarily the quality of a promise with God as continual warranty? For if the first were true, it would seem to be enough if the one swearing about the future had the intention at that time to carry out what he promised under oath, although afterwards he may change his mind. The second seems more consonant with the common opinion, because in that oath it is said that one will always remain obligated until one's promise is carried out.

So far as assertive perjury is concerned, there is no need to treat of anything in particular that is not covered by the article on perjury in general.

But where perjury involves a promissory or obligatory oath, I say such can be deceitful, or rash, or forced, or lacking all these unfitting conditions.

[The deceitful oath] A deceitful oath is swearing to carry out some promise with no intention of doing so or of obliging oneself to what one swears to. In the act of swearing such a person sins mortally, because he calls God as a witness that he will do what he says, when he has no mind to do so. Nevertheless, after he has taken the oath he does not remain obligated, because with private obligations one is not bound to anything one has no intention of taking on. Nor does it follow that he profits by his deceit, inasmuch as he would have been obligated had he not sworn deceitfully. For to bear the burden of mortal sin is bad enough for him, and if he had not sworn deceitfully he would not have sinned mortally. Still, one who does not swear deceitfully is bound to his oath, whereas this one is not, and this intention to carry out one's oath is not so hurtful as is the penalty the other merits in swearing deceitfully, because he sins mortally.

[The rash or incautious oath] One can swear rashly in two ways:

[a] Either the matter is something entirely illicit, for instance, if someone swears to violate some commandment, e.g., takes an oath to kill someone or to commit adultery with someone; and such an oath does not obligate the person further so that he would have to carry out what he swore to do. Nevertheless, when he took the oath, if he did not have the intention to do so, he sinned mortally in calling God to testify to a falsehood. But if he did have the intention to do so, he still sinned mortally, because to will to sin mortally is itself a mortal sin. In either way, then, he sinned mortally in taking such an oath. But after the fact he is not obliged to carry out his oath, because he must not add one sin to another. For the fact that he swore to do something illicit does not make what was illicit licit, since it is a mortal sin.

[b] One could also swear rashly when one takes an oath to do something one could not possibly perform, if at the time one thought one could do it. And one must judge or view this in the way set out in the article on oaths in general, because if it could be done in the future, one would be held to it; but if it could not be done, since one believed at the time one swore to do it that one could do it, one is excused because the matter is in one's favor.

[A forced oath] As for an oath one is forced to take by the sort of coercion that can befall a steadfast person, there are various views. Look them up in the fourth book.

[A promissory oath] A promissory oath that is not deceitful, rash, or forced obliges the person taking it never to retract his will in the matter, and one does not sin, even though how one reasonably fulfills it may differ, according to changing circumstances. Such a person first commits perjury, however, at the moment he or she decides not to fulfill the promise taken under oath, for that is when one first calls God to be a witness to a falsehood.

[Reply to the Initial Arguments]

[To 1] The answer to the first argument is clear from [canon law; see *Decretum Gratiani* II, causa 22, q. 4, c. 5]: "In turpi voto mutua decretum." One sins mortally, however, in taking such an oath.

[To 2] To the other argument, I say that, other things being equal, the strongest oath is to swear "By God," because it is not licit to swear by anything else, except God be present there in some special way, for instance, "By the Gospel" [or Bible], because God is revealed there; or "By heaven," because God dwells there in a special way; or "By the Church," because God is worshiped there in a special manner. Nevertheless, reasonable custom has it that certain oaths are taken with greater solemnity than others, and when such a solemn occasion occurs the presumption is that the oath must never be taken except with deliberation. Other oaths could be taken without deliberation, however. Therefore, God has established it that an oath taken "By the Church" has a certain sense of awe or dread about it, so that it is never taken without deliberation, and where one must assert the truth without qualification or reservation. But the oath "By God" is generally and frequently taken lightly and without deliberation. Nevertheless, I say that, other things being equal, it is always more serious to swear by God. But assuming there is a lack of deliberation when using "By God," and full deliberation in another case, such as when one swears by the Church, one assumes there is a mortal sin here, not just because of the irreverence on the part of the one taking the oath, but because of the deliberation present in the one case but not in the other. And if you object: Why, then, is infamy attached to perjury based on an oath taken on the Gospels [or the Bible], whereas an oath "By God" does not make one infamous? I reply: Infamy is not always attached according to the quality of the fault, but is based on whether the offense is a public or state crime. Now, it is established that an oath on the Gospel is taken or should be taken with deliberation and that it is a public matter and event, and therefore a transgressor, where such an oath is concerned, is presumed to be a violator of the faith and hence is reasonably regarded as worthy of infamy; whereas this is not the presumption in the case of one who lightly swears by God.

[To 3] To the last, it is clear to what extent a promissory oath binds or does not bind one to fulfill what was promised.

33. THE OBLIGATION TO KEEP SECRETS
(*Ordinatio* IV, dist. 21, q. 2)

Regarding the seal of confession I ask: Is a confessor bound not to reveal a sin discovered in confession from the law of nature? . . .

In this question our first conclusion is this: The priest is bound not to reveal a sin discovered in confession from the law of nature. [Secondly, these principles] apply to other secrets about others confided to us under the seal of secrecy . . .

I hold this first conclusion, but present four reasons other than [those commonly given]. The first is derived from the nature of charity, the second from that of fidelity, the third from that of veracity, and the fourth from the grounds for unity or mutual utility.

The first is this. The law of fraternal charity is expressed in Matthew 7:12: "Treat others the way you would have them treat you; this sums up the law and the prophets"; and Luke 6:31: "Do to others what you would have them do to you." But this proposition of the law of nature regarding fraternal charity must be understood in this way. "What you would have them do" means what you would have them do according to right reason. This also applies to that command in Matthew 22:[39]: "Love your neighbor as yourself." Now, everyone according to right reason ought to love his good name or reputation; therefore, he must also want the sins he confesses to remain hidden, and hence his confessor must want the same as his penitent does. The revelation of sins would take away the good name of the one confessing them; therefore, [the sins he reveals must be kept hidden].—The minor of this argument is proved from reason. Everyone according to right reason ought to wish to live the life of a respectable citizen. Loss of reputation would rob him of this, however, for a person is fit to live as a respectable citizen only insofar as he is fit for such legitimate activities as pertain to citizenship; and a loss of reputation would make him unfit for such, because it would cost him his worthiness to perform such functions as he would otherwise be worthy to accomplish. The second part of the minor, namely, that the revelation of the sins he confesses would deprive the penitent of this reputation to which he has a right, is proved in this way. The same reason that would justify revealing his faults to one would permit one to reveal them to others and thus to all. But it is clear that by such a revelation his status of unblemished worthiness, consisting of his good name among his fellow citizens, would be taken from him.

The second reason: Everyone is bound by the law of nature to keep such faith as his neighbor wants him to keep and as he should want his neighbor to keep with himself. But anyone who commits a great secret to another wants it, and should want it, to be kept secret; therefore, the other, to whom he confides such, is obliged to do so . . .

The third reason: Everyone is bound by the law of nature to keep a licit promise he has made; but the recipient of a secret, above all one learned in confession, promises, if not explicitly, at least implicitly, that he will keep such secret, because without such a promise, at least implicitly understood, the penitent would not reveal such a secret to his confessor; therefore, etc. This reason could be gleaned from those words [of Zachary 8:16]: "Speak ye the truth every one to his neighbor."

The fourth reason: A community has a holistic character analogous to the unity of the mystical body of Christ, namely, that here there is an ordered relationship of superior and subject; and the superior is bound to help the subject and the subject is bound to carry out his ministry under the direction of the superior, according to that simile Paul uses of the mystical body of Christ, which he describes in so many places. But in civil life it is the subjects that are less knowledgeable, whereas in the Church it is the sinner that is the inferior and the priest is the superior, who both counsels and reconciles the penitent. Hence it is in the nature of this relationship that nothing should prevent the inferior from having recourse to the superior in his need, or the superior from exercising his beneficent influence on the inferior, for this is the way in which the members are useful to each other. But the revelation of secrets prevents the inferior from taking such recourse to the superior when his soul is in need of counsel, and hence prevents the superior from helping the inferior, because no one would have recourse to someone for counsel or help, if such a one were not bound by rule to keep hidden his secrets. Therefore, the same law of nature whereby one is bound to preserve the unity of the mystical body of Christ, to work for the common welfare of each other as members of a body, also binds one to keep the secrets of confession.

As for the other point, it is admitted that everyone is bound by the law of nature to preserve all secrets, for the same reasons given for the above conclusion. Nor does this law bind only when the one confiding such expressly says he wishes to convey this as a secret, but whenever from the manner in which the secret is conveyed it is clear it was meant to be kept as a secret.

34. THE SIN OF ENSLAVEMENT
(*Ordinatio* IV, dist. 36, q. 1)

Regarding this thirty-sixth distinction [of Bk. IV] I ask: Does slavery impede matrimony?

[Arguments Pro and Con]
That it can:

No one can give what belongs to another; but the body of the slave belongs to the master, according to the Philosopher in III *Ethics*, chs. 3–6 [passim].

Furthermore, religious profession is more pleasing than carnal marriage; but a slave cannot make religious profession against the will of his master; neither, then, can he contract marriage.

To the contrary:

The canon "Dignum est" entitled "The Marriage of Slaves," [*Decretales Gregorii IX* IV, tit. 9, c. 1, states that "marriage among slaves shall in no way be prohibited. And if they shall have contracted marriage against the will and objections of their masters, on no grounds is this to be dissolved by an ecclesiastical court, but they are no less bound to render their own masters their due and customary service"].

[Body of the Question]
Here there are two points to be investigated: [1] How did slavery originate and was it introduced justly? [2] Does it impede marriage?

[Article 1: The Origins of Slavery]
As for the first, it is said that by the law of nature all are born free. However, servitude or, more properly, filial subjection to the father pertains to the law of nature, for instance, filial obedience pertaining to education. For according to the Philosopher in Bk. VIII of the *Ethics*: "The son has existence and education from the father."

But the slavery about which we are talking is that described by the Philosopher in Bk. I of the *Politics*, according to which the master can sell the slave like an animal, for he cannot exercise acts of manly excellence, since he has to perform servile actions at the command of his master. {Addition: And this servitude or enslavement is such that an individual loses all his legal rights to another person, which is something not to the good of the slave, but to his detriment, and this slavery is what Aristotle talks about when he says a slave is like an inanimate instrument, neither can he be good or virtuous. This kind of slavery, as we said, is not good but bad for the slave, and therefore the Apostle says: "Know that you are free and do not make yourself subject to any man."} This sort of slavery is introduced only by positive law.

But how can it be just? I reply: In dist. 15, it was explained how dominion of possessions came to be just [by positive law], and so I say that this vile form of servitude can be just only in two cases: the first is when a person voluntarily subjects himself to such [to pay a debt, for instance]; but such subjection is foolish. Indeed, it may even be against the law of nature that a man abdicate his freedom in this fashion. Nevertheless, once he has done so, he must carry out his part of the bargain, because this is only just. The other way servitude can originate is if one who is justly charged with the government of the community, seeing that some criminals are so vicious that their liberty would harm both themselves and the public, can justly punish them with slavery, just as he could execute them in certain cases for the welfare of the state.

And if you insist that there is also a third legitimate reason for servitude, for instance, that if one captured in war is preserved unharmed, and thus spared from death, he may become a slave destined to serve, I doubt this—unless [playing on words] you mean by "servus" here one who is "pre*served*." Neither is such enslavement a clear case of justice, even if the captor, perhaps, might have otherwise killed his captive (assuming the war was a just one of self-defense and not one of invasion, and that the captive persisted in his obstinacy against the person fighting defensively). Nevertheless, given that the captive could cease to be obstinate, since he has it in his power to change his mind, it seems inhuman to inflict on him a punishment that is against the law of nature. Neither does the second justifying reason for enslavement apply here, since he might very well not remain rebellious or abuse his liberty, but become docile, perhaps, and use the liberty granted to him in a proper way.

[Two objections and their solution] To the first point [that all are born free] you may object that servitude is not against the law of nature, because according to the Philosopher in I *Politics:* "Those strong in mind should rule; those strong in body should serve." Some are naturally strong in mental ability and hence naturally disposed to rule; others are less prudent in mind but more robust in body; therefore some are naturally suited to be masters, whereas others are naturally suited to be servants. In support of this one can cite the example of the members of the human body, where certain parts naturally serve the main part [or head]. To this I reply: What he says there applies not to that extreme form of servitude [i.e., the slavery] we are speaking of now, but only to political service, where superiors appoint inferiors, not as distributing or arranging inanimate things, but rather in the way the less gifted are assigned appropriate tasks by the more gifted.

If you argue against the second point [that positive law can justify servitude] on the ground that, if something is against the law of nature, it can never become just (because crimes are not ratified by their longevity, but are rather more to be condemned; now, all forms of servitude other than these two cases [of voluntary indenture and as punishment for criminal activity] are against the law of nature; therefore, no matter how long such a contrary custom has existed, it would not seem just that a master exercise such dominion over such servants), I reply: In dist. 15 I explained how a right could be acquired by prescription, namely, if certain conditions, determined by law, prevail (namely, that it is acquired by a just title and that the possessor is in good faith, and that he has possessed such without interruption for a period of time determined by law). Now, while this refers to possessions, it does not apply to slavery, for, according to the law of nature, the reasons for possessing gold and persons who serve you are not the same, and it would be difficult to establish the justice, by prescription, of retaining slaves of this sort, unless one assumed they became such from the outset by one or the other legitimate ways in which servitude is introduced. And if you object, Why, then, did the Apostle [Eph. 6:5; Col. 3:22] command such slaves to obey their masters? I reply that many obligations were unjustly introduced, but nevertheless, once they have been established, they have to be observed. Hence, the Apostle, after showing that slavery is not something commendable in itself, and even more, no one should keep one enslaved, says [1 Cor. 7:21]: "Were you a slave when your call came? Give it no thought. Even supposing you could go free, you would be better off making the most of your slavery."

[Article 2. Is Slavery an Impediment to Marriage?]

[The opinion of others] Regarding the second, on the basis of the preceding article, some say that the slave could contract marriage though his master is unwilling, because matrimony is from the law of nature, whereas servitude is not, but rather is against it. But what is of the law of nature is not annulled by what is only positive law. Another reason given is that the slave does not belong to his master to such an extent that he has no right to such natural acts as pertain to the conservation of the individual. For it is obvious that he can use what is necessary for life; therefore, by the same token he has a right to what pertains to the conservation of the species. That the implication holds is proved from the fact that the conservation of the species, since it is a greater natural good, pertains even more to the natural law. Or it is argued in this way. The slave cannot be just a brute animal, and hence all men have a right to some acts on their own; neither can one be just a slave where such acts are concerned. On the contrary, nature makes man so free that he cannot even make himself a slave in these matters. This is so as regards natural acts that pertain to the preservation of the individual and also of the species, and a person cannot obligate himself to any master in what is in violation of such; but a person can so obligate himself that he is bound to his master where other subsequent acts are concerned.

These arguments could be refuted: The first, because an obligation not of the law of nature could impede some liberty that one has in virtue of natural law, and that is the case here. Take this example: by the law of nature I owe you nothing; nevertheless I can vow obedience to you, and then I am bound to obey you. Matrimony, however, pertains to the law of nature only in the secondary sense, as was explained earlier [in selection 18], whereas the obligation to "render to each his due" seems to be equally a matter of natural law; indeed, it is primarily such. Therefore, by reason of the obligation to the master that a slave has imposed upon himself, he is bound to render to his master whatever is his due and to abstain from anything that would prevent him giving such service, even though this other impediment [to marrying] might not oblige him by reason of some secondary law of nature.

The second reason is not conclusive, because it is certain that not everyone bound to conserve himself as an individual is also called upon to multiply the species. If you say that at least it is licit for him to do so and man cannot take this from him, I admit this is true where there is a case of necessity in which the conservation of the species depends upon an act of his. But because many who are not slaves and have embraced the Christian law have chosen to beget, the conservation of the species does not require his particular contribution to this goal, and therefore he can be prevented from making such by some other obligation he has. Consequently, if a prior commitment to perform acts of lesser importance prevents him from performing acts of greater importance, where these are not absolutely necessary for the procreation of offspring, then it does not seem he should put off doing these less important things he owes in order to perform unnecessary, though more important, acts. For it does not seem that the procreation of children through him is necessary in any unqualified sense of that term, for the human species can be multiplied and children begotten by others.

This argument is confirmed, because before he marries, let us say he is bound to perform certain acts, call them A, B, and C. If he marries, however, he may be obliged to something that is incompatible with B and C. In such a case, he cannot justly take on this marital obligation, since in so doing he would violate the prior commitment he has made to another.

[Scotus' solution] I say, then, to this article that the slave can marry if his master is willing, and if the burden of married life causes his customary service to suffer somewhat, the master, by permitting him to marry, has implicitly relaxed to some extent what is required of him. And if the master later takes back his concession to such an extent that he prevents his servant from having any carnal intercourse whatsoever, or sends him to distant parts or imposes such labor upon him that he cannot occasionally visit his wife, then that master sins mortally and clearly needs to be corrected by the Church as well.

Also he can marry, even if his master is not willing, insofar as he has some rights over his own body, for he has not deprived himself of all freedom to perform such marital acts, and so far as his body still belongs to him, he can share it with another. And if this other person, whether free or not, will be content with this modicum of freedom or this limited use of what she knows he can give, then she can give herself to him in marriage without being at a disadvantage, and the exchange of vows is valid. Now, the slave has such dominion over his body when he is not engaged in serving his master; and if he marries despite his master's opposition, then the married partners have no obligation to each other as regards intercourse save what they can fulfill without doing injustice to the master. Hence that chapter [in canon law] entitled "The Marriage of Slaves" says that the slave who marries when his master is unwilling gives what he has, and is still bound to fulfill his service obligations to his master, because he could not give another what he did not have in his possession. But he did not have an unqualified dominion over his own body; therefore, etc.

And from this it follows that a slave could marry a free woman provided she is aware of his servile condition and consents to marry him with this in mind, because then she gives him dominion over her body insofar as she receives from him that measure of dominion he has over his own body, and he can marry the girl. And then it would seem that both give what they can to each other and in marrying in this way they are bound in justice to fulfill their marriage obligations as far as those acts of customary service to the master do not impede them.

But what happens when two slaves marry without their masters' consent, and one master sends his servant to Africa and the other his maid to France? Is it lawful for them to do this? I say that because legally marriage is favored, the masters should be induced not to do this. But if they should insist on doing so, it is not clear how they would be acting unjustly towards their servants, granting their servile condition. For prior to the marriage, his master had the right to send him there, and what is more, to sell him; and similarly she too owed it to her master to be in the place he chose; and by their own actions in marrying without the permission of their masters, they could not liberate themselves in any greater measure, nor justly free themselves from their masters. Therefore, it would still be licit.

But if a girl intended to contract marriage with one she believed was free, but actually was a slave, is their marriage valid? One could say an error in regard to a worse condition invalidates the contract, because it prevents the one making the exchange from receiving what he or she intended to exchange, whereas for the opposite reason, ignorance of a better condition or one that was equal does not invalidate a contract.

[Reply to the Initial Arguments]

To the first, according to this last argument it is clear that a slave does not belong to his master in every respect, because he has the legal right to eat, drink, and sleep, and in short, to engage in all such activities as do not detract from the service he owes his master. Therefore, since under such a stipulation he could engage in carnal intercourse, he could obligate himself to such insofar as this is within his legal rights. And what the Philosopher says of that damnable form of servitude, where the slave is like an animal, can be interpreted to mean he belongs to his master like a possession or like money. But this does not mean that in his actions he is only led and does not lead on his own, because no matter how much of a slave he might be, he is still a man and so has free will. And on this score, it is clear what great cruelty is involved in first imposing such servitude, for it reduces a man who is his own master and free to act in a manly and virtuous fashion, to the status of a brute animal, as it were, unable to choose freely or to act virtuously.

To the second, there is no likeness in the two situations, for in taking religious vows the one making profession submits himself in complete obedience to his religious superior, and in this he withdraws himself entirely from the service he is accustomed to give his master. But this is not the case with one who enters marriage, for what he does for his mate is compatible with the service he owes and is accustomed to render his lord. But the Church wants neither to prejudice the rights of another nor to destroy anyone's privileges in favor of another.

Bibliography

Adams, Marilyn McCord. "The Structure of Ockham's Moral Theory," *Franciscan Studies* 46 (1986), pp.1–35.

———."Duns Scotus on the Goodness of God," *Faith and Philosophy* 4 (1987), pp. 486–505.

———. *William Ockham*. 2 vols. (Notre Dame, IN: University of Notre Dame Press, 1987a).

———. "Duns Scotus on the Will as Rational Power," *Via Scoti: Methodologica ad Mentem Joannis Duns Scoti*, ed. Leonard Sileo (Rome, Antonianum, 1995), pp. 839–54.

Alluntis, F., and Wolter, A. B. *John Duns Scotus: God and Creatures, The Quodlibetal Questions* (Princeton/London: Princeton University Press, 1975; reprint Washington, D.C.: The Catholic University of America Press, 1981).

Anselm. *S. Anselmi Cantuariensis Archiepiscopi opera omnia*, ed. F. S. Schmitt (Stuttgart: Friedrich Frommann Verlag, 1968).

Auer, J. *Die menschliche Willensfreiheit im Lehre des Thomas von Aquin und Johannes Duns Scotus* (München: Max Hüber, 1938).

Bąk, F. "Scoti schola numerosior est omnibus aliis simul sumptis," *Franciscan Studies* 16 (1956), pp. 144–65.

Balić, C. *Les Commentaires de Jean Duns Scot sur les quatre livres des Sentences* (Louvain: Bureau de la Revue d'Histoire Ecclésiastique, 1927), Appendix II, pp. 264–301.

———. "Une question inédite de J. Duns Scot sur la volonté," *Recherches de théologie ancienne et médiévale* 3 (1931), pp. 191–208.

———. "De Ordinatio I. Duns Scoti disquisitio historica-critica," in *Opera omnia I. Duns Scoti* (Vatican edition), tom. I (1950), pp. 1*–329*.

———. "Johannes Duns Scotus und die Lehrentscheidung von 1277," *Wissenschaft und Weisheit* 21 (1966), pp. 188ff.

Binkowski, J. *Die Wertlehre des Duns Skotus* (Berlin/Bonn: E. Dümmler, 1936).

Boler, John. "The Moral Psychology of Duns Scotus: Some Preliminary Questions," *Franciscan Studies* 50 (1990), pp. 31–56.

———. "Transcending the Natural: Duns Scotus on the Two Affections of Will," *American Catholic Philosophical Quarterly* 67 (1993), pp. 109–26.

———. "An Image for the Unity of Will in Duns Scotus," *Journal of the History of Philosophy* 32 (1994), pp. 23–44.

Bonansea, Bernardine M. "Duns Scotus' Voluntarism," *John Duns Scotus, 1265–1965*, ed John K. Ryan and Bernardine M. Bonansea (Washington, D.C.: The Catholic University of America Press, 1965), pp. 83–121.

———. *Man and His Approach to God in John Duns Scotus* (Lanham, Md.: University Press of America, 1983).

Borak, A. "Libertà e prudenza nel pensiero di Duns Scoto," *Laurentianum* 10 (1969), pp. 105–41.

Bourke, V. I. *History of Ethics*, vol. I (Garden City, N.Y.: Image Books, 1970).

Burger, Maria. *Personalität im Horizont absoluter Prädestination: Untersuchungen zur Christologie des Johannes Duns Scotus und ihrer Rezeption in modernen theologischen Ansätzen* (Münster: Aschendorff, 1994).

Copleston, F. *A History of Philosophy*, vol. 2 (Westminster, Md.: Newman Press, 1950).

De Blic, J. "Syndérèse?" *Revue d'ascétique et de mystique* 15 (1949), pp. 146–57.

De Wulf, M. *Histoire de la philosophie médiévale*, ed. 6, t. II (Louvain: L'Institut Supérieur de Philosophie/Paris: J. Vrin, 1936).

Dumont, Stephen. "The Necessary Connection of Moral Virtue to Prudence According to John Duns Scotus—Revisited," *Recherches de Théologie ancienne et médiévale* 55 (1988), pp. 184–206.

————. "Theology as a Science and Duns Scotus's Distinction between Intuitive and Abstractive Cognition," *Speculum* 64 (1989), pp. 579–99.

————. "The *Propositio Famosa Scoti*: Duns Scotus and Ockham on the Possibility of a Science of Theology," *Dialogue* 31 (1992), pp. 415–29.

————. "The Origin of Scotus's Theory of Synchronic Contingency," *Modern Schoolman* 72 (1995), pp. 149–67.

Duns Scotus, Ioannis. *Opera omnia*, ed. Wadding-Vivès, 22 vols. (Paris, 1891–95), referred to as the Wadding reprint edition.

————. *Opera omnia* (Civitas Vaticana: Typis Polyglottis Vaticanis, 1950–), referred to as the Vatican edition.

————. *Quaestiones super libros metaphysicorum Aristotelis, Libri I-IX*. Opera Philosophica III–IV, ed. Girard Etzkorn et al. (St. Bonaventure, N.Y.: Franciscan Institute, 1994).

Dupré, Louis. *Passage to Modernity: An Essay in the Hermeneutics of Nature and Culture* (New Haven and London: Yale University Press, 1993).

Effler, R. *John Duns Scotus and the Principle 'Omne quod movetur ab alio movetur'* (St. Bonaventure, N.Y.: Franciscan Institute, 1962).

Erdmann, J. E. *Grundriss der Geschichte der Philosophie*, Bd. I (Berlin: W. J. Hertz, 1866) .

Frank, W. A. "John Duns Scotus' Quodlibetal Teaching on the Will," Ph.D. dissertation (Washington, D.C.: The Catholic University of America, 1982).

————. "Duns Scotus' Concept of Willing Freely: What Divine Freedom Beyond Choice Teaches Us," *Franciscan Studies* 42 (1982a), pp. 68–89.

————."Duns Scotus on Autonomous Freedom and Divine Co-Causality," *Medieval Philosophy and Theology* 2 (1992), pp. 142–64.

————. "*Sine Proprio*: On Liberty and Christ, A Juxtaposition of Bernard of Clairvaux and John Duns Scotus," *Bernard Magister*, ed. by John R. Sommerfeldt (Kalamazoo, Mich.: Cistercian Publications, 1993), pp.461–78.

———— and Allan B. Wolter. *Duns Scotus, Metaphysician* (West Lafayette, Ind.: Purdue University Press, 1995).

Freppert, Lucan. *The Basis of Morality According To William Ockham* (Chicago: Franciscan Herald, 1988).

Gál, G. "Peter de Trabibus on the Absolute and Ordained Power of God," *Studies Honoring Ignatius Charles Brady, Friar Minor*, ed. R. S. Almagno and C. L. Harkins (St. Bonaventure, N.Y.: Franciscan Institute, 1976), pp. 283–92.

Gilson, É. *Jean Duns Scot* (Paris: J. Vrin, 1952).

Harris, C. R. S. *Duns Scotus*, vol. 2 (Oxford: Clarendon Press, 1927).

————. "Duns Scotus, John," *Encyclopedia of the Social Sciences*, vol. 3 (New York: Macmillan Company, 1937), p. 282.

Hayes, Z. *St. Bonaventure's Disputed Questions on the Mystery of the Trinity* (St. Bonaventure, N.Y.: Franciscan Institute, 1979).

Henry of Ghent. *Quodlibetal Questions on Free Will*, trans. Roland J. Teske (Milwaukee, Wisc.: Marquette University Press, 1993).

Hoeres, W. "Naturtendenz und Freiheit nach Duns Scotus," *Salzburger Jahrbuch für Philosophie und Psychologie* 2 (1958), pp. 95–134.

————. *Der Wille als reine Vollkommenheit nach Duns Scotus* (München: Verlag Anton Pustet, 1962).

————. "Wille und Person bei Scotus," *Wissenschaft und Weisheit* 29 (1962a), pp. 188–210.

Honnefelder, Ludger. "Die Kritik des Johannes Duns Scotus am kosmologischen Nezessitarismus der Araber: Ansätze zu einem neuen Freiheitsbegriff," *Die abendländische Freiheit vom 10. zum 14. Jahrhundert. Der Wirkungszusammenhang von Idee und Wirklichkeit in europäischen Vergleich*, ed. Johannes Fried (Sigmaringen: Thorbecke, 1991), pp. 249–63.

———— et al., eds. *John Duns Scotus: Metaphysics and Ethics* (Leiden: E. J. Brill, 1996).

Hugh of St. Victor. *De Sacramentis Christianae Fidei* (PL 176, 17–618).

Incandela, Joseph M. "Duns Scotus and the Experience of Human Freedom," *Thomist* 56 (1992), pp. 229–56.

Ingham, Mary Elizabeth. *Ethics and Freedom. An Historical-Critical Investigation of Scotist Ethical Thought* (Lanham, Md.: University Press of America, 1989).

―――. *Ea Quae Sunt Ad Finem*: Reflections on Virtue as Means to Moral Excellence in Scotist Thought," *Franciscan Studies* 50 (1990), pp. 177–96.

―――. "The Condemnation of 1277: Another Light on Scotist Ethics," *Freiburger Zeitschrift für Theologie und Philosophie* 37 (1990a), pp. 91–103.

―――. "Scotus and the Moral Order," *American Catholic Philosophical Quarterly* 67 (1993), pp. 127–50.

―――. "Duns Scotus' Moral Reasoning and the Artistic Paradigm," *Via Scoti Methodologica ad Mentem Joannis Duns Scoti*, ed. Leonard Sileo (Rome, Antonianum, 1995), pp. 825–38.

―――. *The Harmony of Goodness. Mutuality and Moral Living According to John Duns Scotus* (Quincy, IL: Franciscan Press, 1996).

Kent, Bonnie. "The Good Will According to Gerald Odonis, Duns Scotus, and William of Ockham," *Franciscan Studies* 46 (1986), pp. 119–39.

―――. *Virtues of the Will. The Transformation of Ethics in the Late Thirteenth Century* (Washington, D.C.: The Catholic University of America Press, 1995).

Klein, J. "Intellect und Wille als die nächsten Quellen der sittlichen Akte nach Johannes Duns Skotus," *Franziskanische Studien* 3 (1916), pp. 309–38; 6 (1919), pp. 107–22, 213–34, 305–22; 7 (1920), pp. 118–34, 190–213; 8 (1921), pp. 260–82 .

Knuuttila, Simo. "Time and Modality in Scholasticism," *Reforging the Great Chain of Being: Studies in the History of Modal Theories*, ed. Simo Knuuttila (Dordrecht: Kluwer, 1981), pp. 163–257.

―――. "Duns Scotus' Criticism of the 'Statistical' Interpretation of Modality," *Sprache und Erkenntnis im Mittelalter*, ed. Jan P. Beckman et al., 2 vols. (Berlin and New York: De Gruyter, 1981a), vol. 1, pp. 441–50.

Landry, B. *Duns Scot* (Paris: F. Alcan, 1922).

Langston, Douglas. *God's Willing Knowledge: The Influence of Scotus 'Analysis of Omniscience* (University Park and London: Pennsylvania State University Press, 1986).

Lee, Patrick. "The Relation between Intellect and Will in Free Choice according to Aquinas and Scotus," *Thomist* 49 (1985), pp. 321–42.

Longpré, É. *La Philosophie du B. Duns Scot* (Paris: Librairie S. François d'Assise, 1924) .

Lottin, O. *Psychologie et morale aux XXII et XXIII siècles*, t. 1 (Louvain: Abbaye du Mont César/Gembloux: J. Duculot, 1942); t. 2 (1948); t. 4 (1954), pp. 551–742; t. 6 (1960), pp. 403–23.

―――. "L' 'Ordinatio' de Jean Duns Scot sur le livre III des Sentences," *Recherches de théologie ancienne et médiévale* 20 (1953), pp. 102–19.

McGrath, Andre Joseph. *Competent Agency: A Study in the Ethics of John Duns Scotus Contained in His Doctrine on Marriage, Ordinatio IV, Distinctions 26-42*, Ph.D. dissertation (Washington, D.C.: The Catholic University of America, 1979).

Minges, P. *Ist Duns Scotus Indeterminist? Beiträge zur Geschichte der Philosophie des Mittelalters*, Bd. V, Hft. 4 (Münster: Aschendorffsche Verlagsbuchhandlungen, 1905).

―――. *Ioannis Duns Scoti doctrina philosophica et theologica*, tom. 2 (Ad Claras Aquas: ex typographia Collegii S. Bonaventurae, 1930).

Mohle, Hannes. *Ethik als Scientia Practica nach Johannes Duns Scotus: Eine Philosophische Grundlegung* (Münster: Aschendorffsche Verlagsbuchhandlungen, 1995).

Noone, Timothy B. "Individuation in Scotus," *American Catholic Philosophical Quarterly* 69 (1995), pp. 527–42.

Pernoud, M. A. "The Theory of the *Potentia Dei* according to Aquinas, Scotus and Ockham," *Antonianum* 47 (1972), pp. 69–95.

Peter Lombard. *Sententiae in IV libris distinctae*, ed. I. Brady (Grottaferrata/Romae: Collegii S. Bonaventurae ad Claras Aquas, [tom. 1] 1971, [tom. 2] 1981).

Prentice, R. "The Contingent Element Governing the Natural Law on the Last Seven Precepts of the Decalogue according to Duns Scotus," *Antonianum* 42 (1967), pp. 259–92.

―――. "The Degree and Mode of Liberty in the Beatitude of the Blessed," *Deus et Homo ad mentem I. Duns Scoti,* Acta Tertii Congressus Scotistici Internationalis Vindebonae, Sept. 28–oct. 2, 1970 (Romae: Societas Internationalis Scotistica, 1972), pp. 328–42.

Quinton, A. "British Philosophy," *The Encyclopedia of Philosophy,* ed. P. Edwards (New York: Free Press/London: Collier-Macmillan, 1965), vol. I, p. 373.

Richard de Saint-Victor. *De Trinitate,* ed. J. Ribaillier (Paris. J. Vrin, 1958).

Rintelen, F. Joachim von. *Der Wertgedanke in der europäischen Geistesentwicklung* (Halle: Max Niemeyer Verlag, 1932).

Rohmer, J. *La finalité chez les théologiens de saint Augustin à Duns Scot* (Paris: J. Vrin, 1939).

Rousselot, P. *Pour l'histoire du prolème de l'amour du moyen âge. Beitrage zur Geschichte der Philosophie des Mittelalters,* Bd. VI, Hft. 6 (Münster: Aschendorffsche Verlagsbuchhandlungen, 1908).

Santogrossi, Ansgar. "Duns Scotus on Potency Opposed to Act in *Questions on the Metaphysics,*" *American Catholic Philosophical Quarterly* 67 (1993), pp. 55–76.

———. "Scotus's Method in Ethics: Not To Play God—A Reply to Thomas Shannon," *Theological Studies* 55 (1994), pp. 314–29.

Schwendinger, F. "Metaphysik des Sittlichen nach Johannes Duns Skotus," *Wissenschaft und Weisheit* I (1934), pp. 180–210; 2 (1935), pp. 18–50, 112–35; 3 (1936), pp. 93–119, 161–90.

Shannon, Thomas A. "Method in Ethics: A Scotistic Contribution," *Theological Studies* 54 (1993), pp. 272–93.

———. *The Ethical Theory of John Duns Scotus. A Dialogue with Medieval and Modern Thought* (Quincy, Il.: Franciscan Press, 1995).

Siebek, H. "Die Willenslehre bei Johannes Duns Scotus," *Zeitschrift für Philosophie und philosophische Kritik* 90 (1898), pp. 179–216.

Sileo, Leonardo, ed. *Via Scoti. Methodologica ad Mentem Joannis Duns Scoti.* Atti del Congresso Scotistico Internationale, Roma 9–11 marzo 1993 (Rome: Antonianum, 1995).

Sondag, Gerard. *Ordinatio, Book I, distinctio 3, pars 3. L'Image /Duns Scot;* with introduction, translation, and notes by Gerard Sondag (Paris: Vrin, 1993).

Stratenwerth, G. *Die Naturrechtslehre des Johannes Duns Scotus* (Gottingen: Vandenhoeck und Ruprecht, 1951).

Von Hildebrand, D. "Phenomenology of Values in a Christian Philosophy," *Christian Philosophy and Religious Renewal,* ed. G. F. McLean (Washington, D.C.: The Catholic University of America Press, 1966), pp. 3–19.

Vos Jaczn, Anthonie, et al., eds. *Contingency and Freedom: John Duns Scotus, Lectura I* 39 (Norwell, Mass.: Kluwer, 1994).

Williams, Thomas. "How Scotus Separates Morality from Happiness," *American Catholic Philosophical Quarterly* 69 (1995), pp. 425–45.

———. "The Unmitigated Scotus," *Archiv für Geschicte der Philosophie,* (forthcoming).

Willmann, O. *Geschichte des Idealismus,* ed. 3, Bd. II (Braunschweig: F. Vieweg, 1896).

Wippel, J. F. *The Metaphysical Thought of Godfrey of Fontaines* (Washington, D.C.: The Catholic University of America Press, 1981).

Wolter, A. B. *The Transcendentals and Their Function in the Metaphysics of Duns Scotus* (St. Bonaventure, N.Y.: Franciscan Institute, 1946).

———. "Duns Scotus on the Natural Desire for the Supernatural," *New Scholasticism* 23 (1949), pp. 281–317.

———. "Duns Scotus on the Necessity of Revealed Knowledge," *Franciscan Studies* (1951), n. 3–4, pp. [231]–[273].

———. *Duns Scotus: Philosophical Writings* (Edinburgh: Nelson, 1962).

———. "Duns Scotus, John," *The Encyclopedia of Philosophy,* ed. P. Edwards (New York: Free Press/London: Collier-Macmillan, 1965), vol. 2, pp. 427–36.

———. "Native Freedom of the Will as a Key to the Ethics of Scotus," *Deus et Homo ad mentem I. Duns Scoti,* Acta Tertii Congressus Scotistici Internationalis Vindebonae, Sept. 28–Oct. 2, 1970 (Romae: Societas Internationalis Scotistica, 1972), pp. 359–70.

———. "The Oxford Dialogue on Language and Metaphysics," *Review of Metaphysics* 31 (June 1978), pp. 615–48; 32 (December 1978), pp. 323–48.

————. "John Duns Scotus on the Primacy and Personality of Christ," *Franciscan Christology,* ed. D. McElrath (St. Bonaventure, N.Y.: Franciscan Institute, 1980), pp. 139–82.

————, trans. *Duns Scotus: Questions on the Metaphysics, Bk. IX* (Washington, D.C.: The Catholic University of America, 1981), distributed by Translation Clearing House, Dept. of Philosophy, Oklahoma State University, Stillwater, Oklahoma 74078.

————. "A Scotistic Approach to the Ultimate Why-Question," *Philosophies of Existence, Ancient and Medieval,* ed. P. Morewedge (New York: Fordham University Press, 1982), pp. 109–30.

————. *A Treatise on God as First Principle: A Latin Text and English Translation of the De Primo Principio,* ed. 2, revised with a commentary (Chicago: Franciscan Herald Press [1983]).

————, trans. *John Duns Scotus: Four Questions on Mary* (Santa Barbara, Ca.: Old Mission Santa Barbara, 1988).

————, trans. *Duns Scotus' Political and Economic Philosophy* (Santa Barbara, Ca.: Old Mission Santa Barbara, 1989).

————. *The Philosophical Theology of John Duns Scotus,* ed. by Marilyn McCord Adams (Ithaca and London: Cornell University Press, 1990).

————. "Scotus' Paris Lectures on God's Knowledge of Future Events," *Philosophical Theology,* 1990a, pp. 285–333.

————. "Duns Scotus on the Will as a Rational Potency," *Philosophical Theology of John Duns Scotus,* ed. Marilyn McCord Adams (Ithaca and London: Cornell University Press, 1990b), pp. 163–80.

————, trans. *Duns Scotus' Early Oxford Lecture on Individuation* (Santa Barbara, Ca.: Old Mission Santa Barbara, 1992).

————. "Scotus on the Divine Origin of Possibility," *American Catholic Philosophical Association* 67 (1993), pp. 95–108.

———— and Blane O'Neill. *John Duns Scotus: Mary's Architect* (Quincy, Il.: Franciscan Press, 1993).

————. "Duns Scotus at Oxford," *Via Scoti: Methodologica ad Mentem Joannis Duns Scoti,* ed. Leonardo Sileo (Rome: Antonianum, 1995), pp. 183–92.

————. "God's Knowledge: A Study in Scotistic Methodology," *Via Scoti: Methodologica ad Mentem Joannis Duns Scoti,* ed. Leonardo Sileo (Rome: Antonianum, 1995a), pp. 165–82.

————. "The Un-Shredded Scotus," *Archiv für Geschichte der Philosophie,* (forthcoming).

Zavalloni, Roberto. *Giovanni Duns Scoto. Maestro di Vita e Pensiero* (Bologna: Edizioni Francescane, 1992).

Topical Index

Absolute and ordained power, 11, 19, 56–67, 191–94

Additiones magnae: author of, 38; published as *Reportata parisiensia*, 38

Affectio iustitiae. See Affection for justice

Affection for justice, 11, 20, 39–41, 153–54, 296, 298–300; Anselm's conception of, 12–13, 298–99; as "libertas innata," 13; as pure perfection, 14; as ultimate specific difference of free will, 13; God's, 14–16, 18–19; perfected by virtue of charity, 13; right reason and, 17; Scotus' notion of, 13, 102–4, 298–99. See also Native freedom of the will; Will

Affection for the advantageous: Anselm's conception of, 11, 39, 298–99; as self-actualization, 39; natural will and, 11; perfected by virtue of hope, 13

Affectio commodi. See Affection for the advantageous

Anger and the irascible appetite, 243–44

Appetites in the will: irascible and concupiscible, 234, 243–46; virtues of the irascible and concupiscible, 246

Appetitive virtues, 243, 244–46; connection of, 84–89, 252–274; definition of, 77–78, 224; enumeration of, 241–42; generic, 83–84, 242, 247–48; heroic, 81, 242; human versus inhuman and superhuman, 81, 237–39; interrelationship with gifts, beatitudes, and fruits, 247–52; in the body, 234; in sense appetite, 234; of the irascible appetitie, 243, 244–46; sevenfold necessary to perfect man, 241–43, 246. See also Connection of virtues

Aristotle: reason for preferring prudence as more noble, 77, 234; Scotus' rule for interpreting, 30

Badness: definition of, 54; degrees of moral, 49–51, 174–76; violation of right reason, 21

Beatitudes: enumeration of, 79; relation to gifts and fruits of Spirit, 79–84, 237; Scotus' view of, 248–49

Bigamy: can it ever be licit, 209–11; if permitted how is justice preserved, 209–11

Bodily skills as quasi-virtues, 77–78

Cardinal virtues: Aristotelian view of, 75–79, 223–24, 225; Augustine's view of, 226; Philip the Chancellor's distinction of, 85; seat of, 223–37; Scotus' view of, 241, 246

Charity, infused virtue of, 89–94, 275–87; basis for a meritorious act, 90; distinct from theological virtues of faith and hope, 277; do moral virtues require it, 270–72; extends to love of neighbor and self, 94–98, 287–92; formal object of, 277–79; more perfect a virtue than moral virtues, 77; relation to faith and hope, 272–73

Civil authority, origin of, 73–75, 221–22

Coercion and free will, 39, 151–52

Color, Aristotle's and Plato's theory of, 44–45

Commandments, Ten. See Decalogue

Confession to a priest, obligation of, 57, 195–98

Conformity to God's will, 53–54, 181–82

Connection of virtues: of all moral virtues with one prudential habit, 269–70; of moral virtues among themselves, 254–60; of moral and theological virtues, 270–72; of moral virtues with prudence, 260–69; of theological virtues among themselves, 272–73

Contingency: a primary truth, 9; proves God has a will, 9

Conscience, 45–46, 162–68; definition of, 35. See also Synderesis

Creation, God's plan in, 19–20

Decalogue: and the law of nature, 60–64, 198–208; observed in every state, 26, 59, 199, 207. See also Law of nature

Demerit, 50–51

Desire: acts of, 102, 296; distinction of will and, 4; for happiness, 43, 156–61, 296–302; inordinate, 101–2, 296–98, 299–300, 301–2; ordinate, 101, 295; nature of, 43, 101, 295; presupposes benevolent or friendship love, 101, 295

Dispensation: definition of, 62, 200, 209

from decalogue, 22–23, 24, 26–27, 60–73, 199–219
Divine positive law, 57–60, 195–98; twofold sense, 59–60
Divorce: and the Mosaic law, 64–65, 72–73, 212–19; an unmitigated evil, 64–65, 72–73; not permitted equally to men and women, 73; views of the schools of Shammai and Hillel, 65

End: alone does not justify actions, 51–52, 176–78; of mankind is supernatural, 13, 20, 24, 28, 61
Ethical system of Scotus: basis of unity, ix; presuppositions of, ix, 5
Evil as a privation, 98

Firmness of purpose, a pure perfection, 14
Fortitude, 72; and the irascible appetite, 242; resides in the will, 76
Freedom: Anselm's definition of, 12, 98, 293; as power to sin, 14, 98–100, 293–95; moral, 28
Free will: coercion and, 39, 151–52; compatible with some necessity, 12, 15; essential perfection of, 11; how God's differs from ours, 9; pure perfection, 10, 12; positive or superabundant indeterminacy, 10; psychological pressure on, 39; ultimate specific difference of, 13

Gifts and fruits of the Spirit, 78–84, 237–52; beatitudes and, 79, 237; distinction from virtues, 79: enumeration of, 78–79; Scotus' view of, 249–51
God: absolute and ordained power of, 11, 19, 56–57, 191–94; and affection for justice, 14–16, 18–19; as beatific object, 279; as perfect lover, 13; co-operation with actions of creatures, 99, 293–94; debtor to his goodness, 8, 19, 57, 184, 190–91; generosity of, 190; infinity of, 8; intellect not dependent on intelligibility of creatures, 17–18; justice of, 16, 18–19, 54–56, 183–91; liberality of, 190; metaphysical notion of, 5–9; mercy of, 54–55; must be loved, 18, 21–22, 54, 89, 184, 189–90; necessarily happy, 14–15; *ordinatissime volens*, 9, 17, 19–20, 55, 57; rectitude of will, 56, 184–85, 187; relationship to creatures governed by right reason, 16–25; reveals his will in nature, 25; self-love both free and necessary, 16; self-love not private or jealous, 12, 20; steadfast-

ness of will, 14–15; three ways of loving, 13, 91, 277–79. *See also* Trinity; Love of God
Goodness: accidental, 51–52; dependent upon conformity with right reason, 4, 22; dependent upon God's will, 3, 16–25, 57; essential, 17; generic and specific, 21; meritorious, 17, 54; moral, 20–22, 47–54, 167–82; natural, 17–20, 52; primary, 17

Habits: as active potencies, 44; defined, 35; differ from acts, 35
Happiness, 42–45, 155–62; as a reflex object of well-ordered love, 13; God's, 14; loved out of an affection for justice, 14, 105, 302
Holy Spirit: gifts and fruits of, 78–84, 237–52; sin against, 303

Indeterminancy, positive and negative, 37
Indifferent acts. *See* Morally indifferent acts
Intellect: as partial cause of will-act, 44, 46; not a *per se* rational faculty, 36; will and, 31–39, 44, 127–42

Justice: as a moral virtue, 76; Anselm's definition of, 12, 55, 184; commutative and distributive, 185; God's, 54–56, 183–91; infused, 102 (*see also* Charity); legal, 21–22, 184; modifies God's creative act, 16, 18–19, 185–86, 188; particular, 184–85; secondary object of, 19, 186, 188, 190–191; Scotus' definition of, 55

Killing, two views on, 200–201
Knowledge of moral law, three requirements for, 27

Law: Church, 196; divine positive law, 57–60, 195–98; eternal, 23; natural, 195; permitting the lesser of two evils, 73, 212. *See also* Law of nature
Law of nature, 22–25, 26–29, 57–64, 71, 195; dispensation from, 22–23, 24, 26–27, 60–73; secondary or extended sense of, 58, 61, 63, 211–12; fitting it be revealed, 59, 206–7; Gratian's notion of, 63, 195, 202, 203; knowledge of finer details of, 27; observed in every state, 59, 63, 196, 207; recognized by all, 58–59, 63–64; rough agreement as to substantive content of, 27; strict, proper, or primary sense, 58, 61, 62, 211; two tables of, 22–23, 27, 28, 29, 63–64, 202–3, 204–7;

written in the heart, 26–27, 207
Lex aeterna. See Law: eternal
Love of God, 18, 21–22, 89–94, 275–92;
    above all is morally right act, 89–91,
    276–77; does nature suffice for such love,
    91–94, 279–82; for his own sake is prima-
    ry object of charity, 277–78; how are we
    obliged to, 284–85; how understand
    "above all," 279–84; includes love of
    neighbor and self, 94–98, 287–92; why is
    charity necessary if nature suffices for,
    93–94, 285
Love of neighbor, 28, 94–96, 205–6, 287–291
Love of self, 97–98, 291–92
Lucifer's sin, 14, 27–28, 100–105, 295–302
Lying, 106–9, 304–14; Bonaventure's view,
    106–9; by perfect, 108–9, 308–11; offi-
    cious or polite, 108–9, 308; pernicious,
    108, 307–8; scandal, 310–11; three views
    why sinful, 106–8, 305–7

Man as end of all sensible things, 20
Marriage, 64–70; bigamous, 64, 70–72;
    Christian or sacramental, 64, 66–68;
    divorce and, 64–66; more difficult than
    religious life, 69; purpose of, 64, 66, 69,
    209; spiritual, 67; under Mosaic law,
    72–73, 212–19
Merit, 17, 49, 50, 51; and demerit, 50–51
Metaphysics: contribution to the Theolo-
    gian's enterprise, 6; faith and, 5; notion of
    God, 5–9; subject and goal of, 6–7
Moderation of the desire for happiness, 27.
    See also Lucifer's sin
Monogamy: Christ restores, 65; dispensation
    from, 69; pertains to natural law in a sec-
    ondary sense, 211–12
Moral badness: definition of, 49–50; degrees
    of, 50–51, 174–76
Moral goodness: conformity to God's will,
    53–54, 181–82; degrees of, 48–49,
    173–74; nature of, 47, 207–10; source of,
    48, 167–69
Morality of choosing the lesser of two evils,
    73; two views of, 213–15; Scotus' defense
    of second view, 215–18
Moral law: accessible to reason, 25–29, 57,
    62–63; content versus obligation of,
    24–25; evolution of, 29; God and, 54–57,
    183–94; in general, 57–75, 195–222;
    scope of, 22
Morally indifferent acts, 51–52, 178–81
Moral virtues, 75–89, 223–74; angel can
    acquire, 231–32; Aristotelian view of,

223, 224, 225–26; Augustine's view of,
    226; Henry of Ghent's view of, 78,
    235–37; connection of, 84–89, 252–74;
    refutation of views of others, 225–30;
    relation to gifts and fruits of Spirit,
    223–37; Scotus' view of, 230–35; will as
    the seat of, 75–78, 223–37
Motion: Whatever is moved is moved by
    another, 36–37

Native freedom of the will, ix, 20–21, 29, 39.
    See also Affection for justice
Natural inclination: as active potency,
    43–44; for happiness, 43; more powerful
    than a habit, 43
Natural law. See Law of nature
Natural volition, 39, 41–42, 154–55
Natural will, 39, 41–42, 154–55
Nature, seeks its own perfection, 13
Necessity and freedom, 14–16
Necessitarianism: Abelardian and Leibnizian,
    16, 19, 57; Averroistic, 16, 55, 56

Oaths: nature of, 110, 316; in favorable or
    odious matters, 319; promissory, 321–22;
    special kinds of, 320–22; as testimonials
    for promotion to offices, 112, 318–19

Perfect, two senses of, 109, 309
Perjury, 110–13, 314–23; against natural law
    and the first table of the decalogue, 110,
    316
Phenomenological axiology, 29
Polyandry, never licit, 212
Polygamy, why it was permitted, 211–12
Positive indeterminacy, 10
Power, absolute and ordained, 11, 19, 56–67,
    191–94
Practical science, 32–35, 127–36
Practice. See Praxis
Praxis, 31, 33–35, 127–30, 132–35, 201
Property, private ownership of, 74–75,
    219–222
Proportionality principle, 73
Prudence, 85–89; connection with praxis, 35;
    definition of, 35; faith a more perfect
    virtue than, 77; generic or specific, 87–88;
    habit of, 76, 87–88; virtue, 34; legislator
    requires, 221; no moral virtue without,
    85, 88; one virtue, 32; practical knowl-
    edge, 34; resides in the practical intellect,
    34, 76–77, 85. See also Connection of
    virtues
Pure perfection, 98, 294; liberty as, 294

Rational appetite, not free will, 11, 103, 298

Reason and faith, 5–6

Revelation of God's will in nature, 25–26

Right reason, ix, 4, 16, 21–22, 49; and affection for justice, 17, 21; governs God's creativity, 19; three requirements to know what is in accord with, 26

Science: technical meaning of, 31; practical, 32–35, 127–36; theoretical, 32–33; unity of, 31

Scotistic Commission, x, 75

Scotistic school, ix

Secrets, obligation to keep, 113–14, 323–25

Self-actualization, 39

Sin, 25, 98–123, 293–95; gravity not determined by habit, 111, 316–17; of enslavement, 114–23, 325–30; of Lucifer, 100–105, 295–302; of malice, 105–6, 302–4; original, 24; the power to, 98–99, 293–94

Skills. See Bodily skills as quasi-virtues

Slavery, 114–23, 325–30; Church's attitude towards, 114–16; legality of, 116–20, 326; marriage and, 329; origins of, 325–26; symbiotic versus parasitic, 115–16; why the Church permitted, 114–16

Social theory. See Civil authority, origin of

Sufficient reason, principle of, 19

Supernatural order, 20. See also End: of mankind is supernatural

Synderesis: definition of, 35, 45–46; introduced by error, 45; various views of, 45–46. See also Conscience

Temperance, 75; relation to the concupiscible appetite, 246; resides in the will, 76; seat of, 75–76, 246

Trinity: inner life of, 12; Richard of St. Victor's explanation of, 12; man's destiny as union with, 13, 54

Vices as habits, 35

Virtues: Aristotle's view of the seat of the cardinal, 75–76; as habits, 35; connection of, 84–89, 252–74; infused charity, 89–94, 275–92; intellective, 242–43; intellectual and moral, 75–89, 223–74; relation to gifts and fruits of the Spirit, 78–84, 237–52. See also Appetitive virtues

Volition, natural. See Will: natural

Will: ability to act deficiently, 99–100, 294–95; all elicited acts are free, 39; always acts according to either of its two inclinations, 46, 102, 296; and intellect as essentially ordered causes, 44; appetites in, 234, 243–46; as a passive potency, 44; as an active potency, 37, 44; as opposed to nature, 16; as pure perfection, 10; as a rational potency, 21, 35–37, 136–50; as self-determining, 16, 37; cannot be forced by God's absolute power, 31; cannot will evil, 44, 105–6, 303; controls thought, 37–38; Henry of Ghent's theory of, 78; how its acts are ordered, 100–110, 295; inclinations of, 11–12, 39–41, 46, 153–66; malice only in an act of, 38; natural, 11–12, 41–42, 154–55; not determined by good, 44, 105; passions of, 229; superabundant sufficiency of, 37